When in Doubt, Sing

Prayer in Daily Life

Jane Redmont

SORIN BOOKS　Notre Dame, Indiana

All of the persons quoted in this book are real. None is a composite. In some cases, I have changed people's names, occupations, and other identifying characteristics in order to protect their privacy.

---

www.sorinbooks.com

ISBN-10 1-933495-16-2 ISBN-13 978-1-933495-16-3

Cover and text design by Katherine Robinson Coleman.

Cover Image © Laughing Stock.

Printed and bound in the United States of America.

Library of Congress Cataloging-in-Publication Data

Redmont, Jane.
  When in doubt, sing : prayer in daily life / Jane Redmont. — [Rev. ed.].
    p. cm.
  Includes bibliographical references.
  ISBN-13: 978-1-933495-16-3 (pbk.)
  ISBN-10: 1-933495-16-2 (pbk.)
  1. Prayer—Christianity. 2. Spiritual life. 3. Prayers. I. Title.
  BV215.R42 2008
  248.3'2—dc22
                                    2008036876

for Peter,
through thick and thin,

and in memory of
David,
beloved friend,
and
Krister,
shepherd and mentor
who knew how to pray.

As a deer craves running water,
I thirst for you, my God;
I thirst for God,
the living God.
When will I see your face?

PSALM 42:2–3

When they had gone ashore, they saw a charcoal fire there, with fish on it, and bread. Jesus said to them, "Bring some of the fish that you have just caught." So Simon Peter went aboard and hauled the net ashore, full of large fish, a hundred fifty-three of them; and though there were so many, the net was not torn. Jesus said to them, "Come and have breakfast."

JOHN 21:9–12A

God, you shape our dreams.
As we put our trust in you
may your hopes and desires
be ours,
and we your expectant people.
Amen.

A NEW ZEALAND PRAYER BOOK
HE KARAKIA MIHINARE O AOTEAROA

CONTENTS

PREFACE TO THE

NEW EDITION

● ●

Books have a life before they appear in print. They also have a life after their creation. Following its publication, *When in Doubt, Sing* ceased to belong only to me. It took on a new life with its readers.

Books also have a context. They live with us in history, in societies and cultures, and in the case of books like this one, in communities of faith and practice.

A couple of years after the book's release, I was scheduled to give a daylong retreat in Grand Rapids, Michigan, on the topic of "Praying with Body, Breath, and Voice." The scheduled date was September 22, 2001.

A few days after the attacks of September 11, 2001, on the World Trade Center and the Pentagon, I phoned my hosts in Grand Rapids and told them that I would keep my commitment and fly from California, where I was living, to western Michigan, but that it might be a good idea to change the title of the retreat. Flights had begun again, though planes were nearly empty. Soft Muzak versions of patriotic songs piped through the loudspeakers during the layover at Chicago's O'Hare airport. The retreat met under the title "Praying in a Time of Terror." We still spoke of praying with body, breath, and voice, having kept that theme in the subtitle for the day, but the mood of the retreat, some of its content, and the tone of our spoken and unspoken prayers were not what they would have been two weeks before.

In other ways the world in which we pray has not changed. The poor, here and abroad, still struggle for food and for hope. Rich and poor still suffer, become ill, give birth, fall in love, make and break friendships, rejoice, work, join and leave and sustain communities of faith—and die.

The speed of life in the United States, and in many other postindustrial nations, seems to increase daily. The years go by faster, and not only because I have grown older. When I wrote this book a decade ago, I spoke of the scarcity of contemplative spaces. This is even more true now. It is true not only in the world of work, in both corporate and nonprofit organizations, but in churches and other religious communities, in civic and charitable organizations, and on college campuses like the one where I am now a professor. Every time I offer a retreat or a workshop on prayer, I find myself simplifying, paring down the content and components of the session. We all suffer from information overload and lack of Sabbath time. I think about this almost constantly.

The Internet has changed our lives as well. It competes with prayer. It also can help us to pray. Its competitive and intrusive aspects are more obvious to us. Like many other people, I read the news online, check my e-mail too often, spend time in front of a screen that I could be spending on my knees or in half-lotus position. But that is only half the story. There is also religious life in cyberspace. The Daily Office of the Episcopal Church is online; so are Catholic prayers and Jewish chants. Communities of support and spiritual conversation have cropped up across geographic and denominational boundaries as well as inside them. Sometime in 2006, I began reading other people's blogs. On Ash Wednesday 2007, I began my own blog. Sometime during this period, I found myself in a community of support and spiritual conversation. Some of us have since met in person. A few of us knew each other before meeting again in cyberspace. Others will never meet, but talk about politics, theology, church, culture, and sometimes ourselves. We pray for each other. We post icons of well-known saints and stories of unsung ones.

Still, the discipline of contemplation is more difficult than it was, though as the desert fathers and mothers of the early church knew, the demons of distraction and doubt live inside us as much as outside. I am certain that the amount of time I spend at my desk in front of a screen is what determined this past year's Lenten practice. I decided that I would take a half-hour walk as my first action of the day after morning ablutions. This got me outdoors; I live near beautiful trees with which I do not spend enough time, and the first class

I taught this winter was not until the middle of the day. The practice also gave me time for quiet prayer (or just quiet), exercised my body, offered me a chance to breathe more consciously, and forced me to start my day away from my desk. It was small and simple and not too ambitious. It was also difficult, since it required changing my morning routine, interrupting a set of reflexes I had developed, keeping me away from words, even those of the morning Psalms; deferring, for just a short while, the mail, the deadlines, the haze of sentences and paragraphs and to-do lists. As I suspected it would, it often affected the rest of the day. But the point of Lenten disciplines is not to produce "results." My new practice changed the gateway to the day and did so with body, mind, soul, heart, environment, and time. Some mornings it was a liberation and a relief. At other times it was a struggle.

The speed of daily life and the Internet: are they related? Certainly. But it would be wrong to blame the dearth of contemplative time on technology alone. The Internet and the ubiquitous cell phone have accelerated our lives and filled them with beeps, rings, and interruptions, as have the letters demanding immediate response, the twenty-four-hour news cycle, and the temptation to seize upon the first piece of information found in an online search rather than to be critical and careful. Nevertheless, these hallmarks of the twenty-first century are not the only reason we lack time and space to breathe, stop, be mindful, and spend time listening for God. Labor practices and the state of the economy also have something to do with this. In almost every industry I know, individuals are doing the work that two or three people were doing ten or twenty years ago. Workdays and workweeks are longer; expectations of availability have changed; household time and work time overlap. This transformation was taking place long before the World Wide Web threaded its way into our lives. Alone among industrialized nations and dozens of other countries (more than 130 at latest count), the United States has no guaranteed paid holidays mandated by law. Urban and suburban people especially have less and less time in nature, with their families, in the company of friends, and in solitude. How can this not affect our prayer?

Since I wrote this book a decade ago, my life as a Christian has remained much the same: I still spend Sunday mornings in communal celebrations of word and sacrament. I do what I can to work for justice and peace. I ask, "How will this affect the poorest among us?" I give thanks for creation, incarnation, forgiveness, healing, and resurrection. I still live by the calendar, celebrating the seasons of the church year: Advent, Christmas, Epiphany, Lent, Easter, Pentecost. I still read and ponder and tell and listen to biblical stories. I still pray the Psalms, tussle with the Prophets, remember Jesus.

In one major way, however, my life as a Christian has changed. I remember thinking, around the time I handed in the manuscript for *When in Doubt, Sing*, "There are an awful lot of Anglican prayers in this book." Three years later, I had become an Anglican. I was formally received into the Episcopal Church in early 2002, after becoming a member of a local Episcopal congregation the previous fall. I had spent a full year in discernment before that. It was not an easy decision: I had chosen to become a Catholic in my formative young-adult years, at the beginning of my twenties; I expected to die a Catholic.

I had, though, delayed my baptism and confirmation for a full year after the decision to become a Catholic in the 1970s. I was experiencing three calls at once: a call to baptism, a call to ordained ministry, and a call to examine Christian tradition from a feminist perspective and to find a way of living faith that would fully embrace and articulate the experience and wisdom of women. The church community to which I felt most drawn was the Roman Catholic Church; it felt like home, and in that decade after the Second Vatican Council, I joined and was received into it, after that year of reflection, with a sense of joy and peace. I have never regretted that decision. At the time, I was a student at Harvard Divinity School, in the Master of Divinity program, the degree usually leading to professional ordained ministry. In November of my third MDiv year, I attended the first conference on the ordination of Roman Catholic women (Detroit, 1975) and was among the women who stood up at a moving and solemn celebration to acknowledge a vocation to ordained priestly ministry.

The story of the intervening quarter of a century is a long tale for another time and place. The short version is that the call to ordained priestly ministry—a call from God, a call from God's people—never left me. This was a driving reason, though not the only one, for my emigration to the Episcopal Church. I have found a welcome home in this church, with its mix of Catholic and Reformed traditions, its reasoned thoughtfulness and passionate sacramental life, its hospitality and forthrightness. I treasure its love of poetic speech. I value its governance allying the ministry of bishops with strong lay involvement. Immigrants do become true citizens. They also bring who they are with them. Would I have written this book differently had I written it five rather than ten years ago? Perhaps a little, but not in fundamental ways, and so my editors and I have chosen to keep this edition of the book as I wrote it more than a decade ago, except for the addition of this preface and a few small updates to the dedication and acknowledgments.

When in Doubt, Sing, which is now yours as much as mine, has accompanied me in retreats, lectures, and workshops—to Arkansas with the Omega West Dance Company, to retreats with Catholic women in Texas and Episcopal women in Florida, to a Presbyterian retreat center in New Mexico with an ecumenical group watching thunderstorms travel over the mesas in the late afternoons. I have listened to stories of prayer and spoken about prayer with Lutheran, Catholic, Episcopal, United Church of Christ, Unitarian Universalist, Quaker, and Presbyterian groups and at a retirement community with a majority of Jewish members. I had the privilege of addressing a community of Catholic sisters at their national gathering, a multifaith audience of Christians and Jews at a Benedictine abbey, and a Clinical Pastoral Education program training rabbinical students and seminarians as hospital chaplains. I kept a straight face through my host's questions on a television news channel that positioned me without prior warning as a stress-reduction expert on a day when the stock market had the jitters.

I continue to pray in community as well as alone, especially at Sunday Eucharist, periodically in the daily office of the church, but also in more informal prayer gatherings, some Episcopal, many ecumenical. Since the beginning of the wars in Afghanistan and Iraq, many of these gatherings have focused on prayer in a time of war and prayer for peace. Others involve healing prayer. Many make space for silence and contemplation. I often choose prayers, meditations, and songs for meetings of the diocesan anti-racism committee for which I serve as chair. I pray as I write sermons and as I preach.

I am a recipient of prayer, a participant in prayer, and a leader of prayer. I am grateful for the grace in all of these moments.

And yes, I still sing, in solitude and, regularly, in community. There, amid a richer harmony than I could ever know alone, I meet Christ, who continues to surprise me.

IN THE SEASON OF EASTER 2008
GREENSBORO, NORTH CAROLINA

$\mathscr{A}$CKNOWLEDGMENTS

My original editor, Kate Ekrem, first imagined this book upon reading my essay "From Where Will My Help Come?' Praying in a Time of Depression." I thank her for her invitation and for her editorial insight, which was at work even before we were in a formal working partnership. Kate's wisdom, eagle eye, and patience with my delays shepherded me through the first two years of this work. I wish her God's blessings as she now prepares for ordination in the Episcopal Church. My second editor, Kristen Auclair, brought to our work her discerning eye and her Methodist love of hymn singing; she was the soul of kindness during the difficult end of the writing process. I thank my third editor, Bridget Sweeney, for bringing her enthusiasm and her Catholic background to the final stages of the book, and for bearing with the detail-intensive production process. I am grateful to my agent, Christina "Kit" Ward, for her negotiating skill and her support of my work. I thank the National Writers Union for defending and protecting writers' rights in this difficult and vulnerable craft, in these precarious times.

Many friends and colleagues spoke with me about their prayer life and that of people they had encountered, about the Bible and about liturgy, about the music that stirs their souls, about their times of doubt and struggle. They prayed with and for me. They confirmed me in my belief in the communion of saints and the power of the Body of Christ, the gathered community of believers whom time and space cannot keep from one another and from God. They challenged me through our differences and helped me to see these differences as holy.

These people are the proverbial "too numerous to name," but to several I give special thanks: to my theological partner, Tom Powers, whose affection and humor help keep me sane, and my other friends at the Jesuit School of Theology at Berkeley, especially Diana Wear;

to my classmates at the Graduate Theological Union, dear friends and respected colleagues Nancy Pineda, Kimberly Whitney, Fred Sanders and Susan Sanders a.k.a. The Muse, and Kevin Koczela, and all the Chickens and the Sisters of the H.H.T.; and to my academic adviser, George C. L. Cummings.

To Elena Stone, Kerry Maloney, Ellen Reuter, and Anita Diamant, beloved sisters, friends, and conversation partners. To the friends whose hospitality has been a blessing during the writing of this book: Peter Klein; Brian Feit and Phil Melemed and the boys; Mariette Murphy and Marisa Murphy; Carter West; Beth "Betuccia" Harrington; Marge and Luke Lamb; David and Sonia Caus Gleason (and Christopher, both *in utero* and out); Laura Ashkin, Chris Stanton, Ethan Ashkin Stanton, and Miriam Ashkin Stanton; and the women and men of Gelos House—Cynthia, Julia, April, Mike, Michael, and Ken—who took me in when I had no home in the late spring and through much of the summer of 1998 and who bore with me through yet another deadline, enduring my quite unprayerful curses through the final rounds of cuts in the manuscript.

To Mark "Marco-Lorenzo" Asselin for editorial and moral support in three languages and Olivier Joseph for transatlantic cheer (*merci Zitoun*). To David Toolan, always. To Carla De Sola, who embodies grace in the multiple meanings of the word, and Deborah Rosen, who helped keep me healthy and sane. And to Alyosha, of course.

To my mother, Joan Redmont, for getting me started on the path of yoga and teaching me how to stay healthy under stress, and my father, Bernard Redmont, fellow writer and constant cheerleader and comforter. To my brother, Dennis Redmont, for providing both clipping service and cheering section from Rome.

I thank the people of St. Columba Catholic Church in Oakland, California, with whom I worship on Sundays, for their faith and their accompaniment, for welcoming me and taking me in, and for providing me with a place to sing my heart out. I thank the people of Boston's Paulist Center Community, who will always be my family, no matter where I live. I thank the participants in the Christian Feminist Spirituality Retreat at Collegium 1997, for blessing my life and prayer.

This book would have been very different without a throng of cyber-friends, who enriched immeasurably both process and content. I thank especially members of Sister-L, of the Vatican-List, and Dharma brothers and sisters of the Universal-Zendo List.

Writing is a joy. Writing is hard work. Writing is full of trade-offs. If you do other work, you have no time, and it is very difficult to write. If you do not, you have no money, and it is very difficult to write. I thank the friends and family whose gifts and loans helped pay the rent and keep food on the table during several crucial summer and winter months. You know who you are. I will always be grateful for your care, and I promise to pass it on to others in similar circumstances.

My deep gratitude to the many teachers, mentors, spiritual directors, and retreat guides who taught me to pray, listened with the heart, and throughout the years have been witnesses to me of God's living presence—especially Christiane Brusselmans of blessed memory, Miriam Cleary, Thelma Hall, Ken Hughes, and Krister Stendahl.

My gratitude also to Vinny, Larna, and the folks at Vinny Greco's Powerhouse Gym in Watertown, Massachusetts, thanks to whose training skills and supportive cheer I was able to sustain the physical energy to write a book proposal in record time while juggling several jobs and packing to move to California, and whose "wisdom of the body" and discipline I took with me to my new home in Berkeley. Guys, I don't win bodybuilding awards like your other members, but I couldn't have gotten started on this project without you. I'll never take your bumper sticker off my car.

Finally, my love and thanks to Peter Klein, to whom this book is dedicated, whose prayer as a Jew accompanies mine as a Christian, and who has been, since our college days at Oberlin, my soul brother and best friend.

Holy One of Blessing
Your presence
fills creation.
You have kept us alive,
You have sustained us,
You have brought us
to this moment.

For this long-awaited new edition in paperback, I owe a debt of gratitude to my publisher, Tom Grady. I am deeply thankful for Tom's initiative and for his hospitality at Sorin Books and Ave Maria Press.

In my new life in the Episcopal Church during the last seven years, the life and prayer of congregations in Berkeley, Oakland, and Greensboro have shaped and nourished my prayer: Good Shepherd, Berkeley; All Saints' Chapel at the Church Divinity School of the Pacific, Berkeley; St. Paul's, Oakland; and St. Mary's House, Greensboro, my current and cherished home. The brothers of the Order of the Holy Cross in Berkeley, Anglican Benedictines, were steady, cheerful, and reverent in hospitality and prayer during my final years in Berkeley. I give thanks that the ties of faith and friendship endure with the congregation and staff of St. Columba Catholic Church in Oakland, especially Bill and Maud Green, Jayson Landeza, Beryl McCrainey-Slevin, Tom Shaver, and Debbie White.

For spiritual companionship and midwifery during those last West Coast years, I thank Sarah Lewis and Gabriel the Wise. Thanks also to Hanna Smidt, my co-leader at the weekly prayer for peace at Good Shepherd; to Ethan Vesely-Flad, my brother on Episcopal, Anglican, and interreligious paths of peacemaking and justice building; and to Bill Countryman, for his mentoring in Anglican spirituality and history, his exquisite love of poetry and music, his preaching, and his friendship. For their friendship and prayers, I thank Melanie Donahoe, Will Hocker, and Jaime Sanders, who have also made the journey to priesthood in midlife.

I thank my community of bloggers who share in a combination of irreverent humor, conversation on culture, politics, church, and food, and the communion of prayer. You know who you are. I'll see you online.

The nearly ten years since the original publication of *When in Doubt, Sing* have seen departures and deaths. Rereading the acknowledgments to the first edition reminds me of the many friends who have stayed in my life and of those who have left, some through death. Along with my dear friend Peter Klein, who, *baruch haShem*, is very much alive, I remember especially, in the dedication to this new edition, two precious human beings: David Toolan, who now rests with the saints and whom I last saw when he had lost his capacity to speak, but not his gentle and meditative spirit; and my beloved mentor Krister Stendahl, who was in his final hours as I was writing the new preface to the book. I give thanks for their lives and their enduring presence.

IN THE SEASON OF EASTER 2008
GREENSBORO, NORTH CAROLINA

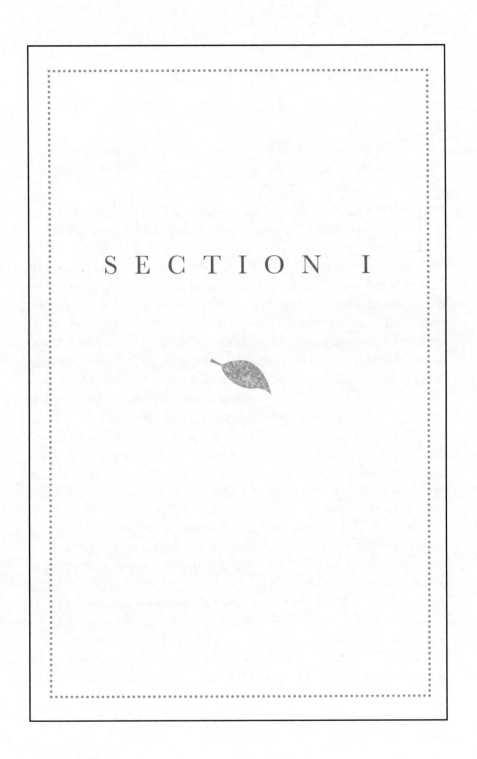

SECTION I

YOURS, MINE, AND OURS:

AN INTRODUCTION

··

This book is for you if you consider yourself a Christian who prays. It is also for you if you do not. You may be active—newly or lifelong—in a congregation, church, parish, meetinghouse, or other assembly for worship. Or you may have left behind the church of your childhood and adolescence, but not your spiritual yearning. You may find comfort and inspiration in religious institutions, or they may evoke in you little besides anger and frustration. In any case, you pray—or in some deep part of your being in the heart of your heart, there is a longing for relationship with God, or for a state beyond those words, what several Christian and Jewish friends of mine call "standing in the Presence." This book is also for you if you live outside the Christian tradition and are exercising the virtue of curiosity. I hope it will speak words of welcome to all those who read it. It is meant to offer an experience of hospitality, just as I believe that God extends to human beings a divine and inexhaustible welcome: the door is always open, the table always set, the arms flung wide, outstretched.

This is not a proselytizing book, but an experiential book, aimed at enhancing your life of prayer, whether you pray daily, have stopped praying, have just begun praying, have recently returned to prayer, or have never prayed in your life. I am a theologian, but this is not a book of theology, though my theological biases will be apparent. It is a book about the practice of prayer, including its struggles. Of course, there is a link. The old Latin saying *lex orandi, lex credendi* is often in my mind when I do my theological work: first come the prayers of the people, later the doctrinal formulations. Not the other way around. First things first.[1]

I began this book alone, or imagining I could write it alone, and soon found that I could not—partly because I am by temperament an extrovert, but mostly because prayer lives inside community even when we do not know it, because we are carried by the prayer of others, and because my own life is graced by friends, colleagues, and strangers whose insights and experiences of prayer accompany and nourish mine. My experience of prayer is shaped by, and grows in conversation with, family and friends, tradition and experience, book knowledge and body knowledge, study and intuition, solitude and community. The grace of God moves and sustains my prayer, but this grace is often mediated. Mediation—encountering God through intermediaries—is no less an occasion of encounter with the Holy One than what we imagine to be "direct encounter." As a Christian I believe in God's incarnation: literally, in God's flesh in the world. Again and again, I meet God in the faces, voices, and actions of others. The writing of this book confirmed me in this experience and in that belief.

Conversing about prayer is not a new experience for me. As a journalist and writer, I have interviewed people of varied back-grounds and ages about both religious and secular matters. As a pas-toral minister and spiritual director,[2] I am accustomed to listening to women and men speak to me about their prayer and its relation to their daily life. A few months into the writing of the book, I began asking friends informally about their experience of prayer. Soon after, I devised a short questionnaire letter and sent it out. Answers began to trickle in in the form of written stories and telephone con-versations.

In Berkeley, as a new PhD student in my early forties, I happily reentered academia but missed the inner-city neighborhoods of Boston where I had worked just before moving west. I began attend-ing St. Columba, a church on Oakland's broad San Pablo Avenue, where stained-glass windows memorializing Irish- and Italian-American parishioners of generations past look down upon a most-ly African American congregation. Gospel music and Catholic liturgy have become one at St. Columba, as they have in many urban parishes in the United States, from Chicago to New Orleans. Three years later, I am still there. My solitary prayer is often in con-versation with this communal experience.

Berkeley is in bloom virtually year-round, with less fog and more sun than San Francisco, just across the bay. My relationship to nature changed when I moved here. On my walk to school and back, I spend much of my time gazing—often gaping—at flowers in a perpetual riot of color. I live with the exuberance of nature and with its fragility on a daily, even hourly, basis. Looking at the hills, coast, and vegetation that soothe my eyes and remind me of the Mediterranean of my childhood vacations, I remember that the beauty of the Bay Area topography and the earthquakes to which we are subject here have the same origin. I also spend more time outdoors, and the outdoors come to visit indoor living space in the form of ants and long-legged spiders. Rose gardens and hot tubs off-set the rigors of academic boot camp. Yoga classes, acupuncture, and massage therapy are as easy to locate as the neighborhood coffee shop. Creation, nature, and the body have moved to the fore in my life of the past three years. Naturally, this has affected my prayer.

Prayer, life experience, and book research have merged. The year I moved west, the funeral of a friend, more than a decade younger than I and dead from cancer after a remarkably rich life, tore open the places where grief and prayer meet, deep in the heart. My Jewish cousins' eldest son became a bar mitzvah, and I watched him lead the Saturday morning Shabbat service with humor, reverence, and aplomb. Classmates and friends invited and accompanied me to Baptist, Episcopal, and Melkite Catholic worship services, and later to Presbyterian, Russian Orthodox, and Lutheran celebrations. I became a regular at my aunt's Seder table on the first night of Passover with the West Coast branch of my mother's family. The circle grew. Having gone online in late 1995, I joined several "lists" (subscribers' discussion groups on the Internet), a few Christian and one Zen Buddhist, and in 1996, using the same informal questionnaire I had sent to my friends, I asked my fellow list members to send me their experience of prayer if they felt comfortable doing so. A wave of stories arrived on my computer screen from as close as Oakland and as far away as South Africa.

Somewhat hesitantly, I wrote my Unitarian Universalist parents, who remain puzzled at their odd duckling of a child's conversion to Catholicism two decades ago, and asked about their prayer, or whatever held its place in their lives. They wrote back with seriousness and care. A Greek Orthodox colleague told me how he and his wife used icons in their prayer and which images they chose to hang in their young daughter's room as a sign of God's blessing and presence. In a seminar on "Theologies from the Underside of History," I read excerpts from slave narratives that spoke of secret gatherings of the "Invisible Institution," where prayer was inseparable from the hope of freedom and the plotting of resistance and escape. In the same class, I heard a South African theologian speak of his companions' arrest for praying in an era—all too recent—when simply holding vigils for those imprisoned for protesting apartheid was a crime. I asked Jewish friends about the meaning of their Sabbath celebrations and the significance of repeating traditional blessings. Liturgical dancer Carla De Sola and I spent a morning on the floor of her dance studio, designing sequences of movements that might help people pray with their bodies.

And, of course, I prayed, prayed as I walked, prayed as I wrote, prayed the gospel music at St. Columba. As most people do, I also had difficulty praying, experienced dry spells, and yes, forgot to pray.

Bringing into this project friends and strangers from near and far has made me even more acutely aware of the importance of the life of prayer of what my religious tradition calls the communion of saints, all those people of faith, dead and alive, whom distance and time cannot separate from me or from each other. Like the rest of my life, prayer lives inside a matrix of friendship—the friendship of human beings, which is sacred to me, and the friendship of the One who creates and sustains us daily, and whom I as a Christian worship in the name and spirit of a Jewish man named Jesus. This Jesus, the Gospel writers tell us, told his followers that he would always call them, not servants or slaves, but friends—a radical statement in occupied territory ruled by the Roman Empire.[3]

In the late 1980s and early 1990s, during the research and writing of my first book, *Generous Lives: American Catholic Women Today*,[4] I pored over thousands of pages of notes and transcripts from hundreds of hours of interviews. I remember realizing, on the fourth or fifth draft of the chapter speaking of the women's understanding of God and prayer, that I needed to go beneath their words to the assumptions underlying what they said. It may be easier for readers to enter this book knowing *my* assumptions. I hope that my naming them will give the reader more freedom in relation to them rather than less, precisely because I have been clear about where I stand.

I write as a person who prays, a practitioner of meditation, an intellectual, minister, activist, and theologian. I write as a white woman who has spent a great deal of time in African American communities, and as an American born, raised, and educated in France. I write as a Catholic Christian of Jewish ancestry who was raised a Unitarian Universalist, spent seven years in the girl scout movement associated with the Reformed Church of France, attended Friends (Quaker) Meeting on and off during my adolescence, and began practicing Buddhist meditation in college. While I am unapologetic about being a Christian believer, I am also deeply committed to, and involved in, interreligious dialogue, and my parents' agnosticism keeps me in close and respectful touch with perspectives and experiences other than my own. In many ways I am typical of the baby boomers depicted by Wade Clark Roof in his book *A Generation of Seekers*—eclectic in spiritual practice, accustomed to pluralism, influenced by the therapeutic culture of the United States, and concerned with the restructuring of religious community.[5] From my family, my undergraduate years at Oberlin College, and my Catholic Christian faith, I have received a strong commitment to social change. I cannot live this commitment apart from the practice of prayer.

I assume that anyone can pray and that prayer can be taught, although the source of our yearnings and learnings is God. I assume that prayer can best be learned in community and with the help of a community—even a community that is not physically present. My developmental bias—that one can grow in the spiritual life—is typically Catholic. One can make progress in prayer. Not all Christians hold this assumption, though all have fervent practices of worship.

In many ways I share assumptions about prayer with the Catholic women I interviewed for *Generous Lives*. That spiritual development is possible in this lifetime is one of them. Four others stand out: the spiritual life is real; God is accessible; God is generous; and the imagination is a good thing, useful to spiritual development, part of a mature religious life.

The spiritual life is real. I do not mean only that God to me is real, but something even more basic: the spiritual life, the life that prayer punctuates and sustains (though it is not identical with it), is its own reality; it cannot be reduced to something else, such as a subset or dimension of psychology. This is not to deny the connection between spiritual life and mental health, between psychology and religion—or between religious and social or sociological realities. But the spiritual life is *itself*—and it is not a projection, not an illness, not something one outgrows after coming of age.

I believe, with the biblical witnesses, that God is profoundly Other. I believe with these same witnesses, and with much of the Christian tradition, including my own Catholic religious family, that God is with us inside the world: that God is accessible. To ordinary human beings, not just to saints. Other, but not unknowable. Creator, but not averse to conversation. Mystery, but also Presence. With presence comes hospitality: the God to whom I pray is a generous God, "merciful and slow to anger," as the psalmist writes. It is not that I spend every day full of trust and peace; the chaos within and the state of the world prevent this. After the Shoah,[6] how can we not wrestle with the question of the absence of God? And in the exhaustion and confusion of contemporary life, how can we not lose a sense of God's presence or the will to pray? In times that starve for hope, it is often memory that saves—memory and community: I know that God is generous because of my own experience but, thank God, not only through my own. I can look back and look around, and in the history of those who have prayed and struggled before me, in the life and prayer of my broader family of faith, I meet the generous and present God and renew my hope.

All religious traditions have a particular form of imagination, but not all treasure openly the use of human imagination in prayer. Mine does, and rather blatantly. From the use of images to focus one's prayer to the use of the imagination or of sensory memory to enter into biblical stories, the Catholic Christian tradition encourages the imagining self; it does not fear imagination nor seek to outgrow it. I sit comfortably within this tradition, practicing a prayer that includes not only the imagination but the senses, the body, the emotions. It is our whole self which prays—heart and mind, body and soul, spirit and flesh. *When in Doubt, Sing* is anchored in this belief.

The language of prayer includes silence, song and gesture, tears and groans, but also words. The words I use in prayer are different from those I used as a child and those I spoke three or seven years ago. Many parts of the Christian tradition wrestle today with the use of male and female images for human beings and for God, but also with the languages—spoken, sung, and danced—that reflect the world's many cultures. As a woman who was raised in two cultures and the name of whose field, theology, can be translated as "knowledge of the divine," but also as "language about God," I am passionately concerned about this question of the language of worship. I know also how much it divides and pains sincere people who pray. In the prayers from many sources that accompany the text of this book, I have included both prayers whose language calls and comforts me and prayers whose language does not, but which I know comfort and call other women and men. I hope readers will ponder these words in the spirit in which I have offered them—and hold them close or let them go, as the Spirit moves.

At the end of almost every chapter of this book is a section that includes Christian prayers old and new, poetry, and some prayers and meditations drawn from other religious traditions. In this eclectic age, such a choice is not unusual, and in the context of my own life, it feels natural. It can raise some problematic questions: Can one really take a Sabbath prayer out of its Jewish context? Can a Christian practice Buddhist meditation without knowledge of the Four Noble Truths? If any find the mix offensive, I ask their pardon. Honoring the integrity of religious traditions is a delicate matter these days, as many of us live on the edges or at the intersection of several communities, or simply learn to appreciate and treasure the gifts of other religious bodies with what Lutheran bishop and biblical scholar Krister Stendahl has called "holy envy."[7] Religious traditions themselves are in flux, and within each of them exist varied perspectives on what constitutes integrity and legitimate boundaries. My goal has been simply to help others pray. I hope that readers will receive the mix of prayers, spiritual exercise, poems, and meditations in that spirit.

The title of this book, *When in Doubt, Sing*, is taken from one of its chapters, which speaks of the role of music and singing in prayer, and with singing *as* prayer. Nearly every person who spoke to me about prayer talked about music. Music, especially song, has nourished my own prayer all of my life. As for doubt: I have found that doubt and faith are not as separate from one another as one may think. Hence the juxtaposition. One can be uncertain what one believes and still pray. First sing; then believe. Or sing your doubt—alone, or better yet, with companions in the struggle.

I speak here of many forms of disciplines and habits and ways of praying. Like the language of prayer, they are only a means to an end, which is drawing closer to God—or letting God draw nearer to you. This is the only thing that matters. If an insight or suggestion in this book is helpful or useful, enter into it. If not, leave it behind. It is the living relationship between you and God that is important—not whether this technique or that, this approach or that, this word or that, has "worked" for you. These are only—let me say it again—a means to an end. But on the path, too, you will meet God. Not just at the end.

Above all, if you can, read the book actively. Make it yours.

What is prayer? A sentence, paragraph, or page of definition would not bring us much closer to the doing of prayer. I keep hearing Jesus' words to his would-be disciples. Curious about this compelling person, his teaching and his life, wondering for what and for whom he was willing to live and die, they asked him, "Where do you live?" "Come and see," he answered. Come and see.

CHAPTER ONE

The Experience of Prayer: Memory, Attention, and Hope

··origin

In the morning, while it was still very dark, [Jesus] got up and went out to a deserted place, and there he prayed.

MARK 1:35

Enslaved Africans took the remnants of their traditional religious structures and meshed them together with their interpretation of the Bible. All this occurred in the Invisible Institution, far away from the watchful eyes of white people. Only in their own cultural idiom and political space could black slaves truly worship God. . . . White folks . . . sought to whip and kill slaves if the latter met secretly to praise God. . . . To belong to God's realm of rule meant African American chattel professed themselves children of God. . . . Under slavery, the children of God secretly hoped for the day of Jubilee, the inbreaking of heaven's Kingdom on earth.

DWIGHT N. HOPKINS

I wonder if I could ever describe what my heart feels. Could it be in words? I couldn't do it justice. In music, in painting? *Pas question*, at this point in my life. So I praise the glory of what I see—a silent hymn to a moment of complete at-one-ness and humble gratefulness.

Last evening I went outside to pick some flowers. There were the wild
yarrow or Queen Anne's lace growing by the raspberry bushes, yon-
der were the phlox. White and fuchsia would be the two colors. I have
a gorgeous bouquet in the living room, which fills me with halleluyahs
each time I go by them. . . . And then, as I picked the flowers, the most
brilliant sunset, which left my heart full of exultation and wonder . . .

JOAN REDMONT (MY MOTHER)

My friend Miriam is fifteen years old. On the day of her bat
mitzvah, the Jewish ritual celebrating her coming of age
as a religious adult at the age of thirteen, she stood in the
synagogue her family attends and chanted in a clear voice the
Hebrew text of the day's assigned reading from the book of Genesis.
During the traditional speech she gave after her reading, part scriptural interpretation, part reflection on the occasion, Miriam
observed, "Today, as I chanted from the Torah, I was doing what I
have watched all my life, and what Jews have been doing for thousands of years. When I hear the eerie tones of the chants, I feel
related to all Jews everywhere." Relatedness, community, and memory cropped up again and again in her remarks: "I am very
intrigued by the fact that today and every day I pray in Hebrew, I
am repeating words sung or said by people who lived centuries
before me," she said. "I was a link in the chain of centuries," she
wrote that night in her diary. "I feel so new," she added, "as if a
spring has glowed over my soul."[1]

Two months later, on the Martin Luther King, Jr., holiday weekend, St. Columba Catholic Church in Oakland resonated with the
sound of keyboard, drums, clapping hands, and raised voices.
During the Prayers of the Faithful, which move from formal, prepared petitions to spontaneous prayers from the community, a
woman whose face I could not see spoke up from the choir. Using
language familiar to generations in the African American Christian
community regardless of denominational affiliation, she prayed "in
thanksgiving for our ancestors. It is because of them that we have
come this far by faith. It is their faith, their lives, that help us to 'keep
on keeping on.'" A few minutes later we celebrated the Eucharist,

listening as we do each Sunday to Jesus' words: "Do this in memory of me." A man who is chief financial officer of a local hospital and another who spends much of his time on the streets were among those who wished each other peace and shared the bread and the cup.

Ancestors. Centuries of believers. Biblical stories heard and retold by aging men and teenage girls, by slaves and exiles, by the settled and the homeless. Jesus' gestures and words. Words of thanks. Hope in hard times. "This far by faith." Hope for our children. "Keep on keeping on." History and expectation met in both these celebrations, converging into the present. Memory and hope are the twin engines of biblical religion. Both Judaism and Christianity are fueled by them, religions not chained by belief in fate but convinced of God's active presence in history—of the possibility of change. We pray inside history, consciously, to the Holy One whom we meet there, God inside our lives and our lives inside God's.

We live by memory, embodied in stories, scriptures, rituals, and festivals. In the Jewish and Christian traditions, there is no prayer without it. Think of the Passover Seder, where the telling of the Exodus from slavery in Egypt—the "coming out of" the country whose name in Hebrew, *Mitzrayim*, means "the narrow place"—is so alive that the language accompanying the ritual meal is in the first person as well as the third. Think of those Christian traditions whose Sunday liturgies follow a lectionary, a set of biblical readings heard by believers all over the world on the same day, in Africa, Asia, the Pacific islands, Europe, and the Americas. Think of the bodily, communal memory-in-action that Christians bring forth when they celebrate communion (the Lord's Supper, or Eucharist), or the washing of the feet, the gesture by which Jesus confirmed his radical statement "I no longer call you servants, but friends."[2] Think of the stories of the saints, canonized and uncanonized, grandmothers and desert mystics, wanderers and householders, scholars and farmers, whom Christians recall and honor in varied ways, pondering texts, lighting candles, venerating icons.

Worship, communal or solitary, is a work of memory. Even the quick prayer many of us toss up or sigh out—at work, on the subway, in the seconds between waking and sleep—is born of memory, a pause in time, to remember. It is also a pause to be mindful, to pay attention to the present. Memory and attention: both hallow our time, make it sacred by knowing it *as time*, not as a commodity to be consumed or conquered. Our society's structures do not encourage this kind of pause, much less the longer, more sustained ones, the Sabbaths of our lives. Contemplative spaces are scarce. Much of our life is speedy, geared toward production, mesmerized with flashing images—not icons whose visual grace we savor, but split-second pictures on a screen with sound bites to match.

And yet: "Presence" was the most prevalent word or metaphor for God among the Catholic women I interviewed a decade ago for *Generous Lives*, before "Father" and every other traditional and less traditional name for the Creator God, the Holy One. The same word cropped up again on the road to this book among Episcopal men, Methodist women, and others; I heard it from Jewish friends as well; it has become a constant in my own life of prayer. "Presence," but also "being present." Edward, a friend in his late forties who is a member of the Episcopal Church, wrote to me, "I suppose that my personal prayer would fall under the rubric of 'standing in the Presence.' Prayer in my life is an ongoing, though at times disjointed, internal conversation. During the course of the day as well as often in the middle of the night, my thoughts are turned to and in God. The prayer of sighing is an essential element. These are not sighs of a disgruntled soul or an angry person, but the expression of a constant sense of the divine, ineffable Presence. I never expect any kind of direct response from this internal prayer, but hope somehow it makes some kind of sense to the divine if not to me."

Being present and knowing that God is present: sometimes that is all prayer is. It sounds almost too simple, but I have found it infuses a day with an attention that charges—or buoys—each moment with layers of complex mystery, a wonderment that stops speech. During the year preceding my decision to enter the Catholic Church, which also happened to be my first year in divinity school, I read Thomas Merton almost constantly. I read not the well-known early autobiography, *The Seven Storey Mountain*, which never "grabbed" me, but the later *Conjectures of a Guilty Bystander*, Merton's journal from the 1960s, as full of social concern as it is of prayer. I also read the very short *Thoughts in Solitude*, which taught me rich lessons about prayer and the Christian life, different as my own circumstances were from Merton's. In *Thoughts in Solitude* Merton writes, "The spiritual life is . . . first of all a matter of keeping awake."[3]

Christianity has always sustained a focus on the present—the reign of God, said Jesus, is among us[4]—but the present has sometimes gotten squeezed between honor of the past and hope for the future (in this life or the next). In this generation, the encounter with religions born in Asia, especially Buddhism, has given us, among many gifts, a reminder of the *now* of spiritual practice. "Mindfulness practice means that we commit fully in each moment to being present. There is no 'performance.' There is just this moment," writes Jon Kabat-Zinn, whose work in behavioral medicine, teaching, and writing draws on the long tradition of Buddhist meditation.[5] It seems these days as if my prayer as a Christian has blended with the Buddhist practice of mindfulness, or at least received a transfusion. Jewish-Christian dialogue is also helping Christians enhance their focus on the present, since Judaism, grounded though it be in remembering, also celebrates the present moment with reverent intensity. At a bar mitzvah I attended last year, relatives and friends of the young man and his family converged upon Oklahoma City from around the United States, Canada, Mexico, Germany, and Scotland to celebrate—religiously at two services, but also with food and dance and conversation and song. Being in the present moment, together, in joy: for nearly three days that was our only charge.[6]

Although the narrow definition of "prayer" that comes to many people's minds is that of petition, entreaty, or supplication, most persons who pray—and the Christian tradition from which I speak—understand prayer much more broadly. Among Christians today prayer takes countless forms, from contemplative, wordless sitting in the presence of God to the ecstatic songs of Pentecostal gatherings, from tearful begging to "Thy will be done." Memory and attention inhabit all these forms, but so does hope. Visions of what biblical texts call the heavenly city and the reign of God permeate the present. Some of these visions concern the hereafter, others life on earth in this time, a new social order. The "day of Jubilee" to which slaves looked and of which they sang in spirituals was never just the otherworldly realm their masters thought they heard described in the songs; it was freedom in this life, in this country, in their own time. Bodily freedom, spiritual freedom, economic freedom, communal freedom.

"All will be well, and all will be well," fourteenth-century mystic Julian of Norwich wrote, "and every kind of thing will be well."[7] Her words, written in an age of plague, have the ring of certainty, but not that of the "power of positive thinking": Christianity is not so much a religion of optimism as a religion of hope. Christine, a professional woman in her late forties working in Atlanta, recently found herself in a situation of intense stress and distress, caught in a maelstrom of institutional evil and ethical dilemmas so complex that she could not speak of it to anyone but her husband and a clergy counselor. Though she is a close friend, I still do not know the details of her ordeal, only the signs and the language of her distress. An active member of the United Methodist Church, Christine spoke to me about the changes her work situation had wrought in her understanding of hope, and in her prayer. "I thought I knew what hope was about before all this," she said, "but I did not know. I have had to discover hope in hard times—to hope against all odds and without the hope of public accompaniment." Alluding in few words to the professional crisis in which she found herself, Christine began speaking of Jesus and the cross. "I don't wish to dramatize my own situation at all—I mean in many ways I haven't suffered: I have a comfortable life, I'm straight, I am married—except to say that in my grief I have come as close as I ever have to understanding some of the agony of the cross. I had always wondered about the language in Evangelical churches about the shame of the cross and the whole business of Jesus dying accused and not defended. There's a particular kind of hope born out of situations like that." She mused, "It's like Paul's image of the whole world groaning in labor and the Spirit sighing in us when we can hardly breathe ourselves.[8] The agony of my isolation in this terrible time has pushed me out into the agony of the world; and the miracle is, I am no longer alone in my pain, and that is the beginning of hope for me. Prayer," Christine said, "is what got me here."

I thought of the starkness of the Gospel of Mark when Christine spoke, a text with which both of us have prayed. It is the least ornate of the Gospel accounts, still raw with the trauma of Jesus' death, the disciples grieving with apparent failure and defeat, and in the midst of this, not outside it, finding hope. Out of this kind of hope comes Christian prayer. And, as Christine learned, to this kind of hope prayer also leads. Suffering is real. Death is real. But they are not the final word.

Often this is where community surfaces: church as friendship in the present, church as communion of memory, church as bearer of hope. Christine said to me after speaking of her loneliness and struggle and of the prayer that emerged out of them: "The only way out of those situations, or through them, is through community. In some ways, it's the only salvation; the only hope is community. Without their even knowing it, you rely on communities to carry out and do the hoping for you. And there is the community of memory as well as the community living today—not just their witness and what they have lived through but sometimes their simple presence. Sometimes you can't have people know what you're going through," she added. "So you have the silent company of the communion of saints."

Christine was speaking of believers past and present in her reference to the communion of saints. As she spoke, I remembered sitting in my church in Boston in the middle of a liturgy during a particularly painful time in my life, praying and crying—which came first?—when the friends sitting on either side of me, noticing my tears, reached out and held my hand, wrapped an arm around my shoulder, did not ask, simply held me and continued to pray, and sing. There was room in the pew for suffering and friendship, for praise and lament—no need to check any part of our lives at the door. In this communal acknowledgment, before God, there was hope, inside the tears.

We pray inside the world in which we live: the world of work and love, transportation and institutions, consumption and longing. Context matters: our friendships, families, and other relationships, the state of the economy, whether our country is at war or at peace, the land and the culture of our ancestors. We pray today in a world riven with division and violence, where the gap between the rich and the poor grows daily in the United States as well as overseas. We pray in a religiously pluralistic society where our neighbors may or may not pray, and where, if they do, they may pray as Episcopalians or Quakers, Mormons or Baptists, Muslims, Jews, or Hindus. We pray in a culture where the roles of and relationships between women and men are undergoing changes that trouble some, encourage others, and challenge all. We pray on a planet encircled by electronic networks of communication that make conversation across continents easier than ever before, where travel is frequent and staying in one place for life has ceased to become the norm.

Our context is not just our social world. We pray also as inhabitants of planet Earth and participants in nature. The mountain ranges, the corn, the grass pushing up between the cracks of an urban sidewalk—they are part of our community.[9] My mother has taught me about this, perhaps more than any other person. She has taught by example, through her stubborn gardening work, year after year, in back of our old vacation house in Vermont; her hikes in the woods and love of swimming outdoors; her conversations with animals settled and stray. My mother is a decidedly social person— "irrepressible Joan," my father calls her—involved in the lives of organizations and of families beyond our own, but in a deep sense she understands the world of nature as her community. It is there she feels most at home. Our parents, whether they intend to be or not, are our first teachers of prayer. My mother taught me to gaze and to walk on the earth. Decades before the environmental movement, she picked up litter and lectured children she saw leaving candy wrappers and paper on the ground—embarrassing me mightily, as she embarrassed me the day she lectured our French greengrocer about apartheid when she saw he was selling oranges from South Africa. "Don't you know what they are doing to people there?" she said in her American-accented French. "How can you support them?" "Don't you see what you are doing to the ground?" she said to the children, my contemporaries, when they littered the grass in the summer camp her parents had founded in Vermont.

I have come to realize only recently that these two actions of hers—her small economic boycott and speech to the grocer, and her picking up of trash on the ground—were part of the same awareness of the relatedness (our Buddhist friends would call this "interbeing") of all beings on earth and with the earth—an awareness that both leads to prayer and is the consequence of prayer. Gazing at creation, walking on the earth, knowing our relationship with all beings—all are part of prayer.

Writing on the subject of prayer in a post-Einsteinian universe, David Toolan, a Jesuit friend, notes a shift in our contemporary awareness of nature and the cosmos, both a return to ancient ways and a jump forward beyond the mechanistic views of the Age of Enlightenment: "Today's Christians, like yesterday's, will want to sense in their bones that the blessing of God is not something apart from, but latent in the very energies of the stars, the planets, and the earth."[10] True. I cannot count the number of people—including active, churchgoing Christians of all communions—who spoke to me of praying outdoors, of being moved by the creation around them to contemplation of its mystery and power and awareness of their relationship with God.

Nature and society are not the only settings for our prayer. We pray—many of us—in the context of our religious community, physically present as mine was in Oakland on that Sunday in January, or absent as it is when Bruce, an economist in his thirties, in Washington, D.C., prays the Anglican Morning and Evening Prayer service by himself, but knowing that around the world people are doing the same. "It is the prayer of the church," he wrote me, "and we are praying together as a church even if we are praying in different places and at different times. It is a form of prayer that rolls on without ceasing; someone, somewhere, is always saying Morning Prayer and Evening Prayer." Our church contexts vary. They may be more or less conducive to prayer than social reality and the natural world. Christians live between the necessity of the church and the sins of the church, but we cannot pray without community. We find it in many places: in cathedrals and in storefront churches, in living-room prayer meetings and public vigils of witness and protest, in twelve-step groups, at weddings and funerals, at special-occasion gatherings of two hours' duration in congregations two centuries old.

Church as community of interpretation shapes our perceptions and our prayer. I passed a magnolia tree in bloom on a crisp day in December, just before sundown. I was walking two streets away from home in the late-afternoon glow, the temperature dipping from the fifties to the forties; the tree was a surprise. I stopped and drank in the sight of it. A grateful moment: presence was everything; only the present was there. I remember thinking, in the next moment, that the magnolia tree with its gray branches and pale flower had a certain

Zen look, reminding me of the sparse beauty of Japanese gardens. Beyond the ecstasy was simply the Zen "only seeing." Almost simultaneously, more layers appeared: I am simply too biblical not to think of Moses when I see a tree with a halo of light. Trees aflame do not exist outside of time for me—not only the time of the cycle of the seasons, but the time in which God and humans meet inside history, the time we learn about in the community of belonging.

❧

B'FEH MALEY SHIRAH—THE GIFT OF GRATITUDE

A Sabbath Day blessing

Our mouths filled with song.
our tongues overflowing with joy—
We bless the source of this life
and so we are blessed.

MARCIA FALK

❧

Lord, oil the hinges
of our hearts' doors
that they may swing gently
and easily to welcome
your coming

A PRAYER FROM NEW GUINEA

REMEMBERING IN HOPE

Possible Settings

- A quiet moment at home, alone.
- During a walk outdoors.
- On a train, bus, or subway ride.
- In front of a sheet of paper or computer, pen in hand or keyboard at your fingertips.
  (You can either write or type, or draw if you are not a "word person.")

Begin

Is there an event, a story, a ritual,
that for you is a bearer of both memory and hope?
Think especially of events, stories, rituals
that are not yours alone,
ones that have a community dimension,
whether the community is religious and cultural
or some other grouping that has shaped your life.
Scan your memory for these bearers of memory and hope.

Focus

Asking the Holy Spirit for guidance, pick one.
One event, story, or ritual that is for you a bearer of memory and hope.

Dwell

Dwell with it.
Recall the memory. Remember the hope.
Why is the memory so powerful for you?
Which community has helped carry it into your life?
Has any community helped to sustain it?
Why does it give you hope? How?
Which hope?
What have been its fruits?
    Take your time.
If you feel drawn to staying
with only one of these questions,
and/or one answer only,
dwell in it.
It is enough.

Give Thanks

Remembering this hope-bearing event, story, or ritual,
give thanks to God for its presence in your life.
Take your time.
Your prayer may lead you to further conversation with God.
Talk to God,
but also listen.

Listen to both the memory and the hope.
Listen for the Voice.

> Holy One, how have You been present to me in this treasure I remember?
> What are You kindling in me through this hope?

Go Forth

As time allows and as you are moved,
return throughout the day
to this event, story, or ritual
and to the insights of this meditation.
How can you continue to keep alive
this hope-bearing memory?
How is God already helping you to do so?
Is there a community that can help to sustain this hope?

❧

This prayer is a favorite of one of my beloved teachers, Krister Stendahl, Lutheran biblical scholar, retired Dean and Chaplain of Harvard Divinity School, ecumenist and worker in interreligious dialogue, and retired Bishop of Stockholm. The prayer's source is unknown.

> O thou eternal Wisdom
> whom we partly know
> and partly do not know;
> O thou eternal Justice
> whom we partly acknowledge
> but never wholly obey;
> O thou eternal Love
> whom we love a little
> but fear to love too much:
> Open our minds
> that we may understand;
> Work in our wills
> that we may obey;
> Kindle our hearts
> that we may love thee.

❧

PRACTICE DOES NOT MEAN REHEARSAL

We use the word "practice" to describe the cultivation of mindfulness, but it is not meant in the usual sense of a repetitive rehearsing to get better and better so that a performance or a competition will go as well as possible.

Mindfulness practice means that we commit fully in each moment to being present. There is no "performance." There is just this moment. We are not trying to improve or to get anywhere else. We are not even running after special insights or vision. Nor are we forcing ourselves to be non-judgmental, calm, or relaxed. And we are certainly not promoting self-consciousness or indulging in self-preoccupation. Rather, we are simply inviting ourselves to interface with this moment in full awareness, with the intention to embody as best we can an orientation of calmness, mindfulness, and equanimity right here and right now. . . .

The spirit of mindfulness is to practice for its own sake, and just to take each moment as it comes—pleasant or unpleasant, good, bad, or ugly—and then work with that because it is what is present now. With this attitude, life itself becomes practice. Then, rather than doing practice, it might better be said that the practice is doing you, or that life itself becomes your meditation teacher and your guide.

JON KABAT-ZINN

Begin Where You Are, Not Where You Ought to Be

The earth is the Lord's and all that is in it,
the world, and those who dwell therein.

PSALM 24:1

Don't set limits to the mercy of God. Don't believe that because
you are not pleasing to yourself you are not pleasing to God. God
does not ask for results. God asks for love.

THOMAS MERTON

In prayer as in many other areas of life, we tend to begin with a
"should" rather than an "is." Often we cannot begin to pray
because we feel we ought to say certain words, or place our body
in a certain position, or show God a certain face. But prayer, like
Zen practice, involves a "beginner's mind." On a psychological
level, this involves letting go of self-judgment and self-consciousness.
On the level of faith, it means trusting—or learning to trust—that
God wants us to come truthfully, without masks, "Just as I Am," as
the old evangelical hymn puts it.

Prayer in daily life is *today's* prayer: not tomorrow's anticipated prayer, not next week's routine (the prayer equivalent of "I will join the health club next week"), and not yesterday's prayer, the one that no longer "works," the prayer we prayed as children, or the one we prayed when we were in another mood, another place, another life situation.

Our whole life belongs in prayer: emotional, intellectual, physical, sexual, social, economic, political in the broadest sense of that word. Our doubts and our pain, not only our wishes and our dreams. Our whole selves. Beware the trap or tyranny of the "ought." Acknowledge what is. Tell the truth about your life. Begin where you are—not somewhere else.

"Ought" is often a rushed or pressured thought or feeling. To practice honesty in prayer, it helps to slow down, enough to notice, to pay attention to our life situation, our feelings and thoughts, the people around us, our growing edges, the places where God may already be waiting for us. Kosuke Koyama, a Japanese theologian, writes in his book *Three Mile an Hour God*: "We live today in an efficient and speedy life. . . . There is a great value in efficiency and speed. But . . . I find that God goes 'slowly'" in helping human beings to grow. "'Forty years in the wilderness'" points to God's "educational philosophy," Koyama says, referring to the time the people of Israel spent in the desert. In the wilderness we slow down to the pace at which we walk: three miles an hour. Entering prayer—I think Koyama would not disagree—is, in many ways, entering a kind of wilderness, where the essentials of life stand in starker relief than they do outside, in the world's rush. "Love has its speed," Koyama writes. "It is an inner speed . . . a spiritual speed. It is a different kind of speed from the technological speed to which we are accustomed. . . . It goes on in the depth of our life, whether we notice or not, whether we are currently hit by storm or not, at three miles an hour. It is the speed we walk and therefore it is the speed the love of God walks."[1]

To encounter the love of God in prayer today, we may need to slow down to "three miles an hour."

All religious commitment costs; how we sustain our commitment in prayer varies. My "rule of no rule," as a Christian who prays and as a spiritual director, is that there is no one way, no "right" way to pray. So much depends on temperament, circumstance, and time of life. Working outside and inside the home, becoming a parent, losing a parent, falling in love and out of love can affect our prayer. How could the prayer schedule or practice of a married administrative assistant who is the mother of three young children be the same as that of a retired celibate professor of theology who does not do his own cooking or cleaning, or that of an adolescent who is homeless in a new city after running away from an abusive home? Since I became a doctoral student, my prayer has become much more bodily, no doubt because I deal so much in the verbal and conceptual on a daily basis; both instinctively and deliberately, I search for contrast or balance. I pray more with the visual, with candles and icons, with nature and the out of doors, than I did three years ago. Ann, a young woman of Catholic background from Pennsylvania, recently returned to school as well. She wrote me: "I'm not sure where I am right now. I feel very resistant to meditating. It is such a transitional time for me in this degree program that sitting still seems to elicit tears or anxiety. The sadness is very difficult. The uncertainty is difficult. Right now I pray by listening to Carlos Nakai, a Native American flute instrumentalist, especially his version of 'Amazing Grace.' And I pray using something I learned in a Tibetan Buddhist class this past year: Breathing in, 'May I be happy.' Breathing out, 'May I be free from suffering.' Breathing in, 'May all beings be happy.' Breathing out, 'May all beings be free from suffering.' And sometimes I light a candle and take a bubble bath and just sit there knowing I am not alone."

Diana, an academic editor in the San Francisco Bay Area, describes her daily private prayer, an early-morning ritual, in these words: "I light three candles for the Creator, Redeemer, and Sanctifier, set my watch for fifty minutes, and nestle into a comfortable sitting position. I let my mind wander with distractions for about the first ten minutes; this is my way of discovering what is uppermost in my mind. Then I center in: 'Holy Spirit, please guide my prayer.' My body language changes; I relax, my shoulders loosen, my hands open upward upon my lap. The quiet deepens. With the in-breath I call, 'God,' with an out-breath I say, 'Creator of life,' in-breath, 'have mercy,' out-breath, 'on me.' I repeat the verse for half the meditation, switching midway to: in-breath, 'I am one,' out-breath, 'with the will of God,' in-breath, 'let it happen,' out-breath, 'as You say.'[2] There is stillness. Sometimes it is so exquisite I get excited and cling to it. But you can't cling. This place of peace is a precious gift. It is to be relished in that moment—not desired, not sought, not grasped, just taken in—in Joy with the Divine. From this might also emerge a revelation or realization—a thought, an idea, a dream interpretation. Not every time is profound, of course, but having reaped the fruits so many times I know they will come again. The alarm goes off. I respond, 'Oh, my loving Creator, how the time flew!' Or equally often, 'Oh, Divine One, that session seemed an eternity!' I wind down with prayers of petition for friends in need, issues of concern, and longings of my heart. I follow with gratitude for the gifts I have received, and prayers for continued hope and perseverance. I rise to my little table where the lectionary sits open to the day's readings: one from the Hebrew Scriptures, a Psalm response, a Gospel passage. I reflect a moment longer, blow out the candles, and rejoice in the blessing that a new day has begun."

Richard, a banker in New York, also uses the Catholic lectionary to read the day's Bible readings, reflecting on them with or without the help of a commentary by a biblical scholar, and more recently, as part of his daily prayer, writing, enjoying the sensuous feel of pen on paper, away from his computer. But his account is different from Diana's, reflecting another temperament: "Private prayer for me is a way to keep in touch. My prayer is nonmystical; too little time, too little patience. Often it is a single word—'Help' or 'Thanks.' At times it is no more than a deep breath, an attempt to pick up signals—no, simply to keep the signal channel open—at an unconventional frequency. At times, prayer is a courage-steeling maneuver; sometimes a guilty spasm spurred by the ghosts of the church militant of my childhood; sometimes, rarely, perhaps almost never, in prayer I catch the shadow or echo of an epiphany."

It helps, as Richard, Ann, and Diana instinctively do, to make allowances for temperament in prayer. Subscribers to one of the Internet forums in which I participate, most of whom are Catholic, engaged in a lively discussion two years ago on plans for the season of Lent. One of us asked: What will you do? How will you carry out the traditional threefold practice of prayer, fasting, and alms giving, especially the first? Shannon is a pastoral minister in a parish, a position no longer uncommon for Catholic women, who may not be ordained but often work full time on church staffs. She wrote, "I've been reading a book in which the authors offer the questions: 'For what moment today am I most grateful? For what moment today am I least grateful?' I've decided to take those to heart, modifying them for my dramatic personality: 'What gave me life today? What drained life out of me?' I have decided I will answer those questions every night from now until Easter, and I will not analyze my answers until after Easter. My task is to simply pay attention to my life and make note. I trust the Spirit will help me with the rest."

Russell, another subscriber, responded: "All I am doing is (1) saying a daily rosary in thanksgiving for God's gift of His Son Jesus Christ to the world, (2) leading a Lenten Gospel Bible study with the catechumens of our parish, and (3) attending weekly Stations of the Cross.[3] You guys have much better stuff to do than me. I will have to be more creative next year." Shannon wrote back: "Russell lamented that 'all he was doing for Lent was praying a rosary a day, leading a Bible study for catechumens, and attending weekly stations of the cross' . . . and I wanted to stand and cheer. That's hardly something to downplay."

She added, "What I have come to learn is that I operate in the world differently. Where most of the spirituality books I read talk about interior quiet, and taking an hour for quiet prayer, this raging extrovert goes nuts. It's not that I'm undisciplined, or unwilling. I just operate in the world differently. So the things I have learned to do for Lent in particular, and in my own prayer life, are different from what others do, because they work for me. Because I work in a parish, and because it is the public prayer of the gathered community which most stirs me, you'll find me at the major liturgies throughout this season. All the prayer in and around the catechumens, candidates, and returning Catholics is part of what I take in to pray with."[4] Elyn, another pastoral minister, interjected, "Funny, this extrovert has the opposite reaction. I work in two very different parishes and, as a musician and RCIA team member, I am involved in a lot of public prayer. So I have resolved this Lent to spend some time in private prayer."

Authors who study and practice both psychology and spirituality have begun pointing out that temperament draws each person to pray in particular ways. Wisely, they encourage people both to pray according to their natural disposition and to stretch beyond their temperament to encounter God in new ways. Human beings tend to relate to the world primarily "through the senses, the intellect, the intuition or the emotions," writes Episcopal priest Nancy Roth in a summary of the popular Myers-Briggs typology.[5] Just as healthy persons would try to bring these dimensions of themselves "into balanced integration," so too they can seek this balance in prayer. "We limit ourselves if we use only the mode of prayer which we happen to find most natural," Roth writes.[6] This book is meant both to help you begin with the practice most natural to your circumstances and personality and to expand your prayer practice. Both are fruitful. Both are necessary. Both require self-knowledge and attention to one's inner rhythms and inclinations.

Our preferred mode of prayer may be related to *where* we feel close to the holy. One of the friends in my new California life is my PhD classmate Nancy, a Mexican-American woman in her late thirties who was raised in El Paso, Texas—desert country where the border looms—and was a longtime resident of the Pacific Northwest before her move to the Bay Area. "I always find the desert very prayerful, and the Grand Canyon even more than the rest," she said to me. "It really is a death-and-resurrection experience, because you go down into the bowels of the earth, and there are all these extremes, and then you emerge. The grandeur of God and creation is so strong." She added, "It's too big for me to absorb."

Another close friend, Sonia, was raised in Queens, New York, and lives in Boston, my former home. An educational administrator and a new mother, she spoke to me of a trip to the Grand Canyon she had taken with her husband before the birth of their child. "Why do I feel the presence of God so much more in the middle of Roxbury [one of Boston's inner-city neighborhoods] at ten o'clock at night?" she asked. "I am such a city kid—I would never win the Francis of Assisi award. When we were at the Grand Canyon looking out over this incredible landscape all I could think was 'Get me away from the ledge.' I mean, God really put out for the Grand Canyon," she said laughingly, acknowledging the grandeur of which Nancy spoke. Asked why she felt the presence of God in the inner city, she answered, "It has something to do with being with the disenfranchised." Sonia and Nancy are both in their thirties; they share a commitment to working with and on behalf of people at the margins of society; they were raised in the same religious tradition, with some ethnic differences—Sonia is Italian-American—but a similar sense of festival and celebration, which both their cultures treasure. Despite these similarities, their response to the Grand Canyon, and the places that move them to prayer, seem to derive from temperament, upbringing, and geography: daughter of the desert, daughter of the city.

Neither Sonia nor Nancy prays only in the places where prayer comes most easily, the ideal environment. The other side of knowing where one prays most easily is recognizing that one can pray anywhere. Anita, a Jewish friend, spoke to me of the many places she has "made Shabbat," welcoming the Sabbath at the appointed time no matter where she finds herself, praying the blessings to sanctify the evening and the day that Abraham Joshua Heschel called "a palace in time."[7] "Shabbat is completely portable," she said. "You can make it happen anywhere. I remember one time in a really shabby hotel room in Québec with my daughter, saying the blessing over the wine in a sanitized-for-your-protection paper cup, and another time when we made candleholders out of shells on Martha's Vineyard."

One can pray also at any time: I remember asking the women in *Generous Lives* when and how they prayed and hearing that they carved out time late at night, early in the morning, and especially while commuting—in the subway, bus, or car. On my return home from one of my interview trips, I called an old friend for a "reality check": Did she pray during her commute too? "Of course," she said with a laugh. "Jesus rides in the passenger seat."

There is no hierarchy of prayer: ranking modes and manners of praying will not help us grow closer to God. I still struggle to integrate this knowledge more deeply into my own life. In my case, the "ought" is the prayer of the contemplative or meditative tradition of the church, which drew me to Catholicism in the first place. I often feel as if any other prayer is "less": not contemplative enough or not still enough or, more often, not disciplined enough—shadows of parental speeches on self-discipline perhaps, unrelated to prayer but settled in my psyche. With this attitude, many of us may feel we are not "praying well" or not praying at all, when in fact we simply need to pray in a different way. My friend Mary, a theologian, responded with characteristic forthrightness when I asked her about forms of prayer in her life: "I'm about on that where I am on fashion," she said. "No prescriptions but whatever feels like it fits, gives good protection from the elements, and otherwise enhances life seems fine with me."

Mary does not seem haunted by perfectionism or by questions about her own worthiness when it comes to prayer. Many are. Even when we have come to understand that we do not need to be a saint to pray (and that those whom we honor as saints, being human, have plenty of flaws), interwoven issues of worthiness and perfection can block our prayer. Often they are related to forgiveness: we are hard on ourselves, have trouble forgiving ourselves even more than we have difficulty forgiving others—which is hard enough.

Both perfectionism and self-forgiveness bear a direct relation to our understanding of God. The first step of prayer is telling the truth about who and where we are. It is also, at the same time, learning the truth about who and where God is. We are the ones who tend to place limits on the mercy of God. Prayer involves a capacity to stretch our imagination, to imagine and therefore to begin knowing a God who is not a projection of our own self-condemnation.

"This is not the spiritual Olympics," I once wrote to one of my directees—a piece of wisdom I often forget myself—when I sensed her prayer had become focused on "getting it right." My quip has become shorthand, in our conversations, for remembering that perfectionism and competition—even competition with oneself—are not standing over us with a stopwatch, nor rating our performance.

There is a relationship between perfectionism and performance or production. The idea that prayer is somehow a production (in the economic or in the theatrical sense—both are destructive) will take us away from prayer. "Begin where you are" means begin where you *are*, not with what you do or what you produce. Certainly the will is involved when we pray; the discipline of prayer is a doing. But prayer is not *about* doing. It orients us toward being, toward the fact that human beings' value resides in their very existence, not in production or achievement. This is how the Creator views us: with love for who we are and because we are.

This is how Jesus, in the Gospels, encounters the rich and the poor, tax collectors and fisherfolk, children and adults, wounded or triumphant, ill or well.

One of the people who see me for spiritual direction is a woman I will call Marie. She struggles with multiple, interrelated emotional and physical problems—including an obsessive-compulsive disorder that causes her to walk far more than is good for her, since she is anorexic and painfully, frighteningly thin. She knows the walking is not healthful, at least in large quantities. She cannot stop. Her therapist wishes she would. So does she—on the days when she has the wish and will to change. When she came to me she was walking, compulsively, for hours on end each day. "Begin where you are," I suggested. "Don't stop walking if you can't stop. Walk mindfully. Breathe. Pay attention to each step. Can you try this?" She tried. The walking became more attentive, slowed down. It has not stopped. But we work together so as not to see the compulsive walking as something outside her prayer, something that is too ill and distorted to be touched by God. In the walking can be attention, gratitude, a different way of being in the present.

Marie's walks, which begin where she is, have become repeated occasions to contemplate God's creation and praise the Creator. This is not the only way she prays. The Bible is a central part of her spiritual life. She is drawn to the Gospels and to stories like the healing by Jesus of the woman who was bent over, her body constrained for years. She also has come to love communal worship. A new way of walking, singing in the church choir, studying, and praying with the healing stories of Jesus: all of these have brought her into a closer relationship with both her body and God.

～∞〜

QUESTIONS TO ASK YOURSELF AS YOU BEGIN

As you enter into your time of prayer, ask yourself:

Am I tired?
How tired?

Am I angry?
How angry?
At what or at whom?

Am I sad?
> How sad?
>> Why?
>> Where in my body does the sadness reside?

Am I afraid?
> How afraid?
>> Of what? Of whom?

Am I grateful?
> For what?
>> For whom?

Is my heart at peace?

Once you have spoken these truths to yourself, tell them to God.
Then listen.

GO DOWN

Go down
into the plans of God.
Go down
deep as you may.
Fear not
for your fragility
under that weight of water.
Fear not
for life or limb
sharks attack savagely.
Fear not the power
of treacherous currents under the sea.
Simply, do not be afraid.
Let go.
You will be led
like a child whose mother
holds him to her bosom
and against all comers is his shelter.

DOM HELDER CÂMARA

Dom Helder Câmara, the author of "Go Down," was Archbishop of Recife
and Olinda in northeast Brazil for twenty-one years. The author of several

books, including *Spiral of Violence* and *The Desert Is Fertile*, he was best known for his love for the people of his diocese—among the most economically poor in Brazil—and for his advocacy of their basic rights, as well as for his infectious smile and deep spirituality. He died in 1999 at the age of ninety.

∽♋✑

Jesus,
receive our love and worship.
Show us how to give you what we have,
for nothing is too big or small
for us to offer, or for you to use.

                              A NEW ZEALAND PRAYER BOOK

AN INCHWORM'S ALLELUIA

Dear God, is any bug more calculating
Than are we inchworms, shyly tiptoeing,
Measuring our steps, so we will know the number
Of thanks we owe you for our empowering?
We may not move as fast as others do,
But we get joy from dancing in a loop,
Omega-shaped, then stretched out toward the future,
Then with feet hunched again, forward we swoop.
Happy, we thrive, yet as we thrive we change!
Alas, we'll soon turn into moths who fly
Uncalculated distances aloft,
Infinite inches, up into the sky.
On that bright day, O God, may we remember
Each journey always with one small step starts,
And trust that, though you once gave us but inches,
You've dreams for us far greater than our hearts.

                              WILLIAM CLEARY

"DON'T THINK GOD IS TRYING TO CATCH YOU"

Thelma Hall, a wise and holy woman belonging to the Religious of the Cenacle, a Catholic religious order, gave this to me at the beginning of my first eight-day silent "directed retreat," a short version of the Spiritual Exercises of Saint Ignatius through which she guided me in January 1977.

If we do not pray, it is because we sometimes hold superstitions, one form being this: if I give myself up too much to God, God will give me something too hard which I cannot do. This is not Christian maturity. It presupposes that Our Lord is playing tricks with us all the time. We have to get rid of the thought that God is a powerful deceiver, that God is ready to catch us in some moment of weakness and impose some terrible punishment. This is a dreadful concept of God. The first thing necessary is to root out every vestige of this thought of God. Don't think God is trying to catch you. . . .

Open yourself to God. God will never, never fail us. We have to really believe we are totally forgiven. Don't set limits to the mercy of God. Don't believe that because you are not pleasing to yourself you are not pleasing to God. God does not ask for results. God asks for love.

THOMAS MERTON

CHAPTER THREE

Praying with the Body

When I run, I feel God's pleasure.

OLYMPIAN ERIC LIDDELL, *CHARIOTS OF FIRE*

How beautiful you are, my love
my friend! The doves of your eyes
looking out
from the thicket of your hair.

Your hair
like a flock of goats
bounding down Mount Gilead.

Your teeth white ewes,
all alike,
that come up fresh from the pond.

A crimson ribbon your lips—
how I listen for your voice!

The curve of your cheek
a pomegranate
in the thicket of your hair.

SONG OF SONGS 4:1–3

God called to him out of the midst of the bush,

[God] said:

Moshe! Moshe!

He said:

Here I am.

[God] said:

Do not come near to here,

put off your sandal from your foot,

for the place on which you stand—it is holy ground!

EXODUS 3:4–5

I cannot imagine praying without my body. My morning "sun salutation"—a classic series of yoga postures—is very much a prayer, a greeting of the day, breathing and stretching, being aware as I awaken of the reality of creation: my own being as well as the world around me, the sun or rain pressing against the window, the goodness of being alive, the reality of middle age showing up in my hip joints, the time taken early in the day to remember, before I begin to rush and run, that I have and am a body, and that this too is where God dwells, speaks, teaches, and heals. I also remember praying at certain times when words failed me and I was filled with either reverent awe, discouragement, or intense weariness, simply by kneeling—almost crouching—very close to the ground, curled forward, head against the floor. My posture spoke for me. It was enough. It was all I could do.

I attend St. Columba for many reasons, not the least of which is the opportunity to pray with the body. I love contemplative, quiet prayer environments, monastic spaces where silence and stillness play a great role. In those places one becomes aware of the body in subtle ways; in the alternation of kneeling and standing, the reverberation of chant and breath, or sometimes the sheer endurance required for regular prayer, which tests body and senses as much as mind and heart. But I am also an extrovert who loves to sing and dance and move and clap. For the past three years I have spent my life in an academic setting, where PhD study requires that I spend a lot of time "in my head." At St. Columba, my whole body is involved in worship. The brain is still ticking, ruminating on the readings, hearing and critiquing the sermon like the academic and preacher I am, but the gospel songs tug at the heart, and often the body prays first: in the call and response of the songs and hymns, I pray with voice, hands, arms, sometimes feet. I pray with the eyes, looking at brightly woven cloth, flowers, and faces, always the faces—fresh, worn, reverent, weary, mostly dark, always beautiful.

At St. Columba, I am also inside a greater body, the community, which literally and figuratively embraces me, Sunday after Sunday. This is a church that welcomes. Some of the old-timers, like my friend Maurice, a retired merchant seaman, do not like the clapping and gospel music a great deal, but they come, and their greeting is no less warm than the greeting of those whose preference is to sway rather than stand still. Each Sunday we invite visitors to stand up and speak their names, applaud them, and ask those in the congregation with birthdays and anniversaries to come forward and receive our blessing—*our* blessing: one of the ministers, ordained or lay, speaks the prayer, but we all extend our hands.

We humans are embodied beings—not souls encased in foreign flesh. The biblical view of the human is not a dualistic one, contrary to popular belief. It is that we are one, body and soul. The Christian belief in the resurrection of the body is a manifestation of this understanding of the person. A spectrum of theologies of the body exists within Christianity, and some, like that of Christian Science, are less incarnational than say, the Catholic or the Orthodox. True, a dualism between body and spirit has crept into the Christian tradition since the early centuries of the church and often competes with what one might call the more holistic dimensions of the tradition. This dualism still haunts us, especially those whom it affected as children and adolescents learning to live inside their bodies. But ethnicity, locale, culture, and family background also play a role, families especially. In my interviews of Catholic women I found that when families were comfortable with their bodies and with sexuality, it did not matter what the women heard in church as children: the family ethos predominated. It was only when negative messages in both church and family colluded that damage occurred.

Practices born in Asia, both in the Far East and in the Indian subcontinent, have worked wonders in reviving in Westerners a sense of the body in prayer. For me this has happened through the practice of hatha yoga, both in the *asanas* (postures) and in *pranayama* (breathing exercises), as well as in Buddhist meditation practices involving a focus on the breath. Remembering the body in prayer has also come to me in the reading of Scripture, especially the Song of Songs, which I often use as a text in wedding sermons. Interpreters have allegorized and spiritualized this book of the Bible for centuries—a legitimate reading of the text. But it is also some of the most beautiful and earthy love poetry in existence, sensual and sexual, delighting in created, bodily reality. This exquisite poetry, which both the Jewish and the Christian traditions lift up as holy Scripture, proclaims that being in love is good. Its witness to us is that physical and emotional passion and longing are holy, that in this longing and passion, God is present. Loving bodies are one of the places where we meet God, where we learn about God, where we look for God.

Taking seriously the Incarnation—God's presence with us in the flesh—and worshiping with awareness and participation of the body are related. We are embodied beings. God is embodied. We are images of God. The word does not exist apart from the flesh. There is also another way of looking at incarnation and Jesus' bodiliness: not just as God's presence with us in the form of a human person, but in the dailiness and detail of it, the way in which Jesus, in his earthly life, dealt with bodies, day in and day out: hungry bodies, sick bodies, bodies of women and bodies of men, bodies of living children and of children who appeared to be dead. The Hebrew Bible is as a rule much more sensual and embodied than the Christian Testament,[1] but the Gospels at least have their own sense of nature and of the body whole and healed, and with this we can pray. Read the Gospels with a focus on the life of Jesus. You will find bodiliness nearly everywhere. Jesus touches eyes, ears, mouths, restoring speech and sight. He heals lame and paralyzed people. He feels the need and the urgent pull of the unnamed woman with the flow of blood who touches his cloak. He eats with reprobates and high officials, drinks wine, multiplies loaves of bread and handfuls of fish. He weeps real tears when Lazarus dies, rests weary feet in the home of Martha and Mary, and receives anointing with fragrant oil from the woman whose name we do not know but whose gesture is recorded in all four Gospels.

Jesus walks in wheat fields and climbs hills, goes out on the water in a boat, tells parables of seeds and trees, rock and sand. In his stories, a young man guards pigs, another seeks out a sheep, a woman kneads dough, and another sweeps her house, looking for a lost coin. A hen is an image of God, covering her chicks with homely wings. A shepherd chasing errant sheep is another figure of the divine. Even after the Resurrection, Jesus is still dealing with bodies: breaking bread on the road to Emmaus, grilling fish on the beach for his friends, showing wounds to a doubting disciple.

Praying with the body is related to knowing with the body. Body knowledge is real knowledge, not lesser knowledge. To know God is to know with one's bodily self. Many of us have learned our religion through the body. Orthodox and Catholic Christians especially have spoken to me of this learning, rooted in childhood. "We Catholics," David Toolan writes, "were a pre-Gutenberg phenomenon with a bias for the charity of God made palpable to the five senses and the sympathetic nervous system."[2] Praying with the body is not a new experiment, born only of a welcome infusion of Eastern meditation and holistic health. It is also an ancient Christian tradition. Protestant traditions too have their bodily worship, though they may not use incense, icons, statues, or architecture in the same way as their Catholic and Orthodox counterparts. In black churches especially, but in almost all religious communities born of the Reformation, song is where the body worships. Prayer reverberates in the body through melody and words, sometimes plainly sung, sometimes triumphant, sometimes ecstatic.

In my own tradition, the Eucharist is central to worship: we listen to the Word proclaimed, we sing our faith, but we also eat and drink it and pass it from hand to hand. The supper that Jesus left his friends is a bodily prayer. Take, eat. Take, drink. There are variations in the ways different Christian communities commemorate and celebrate the Lord's Supper, communion, the Eucharist, the Mass. The symbols are minimal in some places—thin wafers, scarce wine—and extravagant in others—bread dipped in warm cinnamon-scented wine, as in one of the most reverent and bodily services I have attended, a Melkite Catholic Lenten Liturgy of the Pre-Sanctified Gifts. I recently learned again how bodily the Eucharist is, understood it in a new way, at an experimental and public liturgy planned and celebrated by Catholic women working for church renewal, with men and children in the congregation as well. After holding the loaves and bread and cups of wine close to our hearts—"This is my body, this is my blood"—we placed them back on the altar and touched each other with the same words—"This is my body, this is my blood"—sharing the gesture among the whole assembly. You are my flesh and blood, we were saying to one another, and Christ's flesh and blood. "The body of Christ" took on a renewed meaning on that day, for me and for many others.

Bodily expression varies from church to church. After reading an article I had written about the women's eucharist, one of my Wisconsin friends wrote, "Remember that Midwesterners are not necessarily comfortable praying with their bodies!" Regions have their bodily customs, as do ethnicities, churches, and denominations. Churches have temperaments, as people do. Most Baptists I know will hold hands in church at the drop of the hat—or the call of a preacher. At Friends (Quaker) Meeting for Worship, people do not touch each other in prayer, but rather sit, waiting in silence for the Spirit to speak, and at the close of the meeting reach out to one another with a frank handshake. As with styles of prayer, ways of praying with the body have no hierarchy: individuals and religious communities have their own comfort zone. It is forgetting the body, or denying it, that can be dangerous and detrimental to prayer. The next time you are in church, or the next time you pray alone, observe the body, be aware of it. Your attention can be as simple as watching your breath. If prayer is paying attention, it is paying attention also to the body—to the signals it gives us, to the way it wants to pray, to the way it holds tension, fear, even hope.

There are many ways of praying with the body. In querying friends and acquaintances about their prayer, I discovered that more and more seem to be using walking as a meditation or as a way of prayer— an interesting corollary with Koyama's "three mile an hour God." A few engage in structured Zen "walking meditation,"[3] but most do not. My friend Peter had adapted the Zen walking meditation—usually practiced in an enclosed, neutral space with little sensory distraction—

to his morning commute as a pedestrian in downtown New York. It does not replace his Jewish weekly and daily prayers, but adds another dimension to his spiritual practice. Karen, another New York friend, finds church attendance difficult these days. She cannot pray with comfort in the manner of her Baptist and Presbyterian origins. Still, the impulse to worship lives in her body. Her walking, she writes me, has become her prayer.

Shannon, the parish minister of whom I spoke in the previous chapter, told our online forum: "During Lent of 1995, our parish used the image of the burning bush and invited people to take off their shoes during the Sunday liturgy, to recognize that here, as well as all through the week, we stand on holy ground. Originally we thought people would simply slip their shoes off once they were in the pew. But a huge pile of shoes began to appear in the hospitality area. All during the season and on into Easter, people talked about how that simple action made them more aware of what they were doing throughout the rest of the liturgy."

Nancy, a hiker, runner, and trained dancer, said, "For me as a woman, being physically strong in my body is a really important part of my prayer life. So many things in my life, so many systems operate not to support my personhood, especially as a woman of color. So God calls me through body, prayer, feeling, and movement: that enables me to live in situations in communities that are less than supportive, to continue to participate." On a retreat "that ended up being like a vision quest," Nancy said, "I came into an understanding of the deep themes of my life and spiritual journey. One was that of being an athlete, as the foundation of everything else."

Praying with the body is also praying with the senses. On retreat at the ecumenical monastery of Taizé in France, and later at Benedictine monasteries, I remember experiencing a sharpening of the senses. My Zen friends speak of the same experiences when they go on *sesshin*, an extended Zen retreat. Disciplined spiritual practices—regular prayer times; quiet, conscious eating; a simplified rhythm of life—all are part of what the Christian tradition calls *askesis*, a Greek word meaning "training," the root of our "ascetic" and "asceticism." These practices are not a denial of the senses—certainly not a deadening of the senses—but a paring down or simplifying so that the senses can emerge. This is, I think, why after a day or two at a

Benedictine monastery, one hears the birds in a different way, feels the chant reverberate in the body with greater intensity, tastes bread and fresh water with a new tongue.

Ignatius of Loyola, the founder of the Jesuits, encourages the use of the senses in his Spiritual Exercises: the whole person, Ignatius believed, could and should enter into prayer. Ignatius's "composition of place" is based in a biblical meditation: when one reads, say, a passage from the Gospel, one applies the senses, memory, and imagination to the passage to project oneself into it. During the miraculous catch of fish after the Resurrection, Jesus is on the beach cooking breakfast for his disciples on a charcoal fire. What does the beach look like? How cold is the water? What is the smell of grilled fish and bread? How loud are the waves? How resonant is Jesus' voice? Imagining myself as one of the disciples, wet from the spray coming over the side of the boat, relieved and amazed at the catch of fish, realizing suddenly that the stranger on the beach is Jesus, how do I then approach Jesus? What can I say to him? What do I hear? The prayer moves from there.

Some people dance their prayer. Sacred dance makes its appearance in churches in varied ways, joyfully chaotic in storefront Pentecostal communities, simple and solemn in the carrying of incense to the altar in high-vaulted Episcopal or Catholic churches, complex and powerful in portrayals of Mary giving birth to Jesus and other choreographed liturgical dances. Annmarie, a Catholic sister in her late thirties, wrote to me: "For as long as I can remember, I have danced before God. As a child, I went to the basement of our home and danced and danced, in secret, my fears and my joys and my simple love for God. I never told anyone I had danced like this. When I was twenty-one, I saw sacred dance done for the first time in a public prayer service. I was surprised to see someone else do it and amazed that anyone would have the courage and generosity to share it all publicly. I was a novice in my congregation[4] then and was even more amazed when my novice director, who had no idea that I was dancing privately, invited me to do a sacred dance at a prayer gathering of our sisters. Most amazing of all is that I said yes without the slightest hesitation! I am not a person who enjoys being 'onstage' in any way, shape, or form. However, for the past sixteen years of my life, I have been dancing at prayer and liturgies consistently."

Annmarie explained further: "The passion of my dance comes from my almost daily experiences with God in movement. I am a very rational thinker by nature. Dance takes me far beyond the rational and allows me to touch into the mystery of God." She added: "Lots of times too I 'dance in my head.' Often I imagine an encounter with God where we are dancing together. That's when I turn into a 'real dancer' and I leap and turn and run and fly effort-lessly! And God dances with me, around me, before me with equal ease. I encourage people who tell me that they too long to dance their prayer but cannot because of physical limitations to just try imaginary dance. There are absolutely no boundaries or restrictions and you can dance in the most beautiful settings!"

⚬⚬⚬

BEGIN. BREATHE. A SIMPLE BODILY PRAYER

1. Begin seated or standing, as you prefer.

   You can try this exercise both ways and see which is most comfortable for you and/or which draws you more deeply into a prayerful or meditative mood.

   If you are seated, sit with your back straight and your feet on the floor.

   If you are standing, stand with your legs hips' width apart; rock a bit from side to side until you find a centered, balanced position.

2. Place your hands against your chest. Let them rest on the upper part of your chest, touching (but not overlapping) or close to one another. The left one will feel your heartbeat. (Relax the elbows. Do not lift them.)

3. Simply breathe. (Through your nose, with your mouth closed, jaw relaxed, without forcing the breath.) Breathe. Feel the breath. Your breath. The movement of your hands as your chest expands and con-tracts. The beat of your heart.

4. Do this for as long as is comfortable for you before going on to the next step.

5. On the out-breath, extend one hand in front of you, palm open and upward.

6. On the next in-breath, slowly bring your hand back in to your chest.

7. When you are ready, do the same with the other hand and arm: on the out-breath, extend the hand in front of you, palm open and upward.

8. On the next in-breath, slowly bring your hand back in to your chest.

9. Be with your spirit. Be where it is right now. Do not force yourself to pray with words. The language of the body is enough. If you need to give voice to your experience before God—with words, that is—please do so. But if you can, try first the wordless way. See where it takes you.

10. Let this be your prayer.

    Or, once you have engaged in this exercise,
    move gently to another kind of prayer:
    praying with Scripture, praying for others,
    sitting wordlessly in the presence of God.

                    MOVEMENT SEQUENCE BY CARLA DE SOLA
                    TEXT BY JANE REDMONT

Carla De Sola, one of the United States' leading liturgical dancers, trained at the Juilliard School and the Pacific School of Religion in Berkeley, California. She currently teaches at the Graduate Theological Union in Berkeley. She is founder of the Omega Liturgical Dance Company and director of the Omega West Dance Company.

TWO CHRISTMAS PRAYERS FOR THE WHOLE YEAR

    God our beloved,
    born of a woman's body:
    you came that we might look upon you,
    and handle you with our own hands.
    May we so cherish one another in our bodies
    that we may also be touched by you;
    through the Word made flesh, Jesus Christ,
    Amen.
            JANET MORLEY

    Loving Word of God,
    you have shown us the fullness of your glory
    in taking human flesh.

Fill us, in our bodily life,
with your grace and truth;
that our pleasure may be boundless,
and our integrity complete,
in your name,
Amen.

JANET MORLEY

HANDS THAT BLESS, PLEAD, AND DANCE

Bodily Prayer for Shy People, Wheelchair Users, Bedridden Persons, and Sedentary Folk

This is but one model of a "sitting prayer with movement." Experiment with it. If you have movement in only one arm or hand, use the arm or hand you have. Or use your eyes, your neck, your fingers. If you are using an oxygen tank, it is not safe to light a candle; one woman I know was able to spend a bit of time without her oxygen tube; a man had someone bring for him a lamp with a soft, rosy light. If you are blind and cannot work with light and dark, you may want to experiment with a safe source of warmth or heat instead. If shyness rather than mobility is the issue for you, begin with just one step or two of this bodily prayer. Remember that God created and loves you—all of you, every part.

If you need to stop partway through the sequence, perhaps you can express to God what you are experiencing at that moment, what you are discovering—or wondering—about God and about yourself, in this mobile prayer. Take your time.

1. Sit in a comfortable position, with an upright spine if this is possible for you, with a candle nearby, on a table or dresser.

2. Light the candle.

3. Extend your arms and reach toward the light; and with a gentle motion, draw the light toward you. (The light, not the candle.) As you draw in the light, bathe in its warmth. Receive it as the warmth and light of the Spirit. Draw it close to your heart.

4. Repeat this motion twice more, so that you have reached toward the light and drawn it in a total of three times. Take your time. Let your movement be gentle.

5. Now let your hands rest on your chest, near the heart. You can close your eyes if you wish.

6. Be conscious of the rise and fall of your chest. Sense what is in you.

    "When I am doing this, I realize I'm listening in a kinesthetic way to what I am feeling," says liturgical dancer Carla De Sola. "Kinesthetic" means with all your perceptions and senses at once—understanding, touch, hearing, smell, sight—as many as you have at your disposal and can bring into this prayer.

    Keep your listening on the level of "sensing"—do not use your mind to become distant from what is in your heart.

7. Open your hands. And wait.

8. Let the next gesture arise from there.

    This gesture can become your own song or psalm.
    It can stay very simple or become more complex.
    Allow your arms, hands, fingers, eyes to work from your center, from your heart. Let them speak.
    Any gesture is appropriate. Only you and God will know what it is.

9. Return your hands to your heart, as in Step 5, and as in Step 6, sense what is in you.

10. Again, open your hands.

11. And again, move from your core.
    The first time, you just sensed it, just "did it."
    This time, notice what it is you are or were expressing in your gesture(s):
    I am grieving. I am relieved. I am afraid. I am amazed.

12. Become one with your movement. Keep doing it. Repeat it.

13. Once you have repeated the movement once, twice, three times, you can stop in a particular position. Ask yourself: What do I "read" in it? If I saw this gesture in a sculpture, what would it say to me? Or what would I, as the sculpture, be saying? What am I feeling?

14. You do not have to tell God with words what you are feeling, how you are yearning, why you are making a particular gesture. Your body speaks. Your heart feels. God knows.

MOVEMENT SEQUENCE BY CARLA DE SOLA
TEXT BY JANE REDMONT

GREETING THE NEW DAY
....

My practice in the morning is to begin the day with ten hatha yoga sun salutations. For a long time I moved from yoga to sitting meditation to prayer (with
or without Scripture as a springboard in that third stage). More often these
days, movement is my morning prayer. Carla De Sola and I designed the following morning sequence with the sun salutation in mind, but hoping to create a more simple and accessible movement. This sequence can both awaken
your body and begin your day toward God. Try it. If you prefer, begin with
one or two steps, then add one each day. Do not rush or force your body. You
have all the time in the world. See what happens when you repeat this exercise
day after day. Does it make a difference?

You will need a quiet space, but not a very large one. If there is street noise or
the sound of people or animals nearby, try to move slowly and breathe deeply so
as to let your ears receive the noise peacefully, without judging it or tensing your
body. Do keep away the noises you can control: radio, television, recorded
music. In time, you may want to add recorded music, but for now, let the music
of your body and its environment be enough. If possible, do this alone and first
thing in the morning. If you do not live or sleep alone, find an early-morning
time in the bathroom, kitchen, or corner of the living room or back porch. This
may take you as little as five minutes or as long as twenty or more. Adapt it to
your own use. Do it without haste. Greet the new day, which the Creator has
given us.

1. Stand comfortably.

2. Bring your palms together, against your chest, pointed upward.

3. Slowly, turn your fingertips, palms still together, in toward your heart
    and . . .

4. Press the palms of your hands outward and upward,
    opening the chest as you open your arms upward. Slowly.
    You will feel a stretch. Your lungs will open.
    (Your palms will separate during this movement.)

5. Bring your arms widely, loosely down by the sides of your body.

6. Bend the knees slightly—gently—and . . .

7. Extend your left arm toward your right knee and then up,
    bringing it back toward the left above your head
    and back down in a falling motion to the left side of your body,

almost backward—as your body allows; do not strain.
Feel the space as the circle of your arm goes through it.

Keep a sense of fluidity in the movement.
Images that might help you: windmill; waterfall.

8.   Now the opposite side:

Knees slightly bent,
extend your right arm toward your left knee and then up,
bringing it back toward the right above your head
and down in a falling motion to the right side of your body,
almost backward—as your body allows; do not strain.
Feel the space as the circle of your arm goes through it.
Keep a sense of fluidity in the movement.
Images that may help you: windmill; waterfall.

9.   Come back to the center. Keep the knees loose. Remember to breathe.
Both your arms are now by your sides again.

10. As your body allows, arch backward and lift your arms; let them reach
backward, up, as far as you can—do not strain—and . . .

11. Bending your knees, let your arms carry you forward like a waterfall.

12. Touch the earth with your fingertips.

13. Draw your hands upward along the sides of your body, up the legs, thighs,
waist, and torso, as if nourishment from the earth were traveling upward
with them.

14. Keep drawing your hands up, and as they approach your shoulders and
head,

let the gesture open like a flower,
your arms extending up and sideways, arms and palms open.
Breathe in and out, deeply but without forcing the breath. Sigh if
you need to.

15. Draw the arms into the body and place one hand open upon the other.

Palms both face upward.
Your hands are slightly touching the abdomen.
Your upper arms are close to the body.
The feeling of this position is open but contained.
Breathe.

You are ready to face the day,
or to begin the rest of your prayer, as you please.

If you are comfortable praying with your body in the company of others, you may choose to move through this sequence with a partner, or with a small group if you live in community. Let it remain a slow, silent praise. Keep noise and distraction at a minimum. Greet the day and the Giver of the day with your whole self.

If you need to stop partway through this sequence, perhaps you can express to God what you are experiencing at that moment, what you are discovering—or wondering—about God and about yourself, in this mobile prayer.

MOVEMENT SEQUENCE BY CARLA DE SOLA AND JANE REDMONT
TEXT BY JANE REDMONT

Oh God our dance,
in whom we live and move and have our being,
so direct our strength
and inspire our weakness
that we may enter with power
into the movement of your whole creation,
through our partner Jesus Christ,
Amen.

JANET MORLEY

CHAPTER FOUR

Ruach: Breath of God,
Wind of the Spirit,
Breath of Our Life

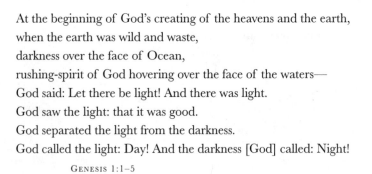

At the beginning of God's creating of the heavens and the earth,
when the earth was wild and waste,
darkness over the face of Ocean,
rushing-spirit of God hovering over the face of the waters—
God said: Let there be light! And there was light.
God saw the light: that it was good.
God separated the light from the darkness.
God called the light: Day! And the darkness [God] called: Night!

GENESIS 1:1–5

When the day of Pentecost had come, they were all together in one place. And suddenly from heaven there came a sound like the rush of a violent wind, and it filled the entire house where they were sitting. Divided tongues, as of fire, appeared among them. All of them were filled with the Holy Spirit and began to speak in other languages, as the Spirit gave them the ability. Now there were devout Jews from every nation under heaven living in Jerusalem. And at this sound the crowd gathered and was bewildered, because each one heard them speaking in the native language of each.

ACTS 2:1–6

Likewise the Spirit helps us in our weakness: for we do not know how to pray as we ought, but that very Spirit intercedes with sighs too deep for words.

ROMANS 8:26

"About four years ago I had a severe asthma attack, which left me with a fistful of inhalers and no energy at all," wrote Kit, an artist in Maryland and a member of the Episcopal Church. "It stopped me in my tracks. For the next several months, as I started to get the asthma under control and to get back my energy and my life, I concentrated on breathing, pure and simple. I spent a lot of time just listening to my breath, 'remembering to breathe,' if that makes any sense, particularly at night when it was harder to do. Somewhere in the middle of all that I ran across Meister Eckhart's words, 'The eye with which I see God is the same eye with which God sees me,' and I realized that the breath that moves in my lungs is also God's breath, God's spirit moving within me, in whom I have my being. I cannot live without breath or spirit. When it was late at night and I was having trouble breathing, I would remember this, and the fear of not breathing, of suffocation, would go away. I can't say it's made me a saint (ask my husband), but it's given me a body awareness of God that I didn't have before. As a result, I tend to use fewer words in prayer and more consciousness, more awareness, more thanksgiving for breath and life."

Kit's experience is reminiscent of the many biblical associations between breath and spirit. *Ruach*, the Hebrew word for Spirit—the Spirit of God or God as Spirit—also means "breath" and "wind." *Ruach* is the Spirit of the Creator moving over the face of the waters; one contemporary translation of the beginning of the book of Genesis, by Jewish scholar Everett Fox, translated the word as "rushing-spirit," an image evoking movement, dynamism, even physicality, not merely an otherworldly reality. In the New Testament, written in Greek, the word *pneuma*, both spirit and Spirit, also has a double- or triple-layered meaning. It is the same root word we find in our English medical vocabulary pertaining to lungs and breathing: pneumograph, pneumonia, pneumocystis. The Latin word for "breath," *spiritus* (the root of a few medical terms; for example, spirograph), in religious texts refers to the Holy Spirit and gave us our English "spirit." Think of some of the words with that root and of their ramifications: *con/spirators*, "those who breathe together, whose spirit is as one"; *in/spiration*, the breath of life, of creativity—of God—rushing in, possessing us; and *spirituality* itself. Breath and God: in our inherited sacred languages, they are never separate.

Writing about spirit, breath, the movement of the heart, and the movement of the body in dance, Quaker author Teresina Havens observes: "The primordial moving energy which we experience in dance cannot be split into 'spiritual' versus 'physical.' It is unfortunate that the translation of the English Bible could not find a single English word for *Ruakh*—and hence separate 'wind' from 'breath' from 'spirit,' the physical from the spiritual. . . . Spirit and breath are one. Through the movement of our own bodies, we experience this unity."[1]

Ruach means common human breath—respiration. It is also the Eternal's Creative Breath—inspiration.[2] Neither exists alone outside the world. The beginning of the book of Genesis describes God's bringing order out of chaos, not creation from nothingness.[3] Breath animates our bodies and those of other creatures. "Our breath," writes Zen master Thich Nhat Hanh, "is the bridge from our body to our mind, the element which reconciles our body and mind and which makes possible one-ness of body and mind."[4]

Many of the world's religions focus on the breath as an aid to meditation, prayer, and other spiritual exercises. In today's Western search for integration of body, mind, and spirit, for health and wholeness, breathing is always present—not only with Buddhist teachers like Thich Nhat Hanh, but in the work of teachers in the field of behavioral medicine such as Herbert Benson, Joan Borysenko, and Jon Kabat-Zinn.[5] Breathing is spontaneous: we all do it, usually without thinking, unless, like Kit, we find ourselves afflicted with an illness affecting the breath. We can also become mindful of our breathing, simply observing the rise and fall of the breath, without modifying anything other than our awareness. Our breathing is also a bodily function we can control, alter, and expand, thereby changing our physiological response to stress. The yoga practice of *pranayama*, which I began learning in my teens, is one such way; the practices recommended by Benson, Borysenko, and Kabat-Zinn, which I discovered in my thirties and forties, are another.

My friend Peter wrote me: "Although my thoughts may wander during formal prayer services, I try to focus on key moments, texts, songs and formulae which have successfully led me into a reverent and mindful state. Whenever I feel that I am not properly aligned, I concentrate on systematic breathing to quiet my soul. Similarly, whenever I feel overcome by the sudden tumults of daily life, I practice the Three Breaths of centering, cleansing, and stillness.[6] The practice was a gift from a friend and, simple as it appears, works instantly. It reminds me of our connection to the Greater Breath, our place in the cycle of creation."

Our breath can quiet us, provide an anchor for meditation, accompany or smooth the way for prayer. But the Spirit of God—the same One Who moved over the waters, the Spirit whom Jesus breathed on his frightened disciples with the word "peace"—also moves within us in prayer, helps us to pray. "The Spirit," Saint Paul writes, "helps us in our weakness: for we do not know how to pray as we ought, but that very Spirit intercedes with sighs too deep for words."[7] One of the marks of the Holy Spirit, in the New Testament, is bold and fearless speech.[8] The same Spirit also groans within us, in what my friend Edward called the prayer of sighing, or even less audibly than a sigh.

"Prayer," writes Episcopal priest Nancy Roth, a dancer, musician, and yoga practitioner and teacher, "is the means whereby we let the Spirit of God breathe in and through us. As breath itself varies with our emotional and physical state, so our prayer varies. It can be a gasp for help, a groan of pain, the disciplined breathing of spiritual 'exercises,' sighs of longing, songs of joy, or the long, slow draughts of the oxygen of contemplative prayer. Just as all kinds of inhalation and exhalation are breathing, all of these ways of 'breathing the Spirit' are prayer." She continues: "Even emptiness can be one of our most powerful teachers, for it is a symptom of our desire for God."[9]

The Spirit helps us to pray in many ways. Each of us may be more aware of a given aspect of the movement of the Spirit in prayer, both communal and individual. If you come from a tradition where set prayers are the norm, you may feel shy or inhibited about

praying spontaneously, or you may find it in some way inappropriate. *The Book of Common Prayer* or another prayer book may provide
you with more security, comfort, and freedom than spontaneous
prayer, and in some ways more challenge as well, drawing you into a
broader prayer than your own. Conversely, if you come from a tradition where all prayer is spontaneous, the set prayers may feel rigid
and confining to you, and you may find them inappropriate to an
authentic relationship with God. My friend and classmate Fred
recounted to me a conversation with his friend Myrna—"Sister
Myrna" to her co-worshipers in the Foursquare Church in which
Fred was raised. Myrna, like other Pentecostals, places a high prior-
ity on the Holy Spirit and the spontaneity of the prayer the Spirit
inspires. She believes that the Holy Spirit simply cannot move in the
more structured forms of liturgy. Referring to the printed order of
worship found in many churches, Myrna declared, "You just can't
run the Holy Spirit off a program, Brother Fred."

The fact is that both understandings are present in Christianity:
the spirit moves in both places and both modes, in either case in
ways that genuinely help us to pray. The Spirit helps us spontaneously and directly, placing the words and the intention of prayer
in our individual hearts, minds, and mouths; but the Spirit also
moves in our collective life of prayer. The Spirit comes in ecstatic
speech, but also in words pondered and repeated. The first coming
of the Holy Spirit recorded in the New Testament, in the book of
Acts, comes to the community. The Spirit, associated with freedom
and bold speech, with healing, insight, and wisdom, the very power
of God—"the giver of life," as the Spirit is called in the Nicene
Creed—is given first to the gathered assembly. Set prayers are the
prayers of the community—the worshiping assembly in the present
but also the community in time, the historically present community.

When I asked Barbara, a recovering alcoholic in Atlanta who
has undergone a profound religious transformation on her path to
sobriety, "To whom do you pray?" she wrote to me: "I pray to the
Spirit. To me this spirit is the Pentecostal Holy Spirit, the love that
God is, the souls that we all have, the energy that created everything
and that everything has today. In this way I feel OK with my
Presbyterian Christianity, the new age spiritual stuff of Unity,[10] and
the feeling I have at an AA meeting. God is warm white light, radiant energy, pure love. Pentecost is my favorite church holy day."

She added: "In the process of having personal experiences in meditation and in the educational process of learning about love, I came to change my mind about myself and about my parents. And I discovered God. The God-is-love God. The energy—the Holy Spirit. So in the [Alcoholics Anonymous] program I say 'My higher power whom I choose to call the Holy Spirit.' I do Eastern-type meditation, but my mantra is a prayer to the Holy Spirit that we used to say after lunch at Our Lady of Victory [a Catholic school]. I chant, but my chant is the hymn 'God is love and he who abides in love abides in God and God in him.'"

God is the One who is as close to us as our own breath—even closer. One of the most ancient Christian prayers is associated with breathing, or more precisely with both breathing and the heartbeat. We know it in English-speaking countries as "the Jesus Prayer." It consists of a simple sentence, usually "Lord Jesus Christ, son of God, have mercy on me, a sinner" (sometimes shortened to "Jesus, Mercy" or even to just the name of Jesus), repeated in conjunction with the breath.[11] Still practiced widely in the Christian East, it has also found its way into the practices of Western Christians. Many of us first read of it in J. D. Salinger's novel *Franny and Zooey* or in the Russian Orthodox spiritual narrative *The Way of a Pilgrim*. In France, where I grew up and where I first learned about it, it is called *la prière du coeur*, "the Prayer of the Heart." If there is a bodily expression as important as breathing in the biblical texts, it is probably the heart, symbol of the whole self, core of our being, the place where God's voice speaks to us most intimately. The association of the muscle pumping blood into our bodies with our most intimate self is an ancient one, not only in the biblical texts but also in other traditions, including Islam, especially in the *zikr* (heart) of the Sufi mystics.

Spirit, breath, and life meet in the Jesus Prayer, or Prayer of the Heart, which, according to Orthodox theologian Kallistos Ware, is "not simply a rhythmic incantation, but implies a specific personal relationship and a consciously held belief in the incarnation. The aim is not simply the suspension of all thought, but an encounter with Someone."[12] It is also one of the ways of entry into *hesychia*, or inner stillness, though Ware notes that "stillness of heart cannot be pursued on its own but presupposes [in its original Orthodox Christian context] all the different expressions of Christian life," including faith in the church's basic dogmas, liturgical prayer, the sacraments, the reading of Scripture, service to neighbor, and the active practice of compassion.[13]

Nancy Roth uses the Jesus Prayer as a model for contemplative prayer, the prayer of quiet: "A simple format for contemplative prayer includes *preparation, finding a focus*, and *passing beyond the focus*," she writes.[14] After one settles physically and mentally into a posture of prayer, the breath and the Jesus Prayer serve as that central focus, whose use "is a means, not an end. The point is not to become proficient at focusing on a mantra, but to focus on God. The word is merely a doorway through which one gazes at God. . . . What one enters through this doorway is not the outside world, but the inside world, at the center of which beats the unending rhythm of God's life in us."[15]

Notice your breath, writes Roth. "Think about your breath at various times in your life. . . . As you think about the moments in your life, you probably realize that your oxygen requirement can be a fairly accurate barometer of your emotional or 'spiritual' state. . . . Both breath and spirit bring us to life, or 'inspire' us. And there, in all its simplicity and depth, we find the connection between prayer and the life-giving breath of God. Just as breath constantly renews the body, filling the lungs with oxygen and emptying the lungs of carbon dioxide, so also our prayer constantly opens us to God's life within us and helps us empty ourselves of those things which are alien to fullness of life."[16]

Trappist monk Thomas Keating writes, "The presence of God is like the atmosphere we breathe."[17]

꧁꧂

Eternal Spirit, living God,
in whom we live and move and have our being,
all that we are, have been, and shall be is known to you,
to the very secret of our hearts
and all that rises to trouble us.
Living flame, burn into us,
cleansing wind, blow through us,
fountain of water, well up within us,
that we may love and praise in deed and in truth.

A NEW ZEALAND PRAYER BOOK

Adorable Spirit,
may the rushing wind of your mercy
blow away all trace of sin within us,
and may your unquenchable fire
purify our souls.
We believe
that you comfort those who mourn,
uplift those who are depressed,
calm those who are angry,
guide those who are confused,
console those who are lonely,
reconcile those who are estranged,
and bring joy
to all who confess Jesus Christ as Lord.
We pray
that you will live
in our simple and humble hearts,
and so make us truly
temples of your glorious love.

DESIDERIUS ERASMUS (1469–1536)

BREATHING—*HA-SHEM*—THE NAME OF GOD

And lo, the Lord passed by. There was
a great and mighty wind; splitting mountains
and shattering rocks by the power of the
Lord; but the Lord was not in the wind.
After the wind, an earthquake; but
the Lord was not in the earthquake.
After the earthquake, fire; but the Lord
was not in the fire. And after the fire,
the soft barely audible sound of
almost breathing.

I KINGS 19:11–12

Moses said to God,

"When I come to the Israelites and say to them,

'The God of your parents has sent me to you,'

and they ask me,

'What is God's name?'

What shall I say to them?"

And God said to Moses,

"Ehyeh-asher-ehyeh."

EXODUS 3:13–14

God spoke to Moses and said to him,

"I am the Lord.

I appeared to Abraham, Isaac, and Jacob

as El Shaddai,

but I did not make myself known to them

by my Name

Yod Hay Vav Hay."

EXODUS 6:2

The letters of the Name of God in Hebrew are *yod*, *hay*, *vav*, and *hay*. They are frequently pronounced *Yahveh*. But in truth, they are unutterable. Not because of the holiness they evoke, but because they are all vowels and you cannot pronounce all the vowels at once without risking respiratory injury.

This word is the sound of breathing. The holiest Name in the world, the Name of the Creator, is the sound of your own breathing.

That these letters are unpronounceable is no accident. Just as it is no accident that they are also the root letters of the Hebrew "to be." Scholars have suggested that a reasonable translation of the four-letter Name of God might be: "The One Who Brings into Being All That Is." So God's name is the Name of Being itself. And, since God is holy, then so is all creation.

At the burning bush Moses asks God for God's Name, but God only replies with Ehyeh-asher-ehyeh, often incorrectly rendered by the static English " I am who I am." But in truth the Hebrew future is unequivocal: "I will be who I will be." Here is a Name (and a God) who is neither completed nor finished. This God is literally not yet. . . .

If God's Name is the Name of Being, then perhaps breathing itself is the sound of the unpronounceable Name. Find a place and a time that are quiet enough to hear the sound of your own breathing. Simply listen to that barely audible noise and intend that with each inhalation and exhalation you sound the Name of Being. It may be no accident that this exercise is universally acknowledged as an easy and effective method for focusing and relaxation.

LAWRENCE KUSHNER

NISHMAT KOL HAY—THE BREATH OF ALL LIFE

The breath of all life will bless,
the body will exclaim:
Were our mouths filled with song as the sea
and our tongues lapping joy like waves
and our lips singing praises broad as the sky
and our eyes like the sun and the moon
and our arms open wide as the eagle's wings
and our feet leaping light as the deer's,
it would not be enough to tell
the wonder.

MARCIA FALK

BREATHING AND MINDFULNESS

TRY: Stopping, sitting down, and becoming aware of your breathing once in a while throughout the day. It can be for five minutes, or even five seconds. Let go in full acceptance of the present moment, including how you are feeling and what you perceive to be happening. For these moments, don't try to change anything at all, just breathe and let go. Breathe and let be. Die to having to have anything be different in this moment; in your mind and in your heart, give yourself permission to allow this moment to be exactly as it is, and allow yourself to be exactly as you are. Then, when you're ready, move in the direction your heart tells you to go, mindfully and with resolution.

TRY: Staying with one full in-breath as it comes in, one full out-breath as it goes out, keeping your mind open and free for just this moment, just this breath. Abandon all ideas of getting somewhere or having anything happen.

Just keep returning to the breath when the mind wanders, stringing moments of mindfulness together, breath by breath. Try it every once in a while as you read this book.

> Kabir says:
> Student, tell me, what is God?
> [God] is the breath inside the breath.
>   KABIR

Practice, Practice, Practice

It helps to keep at it. As you begin befriending your breath, you see immediately that unawareness is everywhere. Your breath teaches you that not only does unawareness go with the territory, it is the territory. It does this by showing you, over and over again, that it's not so easy to stay with the breath even if you want to. Lots of things intrude, carry us off, prevent us from concentrating. We see that the mind has gotten cluttered over the years, like an attic, with old bags and accumulated junk. Just knowing this is a big step in the right direction.

JON KABAT-ZINN

BREATHING AND THE SPIRIT:
AN EXERCISE WITH A QUAKER SPIRITUAL WRITER

Quaker scholar, dancer, and pioneer in interreligious dialogue Teresina Havens (1909–1992) offers several exercises helping us to link spirit and breath, using our bodies. Here she uses the writings of an early Quaker, Isaac Penington, to help groups move and meditate. You may wish to adapt this exercise for individual use. It is the second in a series, following a simple exercise titled "Breathing with One Another" in which partners listen to each other's breathing, one sitting behind the other, palms on the other's back at the level of the lungs and diaphragm.

The divine *Ruakh* (breathing Spirit) brought form out of chaos in the Beginning and continues to renew us in each moment of out-breathing and in-breathing. Our individual life as well as the cosmic life begins with breathing.

Breathing with Penington

Get up and stretch. Sit down, preferably on the floor, with space to extend your arms. Center down quietly. . . . Close your eyes. Let your breath flow out into the wider atmosphere. Let the renewing Breath/Spirit flow in. Let your hands gently support this out- and in-rhythm, at your own pace.

[Havens notes earlier that you can attune to your own breathing rhythm by placing your hands over your diaphragm just below the rib cage on either side. If you wish, reinforce the out-breath by applying almost imperceptible pressure, then lift the pressure on the in-breath. There is no need to take a deep breath: if the lungs are emptied, the air comes in of itself.—JR]

Our teacher in this uniting of breath and spirit is Isaac Penington, an early Quaker who intuitively connected prayer with breathing in his letters of spiritual advice. As you listen to his words, let your body respond, starting with hands and arms. (Where Biblical language hinders you, find your own terms for the universal Ruakh or Breathing Spirit, such as "Great Spirit" or Mystery.)

Let your body respond to Penington's experience of a double movement of Breath/Spirit—the Cosmic Spirit breathing into us, reaching out of us, and our breathing out, reaching out, to the Divine:

> Thus, my dear Friends, let us retire, and dwell in the peace which God breathes.
> In the time of great trouble there may be life stirring underneath . . .
> in which there may be a drawing nigh and breathing of heart to the Lord.
>
> Oh! . . . small breathings, small desires after the Lord, if true and pure, are sweet beginnings of life.
>
> Oh, wait to feel the Seed, and the cry of thy soul in the breathing life of the Seed. . . .

Another letter from Penington makes more explicit what this means: "Breathe unto the Lord that thine heart may be single." Penington is telling us to send forth an intention on the breath. We are to pray/breathe for something. In this case, writing to a parent concerned about how to teach children how to pray, he encourages her to breathe-pray for singleness of heart: "Breathe unto the Lord that thine heart may be single."

Each of us may have our own intention or aspiration or "cry of our soul" to send forth on the breath.[17] Take time now in silence to listen for one. If it feels right to you, let your hands and arms support the intention. Close your eyes. State your intention clearly. Open your mouth; let your diaphragm fall; send forth your intention on the outgoing breath (through your mouth) with a deep sigh. Find your pace. Discover for yourself how to use this practice. You may want to try it daily, to reinforce at the next step in your spiritual growth.

The discovery of a "cry of our soul" may be very tender. Gentle sharing with a single partner may be reinforcing of our intention. Please consider whether you feel moved to share what you have just learned with one other person, or to write it down for your own future explorations. If you wish to share, find someone near you and meet. If you prefer to write, make some notes for yourself about your intention. Those who share orally may wish also to record their intention in writing.

TERESINA HAVENS

TWO COLLECTS TO THE HOLY SPIRIT
FROM THE ANGLICAN TRADITION

Almighty and most merciful God,
grant, we beseech thee,
that by the indwelling of thy Holy Spirit
we may be enlightened and strengthened
for thy service;
through Jesus Christ our Lord,
who liveth and reigneth with thee,
in the unity of the same Spirit ever,
one God,
world without end.
Amen.

THE BOOK OF COMMON PRAYER

Holy Spirit,
mighty wind of God,
inhabit our darkness
brood over our abyss
and speak to our chaos;
that we may breathe with your life
and share your creation
in the power of Jesus Christ,
Amen

JANET MORLEY

CHAPTER FIVE

"At the Still Point of the Turning World": Meditation and Contemplative Prayer

At the still point of the turning world. Neither flesh nor fleshless;
Neither from nor towards; at the still point, there the dance is,
But neither arrest nor movement. And do not call it fixity,
Where past and future are gathered. Neither movement from nor
  towards,
Neither ascent nor decline. Except for the point, the still point,
There would be no dance, and there is only the dance.

   T. S. ELIOT

Practice is very simple. That doesn't mean it won't turn your life
around. . . . Sitting [*zazen*] is essentially a simplified space. Our
daily life is in constant movement: lots of things going on, lots of
people talking, lots of events taking place. In the middle of that, it's
very difficult to sense what we are in our life. When we simplify the
situation, when we take away the externals and remove ourselves
from the ringing phone, the television, the people who visit us, the

dog who needs a walk, we get a chance—which is absolutely the most valuable thing there is—to face ourselves.

CHARLOTTE JOKO BECK

Lift your heart up to the Lord, with a gentle stirring of love desiring him for his own sake and not for his gifts. Center all your attention and desire on him and let this be the sole concern of your mind and heart. . . . In the beginning it is usual to feel nothing but a kind of darkness about your mind, or as it were, a cloud of unknowing. You will seem to know nothing and to feel nothing except a naked intent toward God in the depths of your being. . . . Learn to be at home in this darkness.

THE CLOUD OF UNKNOWING (FOURTEENTH CENTURY)

"Life," my friend Kit observed, "is a pretty noisy place." Most of us can understand immediately what she meant. Even if we are not urban dwellers or suburban commuters, and are among the rare people who live in a quiet environment, we know that inside it is noisy too. Outer noise—which grows louder each day—is not the only cacophony with which we have to contend. There is also the inner chatter, the mind that will not rest, the worry and the turmoil, even the agitation caused by happiness. It can be hard to hear the earth, ourselves, and God in the din.

Ellen, a Midwestern private airplane pilot in her forties who has retired from the practice of psychotherapy to devote more time to her children, wrote to me: "I think I'm probably never far from prayer. Poor God receives something of a monologue from me daily. What needs more work is my ability to *listen*."

Wordless, quiet, often imageless dwelling with God, contemplation is deeper than a prayer of listening, but can often begin with it. From Alaska, Harry wrote: "I try to remember Twain's saying that we have two ears and one mouth and we should use them roughly in that proportion. Most times my prayer is nonvocal." Here in California, Nancy said to me, "In prayer it's important to have moments of quiet, silence, and space. Living is so overstimulating.

Mornings I take time for prayer: just quiet, focusing on my breathing, coming to an awareness of my body and the space around me. There's a hunger for it. And then a kind of sitting in nothingness and being with that."

The contemplative prayer of the church is what drew me to Catholicism in the first place, after forays into Quaker Meetings for Worship in my teens and Buddhist meditation classes in college. I have practiced yoga on and off since the age of fifteen. At Oberlin, I majored in religion with a double concentration in biblical studies and in the religions of classical and modern India; during those years of the Vietnam War, in the late 1960s and early 1970s, I developed an interest in the religious sources of Gandhi's and Martin Luther King's nonviolent direct action. I was beginning to articulate, tentatively, my yearning to find a way of marrying action and contemplation, social activism and prayer. Mainstream Judaism and Christianity had not yet—as they have now—addressed these connections explicitly. In part through a fortuitous visit to my college by Benedictine monk David Steindl-Rast, I discovered that the West had a contemplative tradition of its own and that I did not need to turn East in order to find meditative practices. Through all this and more, from the inchoate childhood desire to pray onward, I found that the heart of all prayer was stillness—even inside music, there was silence calling. I learned one of the truths of prayer: prayer is not words. Prayer is fundamentally attention to God, or listening to God, or simply being in God's presence. Breathing God.

Prayer is being, not doing, at its core. We live in a society overly focused on doing—doing and achieving and performing and producing. Thus, sitting in stillness and quiet can be a profoundly countercultural activity. Prayer, contemplative prayer especially, demands and reveals an understanding of what a divinity school friend, Claire, once called, "the usefulness of uselessness."[1]

I remembered my conversation with Claire two decades later when I read Thomas Moore's *Meditations: On the Monk Who Dwells in Daily Life*. "A billboard near an old house of mind displayed in six-foot type: PRAY. IT WORKS," Moore writes. "I always thought this was the ultimate in American pragmatism. If it doesn't work, do you stop praying? What does it mean to say that prayer works? You get what you want? Life gets better?

"My billboard," Moore continues, "would say: PRAY. IT MAY NOT WORK. Prayer is not an alternative to working hard to get what you want. One discovers eventually that what you want is almost always what you don't need. Pray—period! Don't expect anything. Or better, expect nothing. Prayer cleanses us of expectations and allows holy will, providence, and life itself an entry. What could be more worth the effort—or the noneffort?[2]

We are already in the land of paradox: effort and noneffort, the usefulness of uselessness, praying with no goal. This sojourn begins as soon as we talk about contemplative prayer, the prayer of direct union with the One Whose name we cannot speak. I had more trouble with words on contemplative prayer than with any others in this book, am more aware here than anywhere else of the inadequacy of language. It is difficult to speak of the experience of God, not because it is illusory but because it is so real. Our words turn to poetry. We talk of "unknowing"—as did the nameless fourteenth-century mystic who wrote *The Cloud of Unknowing*. We name what God is not. This is the "apophatic" way, from a Greek verb meaning "to deny."[3]

Bill, a mental health counselor in Oregon, is a forty-nine-year-old Catholic whose years of practice of Zen Buddhism have combined harmoniously with the contemplative practice of Christianity. "Contemplative prayer," he wrote, "is a meditational discipline that prepares you for the gift of contemplation, which is the direct awareness of the Divine Presence. The prayer discipline creates the sacred space, disengages the filter which keeps us from experiencing God in a direct way."

I observed to Bill that here was another paradox of contemplative prayer: in this prayer of "being," there is some clear "doing" involved in the practice of a meditative discipline. "The doing," Bill replied, "is the moment you are hanging on to the limb of the tree, and you let go of the limb, trusting that you will land on your feet and all right. The doing is the act of letting go, again and again, and the discipline of letting go of distraction, again and again." More paradox: we are not used to hearing the words "discipline" and "letting go" together. Paying attention, letting go: in contemplative prayer they coexist. As for our wills, yes, they are involved. But who placed in us the desire to pray in the first place? Who sustains our will?

Contemplation is a gift. Contemplative prayer is a practice. Techniques of prayer are a doing; they do involve the will, but they are only techniques, and they are not meant to "produce." "Our relationship with God is a love affair," Archbishop Desmond Tutu writes, "and ultimately the greatest joy is just to be with the Beloved, to drink in the beauty of the Beloved in a silence that will become ever more wordless and imageless—the silence of just being together."[5]

Laura Ann, a computer professional in Texas and self-described "divorced, middle-aged, white-bread ethnic, nonobservant mainstream Protestant," has for many years felt a pull toward contemplative prayer and meditation. "This is a different form of perceiving," she wrote me, "and it is through meditating that I finally learned what it is that people do. The one thing. The thing that is better than sex. The thing that is more ultimate than death and you can do it a lot, too, whereas you can only die once. This is the thing that we humans do, like wheels roll and flowers bloom, cats catch mice and seeds germinate. It's also different for each one of us, just like being in love is different for each. It's plenty multifaceted, too, but one thing." That thing, Laura Ann said, is "to be unified with God. But you have to forget all the connotations you ever heard! It's hard to put into words." She added, "My own cultural background doesn't have any contemplatives in it, so when I got the call to this way of life I first had to be convinced it wasn't a mass delusion on the part of Buddhists and Catholics."

Contemplative prayer has existed in Christian tradition from the earliest centuries, but has experienced a renewal in recent decades in a variety of forms, including disciplines and practices like the Jesus Prayer, which anchors contemplation in a sentence or word in conjunction with the breath, and techniques of contemplative prayer rooted in ancient Christianity but sometimes informed by Zen or yogic practice. Centering Prayer, which Bill practices, and Christian Meditation, another Christian contemplative practice, are among the two most widespread. Initially started by two Catholic monks—Trappist and Benedictine, respectively—they spread, ecumenically and internationally at their initiative, to communities of lay people. Both practices trace their roots to early Christian asceticism, as does the Jesus Prayer or Prayer of the Heart.[4]

Contemporary contemplative practices also have roots in the prayer of Western monasticism, a method Trappist monk Thomas Keating calls "method-less," consisting mainly of a practice known as *lectio divina*, Latin for "divine reading."[6] "For the medieval monks," Keating writes, "*lectio divina* meant reading Scripture, or more exactly, listening to it. They would repeat the words of the sacred text with their lips so that the body itself entered into the process. . . . *Lectio* . . . was primarily an exercise of listening and attention. The monks sought to cultivate inward attention. Prayer was their response to the God they were listening to in Scripture and celebrating in the liturgy."[7]

The monks then pondered the words of the sacred text—*meditatio*—meditation on the word. They responded with heart and will—*oratio*, affective prayer. Often these two forms of prayer led to *contemplatio*, contemplation, resting in God. Keating notes that these three acts were often interwoven and could take place during the same period of prayer. In subsequent centuries, Keating notes, these forms of prayer became separate from one another, "each with its own proper aim, method, and purpose," a division he calls "disastrous" in furthering the mistaken notion "that contemplation is an extraordinary grace reserved to the very few."[8]

Contemplation is in fact available to all. This does not mean it is easy. "If, in this life, you hope to feel and see God as he is in himself," writes the author of *The Cloud of Unknowing*, "it must be within this darkness and this cloud. But if you strive to fix your love in him forgetting all else, which is the work of contemplation I have urged you to begin, I am confident that God in his goodness will bring you to a deep experience of himself."

Two of my closest friends, from different religious traditions, both living in the intense urban environment of New York City, draw on Eastern meditative practices. One Christian, one Jewish, both are men with busy lives and contemplative hearts. David, a Jesuit priest, writer, and journalist in his early sixties, first went on an Insight Meditation (*Vipassana*) retreat in the 1980s. At first, accustomed to the help of images in prayer, he found the meditation almost unbearable. He wrote in his journal at the beginning of the retreat: "I hate it—the tight schedule, the work, the lack of figure/material for the imagination, the lack of company, the beginner's state—not knowing the way, the unfamiliarity."

The retreat's basic focus was concentration on the breath, with sitting and walking meditation alternating all day. "The whole thing," said David, "had to do with attention, paying attention to subtle movements of body and soul, really noticing what was going on. It was one of the hardest things I've ever done." He developed severe pains in various parts of his body and came to realize as the retreat went on that they were related to submerged feelings—some of doubt and self-doubt, some of grief at the death of his brother two years before.

"After ten days of these exercises," he wrote me over a decade after that first retreat, "my mind felt less busy, less chattering, seemingly had been cleansed, swept clean, emptied. Eyes opened, ears, taste—the senses in general—clarified, alerted. Make every moment count; life is short: this is the general moral exhortation. This moment will never come again; don't waste it."

David's practice has been irregular since 1985, "yet," he says, "the ideal of simple, nonjudgmental awareness infuses my habit of mind—on the subway, walking down the street, sitting by candlelight late at night, listening to the night wind—that before making judgments or decisions, one must simply be aware of what is so, pay attention to what is the case." It has also permanently affected his practice of the examination of consciousness (or conscience). This "examen" prescribed by Ignatius of Loyola, founder of the Jesuits, in his Spiritual Exercises, involves, says David in summary, "asking 'how am I doing?' twice a day." What has changed? "Insight Meditation encourages a nonjudgmental awareness, simply being aware of physical states, feelings, images, thoughts—just as they are, without defenses, denials. Very useful, even if subsequently a negative judgment is appropriate. Also, in my case, helpful in checking guilt trips that block doing what one needs to do to change behavior."

At the same time, he added, he could never make meditation his whole religious practice, though it has definitively influenced his spiritual life. "Insight Meditation isn't sexy enough. Or emotional enough. At heart I'm a *bhakti*," he said, using the Hindu word for devotional religion and its practitioners.

My closest friend from college, Peter, a gay man who is actively and religiously Jewish, has practiced some form of Zen since his teens. A former dancer, choreographer, and director, he works in upper management in Manhattan's fast-paced restaurant and entertainment industries. Peter has formally studied Zen sitting meditation; during retreats, walking meditation and sitting meditation usually alternate. While these concentrated experiences are like treasures, the question remains: "How does one apply that in daily life?" Peter asks. "The baby is crying, you're going to work, you have to cook dinner. . . . How to maintain an inner peace, attentive, wakeful, not overcome by the exigencies of daily life?" He sees in Zen "a *practice* separate from Buddhism though taught from Buddhist context . . . a series of trainings that allow one to filter the external music—to find an internal quiet that allows us to 'move through' and find greater clarity, a detached attentiveness, and to be able to focus on each moment."

I mentioned in a previous chapter Peter's practice of walking meditation, which he has adapted from the enclosed setting of Zen retreats to his walk to work along the Hudson River and on the streets of Lower Manhattan. "It's one of those ways in which you fit your daily life into a practice," he said. "I focus inward, hoping by the time I get to the office I don't think evil thoughts. It's aerobic—I walk at a fairly quick pace—and aspects of yoga and breathing also come into play." Most of the time, the walking meditation is silent, as in Zen practice. Sometimes, on the esplanade by the river, Peter sings as he walks.

"I'm not a great listener for the part-the-Red-Sea VOICE," Peter added. "I sometimes witness the Voice in small human gestures, gratuitous kindnesses which suddenly throw a rabbinical invocation or *mitzvah* into relief.[9] Meditation, the waiting-in-nothingness, is the closest to listening prayer I've experienced."

Contemplative prayer, said Peter, "is most of my current practice, whether it's sitting or walking Zen meditation, or particularly the *Amidah* service." The *Amidah* is a portion of the Shabbat service— and, Peter points out, is part of traditional Jewish services every time the community gathers for prayers. "It is," Peter said, "the silent standing devotion. It is a separation from the tumult of the community and service surrounding you. I often do it facing the wall, combining an old Jewish tradition with *zazen*." In the highly verbal environment of the Jewish liturgy, a silent space has opened: one travels into it on a wave of prayers including some of the most heartfelt of the tradition, and suddenly one finds oneself inside the silence, a live stillness.

David, Peter, and I all worship in our biblically grounded, ritual-intensive traditions, and all three of us practice some kind of sitting, walking, or mindfulness meditation. We have learned these disciplines from traditions other than our own, but they have rooted us more deeply in our respective religions.

Slow down, simplify, and face yourself, says Zen teacher Joko Beck. Let your heart turn toward God, say *The Cloud of Unknowing* and seventeenth-century mystic Brother Lawrence of the Resurrection. In the "how" of practice, these differences—facing ourselves, facing God—become less sharp, which is not to say they vanish. In their recent book, *The Ground We Share*, Zen master Robert Aitken and Benedictine monk David Steindl-Rast, both practiced in East-West dialogue and well grounded in their respective Buddhist and Catholic traditions, discuss philosophical, theological, and theoretical differences but choose to focus their conversation on practice—the meditative contemplation in which both their traditions engage. They also sat *zazen* together morning and evening during the days of dialogue that formed the basis for the book.[10]

Having practiced both Centering Prayer and Insight Meditation, I find that even the one anchoring word of Centering Prayer is too much. I want only the breath itself, with no word. In that silent place, God is so wordless I cannot say "God," or anything else. My own experience has also been that there is not much difference between those two contemplative practices. I was curious about Bill's perception, since his experience with contemplative prayer is more extensive and disciplined than mine. "Centering Prayer, *zazen*, Christian Meditation are all meditational disciplines," he answered, "and not fundamentally different. There may be a little more focus on receptivity in one and on concentration in the other. In my book it doesn't make that much difference. They all basically have the same function, mentally to disidentify with the mental flow of the traffic of the mind and to rest in interior silence."

Is it always about God? I asked Bill about his contemplative experiences. "Yes," he wrote back, "it is always about God, but not the conventional God so often imaged by those around me. It is about a God who lives us, from whom we are never separate, a sense of being in God as are all things, a sense of God manifesting through me and through all Creation." Where and how does Jesus fit into your contemplative practice? I asked. "Somewhere along the way," Bill answered, "I had an experience of Jesus as the Infinite Tenderness of God in human form, and being human, I need to see God as human too—Jesus as being among us, as one of us.

"There is a natural tendency," Bill wrote, "for a 'spilling over' of one's formal practice into everyday life. One tends to act and live increasingly from this interior place of prayer, being anchored in that place. In this way, daily life is not a distraction from prayer, it is prayer, it is new grist for the mill of our deepening union with God. The point of contemplative prayer practice is not to build a wall between prayer/God time and the rest of your life, but rather to so intensify that relationship and practice of Presence that it spills over and pervades all other aspects of daily living."

Thich Nhat Hanh relates the following story: "The Buddha was asked, 'What do you and your disciples practice?' and he replied, 'We sit, we walk, and we eat.' The questioner continued, 'But sir, everyone sits, walks, and eats.' The Buddha told him, 'When we sit, we know we are sitting. When we walk, we know we are walking. When we eat, we know we are eating.' Most of the time, we are lost in the past or carried away by the future. When we are mindful, deeply in touch with the present moment, our understanding of what is going on deepens, and we begin to be filled with acceptance, joy, peace, and love."[11]

Many people reach a combination of inner quiet and union with the Holy One through manual or other bodily practices requiring attention and the engagement of the whole self. I have observed this in my father when he bakes bread, an avocation of his later years, measuring, kneading, letting the dough rest and rise, varying the ingredients in loving experiments which he presents to our family after hours of mindful care. The popularity of fishing and whittling has to do with more than catching fish and making objects, as most solitary fishers will attest, even if they do not speak the language of prayer.

"Against the backdrop of a complex and fast-paced culture," writes Nancy Roth, "the prayer of contemplation is like a deep breath that restores both body and spirit."[12] The psychological and physiological benefits of meditation and the many forms of contemplative prayer are well known, as are those of kindred techniques such as the "relaxation response."[13] Many people have taken up meditation for the legitimate and sufficient purposes of stress reduction and peace of mind. In contemplative prayer, however, while the benefits may be similar to those of a simple meditation exercise, the starting point and center are different. Centering Prayer, says Thomas Keating, "is not just an experience of rest and refreshment—a sort of spiritual cocktail hour. It involves the denial of what we are most attached to, namely, our own thoughts and feelings—our very self."[14] This detachment is neither an ignoring nor a squelching (denial in the popular psychological sense) of our thoughts and feelings; it is simply an acknowledgment that they are not our true self, or our deepest self, our heart of hearts.

Most teachers of contemplative practices recommend sitting once or twice a day, usually for at least half an hour. My own meditation practice, when it was regular, was far less ambitious. After some experimentation, I decided that setting a goal I could not meet would leave me guilty, discouraged, and angry at myself, and that it was better to do something than to do nothing at all.

At the time I resumed a meditation practice in the early 1990s, I already had a regular hatha yoga routine in the morning. Since college I had returned to Insight Meditation episodically, learned Centering Prayer, and more recently, resumed the simplest of meditation practices through a stress-reduction series at my local HMO. Primed by this experience, I devised a morning practice that fit my busy schedule as executive director of a nonprofit organization. I began with yoga: with the day pressing upon me from the moment I awoke, I already needed to quiet my mind and heart, and was able to do this best through the body. From there I made the transition to sitting meditation, at the end of which I made the sign of the cross and moved into a time of spontaneous prayer, with or without words. For a while I read the Bible and prayed from the texts for the day, but eventually silence took over. The whole sequence rarely took more than twenty minutes. I sustained this small practice for two years.

Then during the course of an acute agitated depression in the second half of 1993, I found I could no longer meditate: I was incapable of sitting still. Severe anxiety attacks chased the practice away, major depression kept it at a distance, and no amount of deep and conscious breathing could bring it back. My prayer changed as a result of this experience. I am well again, no longer depressed or anxious, but for a few years sitting straight-backed on a cushion, eyes closed, stilling the mind, was difficult; I also found myself avoiding it, fearing failure or perhaps the assault of an anxiety attack if I began the practice again. I probably also remembered in my bones those two years in which I practiced sitting meditation, a professional nightmare during which this contemplative practice sustained my sanity on a daily basis, but did not save it.

Later, during the writing of this book, my tendency to engage in "spiritual Olympics" came to haunt me. Imagining I could never speak well enough about meditation and contemplation, not trusting my years of contemplative prayer practice—too episodic, amateurish, not enough of this, too much of that—I spent a great deal of time staring at a stack of overdue, mostly unread books on Christian and Buddhist meditation from two different libraries.

Finally, in a letter to a friend, I found myself writing: "What I probably need to do is to stop writing about it and worrying about it and just do it for a while." Less than an hour later I took off my shoes, lit some mild Japanese incense, did not bother to clean the living room—another excuse not to meditate, another escape—took a large cushion, placed it on the floor, and sat down on it in half-lotus position.

I simply sat, first squirming to find a comfortable straight-backed position, then observing my breathing. Thoughts rushed in and about, and soon I remembered: notice the thoughts; do not judge them. Let them go. Do not push them away; do not cling to them. The chattering thoughts continued, but my relationship to them changed. I judged neither them nor myself. I heard street noise, heard the cat crying, then walking in front of me, almost across my lap. I continued to sit. Quiet again, the cat sat down. The street noise continued. I watched the thoughts, feelings, breath. A deeply anchored calm returned, familiar, as if it had never left— no, as if to welcome me back into itself. "Remember? This is it. Not perfection. Not constant calm. But peace beneath the noise, and practice with the noise. Breathe. Sit. Be."

"When solitude was a problem," Thomas Merton writes in *Thoughts in Solitude*, "I had no solitude. When it ceased to be a problem, I found I already possessed it, and could have possessed it all along. . . . We put words between ourselves and things. Even God has become another conceptual unreality in a no-man's land of language that no longer serves as a means of communion with reality. The solitary life, being silent, clears away the smokescreen of words that we have laid down between our mind and things. In solitude we remain face to face with the naked being of things. And yet we find that the nakedness of reality which we have feared is neither a matter of terror nor for shame. It is clothed in the friendly communion of silence, and this silence is related to love."[15]

My return to meditation was only ten minutes long, but it took away my fear of trying again. Beyond, behind, beneath, and above all the words—many of them helpful and all of them inadequate—contemplative practice is really quite simple. Be, breathe, be still—and, in Christian practice, know that I AM. Sometimes only one of these is possible at once. Sometimes all occur. It begins simply, as I did on that exasperated day, the day on which I gave up the desperate search for perfection, with sitting down and taking a conscious breath.

♥∘♥

AN INTRODUCTION TO CENTERING PRAYER

It is most helpful to learn meditative practices directly from a teacher. Check in your local community for Centering Prayer groups, workshops, or retreats, which may exist in any number of Christian churches, or contact the ecumenical organization Contemplative Outreach Ltd., 10 Park Place, 2nd Floor, Suite 2B, Butler, NJ 07405; (973) 838-3384. On the web: www.centeringprayer.com.

I thank Bill Ryan, a student and teacher of Centering Prayer with Contemplative Outreach, for his assistance in preparing this introduction.

1. Choose a sacred word (a mantra) as a symbol of your intention to consent to God's presence and action within. The sacred word is sacred not because of its inherent meaning—though most people pick a word to which they have a deep religious or spiritual connection—but because of

your intent. It expresses your intention to be in God's presence and open to the divine action within you. Spend a few minutes quietly choosing a sacred word which intuitively "fits." A short one- or two-syllable phrase without strong emotional content works best. Possible choices might be: *Abba, Jesus, Yeshua, Spirit, Sophia, Wisdom, Peace, Home,* or *Shalom.* Pick your own. There is nothing magical about this and no "best word." Use your intuition and find the best word for you.

2. Sit comfortably with your eyes closed (see notes below on sitting posture and hand positions), settle briefly, and silently introduce the sacred word as the symbol of your consent to God's presence and action within. Sit with a straight back and head free. Close the eyes and let go of what is going on around you.

3. When you become aware of thoughts, return ever so gently to the sacred word. Thoughts (feelings, perceptions, images, associations) are inevitable. Do not think of them as an obstacle. The action of returning endlessly to the sacred word is gentle and requires minimal effort. The sacred word functions as an anchor to allow you to be in the "depths of the river" while the "boats" of mental traffic float by without your being hijacked by them.

4. At the end of the prayer period of twenty minutes (see below on keeping time) remain in silence for two or three minutes with the eyes closed. This allows time for the psyche to readjust to the external senses and enables you to bring the awareness of silence to daily life.

Notes

Keeping Time

I find kitchen timers tick too loudly. Bill uses the timer on a digital watch. Some people have a clock handy. I take off my watch—an analog with large numbers—and set it in front of me so I can glance at it with eyes barely open if needed. Other people use alarm clocks with a soft alarm. If you are a beginner, some kind of alarm clock or watch timer is probably best since you may be more easily distracted and need to avoid the preoccupation of having to keep looking at something.

Posture

- Keep your back straight, not slumped.

- Let your head remain free (leaning against the back of a chair or other back support is fine, but do not lean the head against anything).

- Remain reasonably comfortable, so as to maintain the position effortlessly and not be distracted by it.

Guidelines for sitting in Centering Prayer are less strict than for *zazen*; most Westerners who practice Centering Meditation choose to do so sitting on a chair. (A straight-backed chair is best.) Experiment and find the posture that works for you. I usually sit in half lotus on a large cushion. Bill sits on a backless posture bench for computer users designed to give excellent support to the spine. He previously used a zafu (a small, round Zen meditation cushion), then a low meditation bench. "My knees don't bend like they used to," he says. "Old football injuries."

Hand Position

The hand position is your choice. I like a palms-open position as a sign of receptivity. Some people fold the hands in the lap, some keep the hands open and extended, some keep them resting on the thighs, palms down. Bill practices Centering Prayer with hands folded in the lap, "modified *zazen* without the thumbs touching" (in Zen sitting meditation or *shitankaza*, the thumbs touch).

THE PRACTICE OF CHRISTIAN MEDITATION

This practice was initially taught by an Irish-English Benedictine monk, John Main (1925–1982), who opened the first Christian Meditation Centre in London in the mid-1970s. He founded an ecumenical network of meditation groups, the World Community for Christian Meditation movement (WCCM), and a Canadian monastery, of which Benedictine Laurence Freeman is now abbot. John Main called Christian Meditation "our oldest and newest form of prayer"[16] and looked to John Cassian and other desert ascetics for the deep roots of this simple practice. Lay people all over the globe now practice Christian Meditation. Practitioners of Christian Meditation recommend group practice to help sustain this form of prayer.

For further information, contact the WCCM at: World Community for Christian Meditation, St. Mark's, Myddelton Square, London EC1R 1XX, England, UK. International Office: +44 0207 278 2070
E-mail: mail@wccm.org
website: www.wccm.org

How to Meditate

Sit down. Sit still and upright. Close your eyes lightly. Sit relaxed but alert. Silently, interiorly begin to say a single word. We recommend the prayer-phrase "Maranatha" [an Aramaic word found in the Greek New Testament meaning "Come, Lord"]. Recite it as four syllables of equal length. Listen to it as you say it, gently but continuously. Do not think or imagine anything—spiritual or otherwise. If thoughts and images come, these are distractions at the time of meditation, so keep returning to simply saying the word. Meditate each morning for between twenty and thirty minutes.

LAURENCE FREEMAN

∽✵∾

Heavenly Father
Open my heart to the
Silent Presence of the
Spirit of your Son
Lead me into that
Mysterious silence
Where your Love is
Revealed to all who call
Come Lord Jesus.

JOHN MAIN

MINDFULNESS MEDITATION IN EVERYDAY LIFE AND THE PRACTICE OF THE PRESENCE OF GOD

It is autumn here and the golden leaves falling one by one are truly beautiful. Taking a 10-minute walk in the woods, watching my breath and maintaining mindfulness, I feel refreshed and restored. Like that, I can really enter into a communion with each leaf.

Of course, walking alone on a country path, it is easier to maintain mindfulness. If there's a friend by your side, not talking but also watching his breath, then you can continue to maintain mindfulness without difficulty. But if the friend at your side begins to talk, it becomes a little more difficult.

If, in your mind, you think, "I wish this fellow would quit talking, so I could concentrate," you have already lost your mindfulness. But if you think, instead, "If he wishes to talk, I will answer, but I will continue in mindfulness, aware of the fact that we are walking along this path together, aware of what we say. I can continue to watch my breath as well."

If you can give rise to that thought, you will be continuing in mindfulness. It is harder to practice in such situations than when you are alone, but if you continue to practice nonetheless, you will develop the ability to maintain greater concentration. There is a line from a Vietnamese folk song that says: "Hardest of all is to practice the Way at home, second in the crowd, and third in the pagoda." It is only in an active and demanding situation that mindfulness really becomes a challenge!"

THICH NHAT HANH

As Brother Lawrence had found such an advantage in walking in the presence of God, it was natural for him to recommend it earnestly to others; but his example was a stronger inducement than any arguments he could propose. His very countenance was edifying, such a sweet and calm devotion appearing in it as could not but affect beholders. And it was observed that in the greatest hurry of business in the kitchen he still preserved his recollection and heavenly-mindedness. He was never hasty nor loitering, but did each thing in its season, with an even, uninterrupted composure and tranquility of spirit. "The time of business," said he, "does not with me differ from the time of prayer, and in the noise and clatter of my kitchen, while several persons are at the same time calling for different things, I possess God in as great tranquility as if I were upon my knees at the Blessed Sacrament."

BROTHER LAWRENCE (SEVENTEENTH CENTURY)

In my small class in meditation for non-Vietnamese, there are many young people. I've told them that if each can meditate an hour each day that's good, but it's nowhere near enough. You've got to practice meditation when you walk, stand, lie down, sit, and work, while washing your hands, washing the dishes, sweeping the floor, drinking tea, talking to friends or whatever you are doing. "While washing the dishes, you might be thinking about the tea afterwards, and so try to get them out of the way as quickly as possible in order to sit and drink tea. But that means that you are incapable of living during the time you are washing the dishes. When you are washing the dishes, washing the dishes must be the most important thing in your life. Just as when you're drinking tea, drinking tea must be the most important thing in your life. When you're using the toilet, let that be the most important thing in your life." And so on. Chopping wood is meditation. Carrying water is meditation. Be mindful 24 hours a day, not just during the one hour you may allot for formal meditation or reading scripture and reciting prayers. Each act must be carried out in mindfulness. Each act is a rite, a ceremony. Raising your cup of tea to your mouth is a rite. Does the word "rite" seem too solemn? I use that word in order to jolt you into the realization of the life-and-death matter of awareness.

THICH NHAT HANH

PSALM 131

A song of ascents

Lord, I am not proud,
holding my head too high,
reaching beyond my grasp.

No, I am calm and tranquil
like a weaned child
resting in its mother's arms:
my whole being at rest.

Let Israel rest in the Lord,
now and forever.

CHAPTER SIX

Gazing: Icons, Images, and the Depth of God

·····································

All things of Earth are holy,
All things are one in you.
The Earth is filled with your beauty, God,
Charged with your love.

BILL WALLACE

What the word says,
the image shows us silently;
what we have heard,
we have seen.

SEVENTH ECUMENICAL COUNCIL (NICEA II, 787)

Contemplation happens in stillness and emptiness. It also occurs in the presence of the visual. Contemplating images has a meditative quality. Icons, one of the great gifts to church and world from the Christian East, are meant to be a window into the reality of the divine: if you look into the eyes of the persons depicted—Christ, Mary, the saints—you are drawn inward, deeper, below the surface, into their gaze toward you. On our own continent, here in the Americas, the image of Our Lady of Guadalupe speaks reassurance, courage, and cultural pride not only to Mexicans and Mexican-Americans, but to people far away from the land where she first appeared to an Indian peasant, Juan Diego, at Tepeyac.

How can a picture—or a statue—help us to pray? Is this not idolatry? Christian traditions have a range of stances toward images and varying practices in relation to them. In fact, the broader church was embroiled in one of its classic conflicts on just this matter, the iconoclast controversy. The writings of the Seventh Ecumenical Council, held at Nicea in the second half of the eighth century before the later break between the Christian East and the Christian West, defended holy images. Links to the past and bridges to the future, images are, the council said, words speaking as powerfully and truthfully as Scripture of the presence of God in the created world.

In a sense the boundaries between apophatic and kataphatic experiences—one a spirituality of emptiness, the other a concrete spirituality of symbol and flesh—which otherwise seem so clear, blur in the contemplation of icons. Praying in the presence of an icon seems to be the height of the kataphatic experience: the image is concrete, mediates the presence of God, provides a focus. Yet the goal of praying with icons is the same as that of Centering Prayer or the Jesus Prayer: union with the One who is beyond words and images, but who inhabits our world and created reality. Before the iconostasis (the screen of icons between the worshipers and the altar and inner sanctuary) at the Russian Orthodox Cathedral of the Holy Virgin in San Francisco, I learned from my friend Kevin that Orthodox Christian art almost never represents the first person of the Trinity—even in this icon-rich, image-saturated tradition. The absence of an image of the Creator is reminiscent of the Jewish practice of not uttering the Holy One's name.

Christianity is a tradition of the word—a tradition where voice is paramount and listening is fundamental to faith.[1] Listening, call and response, God's invitation and our answer, our plea and God's mysterious reply: all these are fundamental to Christianity, as they are to Judaism and Islam. But Christianity is also a tradition of the body and a tradition of image, the tradition of incarnation, God with us, in the flesh. Voice is God's presence, word is God's presence, rushing-spirit is God's presence, Jesus is God's presence, and so too the icon, "image of the invisible."

There is a spiritual discipline of seeing, looking, and gazing. At the same time, images can help us when we are least capable of focusing our attention—tired, distracted, depressed, or ill. "An image is a bridge between evoked emotion and conscious knowledge," Gloria Anzaldua writes. "Words are the cables that hold up the bridge. Images are more direct, more immediate than words, and closer to the unconscious. Picture language precedes thinking in words; the metaphorical mind precedes analytical consciousness."[2]

In the course of reflecting on the place of the visual in Christian prayer, I was in conversation with four colleagues and friends from very different cultural and religious backgrounds. Unlike the more diverse group of women and men whose experiences of prayer inhabit the pages of this book, all are academics—students or faculty—with a hefty investment in words. All are intellectuals, not necessarily a category of people our biases tend to associate with image-based prayer. Yet all, working on a daily basis with words and with ideas, have their own deep involvement—on different terms—with images and the visual as an aid to prayer, a path of prayer, or a preparation for prayer.

Jim, a young Greek Orthodox scholar and professor from a Greek-American family, said to me: "I find icons help to focus my prayer. And I can't pray without them because that's how we grew up praying: in the Orthodox Church, when you walk into church, you're not standing in front of an altar but in front of a screen, facing images of the saints; what is taking place at the altar is hidden, so your relationship is less with the action on the altar and more with the icons and the architecture of the church. That iconographic experience of worship is also in the home. When Orthodox Christians get up in the morning or go to bed at night, they pray in front of icons. Because icons are so pervasive in churches, when you set up your icons in your home you're setting up a house church." Usually icons are put in a privileged position in the home: they create a sacred space. Russian Orthodox believers tend to set them up in corners, and Greek Orthodox, on the east wall of the house.

In the home of Jim, his wife, Stephanie, and their daughter, Anna, the angels and saints speak visually of the presence of God. "We have four main icons: Christ, Mary, Demetrios, my patron saint, and Stylianos, Stephanie's patron saint; you can have a patron saint of the opposite gender. We set them up in our bedroom, but we have icons elsewhere in the house: in the kitchen, in the living room, in my office, and in our daughter's bedroom. You may first think they are there for aesthetic reasons, but they are really placed here to remind us that God is present everywhere in our home." Anna, the mother of Mary, his daughter's and late mother's namesake, is there, as are Ephrosinios, an obscure monk and monastery cook who graces the kitchens of many Orthodox homes, and the three angels of Andrei Rublev's celebrated icon of the Trinity, a reminder also of the hospitality of Sarah and Abraham to the three strangers who were the very presence of God, under the oaks at Mamre.

"They're individual faces," Jim said of the icons. "You can say particular prayers to Jesus and to Mary, it helps you to focus; it makes the prayer more personal. Another thing icons have done for me in my prayer life is to give it a dimension of comfort. There are icons, for instance, of 'the sweet kiss'—[the child] Jesus kissing Mary. She seems peaceful, motherly, not judgmental, accepting, warm." He gave another example: "There is an icon of Christ shown in a gesture of blessing. When I say my prayers I don't always feel like I'm the best Christian, and this brings to mind a judgmental God. I'll look at the hand of Christ in that icon and it gives me a sense of blessing and comfort."

I commented on the eyes of the iconic figures, the gaze. "Yes," Jim said, "you think they're looking at you, but then you look and they're not. They are looking into your soul. The icon spiritualizes the person in the wood. It's not realism. It's not *our* physical reality, though it is a person *within* our reality. It brings us out of the mundane into the spiritual."

I observed that there was a paradox in the icon: it is outside our reality but also part of the ordinary, made of earthly materials and accompanying our daily life. Jim agreed, noting that this is in keeping with the whole of Orthodox Christianity, which "is mystical but also very mundane."

Prayers before the icons can be both spontaneous and formulaic. Orthodox Christians also venerate icons by kissing them, and sometimes, Jim says, by making what the Greek Orthodox call "a full *metaxia*": making the sign of the cross, reverently, bending down and touching the floor with the hand. Why kiss an icon? "It's been part of me so long I can't imagine not doing it," Jim answered. "You would do the same thing with a treasured photograph. I look on it as I do pictures of Anna or Stephanie. It's a way of transferring the kiss to the person who's not physically present.

"My days aren't complete if I haven't said my prayers" before the icons, Jim added. "I don't believe I get any special blessing, but I don't feel complete. For an Orthodox Christian, the presence of an icon is not just a painting or something to remind us of God and the saints, but also the presence of God, *the presence* of saints in a room. It has to do with sacred *presence*, not just sacred *space*."3

I mentioned to Jim during our conversation how many Roman Catholics now have icons in their homes, and sometimes in their worship spaces.4 One Catholic friend who has moved from crucifix to icon in the visual support of his prayer is Kevin, a graduate student in his thirties, of Irish-Polish heritage, who worked for several years at a large shelter for homeless people in Boston. "When I was seven years old, an uncle of mine told me my room looked like a religious goods store," he remembers. "On three long shelves beside my bed stood an eclectic assortment of plastic Marys, dewy-eyed saints, and glow-in-the-dark Jesuses. At the time my uncle made his comment I had just received my First Communion and had asked for, and received, a twelve-inch-tall painted statue of the Virgin. Blue and white, she stood atop the world, her rose-tipped sandals crushing the head of a little green serpent. I thought she was beautiful.

"As a kid, I loved my collection of statues and holy cards. The images I saw on them provided a sense of security, familiar faces on a Catholic road. Above the headboard of my bed hung a crucifix given to my parents at my baptism. Most of my friends had crucifixes in their homes, usually hanging over their beds, sometimes sitting on bookshelves or perched on the television set.

"When I went to church, there too was Jesus, looking down from a thirty-foot cross hanging forty feet above the main altar. Jesus seemed awfully far away to me, up there on his cross. He looked mean and I was glad to see him hanging so far out of my reach. Every Sunday, Jesus writhed in agony above the altar during Mass. Looking up I could see ribbons of blood and sharp-looking triangles of brass stretching away from the nails in his hands and feet. When I knelt at Mass, the blood, the nails, and the thorns on his head loomed large in my imagination. My parents told me that Jesus was alive; they encouraged me to talk to him. I could imagine few good words from the stiff, suffering figure above my head.

"I left Jesus at Mass, and talked instead to the Blessed Mother. Busts, statues, and holy cards of the Virgin Mary crowded the flat surfaces of my childhood bedroom. With her warm face and out-stretched arms, the Virgin invited me to speak my mind. Words of anger, cries of fear, she took them all, a soft smile on her lips. 'There, there,' I could hear her say. Even my earliest religious questions seemed to bring me to the Virgin. A budding theologian at age five, I once asked my kindergarten teacher what people did when they went to heaven; staring at God for eternity seemed a long and bor-ing prospect. Sister Mary Francis thought for a moment, smiled, and told me that heaven was a garden where children sat on Mary's lap while she read them stories. Jesus saved the world by his cross, but his mother read me stories and quieted my fears."

By the time Kevin reached high school, smiling Virgins and glow-in-the-dark saints seemed infantile to him. Only his First Communion Mary and a sleek brass crucifix remained; the other holy objects lay wrapped in newsprint in an attic box. There were movie posters and trophies on Kevin's walls and shelves.

During the summer of Kevin's junior year, his parish received a visit from the "Pilgrim Madonna," a large traveling replica of Our Lady of Czestochowa, a life-size icon of mother and child making its way through Catholic churches across the country. Though many in his small Polish-American parish approached Our Lady of Czestochowa with piety and ethnic pride, Kevin himself, he admits, "had never particularly cared for her." A replica of the image had stood at a side altar of his church, an embossed gold frame studded with glass jewels and plastic pearls covering all but the hands and faces in the image of mother and child. "Like my childhood Jesus," Kevin remembers, "Our Lady of Czestochowa seemed distant and sober."

When the large traveling "Black Madonna" came to Kevin's parish, he went to visit her: "I entered the quiet, dark church and noticed that the jewel-encrusted cover had been removed. I saw instead an ancient image. A Byzantine lady held her baby close, two golden halos glowing red fire. The lady looked calmly forward, regal and profoundly sad. Two drops of blood dripped from sword slashes on her right cheek. A universe of stars sparkled in her blue veil. The baby at her side said, 'Come.' I had met my first ikon."[5] Why and how was this image different from the other images of Kevin's childhood and youth? "The statues and pictures were copies of eighteenth- and nineteenth-century art and tried to be realistic; they also evoked emotion." An icon, a very ancient, stylized form, does not attempt to be realistic. "It somehow cracks open, expands your idea of Mary, of Jesus, of God. It says, 'Look, the world is not what you thought it was.' Your reaction is still emotional, but viewing an ikon also calls forth your beliefs as a Christian. There's a timelessness about the experience."

Almost twenty years have passed since that moment. "Today," Kevin writes, "I am a graduate student studying early Christian ikonography and I study the history and making of ikons. As an adult I cannot escape their gaze. My studies tell me they are works of art, but my instincts and my upbringing tell me they are windows into the Divine. If I'm still and reverent enough, they gaze at me with love and draw me into their world."

Kevin has traded his crucifix for images of Jesus Pantokrator ("all-powerful") and his mother Mary. On a shelf in an alcove in his bedroom stand three icons, one of Mary and two of Jesus Pantokrator. The image of Mary, painted by a friend, reveals the Virgin as "Our Lady Pelagonitissa," a traditional Byzantine icon; it shows a young mother holding her baby close as he squirms to touch his cheek to hers. As he watches the mother and child gaze across the room. Kevin often recalls the warm, welcoming Mary of his childhood and youth. But, he says, "what I see has less to do with me and my needs and more with who God is in the world."

I had never considered myself particularly devoted to Mary, the mother of Jesus, until I wrote *Generous Lives*; when I began asking women about Mary, I realized that I had her everywhere in the house. A copy on wood of a Russian icon of the Mother of God stood watch by my bed. An image by contemporary painter Robert Lentz of a black "Protectress of the Oppressed" holding the child Jesus hung above my desk. In the living room were a mother and child made of banana leaves pasted on cloth, in brown and cream and tan—a gift from a Jesuit friend returned from work with refugees in East Africa—and a "Madonna of the Mango Grove," a greeting card sent by pen pals in India over two decades ago, before I became a Catholic. This Mary, her face in profile, wears a sari and is surrounded by orange light; the brown baby in her arms reaches over her shoulder to a delicate bird in a mango tree.

Mary, more than Jesus, seems to take on the cultural forms of peoples and lands around the world. Apparitions and images make her present in countless local situations, often speaking to children, women, and the very poor. Our Lady of Guadalupe, or the Virgin of Guadalupe, is the most widespread and compelling of these representations here in the Americas—"*la Virgen*," my Mexican-American friends say, and we always know which *Virgen* they mean. Or they say simply "Guadalupe." Mexican-American women and other Latinas I interviewed during the 1980s spoke of her, but so did Filipina, African American, and Euro-American women. When I moved to California ten years later, I began to see her more frequently in the surrounding culture: her feast day, December 12, was celebrated prominently in parishes, her image found in homes, her name on people's lips. Watching a television special on the life of United Farm Workers (UFW) organizer and president César Chávez containing news footage from the 1960s and 1970s, I noticed something I never had before: in every procession and demonstration, beside the familiar flag of the farm workers' union with its stylized black eagle, were banners and poster images of the Virgin of Guadalupe. In a recent farm workers' march and rally in Watsonville, California, a revival of UFW organizing, this time among the strawberry pickers, images of Our Lady of Guadalupe again appeared on posters and flags held high by the marchers.

Virgil Elizondo, for many years the rector of San Fernando Catholic Cathedral in San Antonio, Texas, and a leading Latino priest and theologian, has written movingly of Guadalupe as both a worshiper and a scholar. Retelling the story of Guadalupe's apparition to Juan Diego, Elizondo notes that "the full life-giving meaning of Guadalupe can be seen and understood only in the overall context of the confused and painful reality of the postconquest period. The Aztec-Nahuatl Empire, and with it all the native people, was defeated in 1531. It was the beginning of the end of their world."[6] The new world that the brown-skinned Guadalupe announced, embraced, and symbolized was a mestizo world, a coming together of two cultures, Spanish and Indian, in which the conquered Amerindian peoples could survive without shame and know the power of God's love for them. The story of Guadalupe continues, says Elizondo: "She not only appeared in the outskirts of Mexico City in December of 1531, but she continues to appear today throughout the Americas in the art, the poetry, the dramas, the anthropological studies, the religious expressions, the shrines, and the pilgrimages of her people. Rather than saying that she appeared in 1531, it would be more accurate to say that she started to appear—to be present among us—in 1531 and that her visible, tangible, and motherly presence continues to spread throughout the Americas."[7]

Theologically speaking, Mary is not God. But what I found in researching *Generous Lives*, and again in conversations for this book—those with Orthodox and Catholic Christians especially—is that in prayer she *functions* as God. "Our Lady of Guadalupe has been important in prayer as an image of God who cares and is faithful," Nancy told me.

During her years of work in Seattle, Nancy also earned her first graduate degree in theology. "I was the only Latina in the [degree] program, out of 170 students, and the only person of color as well," she remembers. "I would often go home at night and weep. And I always had her image in front of me. I remember keeping one credit card so I could leave town on a moment's notice; I thought of resigning from the program. I would think, 'This is not the place for me; the religion they express here is not my experience of Catholicism.' Guadalupe enabled me to hang in there. I also did a lot of scholarly work on her: the history of her apparition, its context, its results."[8]

Our Lady of Guadalupe is for Nancy "an image of deep consolation. It's akin to my experience of my grandmother and my mother, whose love was as close to unconditional as one could come:

an experience of being loved and cared for, simply because of who you are—because you are." Guadalupe is also "definitely a Gospel text. There are five Gospels in my life. Her story is a story of death and resurrection—of a people, of one person—on multiple levels. I relate to her, naturally, as a woman of blood both Spanish and Indian and a woman shaped by the border in multiple ways." She quoted to me Virgil Elizondo's words about *la Virgen*, who moved the people of Mexico "from a death wish into a life wish."

In Nancy's living room is a large and beautiful image of Guadalupe in blues and browns. "Her image in my home is a constant reminder of the depth of God's love," she said, echoing Jim's words about the icon of Mary, whom the Eastern churches call the Theotokos, or God-Bearer. Jim spoke of icons "focusing his prayer." Without the image of Guadalupe, Nancy noted, "that knowledge would more easily slip away and be more diffuse. I have her because she reminds me: her image reminds me of the Gospels, the stories, how God loves me. I see reflected in her face the depth of God's love. And she is the image of a woman, a brown woman, of my people and my blood."

Theologian Margaret R. Miles, in *Image as Insight*, advocates "training in image use," a cultural and spiritual discipline vital to this age of advertising and television. It consists of three sometimes simultaneous steps: (1) becoming aware of the messages one receives from the images with which one lives, (2) beginning to ask questions about media images, and (3) selecting or developing a repertoire of images for oneself. These images, Miles writes, "help one to visualize— to envision—personal and social transformation and thus to focus the energy of attention and affection with more clarity."[9]

Fred was raised in the Church of the Foursquare Gospel of Aimee Semple McPherson fame, which he describes as one form of "white middle-class Pentecostalism. I got to know a lot of really good people and a few real saints." He drifted away from Christianity, "read Nietzsche in high school and loved it, and got saved around age sixteen when a youth revival swept the local United Methodist church in western Kentucky." Now an evangelical Christian and theological scholar, Fred majored in art in college, where his spiritual formation included both charismatic and evangelical experiences, many of them communal, all intensely personal;

he continues to study art and to draw. "During the last two years," he told me when I interviewed him in the second year of his doctoral program, "I've made a very conscious effort to train myself in the visual tradition of the church. I'm stocking my head with the symbols that Christian artists have used to portray the mystery visually. This is unconnected with the act of prayer itself, but is part of the all-day charging process"—Fred speaks often of "charging the eyes" with images—"and a big part of my spiritual formation in general."

"I am definitely way too Protestant," Fred later wrote me, "to bring images into an official time of private prayer. That arena has to stay stripped down or I get the heebie-jeebies and my idolatry alarms go off. I could never bring images directly into that moment. Not physical images at least. Mental images are a whole different story, however. Mental images are absolutely unavoidable, especially at that moment when you are consciously trying to quiet yourself for prayer. It's no good saying, 'Images begone, I'm trying to pray,' because my need for images abhors a vacuum. So the only solution is to intentionally choose images that are not distracting, but will in fact spur devotion if they put in an appearance during prayer.

"As a Protestant hooked on images, I've developed a defensive use of images in prayer," Fred continued. "This is probably part of what I meant by 'keeping my eyes charged.' If I've got 'Christ in glory' images taped all over the walls, and have been staring inquisitively at all the odd little devices that artists have used to depict 'glory,' then smokin' Joe Camel isn't going to be invading my sanctuary because there's no room for him. Drive out the unwanted images with desire images."

He clarified immediately: "Do I need to add that 'unwanted images' are not necessarily images of bad or tempting things ('mmm, fudge brownies . . .')? I don't want to give the impression that my prayer life is a constant struggle to suppress sexual imagery, because that's not what I'm talking about. I'm just talking about general visual clutter calling ignorantly for mental attention, causing you to lose your focus. Attentiveness is what I'm after.

"My current practice of glutting my imagination on the church's visual tradition(s) is a good combination of being Mr. actively-in-charge-of-my-spirituality—I choose the images—and passively allowing the images to do their work on me: once I've chosen them, I really do open myself up to them and allow them to 'inform' me, and who's to say that they aren't the ones choosing me, anyway, since it's hard to account for what rivets your attention on one picture but not another"? He mused, "It occurs to me that psychoanalysis was originally called 'the talking cure.' Maybe part of what I'm working on is 'the looking cure.'" He added: "The affective power of images is one of their main draws for me. I'm pretty intellect-heavy, and my emotional range is probably somewhat stunted. Images help me expand that emotional range; they help me to feel as well as just to think. I use them to soften my heart."

"When I got saved," Fred remembered, "the most important development besides a hunger for the word of God taking hold of me was that the natural world took on a vibrancy and magnificence that it never had for me before. I was getting high just seeing clouds for a period of several years. Give me a steep hillside with a tree on it and it was guaranteed rapture. I just had to go to art school, because I was useless for anything else, incapacitated as I was by the sight of any big rock, or a cluster of leaves. When God opened the eyes of my heart, my optic nerves were not unaffected."

Teaching the eye to see is part of the life of faith. After gazing at icons and learning from their gaze, do we look at people differently? I often think of photography, that contemporary form of icon making, when I reflect on the relation among God's gaze, Jesus' gaze, and our gaze on the earth and its people. I love looking at photographs, but also taking them: color photos of nature, black and white portraits of people. Even more, I have learned about gazing in recent years from the photographic work of Mev Puleo, a friend who died three years ago in her early thirties after a painful struggle with a brain tumor. A radiant woman with a dark, intense gaze, Mev photographed people whom we might otherwise never have noticed, both in the United States and abroad. Her gaze remains with us in her photographs and two books, *Faces of Poverty, Faces of Christ* and *The Struggle Is One*,[10] a photographic and verbal account of the church of liberation in Brazil that includes bishops, theologians, and the poorest of slum dwellers, many of them women.

At one of several memorial services for Mev, her friend Don Steele preached from the fifth chapter of Matthew's Gospel, the Sermon on the Mount. "Over the altar in Brasilia Teimosa, one of the poorest parishes in one of the poorest cities in the world, Recife, Brazil, are the Portuguese words of today's Gospel reading. But because Portuguese has the wonderful *vos* form,[11] they translate into English something like 'Y'all beloved ones are salt for the earth; y'all beloved ones are light for the world.' When the world looks at parishioners there, the world sees squatters, sees homeless fisherfolk and prostitutes. The world calls those persons, many of them Catholic Christians, valueless, despised, feared, shameful. Jesus calls them priceless, beloved. Jesus calls them salt and light. Jesus calls them not only those who are saved, but those to whom salvation is entrusted for all."

Don continued: "What you see in photographing these people whose land is being reclaimed from the sea depends on which lens you look through. It is possible to take a snapshot of them and convey misery, dirt, pity, squalor. Or it is possible for the portrait to reveal beauty, courage, dignity, perseverance, strength, and love. Mev chose to look at the people of Brazil through the lens of the Gospel. She saw salt and light—salvation and hope, transformation, and the relentless steadfastness of the love of God. That's what she saw everywhere she looked."[12]

Mev's photographs are among my icons. Gazing at them—at Maria da Silva Miguel, Goreth Barradas, Toinha Lima Barros—and at the image of Guadalupe, at the icons of the Theotokos and Pantokrator, I learn of the presence of God among us, in boardrooms, streets, gardens, and slums. Mother Teresa of Calcutta, who died as I was completing a draft of this book, spoke of Christ's coming to us under the distressing disguise of the poor: she did not say "treat the poor *as if* they were Christ," but "*They are* Christ" among you. This is not a new notion in Christian tradition, though Mother Teresa gave it prominence in a world more sharply divided than ever between haves and have-nots. Icons bring Christ to us. We also meet Christ in the icons of Christ who walk among us. God created us, the book of Genesis says—and the Christian New Testament repeats—in the image of God. In the Orthodox liturgy, the priest or deacon who carries the incense always incenses and bows to the icons of the saints, then to the people in the assembly: for in the congregation too, are the saints, images of the invisible

God, calling us to reverence for one another, gazing upon each other with infinite tenderness and respect.

∾∾∾

ICONS ON THE WEB

Nothing replaces seeing, gazing at, and being with icons in the environment of an Orthodox church or other worship setting. Some people chose to have icons in their homes. But you can begin gazing at icons in a book, at an art exhibit, or, if you have access to it, on the World Wide Web. This selection of sites (updated for this new edition) is not exhaustive, but provides an introduction to different kinds of icons, traditional and contemporary. Most of these sites also include links that will lead you to yet more images.

Gallery of Byzantine images:
www.fordham.edu/halsall/byzantium/images.html#ex1

Byzantine icons—Greek, Russian, and others:
www.iconsexplained.com/iec/iec_masters.htm

A Russian icons index:
www.auburn.edu/academic/liberal_arts/foreign/russian/icons/index.html
This includes several of the most noted Russian icons: Andrei Rublev's "Holy Trinity," his "Redeemer" and "the Ascent of the Prophet Elijah," and the early Russian icons "Vladimir Mother of God" and "Saints Boris and Gleb."

The Ethiopian church is one of the most ancient of Christian churches. There are Ethiopian icons from different periods on this university-related site:
www29.homepage.villanova.edu/christopher.haas/ethiopian-icons.htm

Exhibit of Ethiopian icons from the National Museum of African Art:
www.nmafa.si.edu/exhibits/icons/

Coptic Christian paintings, including icons, are here:
http://touregypt.net/featurestories/copticpainting.htm
More Coptic icons: www.coptic.net/exhibits/Pictures.html#icons

Seventh-century images of four Evangelists from the Lindisfarne Gospels in Britain:
http://catholic-resources.org/Art/4Gosp-Lindisfarne.htm

An Orthodox Christian Fellowship Icon Archive:
www.mit.edu:8001/afs/athena.mit.edu/activity/o/ocf/www/icons.html

Traditionally, icons are unsigned works. "Writing icons" in the Orthodox Christian tradition is a specific, careful spiritual practice. You can read an interview about it here:
www.pbs.org/wnet/religionandethics/week732/belief.html

Christians outside the Orthodox tradition now practice icon-writing, as does this Catholic Benedictine sister: www.mountosb.org/icon/index.html

Photograph of the original image of Our Lady of Guadalupe at the official site of the Basilica of Our Lady of Guadalupe in Mexico with interactive, enlarged details of the image: www.virgendeguadalupe.org.mx/ codice_gpano/menu.swf (Note: This site automatically includes audio with classical music and explanations of image details in Spanish.)

The Saint Andrei Rublev Icon Studio features contemporary icons by William Hart McNichols, a U.S. Jesuit:
http://puffin.creighton.edu/jesuit/andre/

Site for the St. John Coltrane African Orthodox Church in San Francisco, an African Orthodox congregation with a Pentecostal spirit that is home to work by African American iconographer Mark Dukes: www.coltranechurch.org.

Mark Dukes is also the iconographer of the "dancing saints" icons of St. Gregory of Nyssa Episcopal Church in San Francisco:
www.saintgregorys.org/worship/art_section/243/

The work of contemporary iconographer Robert Lentz is now available only on a commercial site, Trinity Images, and features images of Mary, Jesus, traditional saints, and nontraditional saints including Martin Luther King, Jr., Mother Jones, Stephen Biko, Archbishop Oscar Romero, and Harvey Milk. The site also features the work of other artists: www.trinitystores.com

The Nativity Project features the work of Janet McKenzie with images of biblical women from the Christian Testament such as Mary of Magdala (Mary Magdalene):
www.thenativityproject.com/pages/succession_mary.html

ALTERNATIVE TV

The old man on the screen sang
in a loud and shaky voice
and had probably never been very clean
in addition he had hardly any teeth left
a miner with black lung
of course he spoke dialect and his grammar was bad
why after all should he
show his best side to the camera

When god turns on his tv
he sees old people like that
they sing
in a loud and shaky voice
and the camera of the holy spirit
shows the dignity of these people
and makes god say
that is very beautiful

Later
when we have abolished tv as it exists
and are allowed to look at the skin of aging women
and are unafraid of eyes
that have lost their lashes in weeping
when we respect work
and the workers have become visible
and sing
in a loud and shaky voice

Then we shall see
real people
and be happy about it
like god

DOROTHEE SOELLE

SECTION II

CHAPTER SEVEN

Forget What You Learned:
Praying in the Present

When monks spoke about purifying our motives, Father Damasus used to say something that's been very helpful to me. Jokingly but with a great deal of seriousness, he'd say, "Don't worry about purifying your motives. Simply know that they aren't pure, and proceed."

BROTHER DAVID STEINDL-RAST

Holy God,
whose presence is known
in the structures we build,
and also in their collapse;
establish in us a community of hope,
not to contain your mystery,
but to be led beyond security
into your sacred space,
through Jesus Christ, Amen.

JANET MORLEY

P rayer is relationship. It is not unlike a relationship with a friend, lover, spouse, parent, or child. Many of the dynamics involved in a human relationship also apply to prayer, even though God is the other partner. Prayer too has times of absence and longing, peaks and plateaus, a need for fidelity and basic trust, and a requirement of time and presence.

I would take the relationship analogy one step further. Prayer is also like a relationship in the variety of ways that one can help the relationship to develop, survive, blossom, and perdure. It is very much like sex between adults who love one another: *the specifics of what you do* matter far less than the *how* of it—the attentiveness, the intimacy, the expression of desire—and *the fact that you do it*. As in lovemaking, it is what enhances the relationship and its intimacy that is most important, not a given act, position, or technique.

Like any relationship, our friendship with God also undergoes changes. The memory of past give-and-take may remain with us, but often we move into the unknown of God and with God: because our life circumstances have changed, or because God's Spirit moves us in a new direction, or because we come to understand Jesus in a different way. Each time we pray, we step into mystery, and begin again.

In this sense, prayer involves forgetting what we have learned. I am not talking, of course, about forgetting everything we know, especially our own history, but about a kind of letting go, the sort of forgetting which enables us to pray in the present. It is not unlike the mindfulness or attentiveness of which I spoke earlier, part of the truth telling of which I wrote in chapter 2. How am I, and who am I *today*? Today, who are you for me, God? What is your word to me? Where do I hear your voice? Where are you? How can I meet you? Where are you showing signs of your life, of your Spirit moving in the world? As Christians, we answer each day in prayer the question Jesus asked his disciples: *"And you, who do you say that I am?"*

A new way of prayer often emerges with a change in life circumstances. If it does not, it may need to. Look back and remember: How did you pray as a child? As a younger woman or man? What has changed? What has remained the same? Are there any habits, things, people, places, patterns of prayer, notions of God, of which you needed to let go in order to grow in your relationship with God?

Sometimes it is necessary to let go in order to regain a rich life of prayer. This does not necessarily mean letting go of tradition, though in some cases parts of the tradition may be—or may feel like—that which we need to leave behind. I am not talking about change for change's sake or an abandonment of memory. Life-giving change is the point: change for the sake of abundant life.

Sometimes, in the process, God dies for us. If God seems dead, or about to die, it may well be that the God in whom we used to believe must die, because that God has become too small. We humans are the ones who put limits on God. Not just on God's mercy, as I have mentioned before, but on God's capacity to change with us and for us.

Many of us go through a first major change in our prayer life during adolescence, as Fred described in the previous chapter. Another life passage in which prayer is likely to change, in which we have the opportunity to meet God in a new way, is young adulthood. Rachel Ann, a woman in her twenties, describes herself as "a first-and-a-half-generation Filipina-American"—a U.S. citizen born in the Philippines and raised in the United States. "I grew up in Florida, but was rarely allowed to go to the beach," she recounted. "It was not until I got my first job and my own car that I would go off there by myself." During the two years she lived at home after graduating from college, which she describes as "a period of intense personal and professional hell," Rachel Ann "practically dropped out of the Church and began experimenting with other ways of communicating with God, and looking for other places where God might be. Instead of going to Mass with my family," she said, "I would go alone elsewhere, sometimes to a church in another town, sometimes just driving with the windows rolled down so I could smell the sea.

"Perhaps because the beach was forbidden for so long, I did not doubt that God would be very present to me there, albeit probably not in explicitly Christian form," she mused. "One breezy autumn day I pulled up onto a public stretch of beach. I left my sandals in the car and walked slowly over the dunes to the edge of the ocean. My toes grabbed into the dry sand, then slapped hard against the wet sand. I picked up shells and meditated on them. I blessed myself with the water, not caring that my clothes would get wet. And then I walked back a little, the sand sticking to my feet and crusting onto the hem of my skirt, the sun licking the moisture off my ankles, arms, and face.

"On that day, and on others after that, I sat and said, 'Okay, God, here I am. What now?' On windy days I would often speak/scream/whisper/cry into the wind, hoping or trusting that my prayers/concerns/needs/questions would reach God's ear— hence leading us to a quicker, more satisfying resolution. I don't know if I could honestly say I got a concrete answer from God. Maybe I was trying to find God through my senses so that I could be led past them and be convinced of God's existence, care, power, something. It might be more correct to say that doing all these things gave me the time and space for discernment."

Discernment: deciding on life directions, yes, but first creating a space for God's voice to become clear, finding new ways to be attentive, as an adult, to the promptings of the Spirit, to one's conscience, to the best way to use one's gifts in the world, to the important questions about loving well. Clearing a space for the attention to God that is prayer.

Morris, a former Benedictine monk who is now a husband, father, and college professor in his sixties, went through radical changes in prayer as his sense of vocation changed. He entered the seminary in high school. Prayer was formulaic and traditional. In some ways stifling, in others life giving, it planted in Morris a lifelong love of Gregorian chant, even as it left his soul unsatisfied. Ordained a priest at the age of twenty-five, Morris pursued a doctorate in theology. By the time he finished this course of study at the age of twenty-nine, "I was already having big problems with the uniqueness of Christ's and Christianity's salvation—but no big problems whatever with the (my) need for religious salvation and a religious way of life. I was completely committed both to my faith and life as priest and monk on the one hand, and to my search for truth, wherever I might find it. This would cause me lots of conflicts, but I have never lived to regret it. It certainly changed my notions of prayer.

"I remember kneeling in front of the crucifix in the new abbey church of my Benedictine monastery, and talking to my Lord hanging there. 'Lord,' I said, 'you know that I have been brainwashing myself with my prayer-life all of my life. Is that really what you want? The whole structure of my spirituality is clearly constructed by my daily hours of monastic communal Office, the Mass, and the kind of mental prayer that I am doing right now. How do I know that it is not just an artificial house of cards?'"

From that time on, Morris "began to deconstruct my 'mental prayer' of daily reflection on scenes from the life of Jesus, talks with him, and the like. It seemed just too artificial." He had also begun learning "Christian yoga" from a fellow Benedictine, Jean-Marie Déchanet,[1] a Frenchman, and conversing with a Korean Benedictine friend about Buddhist spirituality. He read the work of the atheist existentialists and of the "death of God" theologians.

"Ironically," Morris said, "it was that particular conversation with Christ, precisely the old-fashioned kind of mental prayer at its best, which caused me to change my prayer habits. I slowly but sure-ly stopped programming myself with formulae and mental and emotional attitudes which were prescribed by the theology manuals and traditional manuals of prayer. It dawned on me around this time that I had been following the formula and saying, 'Lord, I love you above all things,' but not only did I not feel this, I did not even know what love was." Emotional deficiencies in Morris's family background had prevented him from having much experience of human love.

Instead of the prescribed kinds of "mental prayer," Morris adopted "a prayer of abandonment: 'Lord, into your hands I com-mend my spirit.'" Looking back on this metamorphosis, he said, "I think it had to do, more than anything else, with my slow realization that prayer was not primarily a rational, theological thing at all, but rather an emotional or pre-rational thing. I came to distrust ideas and slowly came to love trust, peace, and abandonment."

Around the same time, Morris began to discover the importance of human love and intimacy in his life, and to come to terms with the fact that he could not, despite his best efforts, remain celibate. He knew this, finally, "before God." After several years of struggle, he asked for and received a dispensation from his vows. Morris com-pleted a second doctorate and immersed himself in Zen Buddhism for several years, but "found that Zen structures and thought pat-terns were every bit as narrow and stifling as what I had left. So, I returned. Actually I had never left. I had continually been driven to prayer. But prayer had taken on a completely different meaning. When I returned to both the institutional and the spiritual church, I prayed—with an incredible intensity and continuousness—to the Father, and to his son Jesus. But all of the faith which I had reembraced was completely transformed. I knew firsthand what 'emptiness' meant. And I knew very clearly what Aquinas was saying when, near the end of his life, he dismissed words and discounted rational formulas in prayer and theology.

"Prayer became an even more essential part of my life after I left the monastery than while I was a monk. [I pray] daily: in fact I probably usually pray several hours of the day and night (I can't sleep very well). But my prayer is not a burden. Surely it is not something done under obligation. It is a wonderful source of strength and renewal. It is necessary comfort."

Spiritual transitions of midlife or mid-adulthood come in many forms. Some of these transformations occur in the "one day at a time" spirituality of Alcoholics Anonymous and other twelve-step groups. I have not been personally involved in twelve-step groups, but for two decades I have witnessed, both as a friend and as a minister, the ways in which they have functioned as church for women and men of all walks of life, including two women I met while they were in prison and who came from poor and working-class backgrounds, and several upper-middle-class men and women with graduate or professional degrees and all the external trappings of status and social standing. Alcoholics Anonymous and its offshoots have saved countless lives. They have also instilled and nurtured in their members a life-giving spiritual discipline. The intense praying-in-the-moment of twelve-step groups is not a forgetting of the past. The twelve steps require, on the contrary, an honest and rigorous assessment of one's life. They are a combination of remembering, letting go, and embracing—painstakingly, "one day at a time," sometimes twenty minutes, or two minutes, at a time—a new spiritual path, a new way of life. Prayer is often at the heart of this process.

Barbara generously told me the story of her spiritual journey through the twelve steps of recovery: "I came into the program [Alcoholics Anonymous] in 1984 and have been sober ever since—almost thirteen years now, and am still very active. And I guess I found God, or a god, in the process.

"One of the first things they told me in AA was to get a sponsor[2] and work the steps.[3] Either one of these will bring you to the problem of God in a hurry, because a sponsor will usually ask you what step you are on. The second step talks about coming to believe in a power greater than ourselves, and this was the real problem for me. I knew I needed power, but I had been an atheist for so long, an admirer of religious thought from the outside but not a feeler of religious feelings or an experiencer of spiritual experiences. I didn't know if it was possible for me.

"My first sponsor explained it to me like this: She said 'You will pray in the morning and at night. Say anything you want, use prayers you know or your own words, I don't care. But you have to pray.' I said, 'But I don't believe in God so how can I pray, it would be so dishonest.' 'Who cares what you think?' she explained. 'Just do it.' So I said, ever the smartass, 'So I'll just pray to my office wall, will that be okay?' and she said, 'That will be fine.' This was my introduction to the powerful spiritual tool of acting-as-if, coming out of a thought that I want to have instead of the poor thought that I have right now. Her thought was that I could come to believe. And one day, as I was praying to my office wall, I did. I just knew there was somebody there. And that this was the power who had been behind the saving of my life, that had motivated the work of those who had saved me, and whose spirit I felt in the rooms of AA. I started crying. I was so grateful. I had no idea that I was worth saving. So the second step brought me to gratitude and this was my spiritual awakening.

"Then," said Barbara, "I went on a search for God. I had a counselor who laughed at my search. He used to say, 'Barbara, why are you looking for God? He's not lost.' But he had been lost to me all my life. And the Big Book[4] tells me in the ABCs of how it works that no human power can relieve me of my alcoholism but that God can and will if he is sought. Not found. Sought.

"The eleventh step tells me to seek through prayer and meditation to improve my conscious contact with God as I understand him, asking only for knowledge of his will and the power to carry it out.

"My life was saved by a couple of Christians, so I started out on their path, which was the Presbyterian church. I'm still a member,"

Barbara said. "At about three years into the program I hit a wall and had to find something that would help me change my mind about me." She took meditation classes, got involved with New Age spirituality, and attended "nontraditional churches like Unity." Barbara's first solitary experiences of prayer after praying to her wall included meditative reflection on spiritual readings: this spiritual reading became a daily practice, especially during her first few years in the program. For a while, she said, "I started using meditation as my daily eleventh step instead of reading or prayer. Now I try to do all three, and I set time aside for serious prayer and meditation. Over time, prayer and meditation have blended together.

"In the process of having personal experiences in meditation and in the educational process of learning about love, I came to change my mind about myself and about my parents." This is where Barbara discovered "the God-is-love god; the energy—the Holy Spirit." Barbara calls her spiritual practice "integrated." She wrote: "I never left the mainstream but there were those in it, including my spiritual adviser, who thought I was trafficking with the devil and who 'fired' me. I believe my God is the same God as the Bible talks about, at least in places, but there are those who would not agree, especially in Southern Baptist headquarters." She said of her prayer life, "I think it's all about having a spiritual experience. Experience is everything. I believe in praying in gratitude for the solution, but I have also experienced praying in desperation for a sign. Right now my path is to act out the law of love in real life. If I believe, and I do, that God's will for me is to love, purely and simply, then my job is to let go of anything that interferes with my ability to do that on a daily basis. Currently I'm working on letting go of being right. I'm also learning that discipline in daily life leads to freedom."

In the course of asking people about changes in their prayer life, I heard many stories of returning to church or to another religious community, but also stories of new rituals and customs, some of them communal, others solitary. Judith, a woman from Vermont, told me when I asked her about changes in her prayer life: "One of my most cherished yearly rituals is 'mourning the zucchini.' I always do this after the first frost. If you ever grow a garden, you know that zucchini starts yielding early and continues—unrelentingly—until frost. Sometimes you wish those zucchinis would give you a break, but they keep coming and coming. Once some animal ate off the growing tip of a zucchini plant in my garden and I thought it was done for. Darned if the plant didn't send up *three* new growing tips (like pinching back a flower) and maybe produce three times as much! It's amazing that a plant that threatens to take over the world can be done in by a temperature one degree under 32. One day— the Terminator. The next day—a pile of black, dead leaves. So I stand by the dead plant and thank it for being so prolific all summer. I also thank the Gracious Creative Spirit for the vitality of creation. And I say good-bye to the plant as the representative of the tender plants that feed us so bountifully. It makes me sad that the plant had to die; hence, 'mourning the zucchini.' Need I say that this ritual also reminds me of the fragility of life."

⤞∝⤝

YOUR LIFE NOW. GOD'S PRESENCE NOW. YOUR PRAYER NOW.

In *The Story of Your Life: Writing a Spiritual Autobiography*, Dan Wakefield describes a frequent first step in the spiritual autobiography workshops he leads. After asking people to say a few sentences about why they chose to participate in the workshop, "I pass out paper and crayons and ask each person to take fifteen minutes and 'draw the present,' whatever that means to them. Then each person explains their drawing as a way of introduction to the group."[5]

Using this exercise, draw a picture of your life now. (This is not an art contest, and any set of writing or drawing implements will do. Try the felt-tip pens on your desk, or just a pencil, though it is nice to have the possibility of using color.)

You can do this alone or in a group.

I did this exercise for the first time in my life in my late thirties at a session Dan Wakefield taught for potential spiritual autobiography workshop leaders, and have used it since then with nine- and ten-year-olds, people in their twenties and thirties, and people in their fifties, mostly in the context of church programs and retreats.

When I use the exercise with groups, I go a step beyond the book's instructions and ask the following questions (yes, it worked with the nine-year-olds too):

Where is God in this picture? Where is God in your life? Often what is interesting to people is discovering where God is not.

One can then ask:

- Can you bring this in prayer before God?
- Can you ask God into this part of your life?
- Can you see how God might be in this place with you?

Try it.

LIFE CHANGES AND PRAYER CHANGES: A HISTORY

Take your time doing this.

You can answer all these questions in one sitting, or you can answer them over time, one a day, or a few each day. You can make this part of your spiritual discipline or practice for a special week or month or liturgical season—Advent, Lent, Easter, Pentecost—or on your birthday or New Year's Day, or as a way of preparing to discuss with your life partner the religious upbringing of your children. Write down the answers to the questions so you can return to them. There are no right answers. Simply tell the truth.

- What have been the most important transitions or passages in your life?

- What have been the major phases or stages of your life?

- What was your prayer like during each of these transitions, during each of these phases? Write a few descriptive words next to your description of each life transition and stage. ("Lack of" something also "counts.")

- Prayer traditions: How have they been helpful to you? Which ones? How? When? Why? Or why not?

- What new ways of praying have you tried? Have they been helpful? How? Why? Or why not?

- How has prayer helped you work for a more just and compassionate world?

- Has there ever been a time when you made no effort to pray and "gave things a rest," either inadvertently or on purpose, in your prayer life? Why? What was this like? Looking back, can you see any benefit from this experience?

- Are there any ways of praying that you have had to let go in order to grow in your relationship with God? Are there any prayer habits or disciplines you have added to your life? Which ones? When? How? Why?

- Have you ever felt "stuck" in your prayers? When? How? What did you do about it?

- Have you experienced any change in God's faithfulness to you?

- Have you experienced any change in your faithfulness to God?

- How has your understanding of God changed?

- Have you used different names for God throughout the years? What names? Why?

- Do you use different names for God in your private prayer and in communal worship?

- Who is Jesus for you?

- How is the Holy Spirit present in your prayer?

- If you come from a tradition where Mary, the mother of Jesus, is important, what place does she have in your prayer? Has this place changed?

- Do saints figure into your prayer? Who, and how?

- As you look back, what have been the times of death and resurrection in your life? And now? Where is there death in your life? Where is there resurrection?

- What do you fear and desire most?

- Have you spoken to God about these?

- What is your deepest hope?

- Have you brought it before God?

- What has given you the greatest sense of peace throughout the years?

❧

O God, let fear die and conviction be born in our lives.
Let your light dawn in our minds as the day dawns on the earth.
Let us not be so busy hurrying into the future and
worrying about the past that we lose
today—the only one we have.
God, help us to do what we know we have to do today,
and leave tomorrow to you.

MARIAN WRIGHT EDELMAN

SERENITY
....

Prayer for Serenity

The first five lines of this prayer have become best known as the "Serenity Prayer," recited in Alcoholics Anonymous and other twelve-step groups. This is the full text of the prayer; it was written by theologian Reinhold Niebuhr (1892–1971).

> God,
> grant me
> the serenity to accept the things I cannot change,
> courage to change the things I can
> and wisdom to know the difference.
> Living one day at a time,
> enjoying one moment at a time,
> accepting hardship as a path to peace;
> taking, as Jesus did, this sinful world as it is,
> not as I would have it;
> trusting that You will make all things right
> if I surrender to Your will,
> so that I may be reasonably happy in this life
> and supremely happy with You forever in the next.
>
> REINHOLD NIEBUHR

Nada Te Turbe—Let Nothing Trouble You

> Let nothing trouble you,
> Let nothing scare you,
> All is fleeting,
> God alone is unchanging.
> Patience
> Everything obtains.
> Who possesses God
> Nothing wants.
> God alone suffices.
>
> TERESA OF ÁVILA (1515–1582)

WHEN HE CAME (3.)

He gave answers to questions they didn't ask
sometimes they didn't dare
open their mouths anymore
not because they hadn't understood
he was taking from them
everything sacred and safe
he offered no guarantees
Fire was not sacred to him or neon
not singing or silence
not fornication or chastity
in his speeches foxes breaddough
and much mended nets became sacred
the down and out were his proof
and actually he had as much assurance
of victory as we in these parts do

None

DOROTHEE SOELLE

CHAPTER EIGHT

Remember What You Learned:
The Usable Past

We shall not cease from exploration
And the end of all our exploring
Will be to arrive where we started
And know the place for the first time.

T. S. ELIOT

Jesus was at Bethany in the house of Simon the leper; he was at dinner when a woman came in with an alabaster jar of very costly ointment, pure nard. She broke the jar and poured the ointment on his head. Some who were there said to one another indignantly, "Why this waste of ointment? Ointment like this could have been sold for three hundred denarii and the money given to the poor." And they were angry with her. But Jesus said, "Leave her alone. Why are you upsetting her? What she has done for me is one of the good works. You have the poor with you always, and you can be kind to them whenever you wish, but you will not always have me. She has done what was in her power to do; she has anointed my body beforehand for its burial. I tell you solemnly, wherever throughout all the world the Good News is proclaimed, what she has done will be told also, in memory of her."

MARK 14:3–9

113

"Dear Christopher," I wrote. "This is a baptism letter from your Auntie Jane who loves you very much. I am sorry I cannot be with you in person to celebrate your welcome into the family of Jesus' friends, but I will be thinking of you, praying and celebrating, and I will probably sing a little song for you, even though you won't be able to hear it."

Christopher is the son of my friends Sonia and David, born in the first days of 1997 and baptized at the age of five months in late May of the same year, on the feast of Pentecost, in Boston. I sent his parents the letter with some water in a plastic bottle, a mixture of spring waters from the French Alps and from the hills of California—the land of my birth and my adopted home. David and Sonia invited their loved ones to bring or send water, which would be blessed for the baptism, and so the waters came: from Sonia's relatives in Northern Italy and Queens, New York, and David's family in New Hampshire and Massachusetts, water from Lourdes and from the Ganges; well water and seawater, tap water and water from Walden Pond, water from the Pacific and the Atlantic—"part of the web of water that is woven around the Earth which is our home in the sea of creation," one friend wrote. At the beginning of the celebration, participants poured the waters into the large baptismal font, which had been blessed at the church's Easter Vigil, and the priest said the blessing over them all.

On the invitation to Christopher's baptism, David and Sonia wrote to their friends and families, which, like most American extended families today, include people of several faiths and people with no religious affiliation: "Why a baptism? We believe that faith is the greatest gift we have received in our lives, and that the greatest gift we can offer Christopher is to foster his faith. While we have different religious backgrounds, we agree that Jesus' teachings and the Catholic Church will help him find answers to questions he will have about life, truth, and social justice. Baptism will welcome him into this rich tradition.

"The use of water in baptism is a reference to many events in the Bible, and to much that is familiar to all of us. It reminds us of the flood of Noah, the Exodus through the Red Sea, and Jesus' baptism by John. In the womb we were surrounded by water and we are born from our mothers with water. Water is where life began on

Earth, and without it we would all perish." Sonia and David's invitation concluded: "We seek to ground Christopher in one faith, and encourage him to learn from and value other spiritual traditions and philosophies. We ask you all to join us in sustaining Christopher's life and spirit. He is so full of promise, but finding the right path will be hard. He will need much guidance and love."

Sonia was raised a Catholic. She is the daughter of immigrants from Istria. David's religious background is Unitarian. His Anglo-Saxon family has been in the United States for several generations. As an adult he has engaged in serious study of Hindu Scriptures; he often, but not always, attends church with Sonia, for whom Catholicism is both tradition of origin and tradition of choice. His principal spiritual practice is meditation, in which he uses a mantra "mostly for the purpose of seeking inner quiet with conscious attention."

The baptismal ceremony continued with the first sign of the church's welcome on Christopher's forehead, the cross, traced by his mother and godparents; David blessed his child's forehead with a kiss. After the readings from Scripture, homily, and prayers, the catechist and priest invited those who were baptized Christians to renew the vows of their own baptism: the baptism of a child rests also on the prayerful promises of adults. "With all your family and friends," I wrote to Christopher, "I welcome you to the church. It's got its problems, but let me tell you two wonderful things about it. This baptism makes you related to millions of people! People who lived a long long time ago and people who live in Zimbabwe and France and Brazil and Aotearoa New Zealand. People of all different colors and shapes and sizes speaking different languages and singing different songs and eating different foods. They too are your aunties and uncles and brothers and sisters. Imagine that! And all of them are friends of Jesus. That's the second wonderful thing: being a friend of Jesus. He was a real person many years ago, but he's all over the place now too. You can talk to him and listen to him and hear his stories and ask questions about him. You can hear how he was friends with everyone—poor people and rich people, women and men, and little children like you too; he always made room for children. He also liked very old women and men. There was always room at the table for one more person; that's the way Jesus is."

Hospitality is a high virtue for Sonia and David. They are urban dwellers, committed to building humane cities, and lovers of the arts. In the prayers of petition preceding the baptism with water, they prayed, through the voice of a friend and the responses of all present, that they might be "examples of faith for Christopher, and . . . build a home where no one is a stranger." With the assembly they prayed to God, "Help us especially to recognize and embrace you in those who feel marginalized, weak, or alone; help us to work for a just and peaceful world."

"Sometimes following Jesus is hard," I wrote Christopher. "The world has a lot of problems and sometimes we have to make difficult decisions because we are friends of Jesus. We say 'This is wrong' if people don't have food, or a safe house to live in, or clean water, or if they hurt each other on purpose or even sometimes not on purpose. Often there are other people who don't like it if we say those things. People fight a lot on this little planet and sometimes they don't tell the truth. But everywhere there are communities of friends of Jesus—Christians—who will offer you friendship and wisdom. You're not alone, kiddo darling. Jesus walks with you and holds you, and all of us walk with you and hold your hand. There are also good people everywhere who don't say Jesus is their friend, but they are just as good and wise as your Christian brothers and sisters and aunties and uncles. They just belong to a different family of the many families on earth. Ours is the family of Jesus. We promise to raise you well in that family and to give you lots of love."[1]

After the baptism itself, a liberal sprinkling in the name of the Trinitarian God, David lifted Christopher high above his head, as the musicians sang "You are God's great work of art, fashioned with great love." Christopher surveyed the crowd, looking thoroughly pleased; the assembly burst out laughing. After the church celebration came the kind of feast to which Sonia and David's friends have become accustomed, and which their son will come to know is his privilege both to receive and to host.

All ritual is remembering; and all remembering, especially ritual prayer, is re-membering: bringing together, making whole. To bind together, to connect, *re-ligere* in Latin: that is the root meaning of the word "religion." In this communal prayer—the ritual of baptizing infants by sprinkling or by immersion in water—is a sign of the continuity of generations and of God's promise. Baptism in the name of the triune God is the sign of Christian belonging.

There are many ways to pray for a child as we welcome him or her into a community. This is the one celebrated by my religious family, now Christopher's family—baptism, which some Christian bodies, including ours, call a sacrament, others call an ordinance, and a few do not celebrate at all. Events like Christopher's baptism, even when I am far away, make me grateful for the communal prayer of the tradition. In this gathering, we were celebrating birth, but also much more: incorporation into a community of memory, struggle and hope, membership in a body, being surrounded by the promise of companions. *Com/panions*: literally, "the ones with whom one shares bread"; when he grows a little older, Christopher will take part in the meal of Jesus' friends, the Eucharist, in the form of wine and bread.

Death is another time when the prayer of the tradition not only comes in handy, but takes over. When my friend Tom was fourteen, living in a small town in upstate New York, a close friend of his was killed in a car accident. Tom had already lost a grandmother, but this was the first time he had experienced the death of a peer. He remembers two things especially about the aftermath of his friend's death: "The power of the word: I wrote a letter to his parents which was beyond a doubt the most open I had been in my life; and the whole ritual of his funeral: I began to get a glimpse of the wisdom of the ages." What was it about the funeral, I asked, and what was the wisdom in that collective prayer? "The solemnity," Tom answered, "but especially the sense that 'this is not all there is.' The need to mourn, but also to recognize that this life was not for naught. However, there's a difference between that and talk of 'He's in a better place now,' which makes me gag." Collective prayer does not displace the wrenching loss of the family, but places it in a broader context. Prayer is being intensely in the present while at the same time taking the long view. Taking the long view: this is what the church tradition helps us do, in prayer and in other ways.

When a beloved friend died twenty years ago and I had no words of my own to grieve him, in the first numb days after his death, I repeated the Latin words of the Requiem Mass to myself, words I had learned in college, several years before I became a

Catholic, by singing the Mozart *Requiem* as part of a protest and memorial to the dead of the Vietnam War. *Requiem aeternam* . . . "Rest eternal grant them, O Lord, and let perpetual light shine upon them." *Them.* It took years for me to realize that I had prayed for him in the plural, and that this was most appropriate. I said the words, but the words were not mine. I felt the grief; grief was not mine alone. All those who mourn and all those who have died were present in the prayer. The words were not mine, but there was room for all my grief inside them.

Not all times of transition find the tradition of the church so readily consoling, or even available in a welcoming way. Funerals, for instance, can often be the "last straw" for people, when a member of the clergy deals with the celebration in an impersonal way or, in some cases I know of, has refused to celebrate the funeral in a particular church. We feel hurt on these occasions of communal prayer—hurt, or simply not addressed. "It's got its problems," I wrote of the church in my letter to Christopher. Some—myself included—would call this an understatement. The church loses people through abuse of power, but also through boredom, through lack of attention to our adulthood, our language, our daily needs. And it is not just a question of consolation: often we are not challenged enough. If the Gospel does not challenge and change us—if it does not make us uncomfortable—it is no Gospel of Jesus Christ. The church may fail to console us at the right time or to challenge us at the right time. Bad timing, bad judgment, incompetence, lack of sensitivity, lack of insight, dearth of wisdom. This occurs in all religious or spiritual communities, from Orthodox to New Age. I have yet to meet a human community—and all religious communities are human communities—that does not in some form suffer from the breaches I have named. Some are worse than others. None is exempt.

Christopher's baptism, Tom's and my friends' funeral rites, were both rememberings. The prayer of the church is history, is memory, and in this prayer we are re-membered, connected again, made whole. Tradition can also make people feel dis-membered from their own selves—body and soul—and from the body of the community to which they once belonged. What if Christopher had been a girl-child, welcomed into a church where—in practice if not in theory—girls are still second-class citizens? What if his parents had been a lesbian or gay couple rather than a married man and woman? Would they have been able to celebrate as wholeheartedly and in the same place, and with the same words?

And what if a part of our tradition, our past, has been hidden from us? Biblical scholar Elisabeth Schüssler Fiorenza called her groundbreaking book of feminist perspectives on early Christianity *In Memory of Her* after the woman who anoints Jesus, whose name we do not know yet whose story appears in all four of the canonical Gospels.[2] The story of the woman who anoints Jesus is in every Gospel, and Jesus celebrates her love and initiative in each one. And yet we remember the denial of Jesus by Peter, and the betrayal of Jesus by Judas, more often that her extravagant, insightful, and prophetic gesture. "Wherever the gospel is proclaimed and the eucharist is celebrated," Schüssler Fiorenza writes, "another story is told: the story of the apostle who betrayed Jesus. The name of the betrayer is remembered, but the name of the faithful disciple is forgotten because she is a woman."[3] Church tradition helps us take the long view, but which tradition, whose tradition, and who decides? And how does this affect our prayer, whether communal or solitary?

The struggles to answer these questions could, and do, fill books. They also fill lives. It is we who make tradition live—and nowhere else is this more visible and vital than in prayer. Tradition is vast and deep, and is far more than doctrine. Its treasure trove includes all the richness of prayer, visual art, music, Scriptures, spiritual readings, practices and exercises, rituals, devotions, stories, pictures and songs, gestures, ways of interacting with nature, gestural and oral as well as written resources. The oldest of these traditional prayers and practices are "loaded": their history includes the history of their telling. "A lot of mouths have been all over them," my friend Anita said of the traditional Jewish prayers she loves. We could say the same of prayers contained in Scriptures, the Psalms, of the Rosary, of the hymns of Charles Wesley and Isaac Watts, of African American spirituals, Native American blessings, and the birthday blessing song *"Las Mañanitas,"* which my Mexican, Mexican-American, and Salvadoran friends sing with words reminiscent of the Song of Songs. Tradition includes age-old prayers and practices but also tradition-in-the-making: the pouring of many waters in one baptismal font, the telling aloud of the stories of unnamed women, the creation of rituals honoring other forms of love than marriage.

Tradition helps us to take the long view and to take our prayer outside ourselves. The memory of the community does us this favor in ways only it can do. But how do we decide what is, for us, the usable past?[4] In our day, unlike centuries ago, tradition is both a given and a choice. Our relationship to it is necessarily complicated. The very least we can do, in our prayer especially, is to be conscious in and of this relationship. What will our relationship be? Whose history will we celebrate and proclaim? What will we choose? How does the tradition carry us? What do we gain in the process? What do we lose? And what will we become capable of giving to the world around us because we have helped tradition and traditions to live? Only if we wrestle with these questions will we determine what is, for us, the usable past—in prayer and in the rest of our lives.

THE TWENTY-THIRD PSALM

Most Americans are familiar with the Twenty-third Psalm in the King James Version of the Bible:

> The Lord is my shepherd;
> I shall not want.
> He maketh me to lie down
> in green pastures:
> he leadeth me
> beside the still waters.
> He restoreth my soul:
> he leadeth me
> in the paths of righteousness
> for his name's sake.
> Yea, though I walk through the valley
> of the shadow of death,
> I will fear no evil:
> for thou art with me;
> thy rod and thy staff
> they comfort me.
> Thou preparest a table before me
> in the presence of mine enemies:

thou anointest my head with oil;

my cup runneth over.

Surely

goodness and mercy shall follow me

all the days of my life:

and I will dwell

in the house of the Lord

for ever.

Translations and musical settings of the beloved Twenty-third Psalm abound. Perhaps no other psalm has continued to have as much resonance for Christians as this one. And yet, as biblical scholar William L. Holladay writes of the Psalms, "The symbols and assumptions at the time of their composition are likely to be altogether different from those today." For wonderful insights on this psalm, see the first chapter, "The Lord Is My Shepherd, Then and Now," in Holladay's book *The Psalms Through Three Thousand Years: Prayerbook of a Cloud of Witnesses,* which examines not only the origins of the Psalms but their interpretations by Jews and Christians throughout the ages.

THE LORD'S PRAYER

According to the Gospel of Matthew (6:9–13), Jesus' friends asked him how to pray and he gave them words that we now pray in slightly modified form. A distillation of Jewish prayers of his day, the prayer of Jesus, known as the Lord's Prayer, has become the ecumenical Christian prayer par excellence. It is in some ways the fullest and most basic of prayers: it honors God's name, hopes for the realm of God, and places the one who prays within the province of God's will; it speaks of food, wrestles with forgiveness, acknowledges the struggle with evil. Catholics traditionally end the prayer after "and deliver us from evil," though more and more use the ecumenical ending, which is not found in the earliest manuscripts of the biblical text considered by scholars to be the most accurate. The way of addressing God is the one Jesus is reported to have used most often: Abba, "Daddy." Some Christians today choose to change the form of address to one that represents their own most intimate relationship with the Holy One, which may not necessarily be the parental male "Father."

Our Father
who art in heaven
hallowed be thy name
thy kingdom come
thy will be done
on earth as it is in heaven
give us this day our daily bread
and forgive us our trespasses
as we forgive those who trespass
against us
and lead us not into temptation
but deliver us from evil
   for thine is
   the kingdom,
   the power,
   and the glory
   forever.
Amen.

Trisagion

This is one of the oldest prayers of the Christian church. Regularly used in the Orthodox Church, it is also experiencing a revival in some Catholic, Anglican, and Protestant churches. The simple words, sometimes expanded (the second line could read "Holy and Mighty One"), are sung in rich harmony.

Holy God
Holy Mighty
Holy Immortal
Have mercy on us

THE DIVING LITURGY OF SAINT JOHN CHRYSOSTOM

Veni, Sancte Spiritus—Come, Holy Spirit

This hymn for the feast of Pentecost was written by a medieval Archbishop of Canterbury, Stephen Langton (d. 1228).

Come, Holy Spirit,
And send from Heaven
A ray of your light.

Come, Parent of the poor,
Come, Giver of gifts,
Come, Light of hearts.

Best Consoler,
Sweet Guest of the soul,
Sweet Refreshment.

In labor, rest,
In heat, coolness,
In grief, comfort.

O most blessed Light,
Fill the intimate depths
Of the hearts of your faithful.

Without your power
We are empty
And open to harm.

Wash what is unclean,
Water what is dried out,
Heal whoever is wounded.

Bend what is rigid,
Warm what is frigid,
Rule what is wayward.

Give your faithful
Confidence in you,
Give your seven holy gifts.[6]

Give the merit of virtue,
Give salvation at death,
Give perennial joy.

Amen. Alleluia.

....

Sophia

The wisdom tradition is an ancient one in biblical religion, wisdom not only as a quality or attribute of God, but also as God personified, a divine female figure (in Greek, *Sophia*). She crops up again and again throughout the Hebrew Bible and in more veiled ways in the New Testament. Scholars today document her developments and disappearances. Some of the prayers to Holy Wisdom have never left us. Others are new, inspired by ancient texts but highlighting Sophia's presence and power.

> O wisdom,
> O holy word of God
> You govern all creation
> With your strong and
> tender care.
> Come,
> And show your people
> The way to salvation.

This invocation is the first of the traditional "O antiphons" sung during Advent, the weeks marking the preparation for Christmas.

> Wisdom!
> Let us be attentive.

These words precede the reading of the Gospel in the Divine Liturgy and other worship services of the Orthodox Church.

Litany of Praise to the Wisdom of God

> *Leader:* Wisdom, you came forth from the Most High,
> as a mist you covered the earth.
>
> *People:* You were in the pillar of cloud;
> you led our forebears out of slavery into freedom.
>
> *Leader:* You are like a mighty oak;
> you stretch forth your branches—
> branches of glory and grace.
>
> *People:* You are like a vine,
> filled with flowers that yield fruits of glory.

Leader: Wisdom calls: "Come unto me,
you that desire me,
and be filled with good things."

People: For all that eat shall still hunger for you;
all that drink shall still thirst for you.

Leader: You are like a life-giving stream;
you water the gardens you have planted.

People: Let us come enjoy Wisdom's bounty;
let us rejoice in her goodness;
let us find life in abundance.
Amen.

This contemporary litany, adapted from Ecclesiasticus 24, was written by Susan Cady, Marian Ronan, and Hal Taussig. The "leader" and "people" parts can be changed to two sections of the congregation (or two individuals) reading responsively.

Almighty God,
unto whom all hearts be open,
all desires known,
and from whom no secrets are hid:
cleanse the thoughts of our hearts
by the inspiration of thy Holy Spirit
that we may perfectly love thee,
and worthily magnify thy holy Name;
through Christ our Lord,
Amen.

AN ANGLICAN COLLECT

SAINT PATRICK'S BREASTPLATE

This prayer (also known as the Lorica*) is familiar to many Christians both as a spoken prayer and (with an adapted text) as a hymn. Originally written in Irish (Gaelic), the prayer is attributed to the fifth century's Saint Patrick, evangelizer of Ireland, but may be a seventh- or eighth-century document. During the writing of this book, I have come to love the prayer of Patrick, which is at once a statement of faith, a celebration of creation, and a prayer of protection—an exorcism of sorts. It is rare to find all three in one.*[7]

I arise today
Through a mighty strength, the invocation of the Trinity,
Through belief in the threeness,
Through confession of the oneness
Of the Creator of Creation.

I arise today
Through the strength of Christ's birth with his baptism,
Through the strength of his crucifixion with his burial,
Through the strength of his resurrection with his ascension,
Through the strength of his descent for the judgment of Doom.

I arise today
Through the strength of the love of Cherubim,
In obedience of angels,
In the service of archangels,
In hope of the resurrection to meet with reward,
In prayers of patriarchs,
In predictions of prophets,
In preaching of apostles,
In faith of confessors,
In innocence of holy virgins,
In deeds of righteous men.

I arise today
Through the strength of heaven:
Light of sun,
Radiance of moon,
Splendor of fire,
Speed of lightning,
Swiftness of wind,
Depth of sea,
Stability of earth,
Firmness of rock.

I arise today
Through God's strength to pilot me:
God's might to uphold me,
God's wisdom to guide me,

God's eye to look before me,
God's ear to hear me,
God's word to speak for me,
God's hand to guard me,
God's way to lie before me,
God's shield to protect me,
God's host to save me,
From snares of devils,
From temptations of vices,
From everyone who shall wish me ill,
Afar and anear,
Alone and in multitude.

I summon today all these powers between me and those evils,
Against every cruel merciless power that may oppose my body and soul,
Against incantations of false prophets,
Against black laws of pagandom,
Against false laws of heretics,
Against craft of idolatry,
Against spells of witches and smiths and wizards,
Against every knowledge that corrupts man's
body and soul.

Christ to shield me today
Against poison, against burning,
Against drowning, against wounding,
So that there may come to me abundance of reward.
Christ with me, Christ before me, Christ behind me,
Christ in me, Christ beneath me, Christ above me,
Christ on my right, Christ on my left,
Christ when I lie down, Christ when I sit down,
Christ when I arise,
Christ in the heart of every man who thinks of me,
Christ in the mouth of everyone who speaks of me,
Christ in every eye that sees me,
Christ in every ear that hears me.

I arise today
Through a mighty strength, the invocation of the Trinity,
Through belief in the threeness,
Through confession of the oneness,
Of the Creator of Creation.

CHAPTER NINE

Waiting in the Night:
When We Cannot Pray

O God from whom we flee,
whose stillness is more terrible
than earthquake, wind, or fire,
speak to our loneliness and challenge our despair;
that in your very absence
we may recognize your voice,
and wrapped in your presence
we may go forth in the world,
in the name of Christ,
Amen.

JANET MORLEY

The inability to pray is a significant part of the life of prayer, a normal and natural occurrence. It befalls most of us at one time or another. Suddenly God seems absent, as if a telephone conversation had been interrupted. Or we ourselves are absent, restless, or listless, unable to sit, stand, or talk in the Presence.

The reasons people cannot pray are many: Illness, pain, and bereavement. Anger. Depression and other mood disorders, and conditions that may or may not be symptoms of clinical depression: fatigue, sadness, inability to focus the mind. Various stages of addiction and of recovery from addiction. Childbearing and child rearing: the physical exhaustion and emotional demands, the demands on time, sleep deprivation. Lack of time for prayer and resistance to prayer, often difficult to sort out from one another. Life transitions: moving, changing jobs, the beginning or end of a love affair, changes in health, retirement, death of a loved one. Distraction by sorrow, distraction by joy. The inexplicable "dark night of the soul," which most of the great mystics have experienced and of which everyday mystics have their own version. Institutional realities in the church and in society, especially the experience of injustice. Lack of discipline in prayer, or too much of the wrong discipline. A crisis of faith. Some kind of test—from God or from that which is not God. Or simply, a need to let the spiritual land lie fallow.

Any of these factors, or any combination of these, can act as an obstacle to prayer. They may also be opportunities for prayer, but if they are blocks, reframing them as "opportunities" may not help. Acknowledging them first is more likely to "open the channels" again.

Jaime, a friend who was raised in the Presbyterian Church, wrote to me: "About a year and a half ago my mother died of cancer. Since then, I haven't really prayed much in earnest. I used to pray daily—morning meditations, evening blessings over meals. Prayer is a painful place for me now. When Mom was dying, we would pray every day for something, anything, intervention, healing language used by a lot of well-meaning people: 'We'll storm heaven's gates with prayer,' 'We're prayer warriors,' 'Cancer, we rebuke you.' I hated it. I never prayed that way. In fact, I think militaristic language in prayer is sinful." He added: "Thanks. You've given me the opportunity to pause and think about my prayer life, something I hope to one day rebuild." Talking about the inability to pray may be the beginning of the path back to prayer.

What to do when we cannot pray? The first and most helpful step is to take some time to discern what is actually happening. It helps to start with the simplest and most obvious. For instance, it may not be a crisis of faith; you may just be exhausted. Exhaustion is epidemic these days. I do not hear about boredom or distraction from the people who speak to me about their prayer life so much as stress and hopelessness. True, distraction visits most of us in prayer; but despair stalks us more in these early-twenty-first-century days, and fatigue at least as often. We do need to watch the fine line between slacking off and really needing a rest. There is, however, nothing wrong with catching up on sleep and praying for ten minutes, rather than struggling for over an hour with a weary body and an overburdened mind and finding oneself unable to pray.

It may be a time of doubt. On the other hand, trouble in one's prayer life or absence of prayer may be due to discouragement with the institutional church—I see this far more often than lack of faith. The two often become intertwined. Identifying the cause or the nature of the block to prayer will determine what you might do. Begin where you are: having discovered what is causing the block, address it directly. In the case of the "dark night," faithfulness is key. But faithfulness to a particular practice may not be in order if the reason for inability to pray is weariness or sorrow. You may need more sleep, or more time outdoors, or you may want to pray a prayer of lamentation, cry the Psalms, sing, or sigh, trusting the Spirit "who prays within us with sighs too deep for words."

The chances are very high that if we are having difficulty praying, we are not aware of, or are not admitting to, some difficult feeling: sadness, anger, guilt, or perhaps a more positive emotion but one that may also be frightening: desire (sexual or otherwise), lust, intense joy.

When I first moved to California in the summer of 1995, I did not pray much my first two weeks. I attributed this to exhaustion and jet lag and to the demands of unpacking and getting acclimated—though Berkeley was certainly a more relaxing environment than Boston.

What I discovered eventually was a well of feeling I had kept hidden away in the course of the move. Inability to pray can be due to lack of honesty with God, and even before this, with oneself, but it may have its root at an earlier stage: the very lack of knowledge about one's emotions. We do not always know our own feelings. We disconnect from them, and from our thoughts. Sometimes the body provides a clue. After a week or two of unpacking, admiring the local flowers, and experiencing a total inability to pray, I went for a massage. "Do you get headaches?" the masseur asked me. "No," I answered, "almost never." A few minutes later, as he was working on a particularly intractable muscle on the left side of my back, I joked, "Some people get headaches; I bury my feelings in my back muscles." In this case, the feeling I found was sadness. It surfaced as the muscles relaxed. Once I discovered it, hearing its message through my body, it was easier to bring it before God.

Having discovered or uncovered your feelings, take them to God in prayer. My former spiritual director, when I would walk in and pour out the most recent saga, would ask, "Have you talked to God about this?" "I knew you were going to say that!" I answered after several months, half exasperated and half amused. I now ask it of my own directees. More often than not, the answer is a half-puzzled "No." "Try it," I say to them. It is, of course, a reminder to myself as well.

Often, when we encounter difficulties in prayer, our first reflex is to be hard on ourselves. Gentleness and kindness with ourselves may be more appropriate; try them first.

In difficult times such as grief, troubles on the job, a crisis in a relationship—just as in crises of faith, when one questions the very presence or existence of God—the doing of prayer becomes especially important. Fidelity to prayer even in times of obscurity may be one of the most crucial parts of spiritual growth. All prayer is not novelty and excitement, just as committed human relationships are not. Sometimes, as with human love, what matters is faithfulness and presence, being there, giving and receiving even when the will is weak and the meaning of the presence, the giving, and the receiving is not clear. For many, faithfulness to one's habitual prayer practice may be enough. For others, a return to older practices may be useful, helpful, reassuring, opening up the path of prayer again: childhood prayers, familiar Psalms, the Rosary, the lighting of candles or the singing of traditional hymns. Faithfulness to one's habits of prayer may require additional acts of the will. But here, too, it is best coupled with gentleness.

Try faithfulness first. You will not know for a while whether it is the right path. You will not find out unless you take the path itself.

After a time, it may become clear that faithfulness to your prayer practice or routine is not helping your relationship with God, that the routine itself is getting in the way of prayer. If that is the case, try a change in routine, or a new way of praying: silence instead of words, words instead of silence, song instead of speech, walking instead of sitting still. A small faith community may revitalize your prayer, bringing companions into your search, perhaps new language, and a sense that the Spirit moves in ways that transcend your own life.

When I was recovering from depression, I found that the ways I used to pray, including contemplative prayer and meditation, no longer "worked." My spiritual director encouraged me to pray with what "worked" in the present, not with what "used to work." So I left meditation behind as well as the thought that I could now return to meditation; for now, I could not go back to the place I had sat before, metaphorically or otherwise. As it happened, praying with the body and singing emerged as the most appropriate ways of praying for me at the time. Had someone not encouraged me to let go of my preconceived notions of what prayer ought to be, I might have stayed for a long time in a state of spiritual frustration or paralysis.

Again, test this against your experience, be mindful, be honest with yourself. It may be that change is exactly what you need to renew your relationship with the Holy One. It may also be that trying a new routine, a new community, a new mode of prayer, not once but several times, is only restlessness and flight from yourself, and will be fruitless. Only you will know. You may want to speak with friends in your faith community for additional insight, or with a spiritual director.

If times are bleak and God seems absent and prayer is a burden, first, be gentle. Then go to something very simple. Harry, in Alaska, writes that in spiritually somber days, "indigo days," as he calls them, he chops wood—"good indigo meditative practice." A directee of mine whom I will call Susan told me she could not pray. In her busy life, she said, there was no time for this. Besides which, self-judgment was a constant problem. The combination was enough to tie anyone in knots, and it did. Over her whole life was a cloud of judgment, and when it lifted, a kind of urgent rush took its place. I suggested that she simply breathe, whenever the thought

occurred to her, using the three deep breaths of which I wrote in
Chapter 4: cleansing, centering, and stillness. Not at a fixed time—
the clouds of judgment would doubtless overwhelm her—but on
her walk to work, or during a pause in her reading. "You mean, just
breathe?" she said, somehow expecting "homework" of a different
sort. "Yes," I said, "just breathe." The more internal judgment you
bear, the more gentleness you need. The more complex the inner
knots, the more simplicity in practice. Later, there will be time for
more. First, make room for the presence of the One whose love is
unconditional, and who simply wants us to be—not to produce.

Another helpful reality is the presence of others. There was a
year, about twelve or fifteen years ago, when I simply could not pray.
I remember this time as dry and somewhat sad, empty. There was
simply nothing. As I look back, I see that this period was one of the
most significant in my prayer life, because I was truly carried by the
prayer of others, by the prayer of the community of faith to which I
belonged. I belonged to a parish church that I attended almost every
Sunday, and I learned there that I did not have to "do it all" myself,
that I could pray even when I myself could not pray, when I had no
words, when I had no strength. I put myself inside the prayer of the
church. It cradled me. It moved me along. It held me up.

It is quite possible—I say this with hindsight—that I was suffering from low-grade chronic depression. It may also have been a test
of faith. It was certainly related to the despair I felt about the state of
the world at the time, especially the nuclear arms race. In all likeli-
hood it was a combination of all three and perhaps other factors.
From the perspective of my prayer life, the what or why—the
cause—matters little. What remains is the lesson—about being carried and cradled by the prayer of others and the faith of others—
which has never left me.

There are also times, especially after major life changes or when
such changes are brewing, when we need emptiness, as land needs
to lie fallow. "Emptiness is part of the human condition," writes
Nancy Roth. "It can produce despair or dependency, as well as
desire for God. It is not comfortable to feel empty: it is difficult to
accept those moments or even years when we do not *feel* as though
we are filled with God. Because emptiness is uncomfortable, we
often become frantic to fill the vacuum with such things as food,

work, alcohol, or frantic activity. But . . . even when we are not conscious of God's presence, God is there, holding us in life, breathing through us."[1]

One of the most moving accounts I received of the inability to pray was full of mystery, falling somewhere between the blocks occasioned by emotional pain and the inexplicable "dark night of the soul." Phoebe, a fifty-year-old Catholic sister, wrote me: "For about twenty-one years I prayed an hour a day, usually using the Scripture text of the day. Prayer had its ups and down: periods of dryness, periods of intense pain (once for about three years), but somehow I kept going. I almost always had a spiritual director, some women, some men, and they were usually helpful. Everything changed a little over two years ago. My spiritual director, very wise and insightful, opened the issue of a relationship I had with a mutual friend: the relationship was not growing and I was very frustrated at my friend's lack of response. My director prodded me to look at what was happening.

"What happened was that the reflection of the next six weeks or so opened up all sorts of personal issues and I decided to begin psychotherapy. The psychologist really has been God's gift as I have gradually and painfully worked on very complicated personal problems.

"For about six weeks after I began therapy, things were about as usual. Then in June of '94 [she was writing in late 1996] the darkness descended and has yet to lift, though things are different now than they were a year ago. Then, God disappeared, all felt experience of God vanished: all was/is silence and darkness. For many months this was intensified by an intense and unending inner pain during any attempt to pray.

"My director has helped me find ways to 'be' which are somehow also ways to be with God who is the Darkness, is the Pain, is the Silence. The experience of these many months has been a movement from absolute midnight to approaching dawn, yet not dawn, not light, certainly not consolation and joy. But somehow it has been peaceful, though a very different kind of peace than I had ever experienced. I have tried many ways to pray over these months. For a while I did a form of 'breathing prayer,' lying down, focusing on my breathing, not thinking, not doing anything but trying to follow my breathing, trusting that God is in my breath.

"At Easter came a change: a sense of feeling that the movement of death to life was taking place in me and that the 'old Phoebe' had to die, was dying. The next two months of therapy brought even more pain, but 'good pain.' Prayer was a kind of centering prayer, focused on the name of Jesus, not going anyplace; but still I tried to pray. Prayer now is what my director calls 'inner adoration': being (or at least trying to be) utterly still and quiet inside: no mantra, no 'words to God,' nothing: just attention to God who IS."

She added: "These two years of therapy and my continuing journey in faith (dark, dark faith) have taught me that there are no boundaries between the psychological and spiritual dimensions of human experience. We name them in distinct languages, but the process is the same: the journey to our True Self in God. In finding our True Self, we find God: in finding God, we find our True Self. At this point I continue to seek my Real Self. The journey is very, very long."

✺

THE COMPANIONABLE DARK

The companionable dark
of here and now,
seed lying dormant
in the earth. The dark
to which all lost things come—scarves
and rings and precious photographs, and
of course, our beloved
dead. The brooding dark,
our most vulnerable hours, limbs loose
in sleep, mouths agape.
The faithful dark,
where each door leads,
each one of us, alone.
The dark of God come close
as breath, our one companion
all the way through, the dark
of a needle's eye.
Not the easy dark
of dusk and candles,

but dark from which comforts flee.
The deep down dark
of one by one,
dark of wind
and dust, dark in which stars burn.
The floodwater dark
of hope, Jesus in agony
 in the garden. Esther pacing
her bitter palace. A dark
by which we see, dark like truth,
like flesh on bone.
Help me, who am alone
and have no help but thee.

KATHLEEN NORRIS

WHEN HE CAME (10.)

I don't as they put it believe in god
but to him I cannot say no hard as I try
take a look at him in the garden
when his friends ran out on him
his face wet with fear
and with the spit of his enemies
him I have to believe

Him I can't bear to abandon
to the great disregard for life
to the monotonous passing of millions of years
to the moronic rhythm of work leisure and work
to the boredom we fail to dispel
in cars in beds in stores

That's how it is they say what do you want
uncertain and not uncritically
I subscribe to the other hypothesis
which is his story
that's not how it is he said for god is
and he staked his life on this claim

Thinking about it I find
one can't let him pay alone
for his hypothesis
so I believe him about
god
The way one believes another's laughter
his tears
or marriage or no for an answer
that's how you'll learn
to believe him about life
promised to all.

DOROTHEE SOELLE

TRYING TO SEE THE LIGHT

Lord,
> when you send the rain,
> think about it, please,
> a little?

Do
> not get carried away
> by the sound of falling water,
> the marvelous light
> on falling water.

I
> am beneath that water
> It falls with great force
> and the Light

Blinds
> me to the light

JAMES BALDWIN

FOR THE DARKNESS OF WAITING

For the darkness of waiting
of not knowing what is to come
of staying ready and quiet and attentive,
we praise you O God
> *For the darkness and the light*
> *are both alike to you.*

For the darkness of staying silent
for the terror of having nothing to say
and for the greater terror
of needing to say nothing,
we praise you O God
> *For the darkness and the light*
> *are both alike to you.*

For the darkness of loving
in which it is safe to surrender
to let go of our self-protection
and to stop holding back our desire,
we praise you O God
> *For the darkness and the light*
> *are both alike to you.*

For the darkness of choosing
when you give us the moment
to speak, and act, and change,
and we cannot know what we have set in motion,
but we still have to take the risk,
we praise you O God
> *For the darkness and the light*
> *are both alike to you.*

For the darkness of hoping
in a world which longs for you,
for the wrestling and the labouring of all creation
for wholeness and justice and freedom,
we praise you O God
> *For the darkness and the light*
> *are both alike to you.*

JANET MORLEY

Hope without risk
is not hope,
which is believing
in risky loving,
trusting others
in the dark,
the blind leap
letting God take over.

DOM HELDER CÂMARA

CHAPTER TEN

Praying with Anger

Rise up, Lord,
rescue me, my God.
Break their evil jaws!
Smash their teeth!
Favor your people, Lord,
for the victory is yours.

PSALM 3:8–9

Righteous God,
you plead the cause
of the poor and unprotected.
Fill us with holy rage
when justice is delayed,
and give us the persistence
to require those rights that are denied;
for your name's sake, Amen.

JANET MORLEY

When I was about ten years old, one of my playmates, a boy my age, was killed in a car crash. I do not remember much of my feelings except for a kind of numbness and emptiness, and the lack of both a language and a place to express puzzlement, loss, or grief. My parents did not believe in taking children to funerals, and I was left home on that day, without the architecture of a communal ritual to support my experience. What I do remember is the boy's mother, my own mother's friend, who stopped going to church after her son died, unable, she said, to believe in a God who would allow such unspeakable tragedy to befall her.

More than three decades later, I have no answer for the mysteries of suffering and death, but I wonder whether the grieving mother stopped believing in God, or whether she was in fact angry at God and unable to express her anger. Certainly the God in whom she believed before the accident died on that day. Might a new presence of God have arisen for this woman, a God made human who suffers with us, or even a God with whom we can rage and wrestle, a God resilient enough to bear our strongest emotions? No amount of anger can bring back the delicate smile and agile grace of my childhood friend; what anger might have done—might still do—is to restore the relationship with God, once vital and suddenly grown silent.

Anger is one of the greatest blocks to prayer. We fear anger—our own and that of others, our anger and the anger of God. Anger is difficult enough to deal with in daily life even without the "God factor." We equate anger, mistakenly, with hate, though the two can in some cases be partners. We know that unchecked anger can lead to violence, both verbal and physical. We fear that expressing our anger verbally, or even in the privacy of our hearts, to ourselves, necessarily means that our behavior will spin out of control. If we are women, raised to be soothers, mediators, and bridge builders, we may run the opposite risk: we fear our own anger so much that it often turns inward, festering into depression.

Anger is. It is no "should" or "should not" in our lives, but a natural response to loss, illness, personal misfortune, and social injustice. Anger is often a manifestation of love. Love and anger: hold these together for a few breaths, and think of the way in which anger is love with a wound.

When I was interviewing American Catholic women for *Generous Lives*, I found that many, though not all, were angry about women's place in society or in the church. Yet of these women, not one spoke with a hate-filled heart. Their anger was obviously a sign of love, born of intense caring, commitment, and pain. People who do not care do not get angry. Couples know well how much the expression of anger can be a sign of love, trust, and security. I am not speaking of anger expressed in a manner that terrorizes the other or violates that partner's bodily integrity. The wreckage of family violence is all too widespread. What I am talking about is the capacity to express anger to one's beloved because one feels safe—because the beloved will neither react with violence nor run away, nor put up a psychological or emotional wall.

Ginny, a Catholic woman in her late forties living in the Midwest, tells me that at the age of nine she discovered her mother "in the kitchen hauling off at God. Mother was standing at the sink, her perennial place, cutting up vegetables and yelling at God out loud. I was horrified, and certain she'd be struck dead at her temerity! She just said, 'You know I get angry with your father sometimes, right? And he understands?' Yes. Yes. 'Well, I figure God loves me even more than Daddy, and He'll understand too.'" Recounting the story to me, Ginny said, "Even to a nine-year-old that made sense. I've never hesitated since. When I'm angry, God *knows*."

In later years, Ginny carried this awareness with her into her prayer life and into conversations with others. "Seems to me that this is a matter of trusting in God as Beloved Friend," she observed. For a year Ginny, now a scholar, worked as a secretary for two oncologists at a major research hospital in the Bronx, New York. During that time, she "quickly lost count of the spouses—and a couple of parents—who sat at my desk telling me how they had to be strong, while their wife, husband, or child was being examined and evaluated for an experimental and highly toxic protocol. I became very skilled at getting them angry enough to cry—and teaching them, when it seemed appropriate, to have that freedom to be angry with God. They'd say, 'Who am I gonna get angry with? God?' 'Sure,' I'd respond. '*Ginny!!* You?! How could you *suggest* such a thing?!'" Ginny grinned. "So I'd give them Mother's argument, substituting the names. You could see the relief on their faces. My desk became the 'hangout': sit there, cry, and tell off God. No charge. Of course, my work got way behind."

Cecilio is a publisher of newsletters and a journal on publicly funded education and training programs in Washington, D.C. When I queried him about prayer and anger, he bitterly described his father as "an inveterate philanderer in and out of marriage and his association with two concubines." For Cecilio, anger brought about what he called "an epiphany," a manifestation of God's presence. "When my father died, I prayed a written prayer, spelling out all the reasons God the Judge should consign my father to hell. At the end of the enumeration a strange peace descended upon me. I didn't quite forgive, but I did suddenly see mercy taking over."

"When I am mad at someone," one of my correspondents wrote me, "really mad, not just irritated, I can only complain to God because nobody else wants to listen. So I say exactly what I think, including plans for dismembering the person. God doesn't mind." She added, "It is a lot better to be honest than to be 'good'!"

Does this simply make God the Great Therapist, the One with whom it is safe to howl and cry in a controlled environment? No, and yes. To reduce God to the fifty-minute hour writ large is to ignore the biblical traditions in which God, the One who loves justice, rages directly or through the words of the prophets at corrupt rulers, at obtuse believers, and especially at those who neglect or oppress the vulnerable, the poor, and the marginal, "the widows and the orphans" who have no power and cannot provide for themselves.

> Ah, you who make iniquitous decrees,
> who write oppressive statutes,
> to turn aside the needy from justice
> and to rob the poor of my people of their right,
> that widows may be your spoil,
> and that you may make the orphans your prey!
> What will you do on the day of punishment,
> in the calamity that will come from far away?
> To whom will you flee for help . . . ?
> For all this God's anger has not turned away;
> God's hand is stretched out still.
>
> ISAIAH 10:1–4

God does get angry, and that anger is righteous indignation.[1] Anger—God's and ours—is the natural response to injustice.

The question of anger, God's and ours, also brings us up against the seeming contradictions in Scripture, including some of the descriptions of Jesus in the Gospels. We have trouble reconciling, in our minds and hearts, the Jesus who overturned the tables of the money changers with the Jesus who tenderly drew small children into his arms. Is this because we have difficulty with Jesus' humanity and with the classical Christian belief in God as both truly God and truly human? Where is Jesus in our lives and in our prayer when we are angry? Can we also imagine him righteously indignant, furious at injustice, as the Gospels do show him, not only "meek and mild"?

But yes: God *is* the Great Listener. That does not mean replacing the Twenty-third Psalm's opening words with "The Lord is my Shrink, I shall not want" ("I hate these modern translations!" *Kudzu* comic-strip preacher Will B. Dunn would say, shaking his head), but understanding, as Ginny does, that our anger is no burden for God. God can take it. Go ahead, I often tell people who come and speak with me about their relationship with God. Yell at God. God will still be there, God will still love you. The earth will not open and swallow you up.

Of course, I am better at telling this to others than at hearing it myself. For years I struggled to find hope for a world living under the threat of nuclear destruction. I found it hard to believe that the planet onto which I had been born, post-Hiroshima, had a long-term future. During the late 1970s and early 1980s my despair increased, even as I worked in what small ways I could to support efforts toward disarmament and peace. In my twenties and early thirties, I did not believe I would live to see my fortieth birthday. I was not paralyzed: I began to write and publish more frequently, became an activist, read, joined with others who felt as I did, voted in every election, helped organize conferences, took part in public rallies. I went to church, and there in the midst of the community celebration, I could somehow pray, carried by the faith of others. But in private, sometime during those years, early in the 1980s, for a year or so, I could not pray. Inside me was a spiritual blank. The inner space began to color, move, and warm again on the day I got angry at last. Not at people and institutions—I knew that anger,

though it was reasonably contained; I knew my anger at govern-
ments and weapons, at policies and policymakers, at my country
and at myself. It had not occurred to me that I was furious at God.
Every Sunday I went to church and heard, in one form or another,
of One who did not abandon, whose promises lasted forever, who
loved justice and longed for peace. Alone in my room, I lost the
memory of these words, or when I remembered them, they rang
hollow. They did not live inside my body.

They grew alive again, paradoxically, the day I doubted them
out loud—very loud. I sat on my bed and spoke to God. I remember
only that I spoke in a strong voice, my body filled with emotion and
tears, and that the words I spoke were of anger and reproach. I,
reproaching God! I remember only one sentence of what I said:
"Have You abandoned Your people?" At last I was honest. "Better
to be honest," my friend wrote, "than to be good." My despair did
not leave altogether, but God and I began to talk again, and the
despair had a name much deeper than my individual fear of death.
The God to whom I screamed that day was the God of the future
and the God of hope, a God of community and of people, the God
of all creation. Great Listener, yes, but also Holy One of Promise.

Looking back, I see that this was one of the times in life I did not
read the Psalms, a book of the Bible I have visited again and again
since my preadolescent years. I might have spoken to God sooner
had the Psalms been with me. The Psalms are good for anger—in
fact, for most human emotions. I have noticed more and more people speaking to me and to each other about the usefulness, the aid to
life and prayer, of what many of us call in the vernacular "the angry
Psalms"—the ones that used to embarrass us, that we glossed over,
excised from our "Bible of choice," dismissed as primitive, an early
stage of faith, not a mature, *prayerful* prayer. "Rise up, Lord,/rescue
me, my God./Break their evil jaws! Smash their teeth!/Favor your
people, Lord,/for the victory is yours" (Psalm 3:8–9).

More than a decade after the day I sat and railed at God about
the state of the world, praying the angry psalms was part of a
renewed reliance on the Bible during a difficult time. They helped
me to live with depression and to move through it.

I fell prey to a major depression in the fall of 1993, following a
sojourn in what I now call "the killer job." The convergence of a

stressful and eventually traumatic work situation and a moderate mood disorder I may well have had all my life left me stricken with massive anxiety attacks, then haunted by suicidal ideations. Depression is treatable: thanks to a combination of therapy and medication, a brief hospitalization, and the love and presence of my friends, I survived the crisis and was able to heal. I am also certain that the grace of God played no small part in my survival. In the weeks before my hospitalization, I hung on to the Psalms for dear life. As I wrestled with the aftermath of what I experienced as a harmful, destructive work situation, it helped that the Psalms were blunt in their language about good and evil, faithfulness and strug- gle, enmity and vindication. I knew I had dealt with both individual and institutional evil in the killer job, but always the polite, well-bred "good girl," I had sought not to think ill of anyone nor to turn my anger into anything but talk. Depression is anger turned inward, they say, especially in women. The Psalms gave me back my anger, took me beyond gentility into the wrath of God for the unjust. "Smite my enemies, Lord," I would read aloud with tears rolling down my cheeks, and it felt healing. "O Lord, how many are my foes!/Many are rising against me . . . But you, O God, are a shield around me. . . . Deliver me, O my God!" (Psalm 3:1, 3a, 7b). I redis- covered the low-number Psalms, at the beginning of the book, and was amazed at the way they spoke of my own life. Gone were the discomfort and guilt so many of us have felt at the harsh tone of the text. "If you begin to feel suicidal," a physician friend advised me when I called her on one of the worst days, "think homicidal thoughts."

The major depression I suffered in the second half of 1993 was blessed by angry prayer in another way. The "angry Psalms" had stood vigil over its acute beginning; a desperate and furious lashing out at God heralded its end. In the summer, fall, and early winter of 1994, the economic bottom dropped out of my life, mostly due to my illness, which brought with it the temporary inability to work full time, enormous health-care bills despite the fact that I had health insurance, and as a result of this penury, my applications for free care at a local teaching hospital and for fuel assistance to help pay the oil bills for my apartment. The edge of winter found me in a rage: at the health-care system, especially the mental health–care system, at the insurance companies, at the killer job I had left the previous year, at the Republican party for taking measures that would harm the poor and the vulnerable, at the Democratic party for compromising its traditional championing of the poor and the vulnerable, at bureaucracies in general, at the Cambridge Department of Traffic and Parking for ticketing and Denver-booting my car in Harvard Square, at the economy for not getting better. And at God? No, no, I answered when my spiritual director asked whether I was angry at God. It's not God's fault that all this is happening.

Then, finally, one day in early winter, I cracked. I was driving home to Watertown, Massachusetts, by the Charles River. My phone had been shut off—only briefly, because I paid the phone company the money I owed the auto mechanic—and I found myself obliged to pay the auto mechanic with the money I owed the landlord, which I did not have. The oil tank at home read half an inch from "empty" and my application for fuel assistance was still in the belly of the bureaucracy. I was working in a demanding part-time job and several piecemeal bits of employment and was sleep deprived, something I had sought to avoid at all costs in the interests of good physical and mental health. I began to cry in the car, and found myself screaming—at God, I think—"ENOUGH! ENOUGH! ENOUGH!" All I could do was to say "ENOUGH!" and cry. The next day, I felt much better for having yelled at God, and four phone calls came in offering me work, some of it decently paid. Following which I was angry, of course, that even with God, I had to raise my voice, and make an effort, and that nothing was easy these days, not even prayer. Then it occurred to me that I was in a dreadful rotten mood, and that this was perfectly appropriate, given the circumstances, and I began to laugh as I told this to a friend, pointing out to him that there is a difference between being depressed and being in a rotten lousy mood, and that I was definitely not depressed. But in a rotten mood, oh yes, with a vengeance, dear God.

Recounting her spiritual journey and recovery from active alcoholism, Barbara said, "I was so glad when I started hollering at God. It meant to me that I actually really did believe in Him. Unfortunately, I was still blaming and being the victim at that stage, so I was 'stuck,' but at least I knew for a fact that I had some small faith."

❦

PSALM 7

A Lament in Time of Persecution.
Cry out to God, Just Judge and Saving Help

A Lamentation of David,
which he sang to the Lord
concerning Cush, the Benjaminite.

You are my haven, Lord my God,
save me from my attackers.
Rescue me, their helpless prey;
these lions will tear me to pieces.

Lord, if I have done wrong,
if there is guilt on my hands,
if I have mistreated friend or foe
for no good reason,
then let the enemy hound me,
overtake and kill me,
trample me to the ground.

Wake up, Lord!
Arise and rage
against my angry foes.
Provide the justice you demand.
Make the world a courtroom
and take your seat as judge.

Then, judge of all nations,
give me justice.
I have done what is right,
I am innocent.

Put an end to evil,
uphold the good;
you test our hearts,
God of right and truth.
God who saves the honest
defends me like a shield.

God is a zealous judge
ready to say "guilty" every day
if sinners do not turn around.

Instead they sharpen their swords,
string their bows,
and light flaming arrows,
taking up lethal weapons.
See how they conceive evil,
grow pregnant with trouble,
and give birth to lies.

Sinners land in the pit
dug with their own hands.
Their evil crashes on their heads;
they are victims of their own violence.

I praise God who is right and good,
I sing out, "Lord Most High!"

. . . THE GRACE TO SHOUT . . .

Today we ask
the grace to shout
when it hurts,
even though silence is expected of us,
and to listen when others shout
though it be painful to hear;
to object, to protest, when we feel, taste, or observe injustice
believing that even the unjust and arrogant
are human nonetheless
and therefore are worthy of strong efforts to reach them.
Take from us, Guiding God, the heart of despair
and fill us with courage and understanding.
Give us a self that knows very well
when the moment has come to protest.
We ask the grace to be angry
when the weakest are the first to be exploited
and the trapped are squeezed for the meager resources,

when the most deserving are the last to thrive,
and the privileged demand more privilege.
We ask for the inspiration to make our voices heard
when we have something that needs to be said,
something that rises to our lips despite our shyness.
And we ask the grace to listen when the meek finally rise to speak
and their words are an agony for us. . . .

WILLIAM CLEARY

CHAPTER ELEVEN

"From Where Will My Help Come?":

Praying During Depression

Pity me, Lord,
I hurt all over;
my eyes are swollen,
my heart and body ache.
Grief consumes my life,
sighs fill my days;
guilt saps my strength,
my bones dissolve.
Enemies mock me,
make me the butt of jokes,
neighbors scorn me,
strangers avoid me.
Forgotten like the dead,
I am a shattered jar.

PSALM 31:10–13

I lift up my eyes to the hills—
from where will my help come?
My help comes from the Lord
who made heaven and earth.

PSALM 121:1–2

66 "In my second and third years of sobriety," Barbara recounted, "I was in a black cold depression. Most of the time I hated myself. I didn't trust hardly anyone. The people I trusted couldn't fix me. They couldn't reach me through the cold. It was like a January fog.

"I prayed daily. I asked God to keep me sober and help me believe that somehow someday it would pass. I clung to the people that I had in my life and got through it. I believed that the things they told me that helped were messages from God. I knew they were connected. But because I was enveloped in self-loathing, I couldn't feel any love. So I couldn't connect with God. One day I said, 'If I have to feel like this I might as well drink,' and someone said, 'If you drink, you know it will get worse. If you stay sober, there's just a *chance* that it will get better.' That was true, so I knew it was from God. Another day I had the thought out of nowhere, 'If I drink, the best possible thing that could happen is that someday I will be right where I am right now—back in the program with a little bit of time. So why the hell leave?' I knew that was a message from God. These things kept me going. I didn't drink and I didn't kill myself, one day at a time. I went back to smoking, and I gained lots of weight, but I was alive, or as alive as I could be. All through this I talked to God and I listened to people for my answers because I felt totally disconnected."

Depression is the common cold of mental illness. Too often viewed as simply sadness or a bad case of the blues, sometimes even as a character disorder, it is a condition we now know to be biochemical as much as emotional. Sadness is a feeling; depression is a state. These blues do not go away on their own, and character has nothing to do with this. Depression, anxiety, or panic conditions and other mood disorders affect millions of people. They are profoundly debilitating. They are also treatable.[1]

In the early 1990s, I became executive director of a nonprofit organization. Pressed by economic necessity as well as drawn to the organization's mission, I had taken on the directorship upon completing nearly six years' work on my first book. Already tired when I began, I was exhausted by the end of the job's first year. Toward the end of my second year, I resigned. I was weary of having program time devoured by administration and fundraising, increasingly edgy with my staff, unhappy with the person I was becoming, at ideological odds with the most powerful members of my board of directors, and rapidly losing confidence in my professional abilities—something I had never experienced in my life. When all else failed—love affairs, economic stability—I had always been able to rely on my mind and on my competence. I began to feel as if I were losing both.

The early warning signal had come at the end of April 1993. Driving on a road north of Boston, late at night, I became incomprehensibly dizzy, my heart beating fast and waves overcoming me—waves of what? I was not sure. I was close to fainting. My first thought was that I was having a stroke, and that I would die there on the road, in the dark, with the motor running and the car lurching out of control. Twice I pulled the car over to the side of the highway. Finally I got home, singing a chant from the Easter Vigil to steady myself.

Labor Day weekend in Vermont 1993: I had just finished my last week as executive director, though I was due back in the office as a consultant during the fall to help the organization manage the transition. My parents, my old friend Peter, and I were resting after lunch. Around us the countryside was quiet. I became dizzy, unbearably lightheaded, felt my heart rate shoot up. I began to tremble and sweat. I called to Peter, who took my hand, then took my pulse. My heart was beating at nearly twice its normal pace. It took me two hours to calm down.

A few days later, back in Boston, the symptoms returned. Day after day, week upon week they came and went, at all hours of day and night—3 a.m., 5 a.m., 10:30 p.m. I never knew when they were going to hit. Most of the time I was alone. But even at church—for me a place of friendship and safety—in the midst of several hundred people, the attacks came upon me. Externally they showed very little; inside I felt physiologically off balance and emotionally out of control.

I went to the hospital emergency room twice during the worst of the attacks, was hooked up to heart monitors, watched my heart rate go up and down, then down to normal, then up and down again. On the second of these visits I shook so violently that the technician could barely perform an electrocardiogram. "Try to keep still, dear," she said. I thought I was going to die.

Then began the parade to medical specialists, none of whom could determine a physiological cause for my distress. After I had gone for a variety of holistic treatments including homeopathic remedies and two kinds of bodywork, the physical symptoms began to abate. But still the fear gripped me, not a worry about something specific but an anxiety with no bottom—not something I had, but a reality that had me. Sometimes it seemed as if the electrical wiring inside my brain were short-circuiting. No amount of deep breathing, yoga, and fresh air seemed to help.

One of my friends suggested I might be depressed. Not knowing there was such a thing as an agitated depression, I had at first no idea that this could be the case. Anxiety, yes, but depression? Depression, I thought, was moping, slowing down, not getting up in the morning. I was ruminating, speeding, and getting up too early. One day, driving into Boston by the Charles River, I imagined myself—saw myself—jumping off a bridge. I phoned my former psychotherapist and asked to see him, fast.

I began therapy again, willingly and with a sense of urgency. Very reluctantly, a few weeks later, I started taking antidepressant medication, and soon after, an anti-anxiety drug. Even then I was in such a state of terror and agitation—and still haunted by thoughts of leaps from bridges and seventh-floor windows—that I decided to check myself into the hospital. It was late October, nearly two months after the beginning of the series of acute anxiety attacks, six months after the first isolated one.

What happened to my prayer?

Meditation was the first thing to go. I still practiced yoga, and breathing exercises gave me some mild relief from anxiety attacks. But contemplation became impossible. Still, God was present, and I knew it. I did not face the fear alone. Yet the way I prayed underwent a profound change.

One night in September the panic attack came at bedtime, a terrible shaking and fear, causing me to tremble so hard that my steady evening companion, a large black and white cat named Alyosha, jumped off the bed from fright. I breathed as deeply as I could, calmed down enough to open the Bible I keep at my bedside, and began reading Psalms out loud. I read aloud to steady myself, to keep the demons at bay, to make the words more real and hold them in my mouth. At last I was able to cry. The Psalms gave word to my heart, and even to my body. "Oh Lord, heal me," says Psalm 6, "for my bones are shaking with terror. My soul also is struck with terror, while you, O Lord—how long?" They may not have called them "anxiety disorders" thirty centuries ago, but the symptoms sounded suspiciously familiar.

The first change, then, was a renewed reliance on the Bible, especially the Hebrew Bible, and above all the Psalms. Praying the Psalms was not so much a prayer of petition as a prayer of naming, a statement of the situation. It gave me words—ancient words written by people who had the wisdom of experience, prayed aloud by generations of my ancestors in faith, both Jewish and Christian.

I spoke in the preceding chapter of hanging on to the Psalms for dear life, and of the help they gave me in allowing me to pray angrily, to mouth words I had not allowed myself to think, feel, or speak, about the evils I had witnessed and experienced and the way they had found their wounding way into my psyche and my flesh. The Psalms helped in other ways as well. One came into my life and stayed with me for months: Psalm 121. Long after my stay in the hospital I was still reading it each night before turning off the light: "The One who watches Israel will neither slumber nor sleep. The Lord is your keeper. . . . The Lord will keep you from all evil. . . . God will keep your life . . . from this time on and forevermore." I listened to the promise, night after night.

Before meditation left me entirely, one session, a guided one, gave me a revelation that proved to be a treasure. In September or early October, I went to visit a meditation teacher I had met through one of Boston's interreligious dialogue groups. Her school is based in India with branches around the world. I sat with Sharona, a tiny, radiant woman, sipped tea with her, told her about the great fear, and heard of her unexplained headaches and dizziness—one more in the series of people who have spilled out their own stories of depression and anxiety after hearing mine. "Come to the meditation room," she said, and so we went and sat cross-legged on cushions in the quiet apartment, and slowly she began a guided meditation, in a soft voice. My friend's guiding image was God as light, and God as light was neither what I needed nor anything I was capable of perceiving at the time. I remained painfully distracted. But presently she began to speak of God's wanting us to be like children, like small babies enfolded in God's arms.

At that moment in the meditation I saw, felt, imagined arms around me; and then wings—long, vast, protective wings. Then the image of a shield emerged. I need protection, I thought, as the visions rushed in. Opening my eyes at the end of the meditation, I realized I was reacting to, or being reached by, images—*realities*—from the most ancient of biblical traditions. They were not images with which I had spent a great deal of time praying in the past, but they were part of me somehow, planted in me by my Jewish ancestors, by the prayer of the church, by God and God's Spirit—perhaps by all of these.

Only those realities could speak to the depths of my fear, and to the personal and social evils I had experienced with such intensity. No New Age light for me, no nurturing Great Mother, no caring Father. Give me the Watchful One, I thought, the guardian of Israel, the shield, the rock, the fortress, the eagle's wings. In that time and that desire, God had no gender for me; God was personal but not a person. Neither warrior nor eagle, God *was* shield, *was* wings. In that time of trauma, when I felt fragile and raw, only God as heavy metal would do, and this was the God who, from the depths, came to enfold me.

On a quick trip to New York for a consulting job, a week or two into the antidepressant drug and feeling no relief, I fell into a seven-hour anxiety attack with recurring suicidal ideations. On the morning after my arrival I found I could not focus my attention, and focus was crucial in the job I was contracted to do for twenty-four hours, as recorder and process observer at a conference of urban activists that was beginning later that day. I felt as if I were about to jump out of my skin—or throw myself under a truck. An hour away from the beginning of the conference, walking uptown on a noisy Manhattan street in the afternoon, I prayed. I prayed to every saint I could think of in that moment, prayed to Dymphna, the patron saint of people with nervous disorders, to Ignatius, founder of the Jesuits, to Mary of Magdala, Jesus' dear friend and apostle to the apostles, to Mary, the mother of Jesus, and finally to Jesus himself—perhaps out loud, I am not sure. I said with all my strength, "Jesus, I don't usually ask you for much, but I am asking you now, in the name of all those people whom you healed, in the name of the man born blind and the bent-over woman and the woman who bled for years, in the name of the man with the demons and the little girl whom you raised up, HELP ME."

Within an hour, I was calm again.

Back at the religious house where I was staying and where the conference was about to begin, I phoned Mariette, my best friend from church, a Catholic pediatrician. "You've got to pray me through this," I said. "There's nothing else left." It was clear I now needed an anti-anxiety medication, but my psychiatrist, whom I had phoned, could not prescribe a controlled substance across state lines. "I will pray," my friend said, "and my daughter too; I trust the prayers of this child even more than mine." And so the prayers of a child and her mother carried me. Miraculously, I was able to stay focused for the length of the conference.

This was only the most dramatic example of the way I was carried by the prayers of others. Most of the time these prayers carried me in the strong and ordinary ways they always have—through the liturgy to which I returned, Sunday after Sunday, through the daily or weekly prayers of friends of many religious paths whom I had asked to remember me in the course of their devotions or meditation. A few times an ecumenical married couple—she evangelical, he Catholic—prayed over me as evangelical Christians do, and I trusted their presence and their words, and God who gave them words and had given me the courage to step out of my self-sufficiency and ask them for help.

The prayer of others also helped me to weep. One of the worst dimensions of the depression was that I was unable to cry. It was a dry depression, a depression with no tears. There were only two exceptions: my night readings of the Psalms, and in church. The crowded Sunday liturgy was one of the few places and times I was able to cry, releasing layers of sorrow, grief, loss, and fear. Why church? I wondered at the time. Perhaps because I identify crying with being safe, or being held, and because in my local community of faith I do feel held, cradled in a way by this gathering of friends in Christ. And because I am touched at a level so deep I cannot refrain from crying. Somewhere in the killer job my voice had been silenced, and in church, especially in singing, I found it again, in both the music and the words.

I made little effort to pray during my psychiatric hospitalization. Nor do I remember praying with any coherence and clarity during the five preceding days, when I was in such a state of terror following my return from New York that I had friends stay with me around the clock, as I wrestled with the chaos inside, with looming fears of harming myself, and with my emerging decision to check myself into the hospital.

But the spiritual lesson of those two weeks was perhaps the central one of this period in my life. In those five days of being loved by my friends who watched over me and waited with me, in the hospital where our main work was to heal by walking through the pain, I heard: "Let me love you. Let yourself be loved." How hard that was for me. How much easier it became through this illness.

My friend Rosalind, the evangelical half of the couple who had come to pray over me, was one of the several loved ones who came to visit me in the hospital. When friends came, we talked, often joked, hugged, sometimes walked together. The day Rosalind came, I was weary and not my talkative self. She found me lying on my bed, asked what I wanted, then sat in silence by my side, rubbing my back. Half asleep, I gave thanks for the receiving.

It all came together: the knowledge that I was safe, that I was "good enough" and did not need to "try harder," that I would be all right, and that God—more deeply than I had known or let myself believe—loved me; that it was all there, there for me, "without money, without price," in the words of Isaiah.[2]

At night I read the 121st Psalm. The insomnia of the past two months came to visit again the first night of my inpatient stay, then left for good. I slept deeply. Mostly, it was time in a safe place simply to be human and attend to my feelings, not to perform, produce, put the needs of others first, or be Ms. Cheery Supercompetent, the great coper.

With letters and visits came flowers and a collection of devotional objects. Mariette, a Brooklyn-born, Harvard-educated physician, arrived bearing a rosary and a laminated card of Saint Dymphna. I loved the cards and the beads—I, the intellectual, the Catholic meditator. The Catholic tchotchkes to which I had little attraction two decades ago as a convert in my early twenties were perfect for the circumstances. They were concrete and comforting. Like the guardian of Israel, Mary and the saints watched calmly, images speaking when I had no words left to pray.

Leaving the hospital was hard. Today the insurance companies determine what length of time it takes for one's psyche to heal, or at least to be removed from mortal danger. I was discharged after twelve days, still shaky but trusting that I would heal, step by small step. Six days out of the psychiatric unit, on a Sunday evening, the pull toward death came to visit: not from my will, for my will wanted to live, but from somewhere between the biochemical and the metaphysical, a wave of death, a compulsion born of a combination of malfunctioning neurotransmitters and the powers of evil and sin, somewhere demonic, somewhere I knew was not from God or from anything good, a wave of death that would not go away.

I busied myself, paying bills, making phone calls, sorting papers, fighting the demons with tiny acts of the will, barely praying, scattered and tense, all the while thinking I knew exactly where there was a razor blade, in the tool chest, in the guest-room closet, on the upper shelf.

Most of all I felt alone. I knew I could not struggle in solitude. The threat was too great. I began phoning again, this time to call for help. "It's warfare," one of my friends from church said categorically, "spiritual warfare." She invoked angels, archangels, the vanguard of the Catholic pantheon, protecting and armed for battle. I phoned the ecumenical couple with the high-tech careers, who had promised that they were available for prayer anytime, day or night. I asked if they could pray on the phone, with me, for me. In simple words they spoke to God. I remember their saying that I needed safety and protection, that evil was real and present, that they trusted God, God would be with me, please God, they said, be with her, and your angels too.

Remembering what I had learned in the hospital, I made a plan for going to bed, step by step: take a hot bath, drink warm milk, swallow the evening medicine. If sleep does not come, I decided, I will watch and pray, but I will not let this get me—and if worse comes to worst I will go to the emergency room and beg for the psychiatrist on call, since I am, after all, in a state of emergency. After the bath I crawled between the flannel sheets, under the down comforter, taking with me a stuffed bear, a box of tissues, and a broken string of rosary beads. I awoke after sleeping for eight solid hours. Alyosha, the cat, was asleep on the comforter, sloped against my feet. The rosary was still in my hand. "The One who watches Israel will neither slumber nor sleep . . . will keep your life," says Psalm 121.

That evening I sat at the computer and wrote a long poem about the experience of the preceding night. By the time I was halfway through, I knew that I was on the mend, that the antidepressant medicine had "kicked in" or that God had navigated me through the waters, or both. I felt alive, and well. I was no longer silent. My voice was out in the world again.

The next writing to emerge was a reflection on social and political realities and their psychological consequences—an essay on my family's experience with the McCarthy era blacklist and its long-term effects. By summer, I was writing theology again—in a commentary on Pope John Paul II's apostolic letter on the ordination of women, *"Ordinatio Sacerdotalis."*[3] Having had the experience of falling to pieces, I experienced the reunion with my writing self as exquisite mending. It was both sign and cause of my renewed health.

Sometime in the middle of 1994, I realized my prayer had no anchor. I was better. I was working, writing, healing—and yet feeling as if I were wandering in the wilderness. No longer in crisis, not yet in steady peace. I decided it was time to go back into spiritual direction. The informal insight of peers was no longer sufficient. I needed someone older and wiser—and someone new.

Asking for help: again and again, it has come down to this. Help from therapists, from family, from God, from the local bank, from colleagues and friends. Help with the fear, help with the rent, help with untangling the emotional knot, help with employment, help with prayer.

"It doesn't work the way it used to," I complained to my new spiritual director. "I'm out of emergency mode, but I can't pray as I did before." "Begin with your experience," he offered, "begin exactly where you are." I wanted to be gentle with myself. At the same time, I felt I ought to bring back a rhythm of prayer, the kind of discipline and fidelity I imagined to be "right," to be a sign of spiritual health. "Bring back" was not, as it turned out, the operative term. I had undergone—was still undergoing—the most profoundly transformative experience in my life after my conversion to Catholicism. How could my prayer remain the same?

In those days and months of healing, I found that the prayer best suited to me was that which involved my body most. I was still waking up with yoga, the one practice I had not abandoned even in the hospital. Better still was the prayer involving both body and breath: singing. When all else failed that year—and "all else" failed so often that I finally ceased trying to recapture it—I played recordings of sung Psalms, chants, or gospel songs on the tape decks in my kitchen and car. I sang with them, letting the words and music carry me, entering into them with my voice, often repeating the same song two or three times. Some of the most powerful moments of communion with God came in those all-absorbing moments, not so much times of trance as periods of intense presence. A few years later, I am still asking music for help: when in doubt, sing.

For a while, I was so absorbed with daily survival that my prayer, usually made in motion—walking, on the bus, on the subway, in the car—became reduced to two simple expressions: "Thank You" and "Help!"

I struggled, hard, with the realities of evil and forgiveness. Resentment and anger at the killer job sat inside my belly like a lump. "Some demons," Jesus said, "can only be cast out by prayer." I believed it, and I knew this was one of them, but I did not know how to cast it out, nor did I yet know how Jesus would help me do it.

I am still singing in times of doubt.

❦

A SIMPLE EXERCISE: PRAYING DURING DEPRESSION
WITH THE HELP OF WRITING

With depression comes a short attention span. It is hard to concentrate, to focus, to hold anything in the mind. "I felt disconnected," said Barbara of her depression. Sometimes the concrete act of writing can help.

Use this exercise as a way to help yourself write what you are feeling and to express this to God. This is not a writing exercise. It does not matter whether you write in full sentences. Answering with one word only is just fine if you can't get several words out. You don't have to complete all the beginnings of sentences below. Do what you can. Don't censor yourself: what you are feeling is real, it is important, and it is not wrong. If you do not have the energy to copy this page, just write here in the book.

Oh God _____

(Name God as you wish and prefer; you will also find some names for God below.)

I feel _____

I am _____

I wish _____

I am afraid that_____

My help is _____

My hope is _____

I need _____

I don't _____

I do _____

I don't know _____

God, are you ? _____

Jesus _____

Holy Spirit _____

Lord _____

Christ _____

Spirit of life _____

Comforter of the afflicted _____

Holy Wisdom _____

Rock of Strength _____

Ocean of Mercy_____

My Protector_____

I am sad that _____

I am angry with _____

I care _____

I hope _____

Why_____ ?

Where_____ ?

How_____ ?

You, God _____

Now, if you can and if you want to, go back and read aloud what you have written.

Try to do so slowly, taking a deep breath between the lines. If you begin to cry, take time to cry.

If you need to yell, do so.

Write and read this in whatever position or place is helpful to you and makes you feel safe and in some way nurtured or held up: in your bed, at the kitchen table, in an easy chair, on the floor. You are not alone.

Save what you write here.

Repeat the exercise as many times as you need to: tomorrow, the next day, the day after that.

If you cannot bear to do this alone, ask for company and for help from a friend or family member. For this exercise, ask this person for presence—not advice. If you do not have the will or energy to ask for help, show your friend or family member this page and these lines.

PSALM 121

This Psalm was helpful to me in the worst of times. I prayed it each night before turning off the light (or, in times when I was afraid of turning off the light, before going to sleep). I read it in the translation from the New Revised Standard Version (NRSV), since this was the Bible I had at my bedside at the time. Later, I found out that my best friend, in another city, was praying the same Psalm at the same time, in the King James Version (KJV) with which he grew up. Recently, I have read it more often in the new translation of the International Committee on English in the Liturgy (ICEL). But this NRSV translation still carries weight because of the circumstances in which I read it. I usually replaced "he" with "God" or "the One" when I read it.

A song of ascents
I lift up my eyes to the hills—
from where will my help come?
My help comes from the Lord,
who made heaven and earth.

He will not let your foot be moved;
he who keeps you will not slumber.
He who keeps Israel
will neither slumber nor sleep.

The Lord is your keeper;
the Lord is your shade at your right hand.
The sun shall not strike you by day,
nor the moon by night.

The Lord will keep you from all evil;
he will keep your life.
The Lord will keep your going out and your coming in
from this time on and forevermore.

❧

Just as day declines into evening, so
often after some little pleasure
my heart declines into depression.
Everything seems dull, every action feels
like a burden.
If anyone speaks, I scarcely listen.
If anyone knocks, I scarcely hear.
My heart is as hard as flint.
Then I go out into the field
to meditate, to read the holy Scriptures,
and I write down my deepest thoughts
in a letter to you.
And suddenly your grace, dear Jesus,
shatters the darkness with daylight,
lifts the burden, relieves the tension.
Soon tears follow sighs, and
heavenly joy floods over me with the tears.

AELRED OF RIEVAULX (CA. 1110–1167)

CHAPTER TWELVE

"How Can We Sing God's Song in a Strange Land?": Troubles and Laments

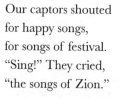

Our captors shouted
for happy songs,
for songs of festival.
"Sing!" They cried,
"the songs of Zion."

How could we sing
the song of the Lord
in a foreign land?

PSALM 137:3–4

Who will separate us from the love of Christ? Will hardship, or distress, or persecution, or famine, or nakedness, or peril, or the sword? As it is written, "For your sake we are being killed all day long; we are accounted as sheep to be slaughtered." No, in all these things we are more than conquerors through him who loved us. For I am convinced that neither death nor life, nor angels, nor rulers, nor things present, nor things to come, nor powers, nor height, nor death, nor anything else in all creation, will be able to separate us from the love of God in Christ Jesus our Lord.

ROMANS 8:35–39

God forgives you.
Forgive others;
forgive yourself.

A NEW ZEALAND PRAYER BOOK

Depression is widespread, but troubles are universal. People have always suffered, still suffer, ill health and broken hearts, bereavement and betrayal, financial and vocational woes. Sometimes these troubles keep us from praying. Often they drive us to prayer.

Our personal or social difficulties may be dramatic or extreme—life-threatening illness, becoming a refugee, involvement in crime. But there are many other circumstances, some of them curses of the present age, that can reduce us to states of desolation: the sheer overload of the lives of working adults, particularly if they are also parents, the despair of youth, the isolation of elders, or the social dislocation that leads to loneliness and lack of a primary community. Many of us find ourselves in a strange land both figuratively and literally. We move across the country to enter a new job or go to school, return home to care for a sick parent, follow a spouse or partner to an unknown city. And there are other lonelinesses: one can experience loneliness as a single person, but also within the life of a couple, as one can in a classroom or office, in a church or synagogue or mosque or ashram, in a community organization or on a board of directors—because of lack of communication, lack of shared values, knowledge that one needs to make an unpopular statement or take an unpopular position.

The prayer of lamentation is a venerable tradition: we name the suffering and groan prayerfully (or not so prayerfully), inwardly or aloud, because that is all we can do at the time. Sometimes there is no naming, only a moan. Rachel Ann, now a graduate student in New York, wrote: "I find my prayer most *in*articulate in the midst of suffering because words alone cannot pinpoint the source of pain nor fully describe its depth and extent. Sometimes tears say things best. Sometimes staring dumbly into silence is enough. I don't think of this as an inability to pray. To me it is more of just letting things out, however they come out, and letting God make sense of it as best God can."

In the late winter of 1994 I was invited to preach for the annual Church Women United World Day of Prayer at Boston's Episcopal Cathedral Church of St. Paul. The service for this day has a different theme each year, and its outline, prayers, and preparatory reflections are composed by a specific group of Christian women. (Church Women United is ecumenical and includes Orthodox, Catholic, and Protestant women.) That year, Palestinian Christian women had written the service. In a devastating coincidence, the Hebron massacre, in which an Israeli opened fire on a group of Palestinian Muslims praying at the Tomb of the Patriarchs, occurred a few days before the service. How then was I to preach? What could I say? In addition, I knew the congregation would be composed primarily of older African American women with deep church and community commitments. Israel and Palestine were not familiar realities to them. The city of Boston was. The weather was cold, wet, and foul, a typical early March day in New England. It was Ramadan, the holiest month of the Muslim year, Lent in the Christian churches of the West, and just a few days before the beginning of Great Lent in the churches of the East.

I did the only thing possible: I began with lamentation. How else to pray together in a time of international crisis and mourning than by stating the truth? We had to begin with naming: Muslims, Jews, and Christians, in this week of tragedy and terror, all were—once again—mired in anguish, violence, confusion, despair. In their names and in the names of the women gathered before me—for preaching is not just speaking to a community but giving voice to it— I spoke of the weeping and of those for whom we wept that day, Israelis and Palestinians, especially the women who were both sisters and enemies to each other. With these women of the city of Boston, so far from Jerusalem and Hebron, I spoke of the biblical vision of the holy city healed, and also of our grief for the city in which we lived. I knew we might be able to make the connection with the women we honored in our prayer because we, too, wept for the children of the city, our city, where there was also violent death, not only that of the streets but a shooting, the previous year, inside a Baptist church—like the shrine at Hebron, a holy place, a sanctuary.[1]

It was only in lamenting, in naming the realities of injustice, suffering, sin, and evil, that we could pray. But lamenting was only the first step: the call of lamentation turned into a cry for justice and a call for healing. We found hope inside our tears; yet only inside our tears could we find hope.

With lament, the Psalms again make their appearance. But in the Psalms (as in the book of Job, known for its description of troubles) lament is not the last word. In *Healing of Soul, Healing of Body*, a contemporary commentary in several voices on Rabbi Nachman of Breslov's ten designated "healing Psalms," Orthodox rabbi Charles Sheer recalls his own sense of helplessness at hearing the news of his beloved's terminal illness: "In such distress, I could readily join our psalmist [the author of Psalm 42]: 'I say to the Almighty, my Rock, "Why have you forsaken me? Why must I walk in dark gloom, oppressed by enemies?" Crushing my bones, my adversaries revile me, taunting me all day with "Where is your God"' (vv. 10–11)." Then, in the last verse of the Psalm, Sheer notes, "Brief, almost terse, the solid faith reemerges: 'Have hope in God; I will yet praise Him, my ever-present Help, my God' (v. 12)."[2]

Sheer asks, how can the psalmist shift from doubt to declaration of faith in the midst of such woe? "His answer is instructive. Having poured his heart out, he does not deny the reality of his pain nor does he present simple pieties to explain God's design. Instead, in the face of human adversity, he presents a human *response* rather than an *answer*." "I will yet praise God," says the psalmist. In this "yet"—two Hebrew words in the text—the suffering one echoes the beginning of the Psalm, remembering in a time of trouble the celebrations of the past, and thereby summoning strength and hope for a still uncertain future.[3] This is hard-wrought, not easy faith.

Psalms are, of course, songs, and many people sing to God despite the pain, with the pain, or through the pain of their sorrow or physical suffering. "Sometimes I feel like a motherless child," the well-known spiritual goes, and it is without doubt a prayer as well as a lament. Theologian Diana Hayes, already living with a degenerative disease in her knees, writes of the assault of chronic and painful rheumatoid arthritis when she was only forty: "There are times when I do not understand why I have this disease. There are times when I feel like giving up—giving in to the pain and simply letting it take over not just my body, but my mind as well. But I find I cannot do that. For I am constantly and persistently called out of myself by those around me who seem to feel that my words bring hope into their lives. They do not realize how much their response brings hope back into mine.

"And so I marvel at this curious thing, 'that God would make a poet black and bid [her] sing!' I, a Black woman, at times completely overpowered by this disease that has taken up residence within me, am bidden over and over by this God, in whom I have put all of my trust, to sing. And so I sing, and in the singing I too am free."⁴ An old Quaker hymn goes: "What though the tempest loudly roars, I hear the truth, it liveth. . . . No storm can shake my inmost calm/While to that rock I'm clinging/Since love is Lord of heaven and earth/How can I keep from singing?" The hymn was probably written in response to social and religious struggle.⁵

Diana Hayes speaks of the role of others in her suffering, calling her beyond herself and in this movement bearing hope to her. Companionship in suffering can take the form of prayer. Churches and prayer groups are consoling, but so is the simple knowledge that people are praying for us. My friend Don wrote me when I was in the midst of a relationship with a man whose behavior had become ambivalent and confusing: "Jane, you are in my prayers." He quoted the words of the liturgical prayer: "Deliver us from all anxiety as we wait in joyful hope," adding, "'Ambivalent behavior': that seems to say it all. That failure to commit to another is what undermines confidence and trust, and, frankly, is what keeps even good marriages from being better. And it is so painful. Lord, take your friend Jane into your embrace and heal the wounds in her heart. Replace the disquiet with peace and assure her of your certain love. Amen." The prayer moved my heart, as did the sympathy behind it, the presence, the fact that Don, married for many years, understood what I was going through as a single woman: this solidarity gave birth to prayer.

Joining with others in prayer is not just for healing oneself. It can also be a reaching out from one's own sufferings, as Diana Hayes indicated. Laura Ann, the Texas contemplative, offered her experience: "When there is some kind of pain, like headaches, one of its excellent uses is as a mnemonic. You're lying around with a headache or an upset stomach and nothing to do, so you pray for everybody with the same condition, then you branch out, and it leads to thinking about a lot of people and things that need praying for. So, it is not a waste of time." There is a communion of suffering—not to wallow in it ("misery loves company"), but precisely the opposite, to deepen our humanity by plunging more deeply into the humanity we share with others.

One of the ways in which Jesus is dear to Christians who pray is in his presence to them in times of trouble. For some, Jesus is a brother and companion, the one who accompanies, who walks along the way with us, who has been where we humans have been. He is the Jesus whom the Gospel of John presents as weeping for the death of his friend Lazarus, whom he loved,[6] who sweats blood during the agony in the garden and wrestles with the will of God and the evil of the world, when all his friends have fallen asleep, who later that day cries out on the cross. For others, Jesus is the one who lifts our burden, who takes it from us so we do not have to bear it on our own. For many, he is both. Either way, Jesus is presence. For those who believe and practice the Christian faith, Jesus is God made visible, God made human: God close to our trials and our everyday life, not distant or uninvolved. This is not the fix-all God or the magician God. The God to whom or with whom we pray in our sufferings is not God as explanation, but God as companion—a God who suffers and knows suffering.

Laura Ann remembered: "I read something once that was so painful to read that I was rolling around and hollering (upsetting my then husband no end), and it was then I realized that sorrow is a good thing because it is true, and God sorrows. To feel the intense pain of God's sorrow is much better than to feel any kind of pleasure except the intense pleasure of unity with God."

God as companion in our suffering is both the One who suffers with us and the One on whom we lean. Psalm 46 says, "God is our refuge and our strength, a very present help in trouble." I remember once, in a difficult time, wishing I could lean back with ease and trust, as on a large pillow, in bed, and realizing that God could indeed be this rest for me. I thought I had read and imagined all manner of images for God until this pillow showed up in my mind! The hymn "Leaning on the Everlasting Arms" is a prayer written for times like these.

Some people spoke to me of turning to meditation in the midst of physical suffering. Morris wrote me two summers ago, "I came down with a severe case of lower-back disk hernia and had to have an operation. I just got out of the hospital after three weeks of successful recuperation from surgery. During this time I was able to listen to tapes by my old friend John Main [the teacher of Christian Meditation, whom Morris had known in his younger days as a Benedictine monk]. What a wonderful treat! And his mantra *'Maranatha'* helped me very much to get through the sleeplessness, pain, and discouragement of hospitalization. I can't say that I really 'meditated' in John's full sense of that term, but it was a better sleep producer than sleeping pills."

Reciting and repetition—another type of meditative practice—often enter into people's prayer in time of physical or mental and emotional pain. Ellen, who has suffered from chronic depression all her life, has for years prayed the Rosary when she has insomnia ("though between you and me, Jane, medication works better," she quipped, in contradiction to Morris). Many sing old hymns and repeat Bible passages in times of trial. I know of several people who have used the Twenty-third Psalm during radiation or chemotherapy treatment to steady themselves and endure the pain. The resources of the "usable past" are often those that rise to the surface in times of trouble.

"Suffering," said Laura Ann, "is a miserable state that should be wiped out, but if you can't eliminate it, you can at least use it. I have experienced a lot of very severe pain in the last year so I named my pain 'Hank Toadwell' and made friends with it. This doesn't mean I like it. Just that when I start to hurt, I say 'Oh, hi, Hank,' and just make (imaginary) small talk. 'Well, how you doing, Hank? I sure wouldn't want *your* job.' 'Me, either,' he says. 'The bad guys are always making me work for them.' 'Well,' I say, 'at least we can look forward to when things get fixed and you don't have to be going around hurting people anymore.' 'Really,' he says. 'No kidding. This gets old.'"

"This does tie in with the subject of prayer," Laura Ann added. "Learning to separate yourself from sensation is closely related to the thing you do when you meditate. You're a lot more motivated to separate yourself from pain than from pleasure or just normal sensation. I owe a lot to Hank—without him I probably would not have started learning contemplation." She concluded: "You probably think I'm nutty as a fruitcake, and I guess you are right, but it has produced good results in my life, and how can you argue with that?"

There is another kind of sorrow besides that of pain, grief, or trial: sorrow at our wrongdoings, which some traditions call contrition or repentance for sin. Kirk, a young man from a Reformed Church background, wrote to me of his understanding and experience of confessional prayer: "I struggle with how to open myself before God as I examine the ways in which I am broken and further the brokenness of the world. We come before God to confess our Sin, and it seems like I often end up confessing particular little actions or omissions—and then I wonder how much I'm just beating myself up for petty little quirks rather than the bigger stuff, the stuff that counts."

Meredith, now a professional in the computer industry, related to me her firing for larceny, an ethical violation which she refused to admit at first and for which she later felt great remorse. "It taught me more about God's love and forgiveness in a few months than I'd learned in forty years," she said. "You cannot plumb the depths of God's forgiveness until you're in the sewer." I asked where prayer fit into the story. "At the time [the violation] occurred," she said, "I had no prayer life to speak of. I only got in touch with God's forgiveness a year later, through my therapist." It was through psychotherapy that Meredith began to face her actions and, eventually, to be led into prayer, which led to her contrition. She also remembers being moved to tears by the lyric of a song by Michael Card that included the words "look into your judge's face and see a Savior there." We are, she discovered, much harder on ourselves than God is on us.

Perhaps no pain is more difficult to pray with than that of violence and trauma. Many people simply lose the ability to pray, which is so related to the ability to trust. Laura, a woman from New York in her thirties, now living in a Western state, admitted: "I don't know exactly where I stand with prayer right now. Yes, I know that everyone's prayer life evolves, but mine seems to be swimming around these days . . . but I'm trying." She recounted her trauma of four years ago: "I was brutally attacked by a man who had broken into my apartment and read my journal. During the attack he wanted me to pray to him and I wouldn't. He kept quoting things that he'd read in my stolen journal. He kept saying, 'Say that to me. Make me your God. I want that power over your life.' I wasn't 'cooperative.'

"Every time that I wasn't cooperative I was punished: among other things, he rotated my neck almost 180 degrees and the muscles split down both sides of my back. As the muscle damage and nerve damage began to heal a muscle problem called fibromyalgia (FM) set in." Laura is now unable to work and is living on disability. "I lost the ability to write. My arms were really weak and everything exhausted them and the pain was tremendous. That was from the attack, but as my muscles began to heal the FM took over and it became impossible to write because of pain. The physical problems made the FM worse and the FM made the physical problems worse . . . a vicious cycle."

The pain itself is exhausting. Laura cannot stay in an upright position for more than four hours. She sleeps part of the day, and nudging her right arm or back can make her faint from pain. "That," she said, "is a normal day. If it's an FM kind of day, don't bump either side of me anywhere or I'll throw up and then pass out.

"So life really changed almost four years ago. It doesn't seem like four years because I was really drugged up and 'out of it' for the first two, so in a sense, I've only been dealing with the situation and learning lots from it for a little less than two years." The event "had a profound effect on my prayer life because I would catch myself praying something that this guy had quoted to me and the result was flashbacks." Often her efforts at prayer, guided by a strong faith, have been brief, like her attention span: "Simply put, when I can't think straight because of severe pain and I can't even follow a Scripture story that I've read a thousand times, I just try to hold on to the idea of doing something each day to *simply make God smile* . . . even if it's just sending a postcard to someone or any other small thing."

As time has passed, Laura has been able to feel safer in prayer. During the course of our correspondence, I commented to her that she was brave—which indeed has been my experience of her, facing each day with heart despite excruciating pain—and she replied, "I don't have to be brave (smile), I have a large Father who really does know it all!" A few days later, coming back to my letter, she corrected me gently. "I *do* take your calling me brave as a compliment. I think that I have been brave in my life, but I don't think that I'm brave anymore. At some point, I think, if you hit 'joyful Christian,' you never have to be brave again. You are simply abandoned to Christ. . . . Brave people are in charge of themselves. Joyful people let God be in charge, not their commitment to God. When abandoned you are not brave; you just do what comes naturally.

"I'm getting better every day," Laura wrote. "What a truth it is that no matter how bad things get or what evil there is out there, God can really reach down, grab you by the shirt collar, and make so much good come out of the situation, if we let Him. I've learned lots and I think that I've helped a lot of people. God has turned it into a very good situation and I am tremendously grateful for that. It doesn't really matter what happens to us in life. It matters how we respond and Whom we turn to."

She added: "About prayer and pain: it seems to me that patience is a big key here. I saw a cartoon the other day: a man holding up a fish in a fish bowl to see the ocean; no caption. It said a lot to me. It was a very freeing realization to start to become 'active in life' again and see all of the truly amazing things that had happened without me. Pain can tend to make us feel bigger than we are (and smaller at the same time). Pain also makes time seem long, and so the theme of patience. Sometimes when we don't feel that we are moving forward in our prayer lives we are correct and we have to put our own foot down and say to ourselves, 'Get on with it.' And sometimes, we are absolutely wrong and things are happening that we can't see or feel, usually deep-seated, slow-growth kind of things, that will move us *far* beyond what our own limited efforts might accomplish (even if we were 'well') and keep us humble, wondering and human. God surely sees our pain, spiritual as well as physical. In His mysterious love, He sometimes chooses to make us wait . . . but He is there."

She repeated. "Pain can make us seem bigger than we really are, and smaller at the same time. But we are, after all, just poor fish: beloved fish, though. We can thrash around all we like but we can't swim outside of God, nor can we swim out of the little bowl that He has provided for us."

❦

PSALM 57

....

For the choirmaster.
According to "Do Not Destroy."
A miktam of David,
when he fled from Saul into the cave.

Care for me, God, take care of me,
I have nowhere else to hide.
Shadow me with your wings
until all danger passes.

I call to the Most High,
To God, my avenger:
send help from heaven to free me,
punish those who hound me.

Extend to me, O God,
your love that never fails,
for I find myself among lions
who crave for human flesh,
their teeth like spears and arrows,
their tongues sharp as swords.

O God, rise high above the heavens!
Spread your glory across the earth!

They rigged a net for me,
a trap to bring me down;
they dug a pit for me,
but they—they fell in!

I have decided, O God,
my decision is firm:
to you I will sing my praise.
Awake, my soul, to song!

Awake, my harp and lyre,
so I can wake the dawn!

I will lift up my voice in praise,
sing of you, Lord, to all nations.
For your love reaches heaven's edge,
your unfailing love, the skies.

O God, rise high above the heavens!
Spread your glory across the earth!

❧

Full is my woe now, speechlessly it all
brims up in me. Rigid am I, as stone
at the stone's core.
Thus hard, I only see one thing:
that you have grown—
. . . and you have grown
into a grief so large,
it is beyond my heart to grasp
and reaches out.
Now you lie right across my womb,
now I can nevermore
give birth to you.

RAINER MARIA RILKE (1875–1926)

MY NAME IS WAITING

I am a child born of the union of tradition and crisis. Sorrow is my grandmother; suffering and striving my aunts; begin anew my great-grandmother. I
am a daughter not a son: My name is waiting.

My name has lived my life under the whip, under the lash; my name has lived
my life within walls, within bondage; my name has lived my life through exodus, through sojourn.

I have waited in the desert of Syria, in the streets of Egypt, in the land of
Babylon. I have waited in the cloisters of France, in the palace of the Oba of
Benin, in the rice-paperhouses of Japan. I have waited in the Glens of
Armagh, in the slave ships bound for hell, in the barrios of southern
California.

I have waited in the tin shanties in Soweto, I have waited in the showers of Buchenwald; I have waited in the hills of the Dakotas.

I have waited in fields and vineyards, picking cotton and beans and grapes, cutting cane. I have brought down my hoe on hard ground; I have gripped the plow firmly; I have forced fruit from the earth.

I have waited in houses—washing, cooking, cleaning, I have sheltered the orphan, welcomed the stranger, embraced the lonely. I have lived alongside pain and disease, poverty and misery, anxiety and affliction. I have pleaded and hurt; I have known the coming of despair; I have given birth.

I have waited in the journey. My throat has grown parched thirsting for truth and justice. My feet have grown bloody cutting a path across the precipice, making a way where there is no way, coursing a road where there was no road. Righteousness was my guide. I have slept under gathering clouds with hope; I have rested near fresh water with faith; I have eaten and grown strong with love.

I have known blood and want and pain and joy. I have drunk water from the well; I have walked the threshing floor; I have been to the mountain top.

I am waiting.

M. SHAWN COPELAND

PSALM 51

. . . .

> Have mercy on me, O God,
>   according to your steadfast love;
>   according to your abundant mercy
>   blot out my transgression.
> Wash me thoroughly from my iniquity,
>   and cleanse me from my sin . . .
>
> Let me hear joy and gladness;
>   let the bones that you have crushed rejoice.
> Hide your face from my sins
>   and blot out all my iniquities.
> Create in me a clean heart, O God,
>   and put a new and right spirit within me.
> Do not cast me away from your presence,

and do not take your holy spirit from me.
Restore to me the joy of your salvation,
    and sustain in me a willing spirit.
Then I will teach transgressors your ways,
    and sinners will return to you.

Deliver me from bloodshed, O God,
    O God of my salvation,
    and my tongue will sing aloud of your deliverance.
O Lord, open my lips,
    and my mouth will declare your praise.
For you have no delight in sacrifice;
    if I were to give burnt offering, you would not be pleased.
The sacrifice acceptable to God is a broken spirit;
    a broken and contrite heart,
    O God, you will not despise.

        (VERSES 1–2, 8–17)

NO LAMB IN THE THICKET

When I am spread out
ready for the surgeon's knife
There will be no lamb caught
in the thicket
to spare me.
I see it now
the knife in the shadows—
Down it comes
gouging out my right breast
leaving only an ugly scar
and a deeper, more enduring pain
while they talk of possible Reconstruction
instead of complete Liberation
into your Arms of Love.

    KATHY KEAY

IN WEARINESS

O Lord Jesus Christ
who art as the shadow of a great rock in a weary land,
who beholdest thy weak creatures
weary of labour, weary of pleasure,
weary of hope deferred, weary of self,
in thine abundant compassion,
and fellow feeling with us,
and unutterable tenderness,
bring us we pray thee,
unto this rest.

CHRISTINA ROSSETTI (1830–1894)

PRAYER AT A FUNERAL

O God who brought us to birth,
and in whose arms we die,
in our grief and shock
contain and comfort us;
embrace us with your love,
give us hope in our confusion,
and grace to let go into new life,
through Jesus Christ, Amen.

JANET MORLEY

CHAPTER THIRTEEN

Pronouns, Poets, and the Desire for God: Language and Prayer

O God Our Disturber,
whose speech is pregnant with power
and whose word will be fulfilled;
May we know ourselves
unsatisfied
with all that distorts your truth,
and make our hearts attentive
to your liberating voice,
in Jesus Christ,
Amen.

JANET MORLEY

Prayer is relationship. And we who pray, with our stumbling human words, try to find, as best we can, a language that will be the language of love, so that our relationship with the Holy One can be one of communication and intimacy.

In the movie *Il Postino* (*The Postman*), poet Pablo Neruda counsels the passionate but inarticulate postman, Mario, on how to woo his beloved. "You have to use metaphors," he says. "Metaphors?" the

181

postman asks. "What is that?" Patiently and clearly Neruda
explains. A metaphor is a comparison, a way of describing one reality by using another: your eyes are like the ocean; your voice is the
wind that sings in my ears. The postman uses metaphors, and soon
the woman he loves, enchanted by his words and by the spirit in
them, begins to love him.

The language of prayer, like the language of love, uses
metaphor. It uses analogy, pointing to God by saying what or whom
God is like. Which is not to say that this—the wind, the rock of
strength, the father or mother, the shepherd, the potter, the storm
and the voice—is what God is. Prayer-talk, says Lutheran biblical
scholar, theologian, and bishop Krister Stendahl, is "primary religious language, the language of religious experience. . . . Liturgy is
play, liturgy is repetitious; when you play, when you worship, you use
language in a caressing manner. It has the same sort of expression as
that kind of language by which one caresses the person dear to one.
That is proper, since the ultimate aim of our whole existence is to
praise God, glorify and enjoy God forever. Liturgy has a caressing
function: its language is a love language."[1]

The language of prayer, both private and public, must reveal
and foster relationship. Words, even pronouns, make our hearts sing
or sink. They can reveal or mask God, caress or injure. God is
beyond language, but our language is powerful.

All the same, one cannot speak of language without speaking of
its limits. Thomas Merton writes in *Thoughts in Solitude* that we put
words as smoke screens between reality and ourselves. Silence and
solitude can put us back in contact with "the naked reality of
things." From that silence which he calls "the mother of truth," we
can then produce "a few good words."[2] Laura Ann put it another
way in a letter to me: "You can use words or any other thing you
think with: prayer is an activity of the will and so you can use whatever you've got. Eventually words fail and you have to do it with you,
instead, just like in love affairs, words fail and you have to get nekked
and climb in bed."

The Pentecostal and charismatic traditions trace their spiritual
roots back to the first Pentecost, when the Holy Spirit gave members
of the early Jesus movement the ability to understand each other's
languages, and to the early Christian churches, in which some

members had "the gift of tongues." In these traditions, this love language moves beyond everyday words to ecstatic speech. Many in the Pentecostal churches refer to this as "praying in the Spirit." Harvey Cox, in his recent book on the worldwide spread of Pentecostal spirituality, calls this language "primal speech" and comments, "In an age of bombast, hype, and doublespeak, when ultraspecialized terminologies and contrived rhetoric seem to have emptied and pulverized language, the first pentecostals [in the early twentieth century] learned to speak—and their successors still speak—with another voice, a language of the heart."[3] In some ways the silence of contemplatives and the ecstatic song and glossolalia[4] of Pentecostals are two sides of the same coin—a moving beyond ordinary language into a communication with God that is direct, unencumbered, bursting or melting out of social and linguistic structures into another dimension.

Why touch on language after speaking of laments? Because for an increasing number of people, women especially, but also men, the language of worship now feels like a place of exile, in which they are strangers in a strange land. "Language and experience are interrelated," writes theologian Kathleen Fischer. "One aspect of the relationship is the capacity of language to control and limit our experience. This is particularly true of the language of the imagination."[5] In the imaginative language of prayer, at least in the Christian tradition, male God-language has been dominant, often exclusively so.[6] Fischer writes that this "is especially destructive for women. From the time we are very young we learn that all the symbols for what is most sacred in life are male. Ultimate religious authority and meaning are found in a male God, a male savior, and male church leaders."[7]

Some remain comfortable with patterns of speech privileging male images of God. Laura, speaking of her prayer and her survival from trauma, has used "Father" over and over again to speak of God, and experiences God as *her* father—loving, protective, and freeing. Julie, a woman in her twenties from Indiana, also finds no obstacle in male God-language. "Over the years I have come to see God as my best friend. He (yes, I see God as masculine—being a tomboy myself is the reason) is always there in good times and bad, and I talk to Him all day, informally."

Cathy, an active Catholic in her fifties, when asked about her daily prayer practice, answered: "I'm very traditional in my prayer 'routine': the liturgy of the hours, especially morning and evening prayer. Am I absolutely faithful? No, but that is what gets me through a lot of life's garbage. Especially the Psalms, and the knowledge that worldwide others are praying the same—a kind of universal community. But I have had to do some major editing to get rid of the exclusive language; I hope someone comes up with an inclusive one that still holds to the universal format, just cleans up the language.[8] More and more I find that tripping over exclusive language is most disruptive to prayer."

For many, the experience goes beyond "disruptive." They find themselves in the wilderness, unable to pray with the old words, no longer at home in their native religious land. Fischer speaks of women whose "desert experience coincides with their increasing inability to relate to the traditional religious symbols that are embedded" in a male-dominated system. She quotes one woman who said: "The old answers that used to speak, no longer speak to me, and the passages of Scripture in which I once felt comfort are no longer comforting. There is a silence in me that as yet has no voice." For many of these women, the apophatic path, the path of silence and non-knowing, the prayer of obscure awareness and imageless contemplation, is the only way into a relationship with the divine. New words arise only later, if they arise at all. Fischer attributes the rise in interest in apophatic prayer in part to dissatisfaction with traditional prayer, since the apophatic approach "sees all particular expressions of God as radically inadequate."[9]

What is the particular inadequacy that creates such a wearying and painful desert experience? It is not so much the use of male metaphors for God as their consistently privileged use, which implies that male metaphors—Father, King, He, Lord—are somehow laden with ultimate theological meaning in ways others are not.

Precisely because the Holy One is beyond all category, we need to be critical of all the categories we use, to make sure that we do not inadvertently fall into idolatry. By privileging the use of one category to present the divine, we inevitably ascribe privilege to it in the human realm. By exercising a preferential option for God-imaged-as-male, we also give to male human beings a godlike

authority. In societies where male privilege was encoded in law for
centuries (and that includes most of the societies we know, both secular and religious), the images of "Father" and "King" are not
benign. They can even be dangerous.

Not all metaphors are equal. Calling God "Father," "King," and
"He" is not the same as speaking of rushing wind, mighty rock, river
of justice. The wind, the rock, or the river, or for that matter the
mother hen or the still small voice within, does not refer to one-half of
a dichotomy that splits the world into two parts of unequal dignity,
worth and power: master/servant, father/child, husband/wife. Our
images of God prop up our images of relationship—and vice versa.

The current conversation about inclusive language is an emotional one because of the polarities and parallels some of the biblical traditions have set up between king/subject, master/servant,
parent/child, husband/wife. Within debates on inclusive language
lie the ticklish questions of what constitutes maleness and female-
ness and what constitutes right relationship between women and
men—and, for that matter, between women and women, men and
men, the governing and the governed, the leaders of assemblies and
the body of the people.

The conversation is highly charged because it is in part about
the nature of God and the nature of human beings. It is also about
the relationship of our experience and authority to the authority
and witness of the biblical text: our quarrels about words are quarrels about the Holy Spirit and the nature of revelation. Does God
stop revealing the divine self at a certain point in history? Is God
more present at certain times and in certain words? Does the Spirit
continue its work in the world, including in our language?

What has brought many women and an increasing number of
men to protest the privileged use of male God-language is not the
desire to be politically correct, but the desire for God. At its core, the
issue of gender and biblical language has to do with prayer and
therefore with relationship. How can we find words that will convey
the height and depth of the love of God? Will the word proclaimed
and sung lead us to God, or away? Will it prompt us to listen to the
voice of God, to breathe in the power of the Spirit, to tell out the
saving news of the One who heals and redeems our world? Or will

this word cause such alienation and pain among us that with this word, some find they cannot pray?

The language of our established prayers, like the language of the Bible, comes to us with baggage—and we to it. There is constant conversation between this language, the many generations of Christian tradition, and our contemporary experiences, which form the most recent stage of tradition. New orientations toward language are emerging in assemblies of prayer large and small, reflecting at least three concerns: the desire that our common praise not lead us into idolatry, but toward justice; the care that the way we name God and ourselves not injure our companions; and the hope that these words, and the holy silence beneath them, will lead us to God.

Ann, the young woman from Pennsylvania, wrote: "My experience of prayer continues to be a journey of renaming the Divine; any name . . . aims to express an infinity of compassion which is beyond any name. So I have prayed in communion with Father, Mother, Mother-Father God, Spirit, Christ, Universe, Master of the Universe, Loving Essence, Holy One, Dear Heart, OM . . ." and, she added, "I have prayed in silence."

Carolyn, an Australian correspondent, noted: "Some of us back home use 'Godde' to get away from the androcentric [male-centered] bias in 'God' but not to move to the gynocentric [female-centered] Goddess." A Canadian cyber-friend, Barbara, used the same word quite naturally in her letters to me, telling me about her prayer life: "For the past few years I have been simply trying to live gently, quietly, in an awareness of Godde's presence which is here, now. I 'pray' to our 'Creator,' 'Sustainer,' 'Friend,' 'Companion,' 'Energy,' using whatever image for 'the Divine' seems to surface in the circumstance. Mostly I'm aware of Presence, without image. I seldom pray to Jesus, but am aware that when I pray, Jesus is praying in me."

Sometimes context makes a difference: language does not sing or grate in a vacuum but in a social setting. For three years now, I have heard and sung the Andrae Crouch gospel hymn "Soon and Very Soon" ("Soon and very soon, we are going to see the King") at St. Columba. I used to be uncomfortable with it: royal images of Jesus and God have never sat well with me as a woman or as an American, though I understand the irony in the Gospels, where Jesus tries to explain to the befuddled disciples that his kingdom is not the one they expect, but a realm of a different order. But "king" takes on a different meaning in a community of oppressed people—oppressed in their ancestral uprooting and enslavement, oppressed by economic barriers and racist attitudes and institutions today. This king of whom we sing at St. Columba in Oakland relativizes the rulers of the world—which of course is one of the purposes of the Catholic feast of Christ the King (one of the days, in addition to the Sundays in Advent, on which we sing this hymn). No king, emperor, president, kaiser, duce, fürher, prime minister, or secretary-general has ultimate power over our lives—only God. No "power-over" claims our allegiance, but rather the revolutionary love-power of Jesus.

Our language, secular and religious, contains dualities and polarities of male and female, but also of black and white, darkness and light. I remember reading Grimm's and Andersen's fairy tales as a dark-haired, dark-eyed child with tan skin. The princesses all had pale skin, blue eyes, small hands and feet, and hair like spun gold. Would I ever, I wondered, get to be a princess? At the age of ten or so, I wrote a short fairy tale in which the heroine was dark and her cruel sister a blonde. I took great pleasure in the change of roles. But in the last line, I gave myself away: I had so internalized the northern European image of fair beauty that I concluded, when the blonde princess admitted her faults, "She realized that beauty isn't everything." How much more the biblical stories affect us and our vision of God and of human beauty and dignity. This was only a set of fairy tales—already powerful messages in the life of a young girl. What if they had been depictions of reality claiming divine sanctions?

The issues of dark and light in prayer are complex. Images of darkness and night occur in many cultures and traditions to describe confused or painful situations, or the spiritual state in which one does not know God, save through what God is not. Black churches themselves use these images, especially those of light and darkness—not the darkness of people as much as the dark of night in which shines the light of hope and faith. The black national anthem, "Lift Every Voice and Sing," often sung in church, uses such an image as well, alongside others: "Sing a song full of the faith that the dark past has taught us . . ." But it also speaks, with positive connotations, of being "shadowed beneath" the protective hand of God.[10] At the same time, African American and other communities of faith are becoming increasingly aware of the need to acknowledge and celebrate dark beauty, to view Jesus and his companions as other than copies of German or Flemish paintings and to celebrate their own blackness or *mestizaje*[11] The first step through this complexity is awareness, and white people especially need to ask: Do we thoughtlessly equate goodness with things light? How often do we equate black and darkness with fear, ugliness, and evil? Why are hard times only dark and not also bleak? What are the many sides of night—frightening, sheltering, dangerous, restorative? Does our prayer, solitary and communal, celebrate or suppress our cultures? Does it sustain racism or subvert it? The answers we give to these questions have consequences for social reality, not just for intimate speech.

Linguistic issues become even more complex when we pray in more than one language. Cecilio, who is bilingual in English and Spanish, wrote to me: "I learned the Act of Contrition [a prayer confessing sin and asking for forgiveness] in English, then in Spanish. The Spanish stuck and I always throw confessors off with it—unwittingly. 'Lord' bothers me. Terribly undemocratic; colonialist. '*Señor*,' equally feudal, does not." I have the same reaction to the French "*Seigneur*," whose tones I associate only with tenderness.

My college friend Laura, a Reform Jew, in whose branch of the tradition the services are in a mix of Hebrew and English, tells me she likes the fact that Jewish prayers are in Hebrew and the experience of praying "in a special and different language. I find that one can easily say much more embarrassing things in a language which is not one's own," she admits. "I also like how when I am praying in Hebrew I am always thinking what the words mean. They don't automatically enter my brain the way English does. I guess some people would dislike this, but it is helpful to me. Do or did some Catholics feel that way about Latin?" she asked.

Mostly not. Quite the opposite: countless Catholics repeated the Latin responses at Mass without knowing their meaning. Part of the movement toward liturgy in the vernacular after the 1960s reforms of Vatican II (and centuries before, in the reforms of Martin Luther) was precisely aimed at helping people know better what they were saying and having a more intimate as well as more conscious, reflective experience of worship. Latin had become an obstacle more than the tie that binds, and local churches had begun to protest its superimposition upon their cultures. They wanted to speak to God, publicly, the language of the heart: Tagalog, Wolof, French, Tongan, Portuguese. This is not to say there is no nostalgia for Latin—but oddly, aside from a small minority of traditionalists, those who are most vocal about it are often people who no longer attend church for reasons most would view as "liberal." It seems to be associated with a nostalgia for a certain aesthetic, for the beauty of chant and the reverence of ritual, not only for the language itself. In churches where the ritual is rich and carefully planned, the music is of high quality, and the preaching and prayers speak of and to the needs of parishioners and their world, there is little if any nostalgia for Latin. Most older Catholics I have met, of varying socioeconomic classes and ethnicities, rejoiced when they could worship in their own language.

My friend Mark spent some time working in Central America a decade ago. During the intensive Spanish course preceding his trip, he chose to learn a few basic prayers from a Spanish-language prayer book. "I found that praying in a foreign language—even with memorized prayers—helped me to focus more intently on the words than when I prayed in English," he said. "The same words in English had, with years of repetition, begun to seem meaningless. After coming back from Central America, I then noticed how much I paid attention to what I was saying in my own tongue. Old prayers seemed new again. Anyone who's read Scripture in a different language other than one's own, or better yet, in the original languages, knows what I mean about discovering new aspects to familiar tales."

Mark's account confirmed my own recent experience. Some time ago, when my prayer had become somewhat dry and unfocused, I found that praying the Psalms in French revived it. This particular translation used *"l'Éternel,"* "the Eternal One," whereas the Hebrew has YHWH, which observant Jews read "Adonai" and which the most common English translations render as "Lord." I had not for a long while focused on God as "Eternal"; language can surprise us, taking us to places where we have not been. The French was melodious when read aloud; in my case it was not a second or a new language, since I have been bilingual almost since birth, but a return to a neglected tongue. Changing the language refreshes the text for me, reinfuses spirit in it. It is literally a change of tune: the melody is new. It also introduces nuances of meaning, since no translation is exact: language is metaphorical, not mathematical.

I asked Nancy, who is bilingual and deeply devoted to Our Lady of Guadalupe, whether she prayed in English, Spanish, or both, especially when addressing—or being addressed by—*la Virgen de Guadalupe*. "I pray in English and in Spanish, sometimes a combination of the two," she answered. "I find singing in Spanish particularly moving emotionally. I often find myself flooded with tears when I sing in Spanish. It feels much more raw, more basic, more stripped of all pretensions.

"When I am in need, I often pray to Our Lady of Guadalupe, addressing her in Spanish by the name Lupe or Lupita [affectionate diminutives of Guadalupe]. I ask, *'Ayuda me con esta problema,'* 'Help me with this problem.' She likewise responds in Spanish. It is as if in using Spanish she triggers in me the sense of endurance that has been so much a part of Mexican experience. This is not simply an endurance that enables survival, but an endurance that is born of *a wisdom which knows*. The knowing comes from courting death and pain throughout a lifetime." She added: "I also find soothing the Rosary prayers of elderly Mexican women like my grandmother. In their presence I find myself simply wanting to be a part of them, to join them by adding my voice to the collective prayer."

With the yearning for new words comes a lot of experimenting— greeted by some with relief and delight, by others with ridicule and revulsion, by still others with indifference. Three decades into the conversation about inclusive language, we now have at our disposal scholarly and pastoral studies, liturgies and poems, and a host of other resources.[12]

God is not bound by metaphor, but is revealed by it, however dimly, and reveals us to ourselves in the process. In every generation, poets, prophets, and mystics have brought forth new words to approximate the burning experience of God's presence, as they did in biblical times. This generation too needs prophetic poets, and the poet in all of us. New metaphors are springing up and taking their place beside the old. Of course this is risky. It is also risky to worship prayers or biblical texts themselves, rather than the living God to which they are witnesses—even more risky. The makers of new metaphors—or perhaps, to honor the unconscious and the Holy Spirit, I should say the receivers of new metaphors—are no less filled with wonder and delight at the adventure of God than the biblical writers or early creators of creeds, collects, and hymns. Sometimes the authors of new prayers are the same people who draw strength, as Nancy does, from the prayers of grandmothers and the rhythms of their childhood.

In the language of prayer, which is the language of love, we can venture into new speech, Bible in hand or not. We may be awkward, like lovers stammering their first tender words to each other or immigrants learning a new tongue. God will understand. More than that: it is God, Holy Wisdom, Rushing-Spirit, who will give us the words we need.

OUT OF THE DEPTHS

Out of the depths I cry to you, O God,
Hear my voice, O God, listen to my pleading.

My voice is weak, O God, my God,
Although it speaks for many.
It is the voice of Sarah, shamed
before her servant,
Barren, and given no worth.

It is the voice of Hagar, abused
by her mistress,
Driven out into the desert with her child.
It is the voice of Rachel, weeping
for her children,
Weeping, for they are all dead.

It is the voice of Mary, robbed
of her humanity.
Woman, yet not woman.
It is the voice of Martha, taught
to be a servant,

challenged to choose for herself.
It is the voice of a nameless woman,
bought and sold,
Then given back to herself.

It is the voice of women groaning in labour,
Sweating in toil, abandoned in hardship,
Weeping in mourning, awaked in worry,
Enslaved in dependency, afraid of their weakness.

Do you hear my voice, O God, my God?
Can you answer me?
The words I hear all speak to me of men.
You said I am also in your image,
You are my father, are you also mother,
Comfort-bringing like the loving arms?

Do you hear my voice, O God, my God?
Can you answer me?
I can sing your song of praise no longer,
I am not at home in this world any more.
My heart is full of tears for my sisters,
They choke my words of joy.

Do you hear my voice, O God, my God?
Can you answer me?
You sent your son, a man, to love me,
But him they killed also.
What is the new life that you promise me?
I DO NOT WANT MORE OF THE SAME.

KATHY GALLOWAY

PSALM 42:1–6: ONE TEXT, THREE TRANSLATIONS

Try out different versions of the same text and see which one helps you most
to pray.

Does it make a difference whether you pray this alone or with a group? Try it
both ways. In a group, try it in unison, responsorially (leader and congregation
alternating) or antiphonally (two halves of congregation alternating).

It may be that inclusive language, or a more contemporary translation, is freeing for you; it is also possible you will prefer the older version. This is your choice. What matters is the vitality of your relationship with God.

These are three different translations of the same text, the first half of Psalm 42 (verses 1–6, with some variation in the numbering—some translations also mark these verses 2–6 or 2–7).

> As the hart panteth after the water brooks,
> so panteth my soul after thee, O God.
> My soul thirsteth for God,
> for the living God:
> When shall I come and appear before God?
>
> My tears have been my meat day and night
> while they continually say unto me,
> Where is thy God?
>
> When I remember these things,
> I pour out my soul in me:
> for I had gone with the multitude,
> I went with them to the house of God,
> with the voice of joy and praise,
> with a multitude that kept holyday.
>
> Why art thou cast down, O my soul?
> And why art thou disquieted in me?
> hope thou in God:
> for I shall yet praise him
> for the help of his countenance.
>
> KING JAMES (AUTHORIZED) VERSION

> As a deer longs for flowing streams,
> so my soul longs for you, O God.
> My soul thirsts for God,
> for the living God.
>
> When shall I come and behold the face of God?
> My tears have been my food day and night,
> while people say to me continually,
> "Where is your God?"

These things I remember, as I pour out my soul:
how I went with the throng,
and led them in procession to the house of God,
with glad shouts and songs of thanksgiving,
a multitude keeping festival.

Why are you cast down, O my soul,
and why are you disquieted within me?
Hope in God: for I shall again praise him,
my help and my God.

New Revised Standard Version

As a deer craves running water,
I thirst for you, my God;
I thirst for God,
the living God.
When will I see your face?

Tears are my steady diet.
Day and night I hear,
"Where is your God?"

I cry my heart out,
I remember better days:
when I entered the house of God,
I was caught in the joyful sound
of pilgrims giving thanks.

Why are you sad, my heart?
Why do you grieve?
Wait for the Lord.
I will yet praise God my savior.

International Commission on English in the Liturgy

An Alternative Lord's Prayer

Eternal Spirit,
Earth-maker, Pain-breaker, Life-giver,
Source of all that is and that shall be,

Father and Mother of us all,

Loving God, in whom is heaven:

The hallowing of your name echo through the universe!

The way of your justice be followed by the peoples of the world!

Your heavenly will be done by all created beings!

Your commonwealth of peace and freedom

        sustain our hope and come on earth.

With the bread we need for today, feed us.

In the hurts we absorb from one another, forgive us.

In times of temptation and test, strengthen us.

From trials too great to endure, spare us.

From the grip of evil, free us.

For you reign in the glory of the power that is love,

now and forever. Amen.

A New Zealand Prayer Book

REFLECTIONS ON INCLUSIVE LANGUAGE

We must speak of God as both male and female in our public prayer and proclamation (however uncomfortable that makes us and those in our congregations) and we must speak of God as neither male nor female. The option to use only gender-neutral language for God (which can be done relatively unobtrusively and uncontroversially) is not finally adequate, as it leaves unchallenged the bedrock bias that God is male. If we are going to refer to God as "he," then justice and theological integrity demand that we also refer to God as "she." To avoid anthropomorphism altogether (by opting to speak of God only as "Holy Source," "Rock," etc.) is to be unfaithful to the tradition and to impoverish our faithful imaginations. Our tradition affirms that humanity has been created "in God's image, male and female," so some of what God "looks like" must resemble humanity male and female. This option will surely disturb many, but our faith should disturb and challenge as much as comfort us. And equivalent imaging of God as both male and female will comfort as well as disturb. . . .

How might we best speak of the Trinity inclusively? Christians affirm that God's very being is relationship, that God is comm-unity. We picture this inner being as three "persons," not in the modern sense of person as "an individual center of consciousness" but rather as interrelated expressions or perpetually mutually-gazing "faces" of God who is always One, not three. The dominant metaphor for this mystery historically has been "Father, Son, and Holy Spirit." But this metaphor is, like all of our God-language, only a metaphor. It does not mean that God is literally a male father, a male son (the historical incarnation of the Christ in the man Jesus of Nazareth notwithstanding) and a (potentially female) Spirit. The central Christian claim about the incarnation is that God became human, not male, in the Christ. God graciously elected to share our humanity, not half of humanity's maleness, in Jesus. As Athanasius affirmed, "God became human that we might become divine." Or as Gregory of Nazianzus asserted, "That which was not assumed was not saved." If God only assumed maleness in Jesus, females would have no share in salvation. . . . We must exercise great care to preserve the insight that God is not a collection of related but distinct "functions" (as in "Creator, Redeemer, Sustainer") but rather an interrelated unity (as in "Lover, Beloved, and Love"—John of the Cross's words—or "the Beginning, the Only Begotten, and their Spirit"—Sebastian Moore's).

THE REV. KERRY A. MALONEY

A FATHER'S MERCY

God our father,
you disarm our judgment
with your outrageous mercy;
and the punishment we seek
you turn to celebration.
Lift our self-loathing,
and embrace our stubbornness,
that we too may show such fathering
to an embittered world,
through Jesus Christ,
Amen.

JANET MORLEY

This prayer was written for the sixth Sunday after Pentecost, when the church reads and hears the Gospel of Luke 15:11–31, the parable of the "prodigal son."

Your Language in Prayer

Take some time for reflection on these questions. Write down your answers if you can. You may want to reflect on the same questions a year from now, then return to what you wrote today. You can also do this exercise in a small group. Make sure everyone has a chance to speak. You may want to set up some ground rules for speaking and listening: going around the circle at least once, not interrupting or asking questions during the first round of questions.

How do you name God in prayer?
Speak and write down these names.
How do they speak to you about who God is?
Why do you use them?

Do you name God in prayer differently from the way you name God in conversation or study? In other words, when you talk *to* or *with* God, is it different from when you talk about God? How? Why?

Do you name God differently in public and private prayer?
How so?
Why?

Has your naming of God changed over the years?
Go back to your childhood, then through your adolescence and young adulthood, and if you are older, to middle age and beyond: write down the many names and images of God with which you have prayed throughout the years.
If your naming of God has changed, why has it changed?
Were there circumstances in your life that prompted this change?

Does it make a difference if you sing the words? If you hear them sung?

Are there names of God with which you have difficulty right now?
Why or why not?

When has your prayer been wordless?
Why?
How?
How has the silence or wordlessness helped your relationship with God?

Now put down your pen or leave your keyboard, find a comfortable position, take a few breaths to calm and center yourself, and sit in silence until a prayer comes to you. Speak it from your heart.

Stay inside the prayer as long as you need to, as the Spirit moves you.

When you have finished this time of prayer—and only when you have finished—come back to this reflection and notice what happened in your prayer. Write it down if you think it will be helpful.

CHAPTER FOURTEEN

Daring to Raise the Alleluia Song: Prayer in Times of Joy

For you shall go out in joy,
and be led back in peace;
the mountains and the hills before you
shall burst into song,
and all the trees of the field
shall clap their hands.

ISAIAH 55:12

As difficult as the prayer of lamentation or anger may be, it seems to come more easily than the prayer of joy. We call on God in times of trouble—at least when we are willing to admit to being in trouble. It is often harder for us to exult than to lament. We may cry "Help!" with great regularity but neglect to say "Thank you!" in times of abundance and joy. I wonder sometimes whether our fear of pain is matched only by our fear of joy. It can be hard for us to let go and celebrate; our old sorrows, our Puritan or Victorian heritage, our cultural background, our old or, alas, our more recent religious education, can get in the way.

Perhaps we wonder—I do now and again—whether deliberately praying in joy, making it a spiritual discipline, is not somehow constraining. Are we going to wreck our joy by paying conscious attention to it?

After hearing very little from people about joyful prayer when I first asked them about their prayer lives, I asked again. I received short, spontaneous answers, reflecting the nature of prayer in times of joy. "Yes, I pray when I'm happy," Mary wrote, "like Thanks and Great Show and Keep It Happening." "I just look skyward and say 'Thank You,'" said Anita. Ellen wrote: "I pray when I'm joyful—but it usually just sounds like 'God! Is this great!!!' I hope that God gets the poetry underneath." Sonia said during a phone conversation from Boston, "My favorite time to pray is during a party that's going very well!" Joyful prayer is almost always a prayer of gratitude.

Jo-Anne, a Canadian theology student in her forties and parent of two daughters, wrote: "In times of delirious joy and jubilation I usually am so busy responding to the situation that I tend to forget to thank God. . . . Sad comment, but maybe my reaction is in itself prayer. However, in all those quiet moments of joy, the ones that impart inner peace, I inevitably find myself whispering, 'Oh, thank you, God.' That's it, no formulae, just acknowledgement. Those moments of beauty: a glorious sunset, a certain angle in the garden that produces harmony in color and texture, a perfect tiny forget-me-not bloom, voices in chant. Those moments of reconciliation when someone finds peace instead of torment or despair. Those moments of pure love, given and received with my husband or our children . . . those looks of wonder and awe from the kids on discovering an idea. At all these times, my prayer is simply thanks for grace."

For some, the prayer of joy is in fact the first reflex or the principal aspect of prayer. Marge, a retired industrial relations specialist, wrote from Wisconsin: "Praying in times of joy—I think most of us do that. We realize how happy we are, and concurrently we move to thoughts of that from which all joys come, and who is joy. When I think about the qualities of God, joy is right up there on top. The angels joyfully announced the birth of Christ. God is love; love is full of joy." Bill, a whimsical seventy-year-old, wrote from Vermont: "My main prayer is whistling the chant melody of the '*Veni Creator*.'[1]

Of course, it 'calls' God, and s/he instantly reads my heart. Happens twenty times a day." Anita, whose communal prayer is structured around the cycles and seasons of the Jewish year and the celebration of the Sabbath, said of her personal prayer, "Most of the time when I'm praying in a private setting it's a big conscious 'thank you' to the universe for letting me be there. There's a morning version—the dog is very good for this, that's why you have dogs: the way they go, 'HOT DAMN! WE'RE HERE FOR ANOTHER DAY ON THIS PLANET!'"

A few of those I queried made a conscious connection between prayer in times of joy and the prayer of more painful times. Ginny wrote, "Basically, in moments of greatest joy I find myself with the same prayer as in deepest doubt or depression: 'God!' The tone changes. The prayer is the same." Joan, a singer and writer who attends a Unitarian church in the Twin Cities, wrote, "Yes, I pray when I'm happy. That's when it's easiest to practice gratitude, a skill that comes in very handy when I'm unhappy. I love to recite e.e. cummings's "I thank you god for most this amazing day,' and I sing a lot, which, of course, is a prayer too." Ruth, a college administrator from a Christian Science background, said, "Praying for thanks when things are going well is like going to a therapist when you are in the best state of mind for making even more positive improvements. Always good for introspection and more objective motivation. It's the difference between feeling strong enough to hit a home run versus simply hoping to get to first base."

Experiences of peace, ecstasy, satisfaction, or creativity can in themselves be a prayer, as Jo-Anne suggested, or can lead to prayer: witnessing a child's first steps, making love, putting in the garden for the season, finishing a construction project, having a good exercise session, solving a mathematical problem, or writing a poem. And again and again, when people wrote of joy, they spoke of nature. Joyful prayer here was gratitude, but also connection, even immersion, and always, attention. All manner of people spoke of this relation to nature, regardless of their religious affiliation. My mother, Joan, who is eighty years old, wrote me two summers ago about her understanding of prayer: "Request, entreaty, supplication, set formula, begging—all those ways I reject. Categorically. . . . But spiritual communion, that I do all the time—leaving out God in the traditional sense." She wrote of doing the backstroke, swimming in the small Vermont lake we both love. "I revel in the beauty of the blue sky with the wondrous cloud formations. As I pass by a ring of birch trees, with their leaves dancing gently and gracefully, I glory in it—my good fortune to move, to swim, to have sight, to live that beauty." She wrote of two days of work cutting the old raspberry canes near the house, and finding that a wild vine had entwined itself around them, "not around the green canes already bursting with blossoms and ripening fruit. How strange and wondrous! The ways of Nature. So many unseen powers of which we are too often unaware. Hymns of praise."

Joe is a sixty-five-year-old retired father of five and grandfather of twelve, living in the Sierra Nevada foothills and active in his local Catholic church. In one of the online forums to which I subscribe, he offered this food for the soul: "Picking blackberries on a cool summer morn, before the sun comes over the tops of the trees, gives one time to reflect. As the sweet juicy berries drop into the bowl and your hands get covered with scratches, one's thoughts turn to God's goodness in the many ripe berries, and maybe penance in the nicks from the thorns. Can one do penance in advance? The berries will bring sweet juicy pies next winter. Sinful blackberry jam also. Are thorns advance payment for future sweets?"

Joe continued: "What else is there to do in two hours of picking bowls of berries, but think of the dawn, the land, the berries, and God who gives it all to us. I wonder if one can gain forgiveness for past sins in the thorns, while gaining sweet berries. No, I think not. The fruit hanging in thick bunches brings to mind the riches of God's mercy, His love that overflows, and pours down over us, forgiveness that is ours for the longing. The morn is warm, sweet fruit in abundance, the sun is still behind the ridge. I pick berries and think of God and forgiveness and love."

Like the prayer of lamentation, the prayer of joy can be wordless. I experience it as a kind of sighing laughter, or a laughing sigh. My mother wrote of the impossibility of describing her feelings about the glory of nature and of praising with "a silent hymn." My friend Harry e-mailed from Alaska, late one night: "I pray sometimes in the manner of shedding tears: this kind of joy is beyond words.—Until the Italian gene fights to the surface and tells me that

I don't deserve such joy," he joked. He continued: "I pray silently while drinking in the greens and magentas and purples of the landscape, in such awe as to bypass my limited vocabulary. By being very still so as to absorb the maximum in the minimum time. By listening to a friend and sharing the joy—or pain. By wishing joy upon those who need some."

Merlene, a Catholic woman from California, recounted an experience of deep joy in prayer during a recent retreat: "I decided to accept an invitation to walk the path of the labyrinth which the retreat facilitator had placed on the floor. As I walked the labyrinth's narrow path, which wound toward its (and my) center, I recalled many of the painful moments I had experienced in the fifty-four years of my spiritual journey. To my surprise, memories which I thought might be in greatest need of healing seemed to trouble me very little. Instead, other memories, either long forgotten or assumed to have been of little significance, surfaced, and I experienced their pain in a quiet and healing way. I cried softly most of my journey to the center of the labyrinth. I felt aware of the presence of other persons along the pathway. Most of all I felt the presence of Jesus and was reminded that he had been with me during all the painful moments of my journey."[2]

Arriving at the center of the labyrinth, Merlene experienced a deep sense of being at home. She lit a candle and retraced her steps, back to the entrance of the labyrinth. She wrote: "My spirit felt lighter with each step I took." She found herself skipping and dancing. Outside the labyrinth once again, "I felt great joy welling up within me as I became aware of being centered, together with my brothers and sisters, in the Holy Trinity. I felt held within the Trinity. As I danced, the labyrinth upon which my brothers and sisters walked became a chalice which I was holding up in consecration before God. In that moment all my longing and desire to be a priest in my church came together. I knew that, even without official ordination, I was functioning in that sacred time and space as a priest and the cup of my heart, the cup of joy within me, overflowed."

One person wrote of consciously setting time aside for thanksgiving and joyful prayer. Diana, a full-time academic editor and part-time graduate student in theology, exclaimed, "You bet I pray in times of joy! At the end of every semester I schedule an entire day with the purpose of expressing my joy and thanksgiving to God for all that I learned and all that took place—not just things like surviving in one piece, or having had no traumas that got in the way; rather, that my spiritual life has been stretched to new heights and lengths. The joy is related not to that which causes a smile on my face, but to the faith deep within. And in that joy, I ask for God's response to my semester. I will never forget the year I experienced God saying, 'thank you.' It was awesome."

Setting time aside for prayer is one facet of the prayer of joy. Repeated, even ceaseless prayer is another. Francine, an educator, married and the mother of a son, attends my church in Oakland. "I say 'Thank you, Lord' all day," she told me. "Sometimes I add little gestures of praise." And in hard times? "If it's not been such a good day, it lifts me up. I say it all the time." Her face showed both serenity and intensity as she spoke.

"Everything I know about praise and joyful prayer goes back to the very beginning of my Christian life," Fred wrote to me. "There is of course the remarkable atmosphere of a living, thriving, charismatic congregation: a loud crowd, lots of emotion, and people just glad to be in church together in the presence of God. There's a celebratory atmosphere there that's really something magnificent when it's going right. Jubilant music, clapping hands, and the more outgoing members of the group feeling free to dance, wave hands, sing too loud, shout, and just generally express joy physically. Not to be underestimated as aerobic exercise, either," he joked. "That's stamped in my consciousness from before I was reflective. It's the matrix for all further understanding I ever got around to."

He added: "Praise can take over the entire enterprise of prayer, and invade the rest of life as well. This is a hard thing to talk about because the last thing I can stand still for is Norman Vincent Peale happy-talk about having an attitude of gratitude. But 'the power of praise' is a big deal in my upbringing.

"During high school, I had a very powerful experience related to praise and thankfulness. We had a long snowy winter and missed a lot of school; this was the winter I had just been converted, and I read the Bible for months on end as if my life depended on it. I was really fascinated with the passages in the New Testament that direct us to 'pray without ceasing.' I couldn't imagine how it would be possible, since you pray with your conscious mind and you need your conscious mind to accomplish anything in the world, so how can it multi-task? Well, at some point and for some reason, I began to praise God for everything that crossed my path. Then it occurred to me: 'pray without ceasing' and 'in everything give thanks' are the same thing: the way to pray without ceasing is to give thanks in everything!

"Well, this was one of those moments when the word jumps off the page and directly into your experience. For a period of several weeks that winter, I prayed without ceasing by giving thanks in everything. Chores, cold weather, trips with the youth group to shovel snow from driveways and sidewalks in town, some homework . . . I was in a state of unceasing, uninterrupted prayer and thanksgiving. Now I'm perfectly willing to listen patiently and even accept any reductionist explanation of the whole thing: I had things happening hormonally that made me prone to prolonged euphoria and melancholy, and I was getting to spend time with a couple of girls I liked a lot. And then there's the obvious fact that I was a recent convert, and this was the period of my falling in love with God. But in, with, and under all that, I believe that God gave me a kind of visionary experience, which is to say a manifestation of what life can and should be. Of course it went away, and I've only made teeny little approaches to it since. But that's the rhythm of spiritual life as far as I can tell: God gives us, as gifts, glimpses of what is possible, and we revel in it briefly before setting out to lay hold of it. This was a formative event for me: the gift of prayer without ceasing."

Fred quoted Cyprian, the third-century bishop of Carthage in North Africa: "New-created and new-born of the Spirit by the mercy of God, let us imitate what we shall one day be. Since in the kingdom we shall possess day alone, without intervention of night, let us so watch in the night as if in the daylight. Since we are to pray and give thanks to God for ever, let us not cease in this life also to pray and give thanks."[3]

"This," Fred said, "makes a deep kind of sense to me: that your basic response to the people, things, and events in your life should be gratitude, and your basic posture joy. Jesus conducted a survey that showed nine out of ten lepers aren't even thankful for being healed.[4] Go figure."

Alleluia is the song of creation, praising the wonders God has made. It is also the song of redemption—God moving in history to transform human lives. And it is, most of all, the song of resurrection. The New Testament recounts how the early Christians were so infused with joy that observers suspected them of being "drunk on new wine."[5]

It was not so at first. At the empty tomb, Mary of Magdala, according to one of the resurrection accounts, did not recognize Jesus.[6] In another account, God's messengers say to her and to the other women who had stood at the foot of the cross and now stood at the entrance of the tomb, "Why do you seek the living among the dead?"[7] Having recognized Christ and dared to rejoice in his risen presence, she goes forth to announce the good news, becoming the one the Eastern churches especially call "Apostle to the Apostles."

We are this way. We do not always recognize Jesus when we meet him, or resurrection when it is occurring in our lives. This is especially true when sorrow, illness, or evil threatens to overwhelm us. It is precisely in those times that we do well to ask: What does it mean to be resurrection people? Can "Alleluia" be our song even now? In his memorial homily for Mev Puleo, Don Steele, grieving as we all were on that day in Oakland's St. Augustine Church, spoke of our being together to witness to the resurrection "—of Jesus Christ, of Mev Puleo, of the poor, the exploited, the sick, the marginalized, the church, the earth, the universe. For to all our experiences of death—personal, communal, or universal—God says life. It is in that context of resurrection that we can honestly express the feelings of loss, of fear, of hurt, of anger, of confusion, of doubt, of pain, and of deep, deep sadness—because all of those feelings are real, especially in the face of such a terrible death. They are real, and they are ours, and so we acknowledge them freely in this safe place of community caring and God's caring—and in acknowledging them, recall that as real as they are, they are not the last word."

∽✠∾

O unfamiliar God,
   we seek you in the places
   you have already left,
   and fail to see you
   even when you stand before us.

Grant us so to recognize your strangeness
that we need not cling to our familiar grief,
but may be freed to proclaim resurrection
in the name of Christ, Amen.

JANET MORLEY

PSALM 150

Hallelujah!

Praise! Praise God in the temple,
in the highest heavens!
Praise! Praise God's mighty deeds
and noble majesty.

Praise! Praise God with trumpet blasts,
with lute and harp.
Praise! Praise God with timbrel and dance,
with strings and pipes.

Praise! Praise God with crashing cymbals,
with ringing cymbals.
All that is alive, praise. Praise the Lord.
Hallelujah!

SHECHEHEYANU

This Hebrew prayer is one of the most beautiful and moving in the Jewish tradition. It is the all-purpose prayer of gratitude. You say it when you have reached a particularly wonderful day in your life or, as Anita Diamant, author of several books on Jewish life, once said to me, "when you've eaten the first peach of the season or your child takes her first steps, or when you're just glad to be alive." The *Shecheheyanu* has traditionally been translated as follows:

Blessed are you, O Lord our God,
king of the universe,
who has kept us in life
and sustained us
and enabled us to reach this season.

An alternative, contemporary translation is:

> Holy One of Blessing,
> Your Presence fills creation.
> You have kept us alive,
> You have sustained us,
> You have brought us to this moment.

The transliterated Hebrew of the traditional version reads:

> *Baruch ata Adonai, Elohenu*
> *melech ha-olam*
> *shecheheyanu,*
> *v'ki-y'manu,*
> *v'higi-anu*
> *la-z'man hazeh.*

PRAISES FOR GOD'S CREATION FROM TWO REGIONS OF THE SOUTHERN HEMISPHERE

Benedicite Aotearoa

> O give thanks to our God who is good:
> whose love endures forever.

> You sun and moon, you stars of the southern sky:
> give to our God your thanks and praise.

> Sunrise and sunset, night and day:
> give to our God your thanks and praise.

> All mountains and valleys, grassland and scree,
> glacier, avalanche, mist and snow:
> give to our God your thanks and praise.

> You kauri and pine, rata and kowhai, mosses and ferns:
> give to our God your thanks and praise.

> Dolphins and kahawai, sealion and crab,
> coral, anemone, pipi and shrimp:
> give to our God your thanks and praise.

Rabbits and cattle, moths and dogs,
kiwi and sparrow and tui and hawk:
give to our God your thanks and praise.

You Maori and Pakeha, women and men,
all who inhabit the long white cloud:
give to our God your thanks and praise.

All you saints and martyrs of the South Pacific:
give to our God your thanks and praise.

All prophets and priests, all cleaners and clerks,
professors, shop workers, typists and teachers,
job-seekers, invalids, drivers and doctors:
give to our God your thanks and praise.

All sweepers and diplomats, writers and artists,
grocers, carpenters, students and stock-agents,
seafarers, farmers, bakers and mystics:
give to our God your thanks and praise.

All children and infants, all people who play:
give to our God your thanks and praise.

A New Zealand Prayer Book

An African Canticle

All you *big* things, bless the Lord.
Mount Kilimanjaro and Lake Victoria,
The Rift Valley and the Serengeti Plain
Fat baobabs and shady mango trees,
All eucalyptus and tamarind trees,
Bless the Lord.
Praise and extol Him for ever and ever.

All you *tiny* things, bless the Lord.
Busy black ants and hopping fleas,
Wriggling tadpoles and mosquito larvae,
Flying locusts and water drops,
Pollen dust and tsetse flies,

Millet seed and dried dagaa,
Bless the Lord.
Praise and extol Him for ever and ever.

TRADITIONAL AFRICAN

In Jamaica, we are poor.
Sometimes, I wake up in the morning,
and there is only tea in the house.
I get down on my knees and say,
"Thank you, God, for the tea."
In America, you have so many things.
Yet I am confused:
I see so much around me, in your country,
but I don't see your people saying,
"Thank you, God."

This poem is taken from a sermon that George Simpson, a Jamaican migrant
worker, preached at Bethany Church, Randolph, Vermont, in 1989.

PEACE IS EVERY STEP

Peace is every step.
The shining red sun is my heart.
Each flower smiles with me.
How green, how fresh all that grows.
How cool the wind blows.
Peace is every step.
It turns the endless path to joy.

THICH NHAT HANH

PSALM 126

A Dream Come True:
Home to Zion after Years of Bitter Captivity.
Laughter, Dance and Song

A song of ascents

The Lord brings us back to Zion,
we are like dreamers,
laughing, dancing,
with songs on our lips.

Other nations say,
"A new world of wonders!
The Lord is with them."
Yes, God works wonders.
Rejoice! Be glad!

Lord,
bring us back
as water to thirsty land.
Those sowing in tears
reap, singing and laughing.

They left weeping, weeping,
casting the seed.
They come back singing, singing,
holding high the harvest.

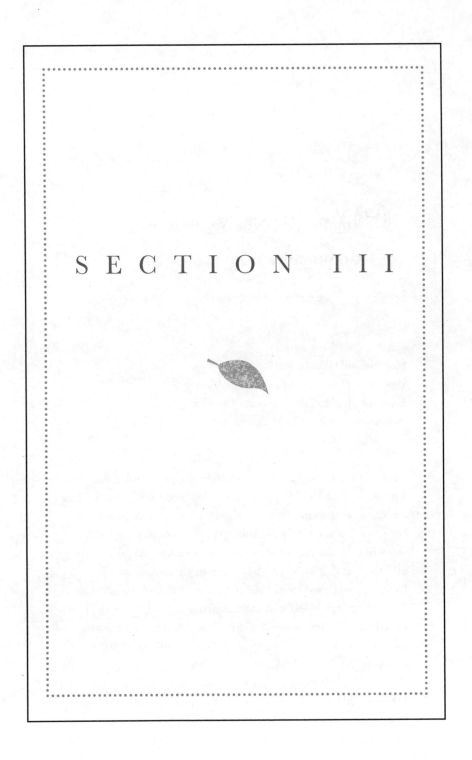

SECTION III

CHAPTER FIFTEEN

Our Prayer, Not My Prayer:
Community Is Fundamental

Here we will take the wine and the water
Here we will take the bread of new birth
Here you shall call your sons and your daughters
Call us anew to be salt for the earth.
MARTY HAUGEN

They are family and more than family, the people of Saint Paul. The blows that would rupture bonds of blood or friendship can somehow be absorbed by a community of faith. There was a member several years ago in the midst of a divorce. One Sunday she watched from the rear of the church as her estranged husband rose in prayer, and from the distance she made out his words. "God bless my wife," he said, "wherever she is." The woman called Reverend Youngblood that night, tearful, insisting she must leave the church. "Where else will you go?" he asked her, and ultimately she chose to stay. Even today in the choir sing two daughters of Reverend Johnny W. Walker, the church's previous pastor, while in the congregation listen the members who unseated him. The same Board of Elders contains Melvin Heyward, who went on strike against the telephone company for months this past winter, and Charles Young, who crossed the picket line as management. One parishioner, Charles Warfield, is married to the ex-wife of another, Ed Lawson. The harmony, if not easy, endures.

"Together," Reverend Youngblood says, "let us pray." Heads bow. Hands reach and clasp. Only now can the rain be heard, drumming its drone on the roof.

SAMUEL G. FREEDMAN

Where two or three are gathered in my name, I am there among them.

MATTHEW 18:20

"I am," the African proverb says, "because we are." One cannot be a Christian away in a corner. Even hermits pray as members of the universal church. We are always linked in prayer with those who share our faith and our tradition, across geography and through history. We speak their words. We speak their names. We draw from their strength.

"How can I find God?" The question came to Jim Martin, a young Jesuit writer and editor, from a close friend who had "lost touch with her church. Like many contemporary Americans, while she viewed herself as 'nonreligious,' she admired friends who lived lives of faith, and desired that faith for herself. Still, she was essentially a skeptical woman—intelligent and well-educated—living in a secular culture. . . . I did the best I could, and then decided to ask other people of faith what they might tell my friend."[1] Like many of the people Jim Martin consulted, and whose answers he later published, I offered the caution that it is more naturally God who finds us. Remembering Jesus' invitation "Come and see" to the would-be disciples, I also offered a pragmatic approach. Don't think too much about finding God: do something, and the finding will follow. Do it on two levels. Find what speaks to your deepest heart. Go to that intimate place where you are infinitely sad, or ecstatic, or creative and talented, or bereft, or deeply engaged, and there you will find God, if you enter into that place and ask what it means for you and for the world that you are there. The other level may be even more important because you have asked, "How can *I* find God?" To "find God," I suggested, "go find yourself a 'we.'" I would have answered in much the same way if she had asked: "How can I learn to pray?"

Go find yourself a "we," I insisted. A community, any community. A Christian community, if the path into which you were born or are drawn is Christian; a Jewish one, if you are a Jew by birth or by choice; a Muslim one if that is your path. I would say the same of the great religious paths that do not have a "God," such as Buddhism—where one "takes refuge in the Buddha, the *dharma* (Buddhist teaching and practice), and the *sangha* (the community)." Find yourself a community of practice and of faith—one that meets your standards of intellectual honesty, lack of hypocrisy, sincere concern for others, non-coercive welcome of the stranger. If the community is Christian, the "we" might be a parish, where worship may be noisy or quiet, structured or chaotic. The "we" might well also be a prayer group—contemplative, charismatic, or other—or a Bible study group, a women's liturgical gathering, a Catholic Worker community, a team that cares and prays for people with AIDS, or an adult education class with some soul and some teeth. You may have to look around, and you may have to try a few different communities, I wrote Jim's friend. Give them a chance. "Come and see." Then stay for a while. See what happens.

I know. Groups are difficult. Common life is messy. Institutional religion may have wounded you, I wrote—hence my listing of several forms of community, in the hope that one might serve as a gateway into the common life that is faith. God alone can answer the lonely yearning inside that heart of yours, which is like no other heart. But God without the "we" experience is not the God of whom the Jewish and Christian Scriptures speak, nor the God whose message the Prophet Muhammad carried to the people who became followers of the path of Islam. God—"I will be who I will be"—is involved in history, in *our* history. In this history, we meet companions. In their friendship, we find God, and God finds us.

Raised a Presbyterian in a Californian, European-American suburban parish which she still considers her home, Katie is also a member of an urban Catholic community, a Catholic Worker house whose members are a mix of immigrants and refugees from Central America, like her husband, José Luis. Speaking of her firstborn daughter, Maria Elena, Katie stressed that she could not separate the teaching of prayer from "faith formation." More broadly speaking, that formation only a community can give. "I don't want her just to have a 'personal relationship with God,'" she said, "but a community that will water that and feed that and challenge that and keep that going—and also provide a community of conscience to stop her when she's going over healthy boundaries." The Christian community where her daughter will grow up "is a community of faith that will include traditions and practices that will develop a *memory*—even if she rejects it, events that bring her through the seasons and give her a sense of some kind of structure."

The prayer of the community—where we pray "Forgive us our trespasses"—has ethical implications for the life of its members in the world. "We have a lot of children's books at home on the people of the Bible," said Katie. "Maria Elena knows about Daniel, Moses, and Jonah. She also knows that when she does something wrong she needs to say she's sorry, and we try to develop a sense of forgiveness— of going to someone and asking them to be your friend even when they bit you half an hour ago. When someone apologizes, it means, 'I still love you and we're still together.' We also have a next-door neighbor who is a retarded man, and she has heard people call him 'Bobo,' which is a derogatory name in Spanish. I said, 'He is not Bobo, he has a name; his name is Cole.' Now she says 'He's not Bobo, that's not good.' So it's a lot more than prayer: she's getting the Gospel message to treat others with dignity, shelter the homeless, feed people who have no food."

The best of worshiping communities both nurture and manifest the faith formation of which Katie speaks. They are, as she puts it, communities of conscience—one could also say communities of accountability, communities of discipleship, communities of interpretation— as well as communities of celebration. Communal prayer is that place of contemplation and celebration where there is room for the Gospel stories and ritual gestures, for the common memory and the Alleluia song—"to tell the story and break the bread" is the way one contemporary writer has put it. For some Christian traditions, hearing the word—and singing it—is central. For others, it is the sacramental life. For many, it is both. In all of these, the prayer of the community is a place of belonging held together by more than the belonging itself.

Richard, the Manhattan banker, after writing me about his daily private prayer and study of the Scriptures, concluded: "Finally, there is public liturgical prayer. I like to sing loud and Mass gives me the chance to bellow. Sacramental liturgy is important to me. I would not willingly give it up, even for consistently finer homilies. The Eucharist is a re-creation of a compelling, moving story, the Passion of God with us in the worst of times, God longing for us and for us to remember. It is the least we can do."

The time and place of hearing the word, listening for God's voice, speaking our needs, singing laments and celebrations, sharing ritual, is also our meeting place, our visible connection, with the church universal. The seasons of which Katie spoke have little weight or color without a community to honor them, whether the community is a household or a cathedral. The language of memory and hope in our mouths is not ours alone.

This is, of course, not true just of Christianity. The weekly Friday prayers, the annual fasting of the holy month of Ramadan, the once-in-a-lifetime pilgrimage to Mecca both sustain and spring from the communal prayer life of Muslims. Malcolm X writes movingly in his autobiography of the impact of the pilgrimage to Mecca, or *hajj*, upon his life and his vision of humanity. "There were tens of thousands of pilgrims, from all over the world. They were of all colors, from blue-eyed blonds to black-skinned Africans. But we were all participating in the same ritual, displaying a spirit of unity and brotherhood that my experiences in America had led me to believe never could exist between the white and the non-white. . . . On this pilgrimage, what I had seen, and experienced, has forced me to *re-arrange* much of my thought-patterns previously held, and to *toss aside* some of my previous conclusions." It was belief in one God, Malcolm X felt, that created the bond between pilgrims and removed the differences caused by race and color in other settings. My friend Anita spoke of the sense of connection she has at Jewish services, both with her local congregation on Saturday mornings and, especially, on the High Holy Days of Rosh Hashanah and Yom Kippur, when "you really have a sense that you're part of a global congregation, and not just through time. It makes you feel very big; at the same time you're also in the business of feeling very small."

Community is also a school for prayer. It teaches the rituals and stories of our faith, but also nurtures the attention, attentiveness, and mindfulness that is prayer. I cannot count the number of times when I have left for church distracted or despondent and found in the liturgy the help I needed to focus my attention, even if I watch my attention wander for the first part of the service.

Parishes are no picnic. My own has its staffing problems, power struggles, and liturgical weaknesses. The liturgy keeps me there, as do the people, who, like the people of my church in Boston, have come to feel like home. I come to remember God and hear words of wisdom, to receive nourishment from both word and sacrament that will help me live through the week. I return also out of commitment to all those who pray with me there, as we sit together week after week singing, reflecting, often struggling, whether with prayer or with the challenges of contemporary life. The repetition, the layering of Sunday upon Sunday, changes me and changes them.

Some worship situations, in parishes and elsewhere, starve the soul. "I don't have a satisfying communal prayer at this time," said Barbara, a Catholic sister in western Canada who described herself as "semiretired." "I get to Mass less and less, and when I do go, I leave feeling disconnected, 'out of synch' with the others, kind of depressed. Our parish and diocese are encouraging small faith communities to develop, and I've proposed starting one with a focus on creative, inclusive liturgies. The one I go to now is dear and pious, but I don't feel comfortable. I find my experience of communal prayer at present to be very lonely." Amy, at least two decades younger, married and living in Boston, asked, "Is there a word for when one's parish is deconverting, becoming more institutional and less related to the Gospel? I think I am giving my parish up for Lent," she concluded sadly.

"Megachurches" are a growing phenomenon in the United States, both in the size of individual congregations and in the number of such churches. Yet an increasing number of Americans are also choosing a living room–size group as a primary congregation. This trend has crossed religious, denominational, and ideological lines in the past three decades; it is not a "liberal" or "conservative" phenomenon but encompasses the *havurah* movement in the Jewish community, Christian base communities, house churches, prayer groups, storefront churches, and the healing circles of Wicca practitioners. Although, as Barbara noted, small size does not guarantee a vital experience of prayer, for most of their members, small groups are a way to deepen religious involvement and bring it closer to home, to satisfy the twin cravings for community and intimacy in the spiritual life. In the Christian context, Bible study groups, prayer groups, and social service groups may be subdivisions of local churches or—less frequently but in growing numbers—alternatives to them. In either case, they often seem to help people pray more than the parish itself.

I call these small communities "the living-room experience," in contrast to what I name "the cathedral experience." I have been involved in a number of them, one of which was a group of a dozen laywomen and -men who celebrated the Eucharist together once a month in a Boston-area living room, another a French prayer group reciting the monastic prayer of the Taizé community at a weekly gathering on the floor of a side chapel of a Paris church. My first living-room experience actually happened outdoors in a circle on the ground with a group of children and early adolescents, sometime during my girl scout years, which lasted roughly from the ages of eight to fifteen. Our scout camps were of the "roughing it" sort, with dirt and hiking and building our own fire—and inevitably, scorching some part of the meal—in the midst of beautiful landscapes, usually mountains. We gathered on Sunday mornings; one person would pick a Bible reading, another a couple of hymns, and a dozen or twenty of us would sit in a circle on the grass and worship. A fervent agnostic at the time, I loved the heroic resurrection hymns.

My classmate Kirk remembers fondly "a group of four men I met with weekly at seminary to pray and talk. The intimacy I experienced with them is something I carry with me still, resigned to the reality that I will likely not ever experience that again. We spent a good deal of time in prayer and singing Taizé chants together. The only time since my Mom's death in 1991 that I have all-out bawled for minutes on end was in that group. That was some real emotion, the likes of which has not surfaced since."

Mary belongs to a community of women and children in Washington, D.C., that identifies with the loosely knit Women-Church movement of feminist Christians, many from Catholic backgrounds.

She says it is now "in its seventeenth year. The original members are all but gone; new ones join each year and the group continues. We do liturgies of all sorts, but the main thing is we get together: community, ministry, and meaning, in that order, are my sense of why people choose to be religious. I like to watch the kids grow up in it—just like a parish only smaller, lots smaller," she added.

"Twice monthly I meet with a few downtown business/law/government types and a priest we know," wrote Richard. "We begin with a formal prayer—a kind of litany of aspirations to use typical business events as opportunities to bring closer the reign of God. Then, a Gospel reading, ten minutes or so of silent reflection, then discussion of the text. I tend to intellectualize more than I should or others would like," he admitted. "But it is in the imaginative re-creation of the events narrated in the text that the Scriptures come alive for me. Compassion does not exist in the abstract; only in the encounter of persons and the ensuing responses. Telling the stories of those encounters, and retelling them in ways that resonate with the experiences we bring to them, that is prayer for me."

I heard fewer stories of what I call "cathedral experiences," though many spoke to me of the sense of relation to the broader faith community they receive on holidays. In a very few cases, the Catholic or Episcopal cathedrals or large Baptist churches of U.S. cities provide that rare and precious experience: a meeting in prayer of a mix of generations, races, and socioeconomic classes. Sunday continues to be, as the saying accurately goes, the most segregated hour in our country's week—racially, especially, but almost as often by class. We do better—though not always—with the mix of generations. During a difficult week in which she and my father were contending with the illnesses of two siblings, my mother took time off from a demanding schedule to attend a midweek event at her Unitarian Universalist parish. Upon returning to the retirement community where she and my father live, she spoke fondly of the mix of generations. "I need it," she said. The intergenerational community of my parents' church does not simply "keep them young." It also offers their presence and wisdom to other generations.

Not all Christian communities center their worship on Sunday services. In some cultures church is only one focus, and sometimes not the main one: the Sicilian and Italian-American Madonna del

Soccorso festival in Boston's North End; the Filipino festivals, processions, and devotions of Santacrusan, Santo Niño, and Black Nazarene, with which Rachel Ann's mother grew up; the Mexican and Mexican-American *Las Posadas*, the re-creation of Mary and Joseph's search for lodging before the birth of Jesus. Festival, procession, and pilgrimage too are prayer, worship in motion and in drama.

Twelve-step programs large and small function as church for many people today, providing both living-room and cathedral experiences. "We pray together a lot in AA, at least here in the South," Barbara wrote me. "We pray twice at each meeting, at the beginning the Serenity Prayer and at the end the Lord's Prayer. This does not mean, however, that we are all praying to the same god. In AA, where God is 'as you understand him,' the community prays together to as many concepts of God as there are alcoholics present, maybe more. It is *not* OK to try to convince anyone else to believe in your concept of God. Some do not even join in the prayer, or [they] silently pray something else during the Lord's Prayer because it is (a) too Christian, or (b) too male-dominant. One friend says a silent prayer to the goddess during the Lord's Prayer—and refuses to lead the Lord's Prayer when asked. No one thinks anything of it as far as I know; I have never heard anyone comment in any way. But," she added, "we are definitely a spiritual fellowship, joined together by the spirit. Whatever it is."

Barbara remembered: "The first time I was introduced to prayer in AA was at my first meeting. They all said the Serenity Prayer. I didn't know it, but wanting to fit in I learned it quick enough. At the end of the meeting they said the Lord's Prayer, holding hands. I liked that—the holding hands part. It wasn't like church. For a bunch of people who prayed and talked about God all the time, being with them did not feel like church, and I liked that. Church had never touched my heart. They did. They talked about pain that I had felt and understood, and then they said that God and the fellowship had showed them a way to live. I needed a way to live. If I needed God for that, I was up for it—even though I didn't believe, and didn't know if I could. You haven't heard anything until you've been to an AA convention and you've heard two thousand sober alcoholics say the Serenity Prayer together."

French theologian Yves Congar asked, "Where would my prayer
be—where would my faith even be—without that of others? We are
all made by others. My prayer is the whole communion of saints:
Saint Augustine, Saint Basil, Saint Paul, Abraham, David. They are
inside my prayer and they help me."[2] Awareness of the communion
of saints, the community beyond the walls and outside the present,
often turns into the prayer form of the litany, a rhythmic, repetitive
invocation that calls upon the presence of those who have gone
before us in faith. The most solemn is the litany at the Easter Vigil,
naming women and men from the earliest Christian witnesses to the
most recent. The litany has also become a popular form at Christian
feminist gatherings, with the congregation naming the courageous
and holy women, formal saints or not, whose memory mainstream
traditions often forget. The very naming of those who have
remained invisible and unheard can be prayer: they exist, they live
in our hearts, they teach us the way of faith and of courage.
Sometimes we pray to them. Intercession, remembrance, making
present: the three often merge. This triple dynamic is also part of
the litanies of names of those who have died in the civil wars of
Central America in recent years. Their compatriots in El Salvador,
Guatemala, and elsewhere speak their names, one by one, as do
their relatives and friends who are refugees here, and those involved
in preserving their memory everywhere, and the assembly responds:
"*¡Presente!*" "She is present!" "He is present!"

Kerry, a college chaplain in Maine who has retained her membership in a large Boston church where she was ordained and to
which she and her husband return as often as they can, spoke to me
of this congregation's practices of communal prayer. "There is a red
book in our sanctuary," Kerry said. "It offers an opportunity to
inscribe your prayers, and at the time of 'celebrations and concerns'
during the Sunday service, a common Protestant custom. We combine statements of these celebrations and concerns at an open
microphone with a reading by the liturgist of the day of what has
been inscribed in the book. One weekend, our wonderful field education student preached, and her text for the day was the 'red book'
since 1985. What a way to get to know a community! She said quite
wisely, 'So much is in here, and so much is not, but your prayers are
inscribed in these pages even when not a drop of ink was there to

speak of them. There are stories that didn't make it into the book because they couldn't [due to their private nature] or because you weren't there and didn't have the book, but they are here in the heart of God and in the heart of the community.'"

On the eve of All Souls' Day, late at night, my friend David in New York wrote me of his vivid experience of the communion of saints, involving "re-membering—of/with/through the dead. My most intense form of prayer in recent years has come through meditating loss and the enduring ache of loss. The presence of the holy dead—brother, father, mother, friends who have taken leave of the earth plane. From another realm, they sneak up on me, catch me unawares, burst the partition between heaven and earth. A secret door, a channel is opened, which I can walk through, tune into.

"Such break-ins usually, but not always, bring the gift of tears," Dave wrote. "The channel is of salty water. 'Altered states,' we used to call them in the sixties. But in this case, they're not something I connive at voluntarily, deliberately. They just come, well up, spring out—depending on the circumstances: late-night musings, a letter to a bereaved relative, a family wedding, encountering a surviving son or daughter. Such moments get me in touch with what I'd call my ghostly cheering section—and more.

"I first became aware of how the dead mediate prayer through my brother, killed in an airplane crash in 1983 at age fifty. In many ways he had raised me—found my glasses when I lost them, fought fistfights for me, mentored me throughout my childhood and until high school. As kids we were inseparable; he was two years older than I. And even later, when as a Jesuit I took part in some very comic 'actions' against the Vietnam War of which he thoroughly disapproved, he—always the provider—had offered to pay for reputable psychiatric care!

"About seven years after his death, late one night, I happened to be talking with an old friend who had just lost his eldest brother. I don't remember now what my friend said, but it was something like 'How's by you?'—meaning, how are you getting along with your own grief? Much to my surprise, the question took my breath away. I burst into tears. Couldn't stop. Guess it was a flood waiting to happen. I had to go outside and be with the enormous ache, the huge hole in my being, the torrent of memory and feeling. Walked around for an hour. Spoke to my brother, who was tangibly there, felt his love of me, mine for him—beneath the pain and anger of losing him, in the flood of sobs. I hadn't realized how intensely I missed him. Ah, but the connection was still a live wire. Still carried me. He let me in on a secret that night, gave me a stomachful, a mouthful of God's love. Still does whenever I turn to him.

"Such moments," Dave continued, "are not always awash with tears. Sometimes they're alight with laughter and the warmth of reunion. For instance, with my father. My father, after a very full, rich life and no regrets, died at age eighty-four in 1979. In death, he's also become a medium, a path to the Lord of Riches—a kind of Christian version of the Hindu elephant god Ganesh. It didn't happen right away. It took several years. But now, to remember him sensibly, in the Ignatian way of 'applying the senses'—tasting, smelling, hearing, seeing, feeling his touch—is to get in touch with a kind of radiance, the glow he cast with his life—of wit, humor, enthusiasm, protectiveness and generosity. An enormously expansive man, and yet one of great simplicity, he'd always told us that at his wake he wanted to be stood up at the door of his home with a glass of whiskey in one hand and the other stretched out to greet the mourners."

Nearly two decades after his father's death, Dave said, "the faults of his single-mindedness, stubbornness, speechifying and rabid anti-communism fade away life chaff, winnowed away now. What is left is himself-as-conduit of grace, blessing, the richness and laughter of God. The God who loves a party, who loves 'here-comes-everybody,' who is one big WELCOME HOME! To remember my father is to get in touch with that, yes, to be touched by the energy of a BIG REUNION."

At one of the Sundays of St. Columba's annual African American series, whose theme that winter was "I am because we are," a neighboring clergywoman, Katherine Ward, was the guest preacher. She returned throughout her homily to the theme of our series: "Alone is not the way we were created by God. We are a body. We are part of each other. We exist together."

❧

VIGIL
....

On behalf of the people of Bosnia and Herzegovina, we formally request
your participation in activating a collective spiritual power in response to the
forces of destruction now plaguing our nation.

REPUBLIC OF BOSNIA AND HERZEGOVINA PERMANENT MISSION TO THE
UNITED NATIONS, IN AN OPEN LETTER, JULY 24, 1995

As a child I lay in bed
and whispered the *Shema* each night,
as if those fevered syllables
could save me from rape
and the Nazis.
Prayer was a bargain with God,
a desperate promise
to be clean and perfect. God
was always angry then,
and I was always afraid.

And so, growing up,
I am having to learn to pray
all over again. Not in the dark,
but in the morning
underneath the skylight,
first sun ranging in
to cast a pool
across the quiet carpet.
I stand, my body open to the glass,
light humming like wings
in the sheltering air.
The old chant
does not pass my lips. Instead,
a gratefulness even more ancient
like the first woman
awakening on a plain of grass
to find that the night has passed safely.

And now, this request:
Two minutes

> *of silent meditation and prayer*
> *at 3 pm in New York City*
> *12 noon in Los Angeles*
> *9 pm in Sarajevo*
> *8 pm in London*
> *will bring millions of hearts and minds together*
> *in the application of spiritual force.*

For one who has always prayed alone,
who even in the soft cacophony
of swaying *shul*-goers takes refuge
in the burning tree of solitude,
this is a challenge.
Not the two minutes,
but to breathe as one of many
fixed on the same hope:

> *Our prayer is that God's will*
> *be done; we trust He wills our people*
> *to be saved.*

The vigil begins.
I close my eyes and wonder
can I ever cross this boundary
feel the old terror that blooms
when it is time
to trust the will of anyone.
And suddenly it is an ancient prayer
that fills my world again:
Ose shalom bimromav
Hu ya'ase shalom alenu.
"May the One who makes peace in the heavens
make peace for us all."

I do not know if prayer
will make a difference.
I only know that I have been asked
to join a great musical chord
that shapes the air
like the vibrations
of a ripe and supple instrument.

I sway in its embrace;
imagine others
who are doing the same.
It is 3 pm in Boston
4 am in Tokyo
11 pm in Moscow
10 pm in Jerusalem
We are all awake in the darkness.

We pray for Bosnia-Herzegovina
And we pray for all the world.

ELENA STONE

LIFE TOGETHER

Because God has already laid the only foundation of our community,
because God has united us in one body with other Christians in Jesus
Christ
long before we entered into common life with them,
we enter into that life together with other Christians,
not as those who make demands,
but as those who thankfully receive.
We thank God for what God has done for us.
We thank God for giving us other Christians who live
by God's call, God's forgiveness, and God's promise.
We do not complain about what God does not give us;
rather we thank God for what God does give us daily.
And is not what had been given enough:
other believers
who will go on living with us through sin and need
under that blessing of God's grace?
Is this inconceivably great gift of God
any less than this on any given day,
even in the most difficult and distressing days
of a Christian community?

Even when sin and misunderstanding burden the common life,
is not the one who sins
still a person with whom I too stand
under the word of Christ?

DIETRICH BONHOEFFER (1906–1945)

CHAPTER SIXTEEN

Healing, Rage, and Thanksgiving: Praying with the Psalms

I love you, God my strength,
my rock, my shelter, my stronghold.

My God, I lean on you,
my shield, my rock,
my champion, my defense.
When I call for help,
I am safe from my enemies.
Praise the Lord!

PSALM 18:2–3

The Psalms are the river of the synagogue's prayer, of the church's prayer. Whatever else is said and done, it is said and done to the flowing of this river. Through the generations, the thanking, praising, cursing, and lamenting of the Psalms have shaped the vocabulary of synagogue and church. This chanting is joined in the public times and echoed in the households and the private spaces. Daybreak and awakening are marked with Psalms as are day's end and night's rest. For Christians, the singing of the church—in every sort of rhythm from Byzantine chanting to the spirituals to the chorales—has drawn abundantly from these Psalms.

GABE HUCK

E verywhere, in every age, in solitude or on crowded trains, Jews and Christians have prayed the Psalms. Psalms become laden with the meanings and emotions brought to them by the communities reading, chanting, singing, and reciting them. I began praying them in my preadolescent or early adolescent years, when both the world and my insides were becoming more complex. My family did not pray the Psalms regularly, nor were they part of any worship I attended save the occasional service of the Reformed Church of France, to whose scouting movement I belonged. There was a Bible at home, I picked it up, the Psalms were there. I read them, mostly, when my spirits were low. That is all I remember. They have stayed with me ever since.

I have prayed the Psalms in the dark of night and early in the day, in my bed and in church, silently and aloud, alone and in community. I loved, still love, their dense humanity and their utter turn toward God, never one apart from the other. They must have reassured me, at the awkward age when I began to read them, that inner and outer turmoil were not my private lot but rather were shared, common—*connected.* Even before I knew that the Psalms are communal prayer in their very intimacy, I sensed that they linked me with other human beings in space and time. They brought me, in the same moment, face to face with the Holy One. The "you" in the Psalms always stands out, engages us, plunges us into relationship with God. We do not need to leave ourselves behind in this encounter. The marvel and relief of this truth moves commentators to alliteration. "The Psalter," writes one, "teaches us that we may and must bring all of life to our prayer. Delight, dailiness, and distress can all be brought to God."[1] Another notes the Psalms' reflection of the width and depth of human experience and emotion: "despair and delight, horror and hope, fatigue and faith, rejection and renewal."[2]

Jonathan, a Malaysian Catholic, wrote to me: "The Psalms express all sorts of emotions including anger, despair, desolation, in addition to praise, thanksgiving and intercession. I used to be

amazed how the Psalmist challenged God by asking God to crush
Israel's enemies, and asking God why God allowed Israel to be
defeated and thus casting a slur on the power of God! But I came to
realize that the Psalmist was correct: God was in everything the
Israelites did, even in moments of desolation. Even if the Israelites
lost a war, they still spoke to God and asked God why!" Jonathan's
favorite Psalm is Psalm 139 ("Lord, you have searched me and
known me . . ."). "The words of this beautiful Psalm have meant a
great deal to me," he wrote. "I was at the crossroads of my faith in
my college days, and in my disillusionment, I felt that God was
speaking to me and encouraging me through the words of this
Psalm."

Peter, an American Jew, prays communally in Hebrew, but he
knows the Psalms and prays them alone, "mostly in English and in
King James English. They get to me each and every time. Like so
many other people I know, in distress and in fear there are some that
I go to time and again. 'I lift up mine eyes unto the mountain,'"—he
quoted the opening line of Psalm 121 "the great crisis prayer of all
times." It was only after the worst of my depression that I discovered
Peter and I, friends for over two decades, shared a love for this Psalm
and had both prayed it regularly in times of woe.

"I go thumbing through them periodically to find new ones,"
Peter said of the Psalms. "They really are occasional pieces. They
are divided into moods and *ragas*.[3] There is something to suit every
occasion, whether praise giving and exaltation or fear and trembling. Most of us go to 'fear and trembling' but when one gets out,
the others are there: joy, triumph."

In English-speaking countries the Psalms have been associated
for generations with the language and rhythms of the King James
Version. Because I was not raised in a traditionally religious family, I
am one of the few English-speaking Christians I know who does not
have at least one Psalm memorized in those familiar cadences. I
wrote earlier of praying in more than one language, especially in the
reading of the Psalms aloud. Not all people have a second language
at their command, but if one does there is no refresher for prayer
like using this other tongue. The words are suddenly new. When I
began reading the Psalms in French last year, out loud as is often my
custom, the change in language made me slow down. I paused over

the words, savored them, received them in a new way. I suspect this would have been true as well for the languages in which I am less fluent: I have read other passages from Scripture in Spanish and German as part of liturgies in which I have participated, or of study in which I have engaged, and again I have found that the change in language refreshes, even if one stumbles a bit. One can also read the Psalms the way one reads the poems of Pablo Neruda in a bilingual edition that has the Spanish on one side and the English on the other. My Spanish is inadequate to read Neruda only in Spanish, but I never read him in English alone if I can help it: the music of his heart's language is as eloquent as the meaning of the words. Setting Psalms to new music, whether the music of chant and song or the music of another language (including the silent and eloquent music of sign language), will breathe spirit into them again. The change in music can even be as simple as an English translation other than the one with which one usually prays.

Every Sunday, Catholics and members of other churches using the lectionary in worship speak or sing a Psalm. We do not choose it. Psalms form the major part of the Liturgy of the Hours. We do not choose them. We thus pray Psalms that do not necessarily correspond to our mood of the moment. The Psalms in the Liturgy of the Hours speak to, and of, the One Who is holy. Precisely because we pray words and emotions not our own, they also place us squarely in the broader church, indeed within the sufferings and joys of all humanity—a reminder of where we are not, which is as important as a confirmation of where we are.

German Lutheran theologian and anti-Nazi resister Dietrich Bonhoeffer wrote of the Psalms, "We must ask how we can understand the Psalms as God's Word, and then we shall be able to pray them. It does not depend, therefore, on whether the Psalms express adequately that which we feel at a given moment in our heart. If we are to pray aright, perhaps it is quite necessary that we pray contrary to our own heart. Not what we want to pray is important, but what God wants us to pray. If we were dependent entirely on ourselves, we would probably pray only the fourth petition of the Lord's Prayer. ["Give us this day our daily bread."] But God wants it otherwise. The richness of the Word of God ought to determine our prayer, not the poverty of our heart."[4] Contemporary scholar

William Holladay suggests reading the Psalms "sequentially . . . without leaving out any sequences that are 'somewhat harsh in tone.' The advantage of the present canonical order," he writes, "is precisely that it is *not* a very 'logical' order—the sequence catches us unawares, forcing us to ponder the sudden actions of God in our lives."[5]

I have had it both ways: the Psalter set out for me, and the Psalter *ad hoc.* I have not recently prayed the Liturgy of the Hours; I used to. I do sing the Sunday Psalms. In my private prayer I pick and choose. Yet even there, as in prepared worship, one can encounter tired routine. Often it is music that breathes life into the words again. The written word comes to life when chanted, the spoken word when sung. When I cannot sit still with a book, I can sway to the sound of a recording, or go to a community where the song will carry me and bring me back to the message of trust, struggle, and hope.

The Psalms appear in fact to have been songs as well as prayer-poems. Tradition attributes the Psalms to King David. It is possible he wrote some of them, and, Holladay writes, "the tradition that he wrote the whole book of Psalms was an expansion of that memory, reinforced by the record of his skill on the lyre . . . of his laments over Saul and Jonathan . . . and over Abner . . . and of his organization of the musicians at the sanctuary in Jerusalem." The variations in style, language, and themes suggest, Holladay writes (in agreement with most contemporary biblical scholars), that the Psalms are "the product of many poets and singers over the centuries."[6] The Psalms, as Peter said, come in many moods. Scholars classify them into different categories: Psalms of lament, penitential Psalms, thanksgiving Psalms, hymns of praise, covenant and festival Psalms, royal and Zion Psalms, songs of trust, wisdom Psalms, and Torah Psalms.[7]

Underlying all the Psalms is trust, and in some there is magnificent rejoicing. But the fact remains: there are more laments in the Psalter than any other genre. Lament is perhaps the most useful of Psalms, if one can dare use the word "useful" to describe a prayer. "Perhaps, this indicates the real suffering of human life," Irene Nowell writes. "The laments teach us to bring everything in our lives to God, even what seems not to be proper. The laments portray anger, hatred, sorrow, humiliation, sufferings, and death. God is not spared the range of human emotion. Nothing is too raw to be brought to prayer. The laments teach us in fact what to do with these emotions: take them to God."[8] "Have pity, for I am spent," Psalm 6 groans, and then wails, and cries: "Heal me, hurt to the bone, wracked to the limit. Lord, how long? How long?"[9]

My own reading of the Psalms does not so much ascribe them a Christian meaning as recall the fact that they were likely among the prayers Jesus learned as a child and recited as an adult. His words from the cross, "My God, my God, why have you forsaken me?" appear to be those of Psalm 22, which ends not in despair but on a note of trust and triumph. "All the ends of the earth shall remember and turn to the Lord, and all the families of nations shall worship before him. For dominion belongs to the Lord. . . . Posterity will serve him; future generations will be told about the Lord, and proclaim his deliverance to a people yet unborn, saying that he has done it."[10]

Other Christians draw a more intimate link between Jesus Christ and the Psalms. "If we want to read and to pray the prayers of the Bible and especially the Psalms," Bonhoeffer writes, "we must not ask first what they have to do with us, but what they have to do with Jesus Christ."[11] Bruce, the Washington economist who prays the Psalms daily as part of Morning and Evening Prayer, wrote to me of his appreciation for Bonhoeffer's *Psalms: The Prayer Book of the Bible*. He finds it helpful to imagine "Christ reciting the Psalms with me— to understand them through his eyes, interpreted in his light, remembering that I am a member of his Body. This brings new or added meaning to Psalms that otherwise might seem obscure or objectionable. It is particularly helpful when the Psalmist proclaims his innocence or his guilt: We are not innocent, but we partake of Christ's innocence, and he bears our guilt. When the Psalmist calls for vengeance against an enemy, we must be careful to understand this not as our own personal enemy, but as the enemy of God—it might even be ourselves—and to remember that this vengeance has already been carried out and borne by Christ."

The Psalms will not let us sit forever inside our lament. Even the Psalms of lamentation are bathed in trust. Trust, healing, victory are the final message of the Psalms of lament. Even more, the Psalms of thanksgiving challenge our prayer, challenge us to look around at creation and inside at our soul and express our jubilation. "Praise! Praise God with trumpet blasts, with lute and harp. Praise! Praise God with timbrel and dance, with strings and pipes. Praise! Praise God with crashing cymbals, with ringing cymbals. All that is alive, praise. Praise the Lord. Hallelujah!"[12] The prayer book of the Bible teaches us to sing the Alleluia song.

Psalms are expressions of joy, but they can also bring us into joy, or reveal joy that had remained submerged or unspoken. A year and a half ago, I immersed myself musically in the Psalms as an aid to writing a journal article about them. One day, on impulse, as I was setting out on a walking errand, I decided to take my portable tape player with me and listen through the earphones to a recording of recent musical settings of the Psalms, a tape I know almost by heart because I have sung so many of the Psalms in church.[13] I walked down the street where I lived at the time, quiet and full of slightly unkempt gardens bright with flowering trees. The air was soft and clear. I was happy to be alive. I had taught earlier in the day and was in the tired but elated state that for me follows a good class, where the students and I have been present to each other and to the subject matter, and we all know learning has taken place and we have left the classroom changed. Walking down the street, hearing the words of Psalm 98, and feeling the music reverberate inside my body, I entered, or was given, a kinesthetic experience of the creation around me. "All the ends of the earth have seen the power of God. . . . Sing to the Lord a new song, for [God] has done wonderful deeds. . . . Sing to the Lord with harp and song, with trumpet and with voice, singing your joy. . . ." As I admired the visual beauty around me with the music and words in my ears, creation and the work of human hands—shrubs, blossoms, architecture, sky—stood in greater relief, not less. It is true that in our culture we suffer from doing too much at once: reading while eating and watching television, talking on the telephone while stirring the soup. More often than not I try to hold myself to one activity at a time, to pare down the sensory input rather than layer it on. But on this occasion the multiplicity of messages converged with grace, the Psalm in my ear teaching my eye to see.

I will never take being alive for granted again. I was predisposed to this outlook by my upbringing. My parents had fallen on hard times economically and professionally in the two years before my birth, in the ugliest period of the McCarthy era, and the difficulties continued—mostly unbeknownst to me—through my early childhood, but my brother and I never felt deprived. We were fortunate to have shelter and food, and our family time and leisure hours were filled with gifts that cost little or nothing and that our parents shared with an affection and wonder equal to ours: a walk by the Seine, a visit to a monument or a museum, and countless picnics in public parks. Hard times, sweet gifts. In much the same way, once my depression and anxiety had come and (mostly) gone, the simplest pleasures were precious, even the fact of waking up without dread. I can concentrate again. I can write. I can sing. There was a time, briefly, when I could not. I am alive. There was a time when I lived in the shadow of death. "Taste and see the goodness of the Lord," the Psalm's antiphon sang in my ears during that walk on my street. "Look to me that you might be radiant with joy."

❧

PSALM 139

O Lord, you have searched me and known me.
You know when I sit down and when I rise up;
    you discern my thoughts from far away.
You search out my path and my lying down,
    and are acquainted with all my ways.
Even before a word is on my tongue,
    O Lord, you know it completely.
You hem me in, behind and before,
    and lay your hand upon me.
Such knowledge is too wonderful for me;
    it is so high that I cannot attain it.

Where can I go from your spirit?
    Or where can I flee from your presence?
If I ascend to heaven, you are there;
    if I make my bed in Sheol, you are there.
If I take the wings of the morning
    and settle at the farthest limits of the sea,
even there your hand shall lead me,
    and your right hand shall hold me fast.

If I say, "Surely the darkness shall cover me,
     and the light around me become night,"
even the darkness is not dark to you;
      the night is as bright as the day,
      for darkness is as light to you.
For it was you who formed me in my inward parts;
      you knit me together in my mother's womb.
I praise you, for I am fearfully and wonderfully made.
       Wonderful are your works;
that I know very well.
       My frame was not hidden from you,
when I was being made in secret,
      intricately woven in the depths of the earth.
Your eyes beheld my unformed substance.
In your book were written all the days that were formed for me,
      when none of them as yet existed.
How weighty to me are your thoughts, O God!
     how vast is the sum of them!
I try to count them—they are more than the sand;
I come to the end—I am still with you.

O that you would kill the wicked, O God,
      and that the bloodthirsty would depart from me—
those who speak of you maliciously,
      and lift themselves up against you for evil!
Do I not hate those who hate you, O Lord?
      And do I not loathe those who rise up against you?
I hate them with perfect hatred;
     I count them my enemies.
Search me, O God, and know my heart;
     test me and know my thoughts.
See if there is any wicked way in me,
      and lead me in the way everlasting.

PSALM 70

For the choirmaster. Of David.
For remembrance.

Help me, God.
Lord, be quick to save me.
People are plotting to kill me;
humble them, shame them.

They want to ruin me;
ruin and disgrace them.
Let those who jeer at me
swallow their shameful taunts.

But those who seek you
and trust your saving love
rejoice and always sing,
"God is great."

I am poor and helpless,
O God, hurry to my side!
Lord, help, my rescue,
do not delay.

PSALM 121

A fresh translation of Psalm 121 from the Roman Catholic International Commission on
English in the Liturgy (ICEL). Compare it with the version of Psalm 121 on pages
164–165. Read them both, slowly, silently, or aloud—perhaps on two consecutive days in
order to let the words, their melody, and their meaning sink in. Does one translation speak to
you more than the other?

A song of ascents

If I look to the mountains,
will they come to my aid?
My help is the Lord,
who made earth and the heavens.

May God, ever wakeful,

keep you from stumbling;
the guardian of Israel
neither rests nor sleeps.

God shields you,
a protector by your side.
The sun shall not harm you by day
nor the moon at night.

God shelters you from evil,
securing your life.
God watches over you near and far,
now and always.

Psalm 65: A Version for New Zealand

You spread your justice, God our Saviour,
  across the world to the farthest oceans.

You have laid down the mountain ranges and set them fast;
  you make the seas calm and the sounds peaceful;
  you reconcile the peoples who dwell here.

So in this corner of the earth we wonder at your deeds;
  at the meeting of east and west we sing your praise.

You water the land and make it flourish,
  from your own bursting river.

To provide our crops, you plough and irrigate the land,
    softening it with rain to make it fruitful;
  a record harvest is achieved, and the stores are overflowing.

The tussock land becomes pasture
    and the brown hills turn green;
  the paddocks are crowded with sheep
    and the plains thick with wheat:
  the world itself a canticle of praise.

A New Zealand Prayer Book

....

After becoming familiar with some of the Psalms, including Psalms of different types (lament, thanksgiving, praise, wisdom), try writing a prayer of your own that follows the structure of a Psalm.

Psalms of Lament

Remember that the Psalms of lament include laments by both individuals (Psalms 3, 4, 5, 7, 13, 14, 22, 25, 26, 28, 31, 35, 36, 42–43, 52–57, 63, 70, 71, 77, 86, 88, 109, 120, 140–142; see also Lamentations 3) and communities (12, 44, 58, 60, 74, 79, 80, 85, 90, 94, 123, 126, 129, 137; see also Joel 12, Lamentations 5, and II Chronicles 20).

The speaker is a person or community in great distress and oppression.

The speaker addresses God first.

The mood is one of anger, hurt, despair, fear, distress.

The psalmist desires God to listen, heal, rescue, save, forgive.

The image of God is most often one of a personal God, who hears my/our cry, who cares for the lowly, who is God of covenant, love, and loyalty.

Structure of Lament Psalms

Addressing God (O God, O Lord)

(The words in parentheses are the words found in the Psalms; you may want to use the same or other forms of address.)

Complaining/Lamenting the distress we/I experience ("Why . . . ?" "How Long . . . ?")

Complaints Against Enemies, God, self

Confessing Innocence of sins that bring on suffering

Confession of Trust in God who has saved us before (beginning with words like "still," "nevertheless")

God's Word of Salvation (very seldom found)

Vowing to Praise God (thanksgiving sacrifice)

Psalms of Thanksgiving

Here too there are Psalms spoken by both individuals (18, 21, 30, 32, 34, 40:1–11, 66:13–20, 92, 103, 108, 116, 138; see also Isaiah 38:9–20 and Jonah 2:2–9) and communities (65, 67, 75, 103, 114, 124).

The speaker is a person or group who has been rescued or saved.

The speaker addresses family, friends, fellow worshipers at a shrine or the temple.

The mood is calm, gratitude, quiet praise.

The psalmist desires that all hearers thank God for the psalmist's rescue, their own saving.

The image of God is that of a personal God, who hears my cry and answers me, who acts for my own good.

Structure of Thanksgiving Psalms

Introduction ("I/we thank you, O God!")

Reason for Thanking God

> Distress I was facing; how I cried out to God in the midst of terror and distress; God delivered me after I cried out

Resolve to make a thanksgiving sacrifice (not always present)

Praise and Thanks to God

WITH GRATITUDE TO JOHN ENDRES, FRIEND, TEACHER, AND SCHOLAR

CHAPTER SEVENTEEN

Not for Parents Only:
Praying with and for Children

People were bringing little children to him in order that he might touch them; and the disciples spoke sternly to them. But when Jesus saw this, he was indignant and said to them, "Let the little children come to me; do not stop them; for it is to such as these that the kingdom of God belongs. Truly I tell you, whoever does not receive the reign of God as a little child will never enter it." And he took them up in his arms, laid his hands on them, and blessed them.

MARK 10:13–16

Dear God,
My dad thinks he is you. Please straighten him out.
    Wayne, age 11

Dear friendly God,
I think you are like a regular person.
I do not believe those people who say you are dead or far away.
You probably live on the next street.
    Marcy, age 8

Dear God,

Do you think there's enough love these days?

I feel there's a shortage.

Love,

>   Ken, age 9

David Heller

H ave you noticed that books on prayer usually leave out children, and books on prayer for or with children are usually
for children only? This is not inappropriate: we need to
pray in a way that corresponds to our developmental stage. On the
other hand, we adults know children to be part of our praying communities. They are our biological, adopted, or foster children, our
nephews and nieces and godchildren, our pew mates in church, and
the children of our friends and neighbors. My parish has a heart-
warming custom during the prayers of the faithful. After the petitions, but before the formal end of this sequence of prayer, the
presider or homilist calls the children forward—it usually takes time,
with our friendly head usher, a longtime member of the parish,
nudging them gently but firmly down the aisle, especially the very
young, who tend to totter and wander. He or she asks the entire congregation to raise our hands in blessing over them. This prayer
leader improvises a prayer that always speaks of the blessing the
children are to us, and asks for protection, wisdom, learning, and
love for them. This time of prayer does not only bless the children.
It blesses all of us. It reminds us visibly, each Sunday, that all these
children, whether we know them personally or not, are our own as
well as God's children.

This blessing is particularly poignant in an African American
urban community where most of us take neither life nor healthy life
for granted, where powerful forces assault our adolescents both literally and figuratively, and where the adults value and treasure education and extended family ties, knowing how both of these have
strengthened the community and helped its young people to survive
and to thrive.

So we pray for and with our children, and our children pray.
Yes, children pray. We—parents especially, even more than the
parish or congregation or religious school or minister of religious

education—are the first teachers of prayer. I cannot count the adults who have told me that they learned to pray literally at their mother's knee, and those, fewer but in significant numbers, who have memories of their fathers at prayer. Yet children also have the desire to pray even before we place it in them.

I found out recently from my mother that as a child of eight or nine I asked insistently that she teach me to pray. My Unitarian Universalist religious education did not include formation in prayer. Prayer was not a part of our family routine, except for the occasional silent, Quaker-style grace before holiday meals. My mother was somewhat stumped by my request, though her own mother, a non-religious Jew, had taught her the Lord's Prayer and a prayer that God bless her family and "make me a good girl, amen," which she abandoned as she got older. "With the Unitarian Universalists we [had] started 'The nicest thing I did today . . .' each night," she recalled many years later. "That, we thought, would be like prayer. Apparently not for you." My seven years in the girls scouts affiliated with the Reformed Church of France gave me occasions for communal prayer, as I have mentioned before, especially hymn singing, reflection on Bible readings, and some intercessory prayer, all in French. Later, or perhaps around the same time, I began reading the Psalms on my own, in English. In adolescence I sought to learn more of the Jewish rituals and celebrations of my ancestors, tugging my parents to temple for the High Holy Days and reading on my own. I loved the architecture of the old churches of Paris and the provinces, but avoided Catholic rituals, which I considered superstitious and silly, probably under the influence of my humanist family. I had, however, envied the girls' white First Communion dresses in earlier years, as well as the attention they received and the pretty holy cards they distributed, even to our public school teachers. Once in a while I attended Friends Meeting at the International Quaker Center with my mother, or a Protestant service with family friends. I began studying hatha yoga as a teenager. Throughout most of that time, from the young age when I first puzzled my mother with my request, something (someone?) moved me toward prayer.

A group of children I know in Boston who meet regularly with their parents for a family-based religious education program answered some questions about prayer conveyed to them by one of their mothers, who relayed the conversation back to me. The children are still young—between the ages of three and five at the time of this gathering. Most, said my friend, associated prayer with "talking with God" and with singing. Prayer, said Madeleine, goes like this: "Close your eyes and put hands together, think about God and say things: say thank you for food and all the people. Sometimes," she added, "I pray when I'm scared because God will help me. Like when I'm thinking about monsters when I go to sleep I ask God to help me think about nice things instead." Another child, Lily, said: "I pray and say what I'm grateful for, and I pray at church." Madeleine, a child of New England, where storms are both frequent and unpredictable, had an afterthought: when it is stormy, she asks God to take the storm away. Emily, who has been attending the same church as Madeleine and Lily since infancy, talked about the Native American "dream catcher" hanging over her bed: "It's supposed to let all the good dreams go through and keep the bad dreams out." Madeleine, eloquent on the subject of prayer at the age of five, talked about "praying for all the people in heaven, and all the people dead in the ground," and added that she would "pray that they come back." Gratitude, food, family, friends, dreams, nightmares, monsters, death, separation, and storms: a child's-eye view of life.

The children's parents began to reminisce. Lily's father, Neil, who is Jewish, said that as a child he would name all the risks in the world he could think of and ask God to protect him against them. Jim, Emily's father, raised in a Congregational church, remembered praying for specific requests: for years, he prayed that an aunt who had died would get into heaven. Susan, Jim's wife, raised a Catholic, had a standard prayer as well as a list of people; when people died, they stayed on the list for a long time, sometimes turning into guardian angels of sorts. The list would be longer or shorter from night to night, depending on fatigue; she still has a powerful image of her father kneeling by her bedside to pray with the list of people.

I asked my friend Tom, a former educational administrator and fundraiser and now a Jesuit priest and theologian, whether he prayed as a child. "Never!" he answered, then corrected himself: "No, I *did* pray. I'm so tainted by the rebellion years that my memory of them spills over into the previous years." He remembers most a sense of wonder—at the warmth of sunshine, at the beauty of autumn leaves in his upstate New York environment, and at the way the nearby lake would clean and replenish itself. Prayer, he said, was private rather than communal and church-bound. "I used to skip school in September and go to the lake. Prayer was also something I shared with intimate friends. When I was about nine years old, two friends with whom I grew up and I sat at the lake and had conversations about nature and the world and why things happen. One of our grandparents had just died. There were no prayer words then; we were just quiet together." Public prayer at Mass, where Tom was an altar boy, was barely prayer for him, and not a time of communion with God. In Tom's childhood in the 1950s and early 1960s, before the changes of the Second Vatican Council, the words of the liturgy were in Latin and "meant nothing." He added, "There was always a moment of panic, and once I messed up one of the prayers. A little girl made fun of me, which of course produced even more panic."

Tom recounted another strong memory of childhood prayer: "I remember as a little kid going to a footbridge near my parents' house. I used to sing hymns underneath there. Then I got caught and was quite embarrassed. I was eight years old." He also recalls "praying fervently for a horse that was being given away" on a children's television or radio show, "making all sorts of promises [to God], and figuring out on my own when I didn't get the horse that it wasn't the right thing to pray for."

Tom's experience of parental prayer was mixed, pointing to the fact that parents teach prayer by example, but not only prayer, and that children are quick to notice when we do not "walk our talk." "I would see my father pray," Tom said. "He was always known and perceived to be a very holy person, but I always saw the other side, which was related to his alcoholism. It was part of my aversion to prayer at certain times in my upbringing. He would be there twenty or thirty minutes before Sunday mass, and attend daily mass and other devotions. But my reality was that he was not a particularly good man. So I was a kid struggling to reconcile the connection between prayer and holiness with a father who was relatively abusive at worst, and completely standoffish at best." Tom's teenage years were "high rebellion years." He added: "That's very important; it doesn't scare me in others today. You have to be free to leave in order to be free to stay."

Sometimes our adult prayer leads us back to the early prayer of our childhood. Bill, after years of Zen meditation and Christian contemplative prayer, looked back on his spiritual journey: "When I first started doing formal practice, one of the consolations and affirmations for me was to discover that this interior place of prayer was a place I used to go to as a child, and I would experience this wonderful, loving Presence there." The discipline of Bill's adult days led him back to the same God he had known spontaneously as a child.

Most children of religious families, like their parents before them, say prayers before going to sleep, alone or with one or two parents. My goddaughter, now on the brink of adolescence, the daughter of a Protestant mother and a Catholic father, grew up saying her evening "God blesses," as her mother called them—a remembering of loved ones both related by blood and unrelated, which expanded to include people in need, like the homeless woman her mother befriended outside our church and always called by name. Many adults I know still pray before going to sleep. Nighttime is a time of rest but also a fearful time, a place of dreams and nightmares; evening is a quiet moment to look over the past day and anticipate the next, in that liminal space between activity and drowsiness.

Often grace before meals is the place where families begin. One of the first acts of prayer is thanksgiving, beginning with thanksgiving for one's daily bread. Some families pray a formulaic prayer that all recite at once; various Christian communions and denominations have their own. Some others improvise a prayer, taking turns—sometimes children only, sometimes either child or adult. Others go around the table, with each person stating a reason to give thanks. Many sing. My friend Kirk, who grew up in Iowa in a Reformed Church family, remembers: "My family had a tradition of singing together at meals to conclude our prayer. Four-part harmony, no less. In any other setting it would have felt contrived and haughty, but with my family it felt natural and good." Today, married and thirty years old, Kirk is still singing, in both community and church choirs, in the midst of a busy life.

Praying with children needs to take into account the developmental stage of the child, the needs of the child, the relationship that exists with the child, and a host of other factors. Fortunately, most faith communities now have abundant resources to help families in this area. When you pray with children, take into account your own faith as a parent, godparent, or friend. Children are perceptive, and they will know if your heart is not in what you are saying. Prayer with children challenges us to examine our own prayer life, our beliefs, our memories.

My friend Anita's involvement with her Jewishness was directly related to becoming a parent. She fell in love with her husband "as someone with whom I could have a child," and began reading more about her tradition in advance of her daughter's conception. At the time of Emilia's birth, Anita and her husband, Jim, had begun celebrating Shabbat, the Jewish Sabbath. When they returned from the hospital after the birth, on the first Shabbat of Emilia's life, they placed her "in a little basket on the table, and lit candles. It was one of the most powerful moments of our lives." Emilia, Anita added, "was the excuse for my discovering Judaism."

Now deeply and still joyfully involved in the celebrations, prayers, and rituals of their tradition, Anita and Jim celebrate them faithfully. They light the Sabbath candles and pray the blessings week after week. Anita said, "Emilia knows it's important to us, and she knows it's not something you outgrow." Many people, she added, feel that after your initial religious education, "you graduate, and their kids know that really clearly" if that is the case. Her daughter, on the other hand, "expects *Shabbas*¹ the way she expects to brush her teeth in the morning; it's part of life. When she was very little she once exclaimed, 'You know there are Jewish people who don't do *Shabbas*?!' This is the main event for us, and very important to her. She's also very grounded at our temple and has her own troupe of friends."

Jim and Stephanie take seriously their daughter Anna's spiritual life as an Orthodox Christian, even at the age of two. "One of the most important things is that she receive the sacrament [of Holy Communion] as many times as we go to church," Jim said. Children in the Orthodox Church receive communion from the time they are baptized and chrismated (anointed, confirmed) as infants. "The services are long. We get there late. We do what we can. But she always seems so much more at peace after receiving the sacrament. There is a twofold reason [Anna's reception of Holy Communion] is important to us. One is that she has received the Body and Blood of Christ: there are benefits even at that age. And the other is that receiving the sacrament regularly is habit forming. We want it to be familiar to her. Too often we see two- and three-year-olds come up who haven't received and they revolt; it can be frightening for them. But Anna is very peaceful in the communion line even if it is long. She opens her mouth, takes the spoon—she has never said no.[2]

"At dinner we do our [sign of the] cross, and she does like this," Jim said, touching his heart. "Mostly I say the prayer, offering thanks for the day and asking Christ to bless the food. We will probably start saying the Lord's Prayer soon so Anna knows it, in both Greek and English. We also have her venerate the icons in the house. It's still a game to her, but it's an action whose meaning will change."

Katie's father is Catholic, her mother Presbyterian. She grew up and is now an elder in the Presbyterian Church, where she was a youth minister for many years. She has also been involved in a Catholic Worker community both before and since her marriage to José Luis, who is Salvadoran. The mother of two children, stepmother of one, and pregnant with another child at the time of our conversation, she was pondering questions of religious affiliation for herself and her children. Ecumenical and interreligious marriages—and in Katie's case, a marriage that is also bilingual and cross-cultural—are more the norm than the exception these days in the United States.

"I have started praying with my four-year-old," Katie said. "Well, actually, my sister started. She's a Seventh-day Adventist, much more evangelical than I. She said grace once with her daughter and my daughter, and they really liked it. My daughter was probably two and a half. 'So let's try something before we go to bed at night,' I said later. I had her make the traditional gesture—close your eyes and put your hands together—and I said a simple prayer, in Spanish: O God take care while I sleep; take care of Mommy, Daddy, and then the names of the people in our immediate family. I would say a little piece of it and she would repeat it, we would say the names, and then 'Amen.' She added names and covered all the bases: the dog, her teacher, friends at school, her great-grandmother."

Children love ritual. It is as important for children to have their own times of prayer and rituals as it is for them to be included in adult celebrations, both at home and in the house of worship, in a multigenerational setting. Here the Christian tradition could take a good lesson from Judaism, which has so much more spirituality and ritual located in the home, particularly around the table.

Living in California, where Mexican religious and cultural customs are common, Katie and José Luis celebrated with her second daughter on her first birthday the Mexican tradition of "Las Mañanitas," in which loved ones come and wake the birthday person in the very early morning and serenade her or him with a traditional song. Katie remembered: "We grabbed Ana Gabriela's baptismal candle,[3] lit it and walked into her room." Katie, her husband, stepson, and elder daughter "kneeled near her crib so we wouldn't hover over her. She slowly woke up with a lazy smile and then pulled herself up and stood while we sang: 'These are Las Mañanitas that King David sang to the beautiful girls. . . . Arise, my love. . . . The day is here, the sun is risen, the birds are singing and the moon has gone to bed. . . .'"

During my last year in Boston, my church asked me to prepare a group of eight- to twelve-year-olds, most of them boys that particular year, for the celebration of their First Reconciliation. The sacrament used to be called "First Confession" and is sometimes still called "First Penance"; its name has been changed to "Reconciliation" to focus on God's acceptance and love. Among other activities, we held prayer services with the children's parents at the end of our sessions together, when parents would arrive early to pick up their children. The services included a mix of set and spontaneous prayer, readings from Scripture, and common reflection on the reading. It was not only a way for us to pray as a group but also a way for the children and adults to experience shared leadership in prayer.

Many of the children's concerns in prayer reflected those we had discussed in our classes, pondering the meaning of "reconciliation" and exploring the areas in our lives in need of God's reconciling love. I was struck by how deeply aware the children were of two areas of need: the prevalence of violence in and around their schools and neighborhoods and in their society (these were middle-class white

children, some urban and some suburban), and the environmental
destruction of planet Earth. They were well aware of thinning
forests and disappearing species, and of the accumulation of waste in
our oceans, lakes, countryside, and inner-city neighborhoods. These
are serious concerns, and several of the children, in our sessions
together, told me their parents had no idea of the extent of the reality of violence in their lives.

Rachel, a woman in her late twenties, is a religion teacher in an
upper-class Catholic school for girls in Connecticut who works with
fifth-, sixth-, and seventh-graders. Besides teaching the academic
study of religion, she also introduces the girls in her classes to various
forms of prayer. She has introduced a simple communal prayer, using
a candle as a visual focus. "Early in the year," Rachel recounted, "I
would walk into a seventh-grade class and they would ask, 'Can we
light a candle and you read to us from the Bible?' I was struck by the
request and overjoyed by it. I couldn't believe seventh-graders would
ask for that. I think in part it has to do with a desire to be peaceful.
The lives of the girls I teach are incredibly overscheduled. They have
their schoolwork and sports, dances or dancing lessons, horseback riding, squash. Often, there are tremendous social pressures placed on
them by their parents as well. That only adds to the pressure to perform for grades and look 'proper' and be THE BEST.

"I believe that the candle affords them the opportunity to slow
down and focus a little. We begin class by turning out the lights and
going around the room saying someone or something that they
would like to pray for. Everyone always has the option to 'pass.'
Petitions range in subject matter: family, friends, 'everyone in the
world,' hope that all do well on a test, a relative who is sick, a pet
who has died or is sick, an absent classmate, the homeless or poor on
occasion, too. It is beautiful to witness them praying for each other.
For example, if a girl says that her dog is sick, from then on, that
girl's dog is in each person's prayer. If for some reason I don't start
class this way, I am always asked why or when we will pray again.
Often someone will say, 'Are we going to pray today? I have something I want to pray for.' Some girls routinely 'pass'; others have different, deep prayers each day. I love the 'candle time' because I hear
their concerns, they hear one another's, and they are listening to
each other."

During Advent, Rachel said, "we had an Advent wreath in the room which served as our candle.[4] We also had an Advent calendar. Each door opened to a Scripture passage that was part of the Christmas story. At the end, we read the whole story from the calendar. During Advent, we also prayed a Psalm antiphonally, so they learned that form of prayer as well. It was great to teach them about Advent with the calendar and wreath; so much about the liturgical year came up: colors, symbols, deepening darkness and increasing light as we wait for the Light of the World to be born, and the fact that Advent is not Christmastime, so no [Christmas] trees should be up!"

Rachel facilitates another form of prayer with her students. "The older girls (seventh and the second half of sixth grade) lead the class in 'meditation.' They must choose some Scripture passage (Psalms are a big favorite), play music (contemporary or not, as long as it doesn't interfere with the reading), a candle, an object or work of art (optional) and a reflection question. In seventh grade, I teach them a collect to close out the reflection time.[5] They work in pairs." Often, these meditations "spark good conversations and faith sharing. I like to see it start at this age."

While adolescents are busy separating themselves from their parents, they do have spiritual needs and gifts, and they can and do pray. Marisa, a teenage friend of mine, excels at science, arts, and sports. She also prays. She has been praying since childhood, both alone and with her mother, who is raising her as a single parent, as well as attending church and participating in a youth group. "How do people make decisions without praying about them?" she asked in amazement at the age of fourteen. For her, the life of prayer and the moral life have become inextricably linked. Other factors besides God enter into her decisions, but God is always present as well, not as Great Outsider, but as a regular conversation partner.

I asked Marisa, now fifteen and a half, how her prayer had changed over the years. "It's more conversational now," she answered. "I used to say mostly set prayers." She does still repeat some of the prayers she learned as a child. "Usually I might say a little set prayer at night, 'Angel of God my guardian dear,' then talk to God, say things I'm thankful for, ask for things: protection if I have a game, help with a test and any problems I have. Sometimes I light candles. If I'm kind of worried about a decision I'm not sure about, if I pray about it, whatever decision comes, I feel more comfortable—that God is backing me up and is going to help me." Did she hear a voice or a specific answer? I asked. Mostly not. Prayer "makes me feel calm—not like God talking to me directly, but a kind of spiritual connection. I have a lot of things going on; it's another person to talk to. It's like a support. Having God there helps, especially if you're kind of confused."

Some of Marisa's prayer is more rote. While most of her friends at school are not religious, she did recount a conversation with a friend who like her is Catholic, "and how we have all these prayers memorized: we say them fast, it doesn't really have any meaning. We race through them, like grace; sometimes I try to think about it, but if I'm really hungry . . ." She smiled. I asked what going to Sunday liturgy meant to her. "After I have Eucharist," Marisa said, "it kind of feels like I'm closer to God. I like saying the prayers with a bunch of other people. It's nice to have the community. Mass is something I just go to every Sunday—I don't really question it—and it feels good at the end of the week to be able to have that. It helps me, because I have so many things going on during the week, to have that set time when we all gather together, and to pray. Sometimes," Marisa admitted, "I'm kind of zoned and I don't really pay much attention." Any particular times, I asked? "During long homilies," she answered. "I like to sing along" during the Sunday liturgy, "to praise God," she concluded.

Marisa's and my most recent conversation about prayer was during the month of January, when she announced, "Today in Confirmation class, we were talking about if God cares who wins the Super Bowl, and we were talking about whether we pray about sports." Marisa is on several sports teams. Does she pray about this? "I sometimes pray for protection," she answered, "or to do my best, not necessarily to let my team win. Well," she added, "*sometimes*, if it looks like a really hard match, I ask, 'Please, God, let us win.' But usually I just ask to do my best."

FOR MY CHILDREN

On this doorstep I stand
year after year
and watch you leaving

and think: may you not
skin your knees. May you
not catch your fingers
in car doors. May
your hearts not break.

May tide and weather
wait for your coming

and may you grow strong
to break
all webs of my weaving.

EVANGELINE PATERSON

"JUNK PRAYER"

Shannon, a minister who worked with high school girls for several years, writes that her best prayer experience with them came out of a so-called "junk prayer" at a youth retreat. She put a brown paper bag at each table of ten girls or so (the prayer can also be done in mixed groups as well—this one just happened to be girls) with miscellaneous things inside: one sneaker, a glue stick, a McDonald's wrapper, a flower, a schoolbook . . . "You name it," Shannon said. "The kids," she remembers, "were given ten minutes to put together a prayer using the items in their bag. So they came up with things like:

Dear God,
Some days I'm always running,   (sneaker)
    sometimes toward you, sometimes away,
but you slow me down with flowers,   (flower)
and teach me to study your creation.   (book)
Don't let me throw away this day.   (McDonald's wrapper)
Stick close by my side always.   (glue stick)
Amen.

Shannon adds: "Kids who'd been sure they couldn't make prayer out of such junk were still talking about it and using it months later. Several of them told me that the experience taught them that anything could be used for prayer, not just 'holy things.' That was well worth it."

You may want to try this at home as well, though adolescents may be less embarrassed and more willing to do this in a large group of peers and in the structured setting of a retreat or youth group.

WITH GRATITUDE TO SHANNON O'DONNELL

O GOD OF ALL CHILDREN

O God of the children of Somalia, Sarajevo, South Africa, and
South Carolina,
Of Albania, Alabama, Bosnia, and Boston,
Of Cracow and Cairo, Chicago and Croatia,
Help us to love and respect and protect them all.

O God of Black and Brown and White and Albino children
     and those all mixed together,
Of children who are rich and poor and in between,
Of children who speak English and Spanish and Russian and
     Hmong
and languages our ears cannot discern,
Help us to love and respect and protect them all.

O God of the child prodigy and the child prostitute,
     of the child of rapture and the child of rape,
Of runaway or thrown away children who struggle every day
     without parent or place or friend or future,
Help us to love and respect and protect them all.

O God of children who can walk and talk and hear and see
     and sing and dance and jump and play and
     of children who wish they could but can't,
Of children who are loved and unloved, wanted and unwanted,
Help us to love and respect and protect them all.

> O God of beggar, beaten, abused, neglected, homeless, AIDS,
>   drug, and hunger-ravaged children,
> Of children who are emotionally and physically and mentally
>   fragile,
> and of children who rebel and ridicule, torment and taunt,
> *Help us to love and respect and protect them all.*
>
> O God of children of destiny and of despair, of war and of peace,
> Of disfigured, diseased, and dying children.
> Of children without hope and of children with hope to spare and
>   to share,
> *Help us to love and respect and protect them all.*
>

MARIAN WRIGHT EDELMAN

Carole, a Catholic sister, wrote me: "After thirty years in teaching and administration on the high school level, five years ago I became the part-time kindergarten-through-eighth grade computer teacher at a borderline inner-city Catholic school.

"When I started teaching the elementary school children, I wanted to begin each class with prayer, even if it was the computer class. I made up a prayer for K–5. The sixth through eighth grades say Francis's prayer for peace. Both of these prayers are printed above the blackboard. The made-up prayer is this one:

> We thank you God
> for all you have made
> For earth and sky,
> wind and water,
> plants and animals,
> For stoves and phones,
> cards and roads,
> radios and computers,
> and especially
> for family and friends
> and people everywhere

I see the students once a week. Each year I am delighted as I watch the kindergartners learn this prayer, I say a phrase, they repeat it. They put their little hearts and bodies into it, often spontaneously making up motions or dancing around as they say each phrase. By the end of the year some of them say it with me, saying each phrase twice.

"By the second or third month of first grade, the kids all try to read the prayer themselves. Second or third graders, even fourth or fifth graders appear to be comfortable with this prayer. How do I judge that? They pay attention, aren't goofing off, and teach new students how to say it: 'This is our prayer.'"

WALKING WITH A CHILD

When you walk, you might like to take the hand of a child. She will receive your concentration and stability, and you will receive her freshness and innocence. From time to time, she may want to run ahead and then wait for you to catch up. A child is a bell of mindfulness, reminding us how wonderful life is.

At Plum Village, I teach the young people a simple verse to practice while walking: "Oui, oui, oui," as they breathe in, and, "Merci, merci, merci," as they breathe out. "Yes, yes, yes. Thanks, thanks, thanks." I want them to respond to life, to society, and to the Earth in a positive way. They enjoy it very much.

THICH NHAT HANH

CHAPTER EIGHTEEN

Mantras for Modern Christians

The light of Christ surrounds us
The love of Christ enfolds us
The power of Christ protects us
The presence of Christ watches over us

CONTEMPORARY *EXSULTET* (EASTER VIGIL LITURGY)

Now you are to love YHWH your God
with all your heart, with all your being, with all your substance!
These words, which I myself command you today, are to be upon
   your heart.
You are to repeat them with your children
and are to speak of them
in your sitting in your house and in your walking in the way,
in your lying-down and in your rising-up.
You are to tie them as a sign upon your hand,
and they are to be for bands between your eyes,
You are to write them upon the doorposts of your house and on
   your gates.

DEUTERONOMY 6:5–9

In recent decades, much of our culture has shied away from the practice of memorizing. But memorizing is making a comeback, particularly among parents who wish it to be part of their children's education once again, from mathematics to poetry. I say "much of our culture" because in some religious circles, Christian and Muslim, Buddhist and Jewish, and others, memorization has never stopped being a part of daily life. I will never forget the evening I spent at a program run by one of my former consulting clients, a church-based economic development group in Boston's Dorchester neighborhood. This training program for emerging urban entrepreneurs has an explicitly Christian base—the church being one of the only institutions that has never abandoned the core of our cities—and the trainer for the evening, in addition to teaching participants how to draw up a business plan, was peppering his presentation with talk of values and spirituality. At one point he mentioned by number two specific verses of the book of Proverbs and asked the class of adult men and women who could tell the rest of the group the content of these verses. Two hands shot up immediately, and both people recited from memory, with heartfelt voices, the verses that spoke of trust in God's presence and wisdom. Memorizing was nothing rote for them; it grounded their lives in a vision and a promise, helped them to make meaning of their daily struggles, and gave them readily available spiritual resources.

"This memorization-prayer is a big part of my own disciplines," said Fred one day when we were discussing the practice of memorizing Scripture passages. "I find it especially helpful because it's one of those exercises that, as my charismatic friends would say, 'you can start out in the flesh and finish up in the Spirit!' That is, sitting down (or walking or working out on a treadmill) to commit words to memory does not require any intimidating gathering of spiritual energy, like the frightful prospect of actually beginning to address God with confession and petitions in mind. But in the midst of the activity itself, you often find yourself already at prayer. It is," he pointed out, "not quite the same thing as praying Scripture."

Fred is one of academe's great researchers. Rummaging through ancient and more recent texts for resources on this topic, he discovered the writings of Matthew the Poor, also known as Matta El-Meskeen, a Coptic Christian "spiritual father" in the Monastery of

St. Macarius in Scetis, Wadi El-Natroon, Egypt. Born in 1919, Matta El-Meskeen became a pharmacist, left the profession in 1948, and became a hermit. A popular speaker, he was one of three nominees for pope of the Coptic Church in 1971. He distinguishes between "intellectual memorization" and "spiritual memorization." The first "requires that the mind progress step by step through investigation until it is on a level with the truth, then little by little rise above it until it can control it, recalling it and repeating it at will as if the truth were a possession and the mind its owner.

"There is another way of memorizing the word of God by which we may recall and review the text, though not whenever and however we wish, but rather whenever and however God wishes." This is what Matta El-Meskeen calls "spiritual memorization," granted by God's Spirit, "the Counselor [who] 'will teach you all things and bring to your remembrance all that I have said to you' (John 14:26)." When the Holy Spirit causes us to recall certain words of Scripture, he writes, the Spirit "does so in depth and breadth, not simply reminding us of the text of a verse, but giving with it irresistible wisdom and spiritual power to bring out the glory of the verse and the power of God in it." While there is "a striking difference between intellectual memorization by rote and recollection through the Holy Spirit . . . we must be prepared for this spiritual recollection by keeping our hearts conscious of the word of God through pondering upon it frequently and storing it up in our hearts out of love and delight. 'Thy words were found, and I ate them' (Jeremiah 15:16) and they were 'sweeter than honey to my mouth' (Psalm 119:103)."[1]

I grew up in the French public school system, in which we memorized and recited scenes from the plays of Molière, Corneille, and Racine and poetry in several languages. My brother and I can still recite the same poems of Goethe and Heine, Victor Hugo and La Fontaine, that we learned ten years apart, several decades ago. On the religious front, "home-schooled" as a Unitarian Universalist, I was not raised to memorize verses of Scripture. I have come to this practice in bits and pieces, often with a particular need at heart. Some years ago, I became executive director of a nonprofit organization with close ties to the corporate world. I entered the job after a long period of writing and consulting, trading casual clothes for pearls and pumps and quiet mornings at home for subway rides at rush hour. In those first days on the job, I memorized the Beatitudes from the Gospel of Matthew (there is another version in the Gospel of Luke).[2] I did so to keep my priorities clear in a downtown urban world that was often neglectful of the poor, the marginal, and those who suffer. Each morning, in my suit or tailored dress, I walked from subway to office mumbling, "Blessed are the poor in spirit." The contrast between my clothing and demeanor and the content and tone of the Sermon on the Mount was not lost on me, and the morning recitation helped me get a good start on the day. I regret that I eventually stopped the practice. But it had its usefulness, perhaps more than I will ever know.

Repetition has a meditative quality. Set prayers and beloved passages of Scripture are really Christian mantras. People who have abandoned Christianity and taken up meditation sometimes find, on a return trip to church, that the Western biblical traditions have had their own version of mantras for centuries.

Examples of these Christian mantras abound: the return to a single, simple word during Centering Prayer, a practice launched in its current form in the latter half of this century but a direct descendent of techniques spoken of in the fourteenth-century text *The Cloud of Unknowing* and practiced for centuries before; the repetition of the word *Maranatha* during the practice of Christian Meditation, another contemporary descendent of ancient practices, especially those of the early desert mystics of Christianity; the repetition of the Jesus Prayer, or Prayer of the Heart, in its traditional form, "Lord Jesus Christ, Son of God, have mercy on me, a sinner," or in adaptations like my friend Diana's, "I am one with the will of God, let it happen as you say," which includes words of Mary; the Angelus and the Hail Mary; and the "Thank you, Lord" that Francine, the woman from my church, repeats throughout the day, as a way of bringing to mind the goodness of God.

Rachel Ann remembered: "When I was in ungodly-long staff meetings in a particularly hellish job, just being in the presence of my boss would consume me with irritation and make my blood boil. One morning, I suddenly found myself doodling the words 'Patience. Wisdom. Strength.' in random circles and lines across the page, over and over. At first I wrote so hard that the letters practically gouged the page. As time dragged on, the grooves did not cut so deep. This continued every week for months on end until I finally got the courage, calm, and centering to quit the job with dignity." She continued: "As many times as I've flown, takeoffs and landings still make me nervous. For the past ten years now, I have had my singsong-y airplane prayer, which popped into my head one day as we were in queue on the runway: 'God, please protect us/God, please protect us/God, please protect us/As we go now on our way.' For full effect," she added, "it should be said with eyes closed, knuckles clenched white, and fingernails buried in the ends of the armrests."

The Rosary is one of the best known and most widely practiced of Christian mantras besides the repetition of Scripture. It is in fact taken partly from Scripture and is meant to be an opportunity to reflect on the life of Jesus as well as that of Mary his mother. Prayer beads exist in many cultures and religions. A rosary is a string of beads used in Christian prayer; the prayer sequence that the beads support with their physical presence is the Rosary. Legend has it that Mary herself gave the first rosary—at least as we know it in the Christian West—to the thirteenth-century Saint Dominic, preacher and fierce opponent of the Albigensians. In fact, the Rosary, like most prayer practices, is the product of a gradual evolution. It seems to have begun as an aid to praying the Psalms, then as a substitute for praying the Psalms, which monks were required to say each day but laypeople could often not memorize. In the Middle Ages a prayer to Mary—the "Hail Mary," which itself evolved over the course of several centuries—joined the "Our Father," the prayer of Jesus. It is also in medieval days, around 1250, that the name "rosary," *rosarium*, a rose garden, became attached to the prayer beads and their prayers. A late-fourteenth-century Carthusian monk, Henry Egher of Kolkar, was the first to set forth the Rosary in its current form of fifteen "decades" with an "Our Father" and ten "Hail Marys" (Latin *Pater Noster* and *Ave Maria*). Before the end of the fifteenth century, the Rosary had taken its current form of fifteen "mysteries" upon which one concentrates during the reciting of each decade, five "joyful," five "sorrowful," and five "glorious." The Rosary has become associated with Mary, mother of Jesus, and exists in several variants besides the traditional version I have briefly described.[3]

Almost all of the people whom I asked about the Rosary or who mentioned it of their own initiative were positive about this ancient devotion. (Cecilio was the sole exception: "I loathe the Rosary," he said. "I remember women and children in processions moaning it out. Sheer opium.") More surprisingly, they turned out to be a rather diverse group of people, not just Catholics, as I expected. Former Catholics who had left for other churches also had retained the practice of praying it. "Although I now am a member of the Congregational Church," said Harry, "I still do the Rosary in whole or in small bits almost daily." "It's very powerful," said Leith, a married Episcopal woman whose work involves hospitality and spiritual direction at a monastic community. "I have found that more and more people are doing it who are not Roman Catholic. It's very portable and adaptable. I don't use it much," she added. "I don't get very far: two or three decades and I'm gone. It puts me in a kind of trance. I don't even get to do all the mysteries." Bill, who practices Centering Prayer daily after years of Zen meditation, has kept various traditional devotions from his Catholic upbringing: "I do the Rosary as a contemplative kind of repetitive prayer. The contemplative dimension adds to the devotional prayers."

Prayer takes many forms, some silent, others spoken or sung, solitary or communal. A majority of people I have met experience private prayer as some form of informal, often ongoing conversation with God. For a few, a free-form, improvised prayer, or even the combination of free-form and "set prayers," is uncomfortable, or less than helpful. They prefer the set prayers. Why is this? My friend Laura wrote from the Sierra Nevada, where she and her husband, the son of a Presbyterian minister and a convert to Judaism, are raising their children as Reform Jews: "I don't pray in the way you talk about. It would make me highly uncomfortable. I don't think I could do it. One of the things I like about Reform Judaism is that there is a place for semi-agnostics like me. I have always had a 'problem' with prayer. I'm not exactly sure what I believe about it. I certainly don't believe that I personally can communicate with God. I'm sort of envious of those who do feel that way. On the other hand," she continued, "ritual prayers give me a sense of peace. I don't feel ridiculous saying them because they have been said by so many people for so long. I don't seem to worry about whether I absolutely believe in every word. The prayer just 'is.' I don't have to question it. Sometimes I just savor the ancientness of it, the connection with all those individual Jews who were saying the same prayer I am saying. It's the way I sometimes felt when I was breastfeeding my babies, a connection with all mothers in all times and places. Other times I guess I do feel a communication with a 'higher power,' but it's more of an acknowledgment that there *is* a power higher than humans, rather than a feeling that this power is paying attention or doing something for me specifically. I suppose that wouldn't sound very satisfactory to many people, but it's comforting to me."

Several other Jewish friends offered helpful perspectives on set, memorized traditional prayers. "Set prayers," said Peter, "are very much an engine. Because the form is so well known you very seldom read it: you have the chant in your body. It's a procession, just as the Mass is a procession and a recognition of moments leading to that ecstatic union [with God]. Set prayers are a highway: once you've hit the ignition and the prayers and responses get going, it leads you inexorably forward and focuses you toward that next moment, where you suddenly are cast into that openness of prayer." He added, "Not only are you praying, and praying with people who are with you, but you have all your ancestors surrounding you."

Elena, an artist and writer, wrote to me: "My quite traditional Jewish education did not encourage personal prayer or talking to God on one's own. My understanding of traditional Judaism is that the prayers are vessels into which one pours one's love for God. They provide a structure. I've heard it suggested that when one says the traditional prayers it relieves one of the pressure of having to focus on and formulate language for one's own sentiments. It's almost as though the prayers are a purifying force that binds the individual to the community and guards against too much focus on oneself as an individual."

Set prayers, said Anita, "are the prayers that are most part of my life. It's a very unmodern, un-American form of prayer—not spontaneous, not from the heart; you say it because it's sunset on Friday night, because the calendar says it's the new moon. . . . Friday night Shabbat prayers are the most powerful prayers in my life. They are spoken in my house around the table when everyone gets home, with our arms around each other. It's very much about reconnecting to what's important—in some ways the words are irrelevant. It's set to song and very powerful; the blessing over the candles has a very haunting melody. It's sort of a songfest, and you look around the table at who else is there, singing. There's a special blessing you say over your children—that they should grow up—and it's getting back in touch with the fact that you're grateful that these people are here and you're here and you have the gift of this child. That's what those prayers are about."

The Hebrew prayers, she added, "are often about food; they're tactile; they have a kind of dimensionality. They're really old—a lot of mouths have been all over them. I don't own them. They're not mine in a personal way."

Raised without memorized prayers, I learned all my set prayers as an adult—though I managed to pick up "Now I lay me down to sleep" through some piece of childhood reading, and the Lord's Prayer during my long sojourn with the French Reformed girl scouts. In my public prayer life, my set prayers belong to the community, and to me with and inside the community. They are the sung Psalms, the hymns, and the words of the Eucharistic liturgy. Some words move me more than others—especially words set to song and the brief sentence at the start of the Eucharistic Prayer, which opens the sequence leading to the receiving of communion, "lift up your hearts." It does in fact make my heart leap—every time.

In my private prayer life, I have made up prayers as I go, or remained silent, with a few exceptions. Interestingly, the two set prayers that stand out, from my early twenties and late thirties, both involve Mary. I was quite surprised when this happened. It was unexpected, unplanned: when I became a Catholic, Mary and the saints were the last figures with whom I thought I would "connect." Over the years, I have become devotedly attached to them. One never knows the surprises God will bring.

My third year in divinity school, the first full year I was a Catholic, was a spiritually barren year for me. The year before had been full of a sense of the presence of God, a year of fire and consolation. No sooner had I been baptized, confirmed, and received into the church than (as I later put it) "Bingo! The Big Desert." It was, to be blunt, a horrendous year. The spiritual bonuses of my time of early conversion had gone underground; it was a trying time in my inner life. I was in the process of breaking up with—or being left by—the man I had thought I was going to marry. I was studying for integrative exams for my Master of Divinity degree. My family was still not reconciled to my conversion to Catholicism. It was winter in Boston, cold, damp, and miserable. That winter, inexplicably, I found myself saying Hail Marys—only Hail Marys, not the Rosary—walking home from school in the cold. The prayer was like an anchor in the storm.

The other appearance of a Mary-prayer was more recent, the early 1990s, but had its genesis about ten years before. The pastor of the church I was attending then, who also happened to be my former Canon Law professor, took me aside one day at a party, entirely out of the blue, and said, "You know, if you're ever really having a rough time, you should pray the Memorare." The Memorare is a prayer to Mary for her intercession. *Memorare*, "Remember," is the first word of the Latin version of the prayer.

My pastor, Jack, chatted briefly, and went back to his drink and conversation in the other room. I filed away the information, assuming I would not have occasion to use it. But I prayed the Memorare, years later, the summer I was finishing my first book. I had been working for five years on this book on Catholic women, I had no money left and was deeply in debt, my family thought I was mad because I was still working on the book and not earning a decent living, I was months past my publisher's deadline, and I often sat at the computer crying and tapping out the words. I taught myself the Memorare that summer, memorized it sentence by sentence, and said it all summer and all fall, until I finished the book. Did it make sense? I didn't care, and still do not. I never expect life to be clean and logical. I tend to think, when something like this happens in prayer, "Ah—I am doing this," and then, having noticed it, to keep on. During that time I was still practicing yoga, going to Mass, and attending the occasional Women-Church independent feminist liturgy. But I prayed the Memorare, and again the prayer to Mary was a kind of anchor in the storm. It really was a prayer of desperation— absolute, utter, total desperation: "HELP!"

During the writing of this book, I memorized again, this time a much longer prayer, Saint Patrick's Breastplate, which I am still in

the process of committing to memory; it also is one of the last texts
I thought I would learn or desire to learn. Part exorcism, part hymn
to creation, part creedal statement, the seventh- or eighth-century
prayer attributed to fifth-century Patrick is lyrical and powerful. It is
eight sections or stanzas long and contains a few words with which I
am uncomfortable and many others that go straight to my heart. I
recite it aloud, like the other set prayers. It is bodily as much as mental, freighted with the power of all the voices that have spoken it
throughout the centuries. It is no accident, I think, that one of the
best television dramas in history, *Nothing Sacred*, chose to feature it in
a show about a Catholic parish on Halloween, the eve of All Saints'.

Carole, a Catholic sister, does not limit either her own prayer or
her teaching of prayer to memorized, set prayers. She does, however, keep them in the mix: "At the high school where I taught for
many years, the homeroom teachers and students stayed together
for all four years of high school. I had six homerooms [in succes-
sion]. For the first five I tried all different types of prayer: Scripture,
student-planned, spontaneous. For what ended up being my last
homeroom, I gave the students a card with the prayer of Saint
Francis on the first day of their freshman year, and they said that
prayer every morning for the rest of their high school years. My reason for doing that was my own realization that the different prayers
we said at different times of the day during my own high school
years had a great influence on me. I never told the kids that, of
course," she added. "That was a very difficult group of students; it
was all I could do to get them to be quiet for prayer, much less participate. On the morning of their graduation, a bunch of the worst
troublemakers came to me with a large package, the gift of the
homeroom to me. When I opened it I realized it was a plaque and
thought, 'Ugh, just what I don't need or want.' I remember the
moment clearly, for when I read the plaque I was in tears. On one
side was the prayer of Saint Francis, on the other 'You have
inscribed this prayer in our hearts . . .' and their names."

๛๑๛

THE PRAYER OF SAINT FRANCIS

Lord,
Make me an instrument of your peace.
Where there is hatred, let me sow love;
Where there is injury, pardon;
Where there is doubt, faith;
Where there is despair, hope;
Where there is darkness, light;
Where there is sadness, joy.

> O divine master,
> grant that I may not so much seek
> to be consoled, as to console;
> to be understood, as to understand;
> to be loved, as to love.
> For it is in giving that we receive,
> it is in forgiving that we are forgiven,
> it is in dying that we are born
> to eternal life.

FRANCIS OF ASSISI (1182–1226)

THE MEMORARE

Remember,
O most gracious Virgin Mary,
that never was it known
that anyone who fled to thy protection,
implored thy help,
and sought thy intercession
was left unaided.
Inspired with this confidence,
I fly unto thee,
O Virgin of Virgins,
my Mother.
To thee I come,
before thee I stand
sinful and sorrowful.

O Mother of the Word Incarnate,
despise not my petition
but in thy mercy
hear and answer me.
Amen.

HOW TO MEMORIZE A TEXT
IF YOU'VE NEVER DONE IT

The text can be a prayer, a Scripture passage, a poem, a piece of spiritual writing.

Pick a short text.

Pick one that speaks to your heart and/or to your current life situation.

Read it once silently.

Read it once aloud, slowly. Feel the words in your mouth. Listen to their sound.

Close your eyes, breathe in and out, and opening them, read the text again silently.

Read it aloud again.

Then repeat and memorize cumulatively, i.e., line by line. Or phrase by phrase.

When you are repeating your one-phrase-at-a-time, or two, don't look at the text!

Use as a measure of how short the line or phrase should be whatever you can hold in your mind at one time. If that means three or four words, so be it. This is not a race.

You can do this in one sitting, or one or two lines a day if you prefer.

Commuting time—walk, subway ride—is a good time to do this.

You can repeat your sentence or sentences internally (for instance, if you are doing this on the subway), though it helps to memorize with your voice, too.

You can do this while you exercise: walk, run, pedal on a stationary bike.

Once in a while, stop in the midst of the memorizing and think of the mean-ing of what you are learning to remember. Savor, treasure the sentence, line, phrase, or cluster of words.

If you forget from day to day, stay with one sentence as long as you need to. It may be your memory; it may also be the Holy Spirit urging you to meditate on that part of the text.

Eventually, if you make this repetition a daily practice, you will remember. This does involve discipline. Try it, for instance, for a week.

Don't start with a reading that makes you angry.

Don't memorize in the bathtub. Just enjoy the water.

PRAYING THE ROSARY

There are many ways of praying the Rosary. Traditionally people have prayed the Rosary both alone and in groups, and today many adaptations exist. Trappist monk Basil Pennington speaks, for instance, of the literal, meditative, and contemplative approaches, and Benedictine sister Joan Chittister offers a model for contemplative group prayer of the Rosary as well as Rosary medita-tions focusing on peace and using the Psalms. What follows is the most basic structure of the Rosary. It is only a starting point. Remember that the Rosary, like all methods of prayer, is only a method. What matters is your communion with God.

A rosary (the beads) is composed of:
• a cross
• five beads
• a medal and
• five "decades" (sets of ten beads) separated from each other by a small chain with another bead in the middle of the chain.

The prayers used in the traditional Rosary (the sequence of prayer using the beads) include:
• the Lord's Prayer ("Our Father," the prayer of Jesus)
• the Hail Mary
• the "Glory Be" or Doxology
• the Apostles' Creed, usually said at the beginning of the Rosary while holding the cross; some people prefer to simply bless themselves (make the sign of the cross) with this small cross in hand.

Praying the Rosary:

- After blessing yourself or reciting the Apostles' Creed:
  On the first large bead (closest to the cross) recite the Our Father, followed by a Hail Mary on each of the next three beads. On the chain before the next large bead, recite the "Glory Be."

- Now begin the meditation on the mysteries (five "joyful," five "sorrowful," five "glorious"):
  If you are beginning with the joyful mysteries, recall—or announce aloud—the first of these mysteries, the Annunciation. You may stay brief and literal, or reflect on this mystery by adopting a meditative approach, pondering the scene of the Annunciation, reading the corresponding reflection in Joan Chittister's book or another commentary on the Rosary.

- Then recite the Our Father on the large bead and the Hail Mary on each of the ten smaller beads. After the tenth bead, recite the Glory Be. When you have completed that set, you have prayed one decade of the Rosary.

To complete the circle, literally and figuratively, pray through five decades, all around the string of heads.

The Joyful Mysteries
- the Annunciation
- the Visitation
- the Nativity
- the Presentation
- the Finding of the Child Jesus in the Temple

The Sorrowful Mysteries
- the Agony in the Garden
- the Scourging
- the Crowning with Thorns
- the Carrying of the Cross
- the Death of Jesus

The Glorious Mysteries
- the Resurrection
- the Ascension
- the Descent of the Holy Spirit
- the Assumption of Mary
- the Crowning of Mary as Queen of All Creation

A Celtic Blessing

Deep peace of the running wave to you.
Deep peace of the flowing air to you.
Deep peace of the quiet earth to you.
Deep peace of the shining stars to you.
Deep peace of the Son of peace to you.

Iona Community, Isle of Iona

CHAPTER NINETEEN

Petition, Protection, and Praise: Praying for Others and Asking for Prayers

You have heard that it was said, "You shall love your neighbor and hate your enemy." But I say to you, "Love your enemies and pray for those who persecute you."

MATTHEW 5:43–44

At the end of the road they will ask me
—Have you lived? Have you loved?
And not saying a word I
Will open my heart full of names.

DOM PEDRO CASALDALIGA

Prayer, including Christian prayer, is far more than "bidding prayer." Nevertheless, bidding, begging, crying, beseeching have their place in prayer if we are to pray from our full humanity, which is, after all, the only place we can begin. Always, the reality of suffering and the power of evil lurk beneath human petitions. I asked Ann, the young woman from Pennsylvania, what she prayed for: "Protection," she answered. "Praying for protection, for myself, and as intercessory prayer for loved ones in times of illness, crisis, or danger, is a long-standing thread in my life of prayer. I guess I've always had the conviction that the will of the holy is the will for well-being. I pray to the saints, the angels, the guardian angels, Mary and Joseph, the Sacred Heart of Jesus."

"Help!" is perhaps the most common of prayers and the most spontaneous. The question is, what kind of help do we want? Sometimes we ourselves do not know; the cry of help escapes us first; then we think. Or it may take us awhile to reflect on the kind of help we really need—remember Tom, as a child, praying for a horse. Lee, a Buddhist cyber-friend, told the following story: "Back in my college days, I found myself in a park, where I bumped into a coworker's father, who was sitting on a picnic table enjoying the summer air. He said he was broke and asked me if I'd like to buy a beer and split it with him. I said yes, and as we sat and talked and sipped, he mentioned to me that he used to find himself in the drunk tank every Saturday or Sunday morning after drinking too much. He would always pray to Jesus and ask him to get out of the mess he was in. The prayer never worked and he kept finding himself with a hangover in jail on the weekend. Then, one day, he realized that he was praying for the wrong thing. Instead of praying to be removed from his troubles, he began to pray to Jesus that he might learn to accept and deal with his situation. After that realization, he never found himself in the drunk tank again."

My friend Ellen wrote from Wisconsin: "As you know, I've read a lot about spirituality, and I know that it's supposedly somewhat immature to continually beseech God to 'Pleeeese make good things happen.' But I do it all the time. . . . I do remember a moment of significant shift in my prayer life. I was a very young social worker, working in very rural counties with handicapped infants and children in their homes. I often went into homes that were somewhat rough and, to me, scary. As I would drive into one particularly difficult farm I would pray, 'Please God, don't let me find any bodies.' (I tended toward the dramatic intercession.) One Sunday the preacher at church said something that somehow addressed my situation exactly. The next week I consciously changed the whispered prayer as I drove into the yard to 'Please God, let me know what to do with any bodies that I find.' As the years have gone on, and I'm no longer likely to discover actual violence in my days, I still find myself whispering before a scary event, 'Let me know what to do with any bodies that I find.' I do believe that that shift has allowed me to know that within myself is the capability to handle whatever comes along. God simply helps me find that capability."

What about matters that are simply out of our control, like the weather? Carrie wrote in August from California's scorching Sacramento Valley, where it never rains in the heat of summer, that she was looking out at an unexpected shower, blessing God "for hearing my 'special intention' at Mass this morning, and the more potent, because more desperate, prayers of all the people who have to work outdoors today." The next day, with temperatures close to 110 degrees, the lightning accompanying the rain touched off over 150 fires in and near Sacramento. Carrie heard from Michigan that the weather there was unusually cool, threatening gardeners' crops of tomatoes, and from her mother in West Virginia that the local peach growers were "grumbling about the cool weather that prevents the peaches from ripening. Meanwhile, we have farmworkers, firefighters, and the usual people (police, road crews, food-stall vendors, air-conditioner repairers) who have to work outdoors in this heat. I would ask your prayers that God move about ten degrees from the Sacramento Valley to Michigan, and another ten degrees from here to West Virginia," she wrote to an online forum of approximately a thousand people where prayer requests are as frequent as academic discussions. She said quite seriously, "We have plenty to spare. If He can make the sun stand still and calm storm winds, He can shift some heat."

Kirk, who grew up in rural Iowa, commented after moving to the San Francisco Bay Area: "I am struck by people's disdain out here over praying for the weather. In a class I had last fall, we were reading an essay that used praying for rain as an example. One student thought that this was a particularly poor choice of petitionary prayer because the weather just happens. I sensed the scientific confidence underlying disdain, and share this to a certain degree, but also knew immediately that she had not grown up in a farming community. When water comes out of the tap on demand, why pray? When either water comes out of the sky or thousands of families are forced into bankruptcy, prayer for rain is no longer an intellectual folly but a psychological obligation. No matter how silly, people pray for what they need. I don't think Jesus ever told us to do otherwise."

From praying for ourselves to praying for loved ones is only a small step. When Ann pleads for protection, she knows the threats to others as well as those to herself, and prays accordingly. The sun and rain shine and fall on us all. In church on Sunday, I hear petitions for relatives with cancer, a family losing its home, homeless persons sleeping on the street, war and conflict in the Middle East, Ireland, and Rwanda. Friends ask me to pray for them—a job search, a relationship conflict, a family illness. In cases like these—work, love, health, where causes and factors are so complex—we move back and forth along the spectrum: Please, make it better. Help me make it better. Your will be done. Help me to understand. Help them to endure. It is easy to shift from one to the other, carrying our loved ones or our own situation of pain and need into the different moods and modes of prayer.

Kirk remembered the years before his mother's death: "With my mom's illness having lasted so long, thirteen years before she died, my family struggled a great deal with how to pray and what to pray for. Toward the end of her life we had moved from praying for specific outcomes to praying generally to be kept in the 'center of God's grace.' Anything else felt controlling."

Praying for a miracle, praying as a way of remembering, praying as accompaniment and presence: they may overlap. Sometimes there is only remembering. When I pray for my beloved friends who live with AIDS, I ask and do not ask. When a friend was diagnosed with breast cancer last year, I asked and did not ask. Like them, I go from howling to being mute. More and more often I place them before God, or perhaps—since I doubt God has ever forgotten them—remind myself before God that they are in God's sight, God's hearing, God's arms, God's care, God's heart. Often my prayer is simply the names of my friends, with feeling.

My friend Tom nearly died over a decade ago, in his early thirties, when he was living in Hawaii. Brutally attacked from behind, he does not remember anything beyond the first blow. He was found with no identification on a Honolulu sidewalk and regained enough consciousness to ask to be taken to St. Francis Hospital, a Catholic hospital with which he had professional ties as well as a common religious affiliation, rather than Queen's Medical Center. He went into cardiac arrest twice and spent five days in the intensive-care unit. "My first conscious realization," he remembered, "was seeing a Sister of St. Francis I knew saying the Rosary." "What was it like," I asked, "to know she had been sitting there praying for you?" "I knew her through my work," Tom answered. "She was the head administrator there and a very, very tough woman. It meant a lot that this person, whom I only knew as a hard-core businesswoman, was just there praying the Rosary by my bed."

I have taken to keeping a little book in which I write, irregularly— someday, I think, I will do this faithfully, on a daily basis—the names of those who have asked for my prayers or whom the Spirit has moved me to remember. The act of writing their names focuses my attention. I also fear forgetting others' requests and my own resolutions, on the days—which seem to grow more frequent—when more than ten people are on the list. My friend Nancy keeps a shell in the corner of her apartment where she prays most often, and places in it slips of paper with the names of people or intentions for prayers.

Petition expands our circle: I find that one name brings to mind a second and third, one area of conflict another. Praying for others is also a way of bringing the wide world into our prayer. It enlarges our spiritual life. Remembering in prayer those who rejoice or grieve, those who govern, those who suffer from war, poverty, or racism expands our heart to include them, to move beyond our self-centeredness. It can also—though it does not always—move us to action on behalf of those for whom we pray. It is certainly no substitute for taking responsibility in the day to day. The question, says Tom, is always this: What will allow you—you who pray—to lead the life Jesus called you to live in the first place?

The prayer of petition also reminds us of the otherness of the ones for whom we pray. Two and a half years ago, after years of not being a member of a couple, I became involved with a man, and, as often happens in romance, complications arose. The details matter less than the fact that, after heady beginnings, our relationship ran into some difficult times. All too aware of what I wanted—emphasis on both "I" and "want"—I began praying for him. Praying *for him,* as opposed to praying for what I wanted. It was not easy. Those times of prayer taught me that loving meant understanding my beloved's otherness. Praying for him helped me love him, not only because I wanted to place his well-being before God, but perhaps more important, because I wanted to be reminded that praying for him was praying for *him*, in all the ways in which he was not me: to keep the line from blurring, to love and honor him as he was, including the ways in which I did not understand him, including the boundaries between us.

I remember not just praying for my loved one but asking, "God, help me to pray for him." Loving him seemed to come naturally. Praying for him, sometimes, did not. I was also well aware of the need to maintain a balance between this orientation toward the other and healthy self-care. Prayer is no substitute for receiving what one needs emotionally, nor for asking for what one needs from one's beloved, directly and clearly. Human petitioning and communicating are not easy; they require assertiveness and courage. Balancing them with the difficulty of praying for the other is complicated. The relationship ended. What I have kept and learned, among other things, has been a lesson in the act of praying for others as a way of honoring them: their existence, their difference.

Praying for others does not always change them. It does, however, change us. Rebecca, a nonprofit administrator in San Francisco, lost her husband to AIDS. "A very powerful lesson I learned when John was very ill was how prayer really works," she said. "I was saying healing prayers daily for him, thinking that his physical health might improve, but his health only declined, so I thought the prayers didn't have any effect. Only later on did I realize that the prayers worked on me—I was healed or transformed spiritually by saying them. I never held any anger towards him for dying or infecting me with HIV, even to this day, which most people have difficulty understanding. Also, I have had several dreams that assure me that John's spirit is extremely happy in the next world. So I know my prayer healed both of us spiritually, something I was not expecting to happen."

Healing and forgiveness are relatives. What if one's now former beloved has acted like a lout? "Forgive us our trespasses," Christians pray, "as we forgive those who trespass against us." Does the path to healing go through prayer? Does it go through anger? Through both? For how long? Healing involves forgiveness, but how soon is too soon? Let the other be other, I think, and far away from me—the lout, the former beloved. Meanwhile, I continue to pray Jesus' prayer, and come to understand why it is meant to be daily, regular, a constant meditation. *"Forgive us . . . as we forgive.* Unfortunately," writes C. S. Lewis, "there's no need to do any festooning here. To forgive for the moment is not difficult. But to go on forgiving, to forgive the same offence again every time it recurs to the memory—there's the real tussle."[1]

The other whom we love can also be the other who has hurt us, or the other whom we have hurt. From praying for another with whom one is entangled in love, friendship, and conflict it is not terribly far to that hard saying of Jesus, the urging—no, the command—that we pray for our enemies, the ultimate other. There we are, at the place where anger meets forgiveness—or far beyond it. Who wants to pray? How can we pray? Why forgive? How to act?

Alexia, an Episcopal woman in her late forties, recounted: "I have noticed that when I absolutely can't go into the Christian tradition and find help, I go elsewhere. For instance, my stepdaughter married a young man and they had a service that they wrote themselves and was done by a Unitarian minister, and that I found so appalling I thought, 'I've got to do something beside just sit there and radiate ill will.' My massage therapist said, 'Here is a Buddhist prayer practice where you try and reflect and radiate goodwill to all those surrounding you.' This included my husband's ex-wife, who was sitting in front of me at this ceremony. I thought, 'I'd better do it.' I did it. You just open yourself and ask that you be used to reflect the good of the universe. It got me through the ceremony. I didn't have a huge goal here; I just didn't want to create bad vibrations. I found it very powerful." She added: "I lost it, of course, once I started moving around, at the reception."

In some ways this practice is a meeting of petition and contemplation. "One other time," said Alexia, "in Maine, where we vacation, I was at a very polarized meeting, local town folks versus summer people. Many at the meeting kept talking about 'you people.' So again I kept doing this same practice; somewhere the mood shifted and there was no 'you people' being said and more listening going on, and I didn't say anything and I don't know if this had anything to do with it—but I don't know what else it would be.

Somehow my not getting into the polarization, by not being one of the parties, being other, it worked for me; there was one little spot in the room that wasn't hot or cold."

Stretch the prayer from personal to national enemies. What then? Several years after the first Gulf War, a Catholic online forum to which I belong had an extended discussion about the war and our prayer. What did your parish do, we asked each other. Were all remembered in prayer, including those our soldiers were fighting? Peggy wrote from Syracuse, New York: "During the Gulf War, my parish did pray for all those affected by the war, including Iraqis. More powerfully, on the front of the altar, there was a map of the Gulf War area (Kuwait, Iraq, etc.) with a transparency of a cruci-fied Christ superimposed on it." Gary, in Chicago, responded: "In the parish I was attending at the time, our staff produced a banner for the altar of a dove descending to the desert ground. The floor of the desert was an American flag. The dove looked like a B-1 bomber. Just took your breath away," he wrote sarcastically.

Shannon wrote from the Pacific Northwest: "When the Gulf War happened, I was in my second year as liturgy director at a parish in western Washington. Come the war, we arranged to leave the church open Sunday afternoons and invited different groups to be responsible for prayer at the top of each hour. The environment for the afternoon included our simple wooden Lenten cross standing behind a table which held a vigil candle—with a yellow ribbon around it; I'm still not sure how I feel about that one—and a note-book in which people were encouraged to write down the names of people they were praying for. One Sunday, I was setting up the envi-ronment for the afternoon prayer, and hauling the American flag out of the sanctuary, and the pastor, a retired Navy chaplain, con-fronted me and told me to put it back. I told him that it was not a part of the environment for that afternoon prayer, that we were here not to pray for 'our side,' but for an end to war and suffering for all people. He was not happy. He never did come to any of those prayer times." Shannon added, "Tacoma is home to two major military bases, both of them very much involved with the Gulf War. It would have been easy to assume God was on 'our side,' but I heard over and over from people how much they appreciated having the time and the space to pray, and the reminder that we are first sisters and brothers, children of one God."

Ingrid recounted discussions at an ecumenical seminary about Christian symbols and the war. One young woman had said that she saw the war in terms evocative of the book of Revelation, as a battle between good and evil, with the United States embodying good against Iraq's evil. "The following week," Ingrid wrote, "the mother of a twenty-seven-year-old soldier in the Gulf wept as she haltingly shared her thoughts. She explained that she had found a way to keep from self-serving, one-sided, un-Christian prayer. In her mind, she has adopted an anonymous Iraqi mother of an equally anonymous twenty-seven-year-old son. Every night she prays for and with her spiritual sister who may be religiously different and politically in the enemy camp, but who loves her son no less than the American woman. There is an awareness in this woman's decision of the tragedy of war, of shared humanity, and of the transforming power of love."[2]

The discussion on prayer brought about some hard questions. Bob wrote from California: "I certainly agree that the victim deserves comforting, prayer, support, first and always. The perpetrator, however, becomes a test of faith. There is a book with a title like *The Impossible Sayings of Jesus*. 'Love your enemies.' 'Turn the other cheek.' 'Do good to those who hate/persecute you.' 'Sell all you have and give.' . . . They do seem impossible, contrary to nature and reason. Did Jesus really say them? And mean them? How do we deal with them in real life? What does it mean to 'put on the mind of Christ'?"[3]

As I write [in the late 1990s], Iraq is again in the news, and the airwaves are full of strategic discussions, many of them comparing Saddam Hussein to Hitler. A bishop is fasting and praying with the civilian children of Iraq at heart. Prayers about Iraq slowly make their way back into public worship. What difference will they make, and to whom? "To whom do I pray?" said Mary. "Nobody. Nothing. But I pray *about* things—focus energy, give attention to, think about, hope for, and in that way pray. It works in that the attention stays there and perhaps has some impact."

People of faith have long believed in the power of prayer, not only to change the community or person who prays and to focus the attention on the person or situation prayed for, but also to effect visible and tangible change through the power of God. More recently, the medical profession has begun to take an interest in intercessory prayer, going beyond the behavioral research on meditation and relaxation to studies on the effectiveness of prayer.[4]

Ruth, a college administrator in her forties, said, "I grew up in a Christian Science church, with the knowledge and reinforcement of the power of prayer. Although I do not continue to practice church participation, I have very much continued to accept the religion's framework of the power of prayer. I accept that I need no intermediary in my communication with a higher being. I pray every morning in the shower. I no longer pray for outcomes, but rather to be a force for the right outcomes. My standard prayer is to 'follow Him/Her more nearly, love Him/Her more dearly, see Him/Her more clearly.' All else is in this context of wanting these things and being 'an instrument of Thy peace.'"

Ruth later wrote me about a fellow staff member who lay ill in a coma with slim hope for recovery. Administrators, students, and faculty at the nonreligious liberal arts college where she works held a large silent vigil on the college green where each prayed in his or her own way. Individuals unaffiliated with the college also prayed for the staff member, intensely and intentionally. The staff member recovered.

Trudi, a member of St. Columba for over ten years, decided to write me some of her experience of prayer. "I am a forty-one-year-old single/divorced/sort of widowed mother of two daughters aged nineteen and twenty-one. An incident reinforced my belief in prayers. It made me want to thank God in prayer. It was 1991 and I was going through a particularly difficult time. I was living about thirty-seven miles from San Francisco. I had bought a house, and during the freeze of 1990 the pipes froze and burst while I was away at work and ruined the house. In addition, we had two fires, my fiancé was killed in a motorcycle accident, my job had changed because of downsizing and a hearing loss. I was on disability and I was worried about money and my oldest daughter was running away for weeks at a time. I spent most of my days crying. I had turned to God for help. One day when my daughter had gone away again, I had lit a candle and opened a book called *Power of the Psalms*. I chose a Psalm that was indicated for the purpose of overpowering someone with a bad attitude. I read the

Psalm and after each reading said, 'I sought the Lord and he heard me and delivered me from all my fears.' I had been praying silently and fervently for over an hour. A friend and her son came over for a visit. [My friend] asked me what I was doing and she joined me. We were praying out loud for about fifteen minutes when my other daughter and my friend's son came in the living room to see what we were doing. Once they found out they began to pray also. After another ten to fifteen minutes had passed the phone rang. My friend said, 'That's Carmen!' I answered the phone and it was a crying, contrite Carmen ready to come home. We immediately said, 'Thank you Father!' I am happy to say she never ran away again. I cannot believe that was coincidence.

"Prayer makes God real," Trudi added. "I know He must be kind. When I have raged against Him, He forgives because He has answered my prayers after every horrible thing I might have said. Everything I ask for does not get answered in the manner I want. My current prayers are for strength, inner peace, to become tolerant and generally a better person. There is a song that says, 'He may not come when you want Him, but He's always [right] on time.' I believe this with all my heart."

Some people speak to God. Others also ask the intercession of the saints. I have found in both formal interviews and casual conversations that intercession has little to do with formal canonization. Judy is a teacher in the public school system in the Boston area, in her late forties, married and the mother of two. "Every day," she wrote me, "I pray to Father Walter Ciszek, S.J., for his intercession in the lives of people on my prayer list. Walter Ciszek was an American Jesuit who went into Poland in the 1930s to minister to workers. He was trapped there by the advent of World War II and managed to slip into Russia. He was arrested as a spy and spent the next twenty-odd years in prison—some in solitary at Lubyanka, some at hard labor in Siberia. His family presumed that he was dead. In the 1960s he was exchanged for a Russian 'spy.' Eventually he spent time at the John XXIII Center for Eastern Christian Studies at Fordham, where Jim [Judy's husband, a former Jesuit] lived and worked with him.

"Jim has told me that Father Walter was a gentle, spiritual man. He was also (as you can imagine) very stubborn. Well, shortly after his death in the 1970s a group was formed to advance his case for canonization." In the early 1990s, Jim was invited by the Ruthenian bishop of Passaic, New Jersey, to give testimony about his friend, around the time his and Judy's daughter developed asthma. "She was having a difficult time with it," Judy remembered, "and we had spent a number of nights with her in emergency rooms." She drove to New Jersey with her husband, and as she was waiting for him to finish his meeting and worrying about her daughter, Claire, she thought of Walter, and asked Walter to intercede for Claire. "Within weeks, Claire's asthma disappeared and she didn't have another attack for a year and a half." Judy began praying to Father Walter for church members and friends, especially those who were suffering from physical and emotional illness and distress: uterine pain, cancer, depression, difficulties between children and parents. The pain disappeared, two cases of cancer went into spontaneous remission, an infant needing heart surgery was cured without the need for surgical intervention. "I think of Father Walter as 'my' special saint," Judy wrote. "Even though I've never met him, I feel strongly connected to him, so I pray every day for his canonization and for the people on my lengthy list."

"I was always curious about the efficacy of prayer," said Peter. "When I was a child prayer was pretty much rote; it was musical, enthusiastic, but it wasn't needful. Being a good contemporary Jew, I found myself with agnostic questions. Whereas I could understand the solemnity of the moment, it seemed rather importunate to ask God for anything. It wasn't enough [for God] to create the world? Why do we have to keep whining? Can't we solve some of these problems ourselves? I would look around and see these people petitioning and think the equivalent of 'get a life.'

"But life," he said, "takes these turns: the eighties were not an easy time for many of us, our parents were aging and my friends were dying [of AIDS], and at one of those junctures in time I began attending services. I looked for a temple where I could be comfortable attending High Holy Days and ended up at Congregation Beth Simchat Torah, which had developed around the gay and lesbian community in New York at the time. They provide an umbrella for a whole range of religious practices—no one asked how traditional, Reform, or radical you were, they left me alone, it provided a haven.

There were times I would come in after services and just pray the *Amidah*. It gave a stability my inner life desperately needed. You know your life isn't working out right when you know the first names of all the nurses at New York Hospital emergency floor.

"That was my consolation; it gave me a chance to ventilate a lot of the fears and wishes I had at that time and to begin praying for friends' health, which was completely unique for me. There is no Jewish equivalent of Lourdes—there are shrines and tombs of various rabbis, kind of a cult; I am not of that tradition, though I can understand it—but one thing you can do while working your way through the *Amidah* is to create conversation. It's mostly supplication. Coming from a theater background, I started vetting these little dialogues, hat and cane, between me and God. I started asking questions. My mother had been in hospital for some time, having had a coronary episode, and my father had had surgery not long after. I asked, 'Do my prayers keep my parents alive?' and the answer immediately came back, 'Yes,' and I was completely devastated. It was not what I expected. I was prepared for 'You'll have to try and find out.' I cracked completely. According to all reports, I was just wailing uncontrollably—I was in *shul* [synagogue] at the time and my friends tried to comfort me.

"After that," Peter said, "I never questioned the efficacy of prayer. I may have lots of other doubts, but that's one I don't have. From that instant I have had more respect for the prayer life of others and an interest in the phenomenon of prayer. Now more than ever after that epiphany, I feel I can pray for people and on behalf of people. I never neglect my short list. It's very simple—it's generally in English and I name names."

"Is it a remembering to God?" I asked.

"Yes," Peter answered, "and remembering the connectedness to God of the people I love who may never pray, but I think it's part of my job [to pray for them]. I don't really pray for myself that much," he added. "I'm still apprehensive about that. But I do give thanks a lot."

THE WORD THAT IS A PRAYER

One thing you know when you say it,
all over the earth people are saying it with you:
a child blurting it out as the seizures take her,
a woman reciting it on a cot in the hospital.
What if you take a cab through the Tenderloin,
at a streetlight, a man in a wool cap,
yarn unraveling across his face, knocks at the window:
he says, *Please.*
By the time you hear what he's saying,
the light changes, the cab pulls away,
and you don't go back, though you know
someone just prayed to you the way you pray.
Please: a word so short
it could get lost in the air
as it floats up to God like the feather it is,
knocking and knocking, and finally
falling back to earth as rain,
as pellets of ice, soaking a black branch,
collecting in drains, leaching into the ground,
and you walk in that weather every day.

ELLERY AKERS

DELIVER ME

From the cowardice that dare not face new truths,
From the laziness that is contented with half truths,
From the arrogance that thinks it knows all truth,
Good Lord deliver me.

A PRAYER FROM KENYA

PRAYER FOR PEOPLE I DISLIKE

Loving God, Mysterious Wind-like Spirit,
blow strongly if you will
and surround with joy all those people whom I dislike.
Be gracious to those whose giftedness I envy.
Bless with wealth and success
those already annoyingly more successful than myself.
They deserve my encouragement, never my scorn.
I pray especially for all those
who do not particularly reverence me,
or may, in fact, dislike me and shun my company.
Give me eyes to see beauty and winsomeness
where I have not seen it before,
and give us all the self confidence to believe
that we would have no enemies at all
if we were known as you, Holy Wisdom, know us.
Amen.

          WILLIAM CLEARY

Lord, help me enter into that peace
which consists in having put my life in your hands.

          CARLO MARIA MARTINI

To God be glory;
To the angels honor;
To Satan confusion;
To the cross reverence;
To the church exaltation;
To the departed quickening;
To the penitent acceptance;
To the sick and infirm recovery and healing;
And to the four quarters of the world great peace and tranquility;
And on those who are weak and sinful may the compassion and
    mercies of our God come,

and may they overshadow us continually.
Amen.

A PRAYER FROM THE OLD SYRIAC
USED BY CHRISTIANS IN TURKEY, IRAN, AND SOUTH INDIA

∾⚭

THE LAST PRAYER OF PETITION EVER

(written between New York and Chicago 35,000 feet up)

Sigmund Freud has put me wise
that God is merely the me
afraid to face the exploding crash of a 747
from the inside.

Also it is common knowledge
that doctors reserve the back wards
for people who daddy God for daily bread.
Of course theologians, always the last to know,
keep asking for little red wagons
while everyone else is buying them at Sears.

So
heaven is not stormed by my "gimmes."
I no longer beg God
"to make mine enemies the footstool under my feet."
I am busy with the upholstering myself
My prayer life has taken a collegial,
adult, Vatican II-ish turn.
I do not beseech a mercy or beg an intercession
(needless to say importuning is out)
but consult with the Senior Partner on affairs personal, social, and cosmic.

So it is
I wonder who was addressed
when in the sudden drop of an air pocket
my heart relocated to the space behind my teeth
and someone sitting in my seat screamed,
"O my God don't let the plane fall!"

JOHN SHEA

CHAPTER TWENTY

Reading with the Heart:
Lectio Divina Revisited

Listen, my people,
mark each word.
I begin with a story,
I speak of mysteries
welling up from ancient depths
heard and known from our elders.
We must not hide
this story from our children
but tell the mighty works
and all the wonders of God.

PSALM 78:1–4

For as the rain and the snow come down from heaven,
and do not return there until they have watered the earth, making
    it bring forth and sprout,
giving seed to the sower and bread to the eater,
so shall my word be that goes out from my mouth;
it shall not return to me empty,
but it shall accomplish that which I purpose,
and succeed in the thing for which I sent it.

ISAIAH 55:10–11

There is an inner dynamic in the evolution of all true love that leads to a level of communication "too deep for words." There the lover becomes inarticulate, falls silent, and the beloved receives the silence as eloquence.

Thelma Hall

We read for pleasure, to acquire information, to fulfill an assignment. We can also read in a meditative mode, slowly, chewing on and digesting the words. Reading may also lead beyond itself, to the place of contemplation "too deep for words," as Cenacle sister Thelma Hall names it. This is the end point of *lectio divina*, the recently revived monastic practice of which I wrote in chapter 5.

The four steps of *lectio*—reading *(lectio)*, meditation *(meditatio)*, prayer *(oratio)*, and contemplation *(contemplatio)*—are not so much a method as stages of a relationship with God that deepens or unfolds in many of the ways human relationships grow. Hall writes that *lectio*, "a proven path to contemplation for centuries . . . engages the whole person: mind, heart and spirit—the intellect and imagination, the will and the affections. All are at some point activated by grace, reaffirming the fact that Lectio Divina is not an objective technique to be learned and followed as a system which will 'produce' deep prayer. On the contrary, it is an organic process, which takes place over a period of time, both in the *microcosm* of a single prayer period, and in the *macrocosm* of a lifetime engagement with God in the lived prayer of faithful love."[1]

Hall distinguishes, as other spiritual writers do, between spiritual reading and *lectio divina*. I have described earlier the four stages and some of the history of the practice of *lectio*. Trappist monk Thomas Keating, Hall, and others call it a "method-less method," of which reading and meditation on the reading are only the first half, though certainly not separate from the affective prayer and contemplation that form the other components of *lectio*. *Lectio*, and the resting-in-God that is its deepest gift, are indeed accessible to all. They are not dependent on education or class, gender or race. Dwelling in God and knowing God's love: the invitation is open to all. It is as rich and generous as the opening words of the fifty-fifth chapter of Isaiah:

Ho, everyone who thirsts,
come to the waters;
and you that have no money,
come, buy and eat!
Come, buy wine and milk
without money and without price.
Why do you spend your money
for that which is not bread,
and your labor for that which
does not satisfy?
Listen carefully to me, and eat what is good,
and delight yourselves in rich food.
Incline your ear, and come to me;
listen, so that you may live.[2]

While I would make the same distinction between *lectio* and spiritual reading, I suggest making a stop, for a while, at the practice of spiritual reading—not to the detriment of the full sequence of *lectio*, but as a discipline in itself, an option among many. There are several related spiritual disciplines that begin with the book, or with the word, among them spiritual reading, reading as a spiritual practice, prayer from Scripture, and *lectio*.

Rediscovering the practice of slow meditative reading in the age of computers and MTV can be fruitful. This kind of reading may be more difficult for us than in the past. Can we sit still that long? What is our relationship to books? What is our relationship to words, especially slow, savored words? Spiritual reading is now a countercultural activity. It has by no means disappeared, and in some circles is on the increase, but it vaunts neither the preferred speed nor the preferred medium of the hour. Slow words: taste and see them.

Spiritual or meditative reading can take place anywhere: a quiet corner or outdoor location, the bus or subway, a doctor's waiting room, the queue at the bank, the unemployment office. I am a member of the crossover generation: I can no longer live without my computer, but I grew up on books and was one of those children who read under the covers with a flashlight after the lights were out, when I was supposed to be asleep. The Internet has many spiritual resources,[3] but nothing can replace the intimacy between a person and a book—and I say this both as a book lover and a well-hooked user of the e-waves. Holding the book, reading it, returning to a phrase or a word, pondering and letting the imagination do its work, opening the heart to the images: all this, part of any act of reading, is very close to prayer.

Ever since the texts have been with us, reading the Bible has been an entryway, a gate, a springboard or starting point for prayer; it has even been prayer itself. Fred spoke to me of using the words of the Bible as prayers—Psalms as well as several of the Epistles of Paul. "It's so hard," he said, "knowing what to pray for other people. Paul's prayer in Ephesians 1:17–19 or 3:14–19 is a prayer for someone else, and it helps.[4] Otherwise I'd tend to pray, 'I wish this person would just get their act together.' The Lord's Prayer is the same: we pray 'your kingdom come,' *then* 'give us this day . . .' so we get God's program in mind first."

Cheryl, who described herself as "a single woman in her early forties and a born-again evangelical," spoke also of the relationship between Scripture and prayer. She had recently been told her project management job in Boston was coming to an end; she was also suffering from depression at the time we spoke. "I'm in a funk," she said. "I'm not suicidal, but I'm just getting through the days. . . . The Psalms seem to reflect accurately what's in my heart; it happened last night before I went to bed; I started reading the Psalms, and there was God speaking to me through the Psalms, helping me to pray to Him." She added, "Because I have the Holy Spirit inside me, because I made a decision to follow Christ, I believe God reveals Himself through His word. I have the ability to understand what He reveals because I have the Holy Spirit inside me; someone who doesn't will find it foolishness. The Scripture was comforting and healing because it spoke through the Holy Spirit."

Other Christians pray the Scriptures in the more structured setting of the Daily Office or Liturgy of the Hours. Andrew, a colleague in California, related: "One of my Episcopalian friends reports that when a Presbyterian visited and saw the readings in the Book of Common Prayer Daily Office, the Presbyterian said, 'You people must think that God likes to be read to. . . .'" Bruce, a high church Episcopal, told me: "At Mass, my most profound experiences have come as a result of focusing on some bit of truth gleaned from the Scripture readings or the sermon, tying it in my mind to the Eucharist, and taking it to myself in receiving communion." Even without explicit reference to the Eucharistic meal, the Jewish and Christian Scriptures themselves are dotted with language about the sweetness of God's word.

"From one end to the other," writes Yves Congar, "the people of God is characterized and constituted by the acts of listening to the word and welcoming it in an active faith. It has become almost banal today to say that the Jewish people, people of the Bible, is characterized by hearing, whereas the Greek people, initiator of the arts and of our human culture, is characterized by sight. This seems incontrovertible." The relationship between God and human beings always involves hearing, and even manifestations of God reach their final form through message, word, and voice, not through vision. "Nothing is more significant in this respect than the episode of the burning bush in the third chapter of the books of Exodus," Congar writes. "Moses draws near to *see*, but he only *hears*—and, in fact, he veils or hides his face for fear that his gaze might fix itself on God, for 'No human person can see God's face and live.'" To see God is a reality marking the end of time; it "would abolish history and be the end of it."[5]

Spiritual reading is not just Scripture reading. The same meditative, sometimes repetitive, savoring method applies to other kinds of literature. "The first kind of meditation that I was exposed to in the [AA] program," said Barbara, "was reading spiritual literature every morning. There are all these little books—they gave me three in the hospital where I got sober. One I still carry with me everywhere, almost thirteen years later, the 'twenty-four-hour-a-day' book. Most of these books are not approved AA literature, but almost all of us, in my area anyway, have been exposed to at least that one. By the time I had three years [of sobriety behind me], I had a stack of little books that I read every morning. I had one book that I kept at work and propped up on the keyboard of my computer so I could remember the 'thought for the day.' This is the godly reading, but it is also the daily discipline. Before I got sober, the only thing I did every day was drink. The only discipline I had was to go to work. Now I was learning discipline in things where nobody could see me if I didn't do it. My sponsor would know if I skipped a meeting, but daily prayer and meditation is something I do because they have convinced me it is a part of this way of life that I want so much. 'If you want what we have,' our literature says, 'and are willing to go to any lengths to get it.' I still do spiritual reading almost every day. Now it's more likely to be the *Course in Miracles* or something from Rabbi [Harold] Kushner or Emmet Fox, but it [remains] part of my routine."

"My thing is prayer with poetry," said Leith, who offers spiritual direction and serves on the hospitality staff of an Episcopal monastery. "I use a lot of poetry in spiritual direction and with people on retreats. Sometimes for a variety of reasons people who come to see me cannot stand the Bible: they may come from fundamentalist backgrounds where they have been clubbed to death with it, or they may be women sensitive to hierarchical exclusivist language in the Bible. I don't make them like the Bible, but I am interested in their having a relationship with the holy and also with Jesus—but it doesn't have to be scriptural; it could be visual." In her work of spiritual direction and hospitality, Leith encounters a large number of artists, therapists, and priests. "Many of those people tend to be visual in their response to reality, so poetry works really well. It gives you a way in if you say to someone, 'What's your image of God?' and they answer, 'I don't know' or 'I have one I formed when I was seven years old and I hate it'—so you try to expand it through poetry."

Cecilio, a manager and publisher in Washington, D.C., reads theology and Christian spirituality. "For the past year (or two?), I've been reading Romano Guardini's *The Lord* on the bus to work every morning. . . . You can't go past a paragraph without stopping. And Rahner's page-and-a-half discussion of the word 'God' kept me going for days in a prayer cloud: the emptiness, the otherness, the disemboweling of all that I knew until there was nothing else." For others, the theological and spiritual text will be Juliana of Norwich, Flannery O'Connor, Thomas Merton, or Langston Hughes. When I was working on *Generous Lives*, the interviews with Catholic women of all stations in life, their words and their wisdom, became my spiritual reading and yes, my *lectio divina* gateway for at least five years. I still draw on the insights of these women today. Some of their words are now recorded in a book, but it was the broader conversation, the interview, a primarily oral form, that was my spiritual "reading."

Another set of words, inscribed not in a book but on two public monuments, one of stone, one of cloth, serve as gateways to prayer, not just for us as individuals but in a much more communal and powerful way for our society, or at least for substantial segments of it. Both their creation and their broad appeal testify to our hunger for memory and our need for meditation. Secular monuments, with their own rituals, have acquired the weight and substance of prayer.

I remember my first visit to the Vietnam Memorial in Washington, D.C., as an event of memory and prayer, though I did not name it as such on that raw, rainy day. The Vietnam Memorial has changed forever our experience of monuments to the dead. The dark wall inscribed with names grows bits of life. People bring flowers and medals, make rubbings of their loved ones' names, meet and embrace, weep and tell stories. So it was too in my encounter with the Names Project AIDS Quilt when it first came to Boston: like the Vietnam Memorial, the Quilt is a live place, no lonely obelisk in the town square but a place of meeting and community. At the Quilt too, people come together through the power of names. It tells stories, spells out the memories in material that almost seems made of flesh. Encountering the Quilt is in itself an act of spiritual reading, part contemplation of icons, part reading of stories, names, poetry, and prayer. Exhibits of the Quilt panels—now too numerous to be shown together in one place—often occur with a formal reading aloud of the names of the dead.

Both the traveling AIDS Quilt and the Vietnam Memorial call us to a slow reading of names, weighty, layered, evoking faces, lives, blood, love, unfinished business. "*¡Presente!*" This too is what Barbara called "the godly reading" in holy time. The dead are present, a vast communion of saints, and with them our love, struggle, anger, and grief—and, because we have named them, our hope.

PRAYING WITH THE SCRIPTURES

Summary: 6 "P's"

Prepare a passage from Scripture and have it marked and ready.

Place. Where you are alone and uninhibited in your response to God's presence.

Posture. Relaxed and peaceful. A harmony of body with spirit.

Presence of God. Be aware of it and acknowledge and respond to it. When you are ready, turn to the

Passage. Read the passage from Scripture slowly and listen attentively.

PAUSE.

Don't be anxious. Don't try to look for implications or lessons or profound thoughts or conclusions or resolutions. Be content to be like a child who climbs into its father's or mother's lap and listens to his or her words and stories.

Carry on a conversation (sometimes called a colloquy) with God about what you have heard. Think of God in the second-person singular ("You"). Tell God what you are thinking and feeling. What would you give to God? What do you want of God?

Praying Scripture has nothing to do with "getting through" passages and books; it has everything to do with letting the meaning and the values of each single word sink into your life.

After the period of prayer is over, it may be helpful to reflect back over the experience of prayer. This review will help you notice what the Lord is doing in your experience.

ADAPTED FROM ARMAND NIGRO

LECTIO DIVINA

Saint John of the Cross's paraphrase of a verse from Saint Luke's Gospel (11:9) provides us with an outline of the four steps of *Lectio*:

Seek in READING,

and you will find in MEDITATION;

knock in PRAYER
and it will be opened to you
in CONTEMPLATION.

. . . The experience of this movement is not a programmed or automatic 1-2-3-4 progression. . . . Prayer is always a gift. *Lectio* is an attempt not to fabricate it, but to enable us to respond to the gift from its first invitation, and to dispose ourselves for its development. We can bring no "time table" of our own to the process.

1. Reading: *lectio*

    Quiet the body and mind. Choose a text—preferably a short one—and read it slowly, listening to it interiorly with full attention. Personalize the words as God speaking to you, now.

2. Meditation: *meditatio*

    Respond by receiving the reading at a deeper level. Move into it in faith. Dwell on and in it with imagination or intellect. Let it move you.

3. Prayer: *oratio*

    This is not something to do, but a spontaneous movement of the heart in response to the leading of the Spirit. In *oratio*, the heart takes over, longs and calls out for God.

4. Contemplation: *contemplatio*

    In the three other phases, activity has remained a dominant factor. As we move more deeply into relation with God, God takes over more and more by "closing down" our natural facilities of reason and imagination. We experience a kind of drying up of devotion and feeling, an inability to meditate as before. We are drawn to solitary prayer, attentive and loving, but obscure, a "passive attention."

    Receive and place no obstacle to the movement of the Spirit. Follow the attraction to interior silence and remain in loving attentiveness, drawn into the darkness of God's love. Contemplation is a strange new land, where everything natural to us seems to be turned upside down: we learn a new language—silence—and a new way of being—not to do but simply to be—and come to understand God's seeming absence as presence.

    ADAPTED FROM THELMA HALL

CHAPTER TWENTY-ONE

Ritual and Healing Touch

Now he was teaching in one of the synagogues on the sabbath.
And just then there appeared a woman with a spirit that had crip-
pled her eighteen years. She was bent over and was quite unable to
stand up straight. When Jesus saw her, he called her over and said,
"Woman, you are free from your ailment." When he laid his hands
on her, immediately she stood up straight and began praising God.

LUKE 13:10–13

During supper Jesus . . . got up from the table, took off his outer
robe, and tied a towel around himself. Then he poured water into a
basin and began to wash the disciples' feet and to wipe them with
the towel that was tied around him. He came to Simon Peter, who
said to him, "Lord, are you going to wash my feet?" Jesus answered,
"You do not know now what I am doing, but later you will understand." Peter said to him, "You will never wash my feet." Jesus
answered, "Unless I wash you, you have no share with me." Simon
Peter said to him, "Lord, not my feet only but also my hands and
my head!" . . . After he had washed their feet, had put on his robe,
and had returned to the table, he said to them, "Do you know what
I have done to you? You call me Teacher and Lord—and you are
right, for that is what I am. So if I, your Lord and Teacher, have

washed your feet, you also ought to wash one another's feet. For I
have set you an example, that you also should do as I have done to
you."

JOHN 13:2B–9, 12–15

O Christ for whom we search,
our help when help has failed,
give us courage to expose our need
and ask to be made whole;
that, being touched by you,
we may be raised to new life
in the power of your name,
Amen.

JANET MORLEY

Every two weeks or so, an ecumenical AIDS healing service
takes place somewhere in the Boston area or elsewhere in
eastern Massachusetts, sponsored by the Ecumenical Task
Force on AIDS and by the local congregation hosting the service.
The service is open to all. The flyer always reads, "For persons with
AIDS. For their families and friends. For those in the healing profes-
sions. For those who are afraid and angry. For those who wish it
would go away. For all who seek God's healing power." This traveling liturgical road show has been taking place for over a decade in
Episcopal, Roman Catholic, United Church of Christ, Lutheran,
Methodist, Quaker, Baptist, and a few Jewish communities. The
service usually reflects the tradition of the host congregation, but
almost always, it involves prayer and laying on of hands: words of
invocation, lamentation, petition, and consolation, accompanied by
a gesture of healing: gentle touch, person to person, flesh upon
flesh.

The AIDS healing services are probably the most powerful times
of communal prayer I have been privileged to experience. Most of
the time I have attended them, it has been as a "minister of healing,"
sometimes at my own church, once or twice at others. The ministers
of healing are both lay and ordained men and women, from different

traditions; their role is to pray, silently and aloud, and to lay hands on those who request the healing gesture and prayer during the service. At my church in Boston—I still think of it as home, although I left Boston in the summer of 1995—the liturgy always involves music, especially singing, as well as readings from the Bible and occasionally another text, a homily, and prayers of petition. After this, there is a long period of music, during which teams of two or three ministers of healing go to the four corners of the church, and people come up, alone or sometimes in pairs, and name their need, asking for prayer. The ministers of healing place their hands on people's heads, shoulders, or hands, embrace them, or offer whatever the appropriate physical touch seems to be. One of them speaks words of prayer. Some congregations add to this an anointing with oil, long a symbol of healing in biblically rooted traditions.

Participants in the healing services come from different socio-economic and educational backgrounds. Some are straight and some are gay. Most hear and use audible language, others communicate in American Sign Language, and a sign-language interpreter is always present. Some of the men and women in attendance are infected with HIV, others not; I have never sensed a feeling of division between the two groups of people, nor any query about "who is and who isn't." As the saying now goes, "not all are infected, but all are affected." At the same time, participants are honest about who they are. This is part of the healing. When people come up to be prayed with, they say what is happening in their lives. The intimacy of these moments is precious, delicate, and humbling. No one wears a mask. Many of the facts and feelings we share are deeply sad, but the honesty is not brutal; there is a gentleness in it, wrenching though it may be.

Every time I have served as a minister of healing, I have felt healed, although I was supposed to be an instrument of healing—perhaps *because* I was supposed to be an instrument of healing. Much of this has to do with the welcoming and compassionate nature of the services, their aesthetic beauty, and the exquisite honesty of which I just spoke. Much of it has to do with the ancient gesture of laying on of hands. Human beings need to be touched and to touch. There is real spiritual power in the laying on of hands, magnified by the ritual context of these celebrations. The power and intimacy flow in all directions: not only from the healing God to us and through us, but through us to those who request prayer, and also among the team of healing ministers. One time, the person who was assigned to be my partner in this ministry of healing was a man I had not seen in ten years and whom I knew from divinity school days. What a way to meet again—holding people in pain and finding words of prayer for them.

Touch can be harmful in religious settings, as we well know, when spiritual leaders abuse their power through sexual touch. Still, under appropriate circumstances, touch is a concrete sign of God's welcome and of the embrace of the community of faith. It can be as simple as the handshake at the end of a Friends Meeting for Worship or the Sign of Peace at a Catholic Eucharist. It can also be a healing minister's blessing and hugging a man or woman with AIDS whose family has rejected him or her, or who feels, even with the love of family and friends, that she or he is unworthy of love— or simply wrung out from the symptoms of illness, from pain, anger, or grief.

As Marge, my friend from Wisconsin, reminded me when we were speaking of prayer and the body, comfort with touch and phys- ical closeness in general can vary, depending on region, ethnicity, or even religious affiliation. I have become so accustomed to worshiping in a congregation that is both Catholic—thus deeply sacramental— and African American—thus finding joy in the chords and rhythms of gospel music and the embrace of one another—that I have begun feeling slightly out of place in other communities, an odd feeling for an "ecumaniac" like me, used to traveling through many traditions and comfortable with varied forms of worship. Last year, on a week- end visit to friends, I went with them to their parish, a largely white and suburban Presbyterian church. Prayer with the body? There was very little of that: neither the swaying in the pews during hymn singing, which I now do without thinking, nor the sitting or kneeling in silent recollection, which happens at my church and in other Catholic parishes. Later, I thought: some of the lack of touch in this church may well have been related to the practices of mainstream Presbyterianism, where worship is "in good order" and much of the physical energy of congregation and choir is channeled into making beautiful music that lifts the soul. Some of it may have had to do with the church's being in a white upper-middle-class community in northern California.

Much as I love my own parish's more bodily worship, I learned again on my visit to my friends' church that one needs to be careful to differentiate physical stance from warmth and good intention: members may have sat fairly stiffly in the pews, but they were welcoming and kind, noticing with care the stranger in their midst. I have also never received so much hospitable follow-up. I had filled in a pew card, and within a few days of my visit, I received calls from both the assistant pastor and a member of the church. They hoped to see me back, but also asked whether I had any questions or concerns. Their calls were welcoming without being intrusive and helped me to feel at home. My own church welcomes visitors with glee on the day of their first visit, asking them to stand and introduce themselves, the applause leading to informal conversation after the service, but we have no mechanism in place for follow-up and more extended hospitality. Which church extends the more welcoming and healing touch?

By its very nature, all ritual is to some extent a healing service. It is always bodily, quintessentially public and communal, rich in symbolic language, usually focused on both the spoken memory of "good news" (the literal meaning of the word "gospel") and the building up of the assembly. This is true of weekly worship, whether sacramental or held together by word and music. It is true of baptisms, weddings, and commitment ceremonies, of funerals and healing services, of the commemoration of Jesus' washing of the feet of his disciples, of the breaking of the bread and sharing of the cup. "Men and women need the stair steps of symbolic prayer to order and heal their all too often mangled emotions and chaotic thought," Morris wrote me from Japan. "Ritual itself can heal." Artist and liturgist Gertrud Mueller Nelson writes, "Ceremonies abound whenever a people mark and make an important new transition. . . . The core of a celebration speaks to the ears of all humankind—in all times and in all places. It speaks the symbolic language of the soul and is hardly ever practical, but more poetic, playful, prayerful. All good ceremony asks us to engage and make real the problem at hand and to feel and express fully . . . its joy and its fear or pain. Ceremony makes the ordinary extraordinary."[1]

The church is far more than a dispenser of doctrine; in fact, it is not even primarily that, but a community of prayer and discipleship—of contemplation and action—of which theological or doctrinal speech is one expression, one form of language, speaking to one dimension of our being among many. The church at prayer, the ritual-making community, speaks another language, addresses another dimension. "This creative and poetic Church helps us to pay attention to what we might otherwise deem ordinary and commonplace," writes Nelson. "Rites and symbols use the ordinary and earthy elements of our existence and, by encircling them, ratify, sanctify, complete. The ordinary becomes the container for the divine and safely contains what was uncontainable. The transcendent is disclosed in what is wonderfully familiar: bread, wine, fire, ash, earth, water, oil, tears, seeds, songs, transformations. It draws its action more from what is most human in us than from theology. In its creative function, the Church speaks directly to the heart, a heart which hears symbols, not rational vocabulary."[2]

AIDS healing services are only one of the contexts where there has been a return of the practice of laying on of hands—which in some parts of the Christian tradition has never been lost. Charismatic and Pentecostal communities as well as a good number of denominations and congregations have throughout the centuries called upon the healing Spirit, which is also the spirit of Jesus, in small and large services of prayer. Psychologist and minister Tilda Norberg and New Testament professor Robert Webber attribute the renewal of Christian healing to broad cultural-intellectual movements as well as to the movement of the Holy Spirit.[3] "It may be misleading to speak of a 'revival' of Christian healing," they write. "Christians have always prayed for healing; they have always been used for healing, even though they did not expect or understand such things. What is relatively new today is that the idea of healing is finding more fertile cultural soil than in the past and is reaching a broader audience of people aware of their own need for healing and willing to trust in God's will for their wholeness."[4]

"Holiness," "wholeness," and "health": these words have the same root. "All refer to a state of being *together*, body and spirit, rather than divided," says Nancy Roth.[5] The renewed interest in healing and healing ritual is one more manifestation of awareness of the relation between spirituality and health and of the deep and complex meaning of the biblical phrase "life abundant." The return of healing and its rituals consoles and soothes us. It also raises challenges and questions: What is the meaning of "life abundant"—in our bodies, our spirits, in our families and clusters of friends, but also in the broader bodies, the body politic, the body of the church, and earth's body?

Physicians' and, earlier, medical consumers' rising interest in meditation and intercessory prayer is directly related to healing, its nature and its causes. The relationship among medicine, spirituality, and healing is no longer a marginal subject in scientific or public conversation. Physicians' books on healing prayer climb the best-seller lists; they have titles like *Healing Words: The Power of Prayer and the Practice of Medicine*, *Prayer Is Good Medicine: How to Reap the Healing Benefits of Prayer*, *Timeless Healing: The Power and Biology of Belief*, and *Love and Survival*, and they contain both prayer advice and accounts of clinical trials, scientific studies conducted under the most stringent controlled conditions.[6] "The power of love to change bodies is legendary, built into folklore, common sense, and everyday experience," writes physician Larry Dossey.[7] Now scientists are charting this power, measuring its force. Most, however, are careful not to turn prayer into a utilitarian tool. On a television program on which I used to appear, I was once a guest with Drs. Herbert Benson, best known for his work on the "Relaxation Response," and Timothy Johnson, medical correspondent for the ABC network, who is also an ordained minister: The subject was prayer, especially prayer and healing. One of the most interesting aspects of our conversation was that all three of us made a distinction between healing and curing, and that all of us were reluctant to view prayer as only a technical (or magical) tool under our control.[8]

Among religious communities, the Christian tradition is not alone in experiencing this interest in healing, with its liturgical manifestations. My friend Anita has been involved with others in (as she puts it) "test-driving" new models of healing services for Jewish congregations, an experiment that she says is "more process- than product-oriented, and very powerful for people." Her own congregation does not hold healing services: "Every service is a healing service," her rabbi says. In larger congregations, however, especially

Reform Jewish congregations, where ritual has not always been the strong suit, Anita says that "healing services have become popular: they give people a chance to say they're in pain or someone they know and love is, and to sit with it—and to talk about how Judaism acknowledges pain." She added, "It's not about curing, it's about healing. Medicine cures; prayer heals." As the guests on the television program noted, healing and curing are not the same. One may die of a disease and yet be healed.

Anita noted that "all these services come out of the AIDS healing services [of the past decade]. It's now mainstream. Synagogues are finally realizing they are places where people have the opportunity to have the laying on of community, whether their hands are there or not." Preaching on the story of the raising of Lazarus in the Gospel of John, a minister I know spoke of the role others play in helping us to live anew—to live without being bound by all that enslaves, wounds, and oppresses us. In the Gospel story, she pointed out, Jesus turns Lazarus over to the community to become unbound at the hands of those who love him. Lazarus cannot take off the death wrappings by himself.

We are all, at different times or even simultaneously, healers and in need of healing. Shannon wrote to an online forum: "A friend of mine called over the weekend to tell me he was facing surgery for a benign tumor that was pressing on his brain stem and causing a hearing loss. He invited me to a celebration of the Anointing of the Sick.⁹ His parents were in town from California, and I knew he'd called other people. I expected maybe 30 to be present. But when I pulled into the parking lot, I had to hunt for a space; it was packed. Inside the church, more than 150 people had gathered, mostly because my friend had insisted on a celebration that was open to others who might need the sacrament, and, as he said so eloquently at the end, so he would know he was not alone in need of healing. When invited, more than half the assembly went forward to receive the laying on of hands, and then they were anointed on the forehead and on their hands."

More and more, healing rituals also happen outside the parish setting. Diann, a feminist liturgist and psychotherapist, works with a broad variety of individuals and groups, among them lesbians with cancer. Some of the women in these therapy and support groups are

Christian, others not. More and more, Diann is asked to help plan and officiate at funerals of these and other women who have died of ovarian or breast cancer. When we spoke, she had recently met with a couple before the death of the terminally ill partner. "I planned the liturgy with them while the one was still living, which was a very touching and difficult thing to do," she said. At the funeral, the participants planted a tree, and all came up to the tree and placed a piece of moss around its edge, patting it down, marking their presence. At the time of the funeral, the tree was in a pot indoors. "On the thirtieth day after Susie's death," Diann said, "the tree was planted outside." Not long after, Rebecca, another member of the group for lesbians with cancer, died. Diann remembered, "She had been a good friend of Susie's, and both were cremated. Susie's ashes were put around Rebecca's tree, and Rebecca's ashes put around Susie's tree, so they would be connected through the earth as they had been through life and hopefully would be in the life after. They had known each other through learning to die." Their life partners felt it was important to mark the connection between these two friends by sharing this ritual. The gesture was healing for the surviving partners and their friends at the same time as it acknowledged the bond of friendship between the two women—a binding of the community of friends-as-family.

Some rituals are so old and well known that their gestures speak without a need for words, bringing with them layers of meaning and adding still more layers. "I remember a beautiful moment the day of my ordination with Phyllis, an Episcopal priest friend," said my Jesuit friend Tom, a strong supporter of the ordination of women. "I went up and hugged her and we started crying. That's when she laid hands on me. She knew she could not get in the lineup that day, but she did lay hands on me, and she did it without either of us saying a word."

Ordination to the ministry in most Christian traditions takes place through prayer and laying on of hands. Different communions have different customs about who participates in the laying on of hands, reflecting differing theologies of ordination and ministry. At a Roman Catholic ordination, the bishop ordains; the clergy procession (what Tom referred to as "the lineup," though he also meant, by implication, the ordination itself) usually includes only

Catholic clergy. At the ordination to the priesthood of an Episcopal woman friend of mine, the ordaining bishop (also a woman) was joined by Episcopal priests only. Other clergy and laity were not invited (though my friend had specifically asked whether they might be), because this would not have conformed to church custom; the procession was, however, an ecumenical one, including members of the clergy of several churches as well as lay ministers. At the United Church of Christ ordination of another friend, the laying on of hands was ecumenical and involved both laity and clergy—in fact, the entire congregation that was present that day, which included members of at least six different Christian communions.

In the spring of 1994 my friend Jeanne became ill. A sixty-year-old Episcopal priest, she had been an elder sister and wise woman to most of the women clergy and seminarians in the local Episcopal diocese and to women of all communions who worked for churches in downtown Boston. She already suffered from chronic severe asthma, absent which, some say, she would have been elected bishop a long time ago. Her physicians discovered cancer of the spine. Shortly after, she had a heart attack. It seemed at the time she had only weeks to live, perhaps days. She survived the crisis. It was clear her days were numbered—though she lived an entire year beyond that time—and she decided to stay at home and not receive extraordinary treatment. After having a hospital bed moved into the first-floor dining room, she settled in and spent the last year at home with her companion and their pets, and friends who came to stay so she would never be alone in the house. I began visiting her regularly after the heart attack, bringing vegetables from Vermont in the late summer and giving her a massage during each visit, every week or two. Often I prayed silently while I worked on her body with scented oil, asking Jesus to heal and be present. Sometimes I prayed that God would use me as a channel of healing—whatever God meant by that. The image that came to my mind most often was fire—a concentrated fire from God, almost like a laser beam, touching Jeanne's bones, her muscles, her tendons. Often the massage itself was a prayer. Sometimes we spoke, of God and politics and other things, and sometimes not. In both words and silence, and in hands that seek to heal and flesh that receives, in the interaction, there is God. The bodywork becomes a prayer. I was never tired when I left, probably because Jeanne was, I am convinced, a truly holy woman, so full of prayer that her being passed it on like a communicable disease.

Jeanne died in the early summer of the following year. The last time I saw her was in midspring, the day before Holy Thursday. She was in too much pain for a full body massage, and could not lie down. That day, I washed her feet with warm water, bathing them in a small tub, then dried and massaged them, and massaged her hands. The symbolism did not escape either of us, but we did not speak about it. We knew this was the week both our churches celebrate the washing of the feet by Jesus of his disciples, the leaving of this gesture and all its connotations to us of mutual service, power transformed by love, friendship as the standard of all relationships, human and divine. We never said a word about it. There was no need.

❧

Two Collects for Maundy Thursday, also called Holy Thursday

Christ, whose feet were caressed
with perfume and a woman's hair;
you humbly took basin and towel
· and washed the feet of your friends.
Wash us also in tenderness
as we touch one another;
that, embracing your service freely,
we may accept no other bondage
in your name, Amen.

JANET MORLEY

Infinite, intimate God;
this night you kneel before your friends
and wash our feet.
Bound together in your love,
trembling, we drink your cup
and watch.

A NEW ZEALAND PRAYER BOOK

In Praise of Hands

Blessed be the works of Your hands,
O Holy One.
Blessed be these hands that have touched life.
Blessed be these hands that have nurtured creativity.
Blessed be these hands that have held pain.
Blessed be these hands that have embraced with passion.
Blessed be these hands that have tended gardens.
Blessed be these hands that have closed in anger.
Blessed be these hands that have planted new seeds.
Blessed be these hands that have harvested ripe fields.
Blessed be these hands that have cleaned, washed, mopped,
    scrubbed.
Blessed be these hands that have become knotty with age.
Blessed be these hands that are wrinkled and scarred from doing
    justice.
Blessed be these hands that have reached out and been received.
Blessed be these hands that hold the promise of the future.
Blessed be the works of Your hands,
O Holy One.

                    Diann Neu

Praying for Another's Healing

Before We Pray for Healing: The Discernment Process

These suggestions are meant not only for individuals but for healing teams, which exist in many parishes as well as independently.

- Invite God to use you as a channel of healing and to continue to give you whatever faith, discernment, and love is necessary to help the person you are praying for.

- Ask God to melt away anything in you that might get in the way—your need for power, your hang-ups or judgment, your brokenness, or your desire to cling to your own agenda. Know that God is able to use you despite these things.

- Feel your love and compassion for the person. Sometimes this is even more important than faith. Your own love for the person will probably carry with it your human desire for the person. Your instinct may be to say, for example, "I want this person to be healed, physically."

- Speak your desire to God as honestly and plainly as you can. Put your agenda in God's hands.

- Then, in silence, allow your agenda to be changed. Listen for the way in which God might want to heal this person. Ask God for what you should pray. Remember, even if a person is eventually healed physically, some other kind of healing may emerge first, for example, the release of anger.

- After inviting God to correct your agenda, trust that God will communicate with you in some way! Pay attention to pictures in your mind, hunches, intuitions, verses of scripture that come to your mind, sensations in your own body, and the like. You might try to pray with faith imagination, seeing Jesus with the person. Remember, God speaks in many ways. It may be easier to trust what you discern when you're with one or more persons rather than alone.

- Once you sense God speaking in some way, ask yourself: "Does this seem consistent with the character of Jesus?" "Does it sound like the God of the Bible?" "Is it consistent with the best we know of theology and psychology?" "Does it echo the wisdom of the church?" For example, discernment that suggests someone is being punished for sins by God through illness and pain is very questionable, indeed. It is questionable because it does not meet the criteria of love and compassion. ·

- Proceed with your prayer, humbly using whatever discernment you were given. Act in faith, holding open the possibility that your discernment is incomplete or even inaccurate. Continue discerning each time you pray.

TILDA NORBERG AND ROBERT D. WEBBER

CHAPTER TWENTY-TWO

Writing as Meditation
and Prayer

One day I was walking along Tinker Creek thinking of nothing at all and I saw the tree with the lights in it. I saw the backyard cedar where the mourning doves roost charged and transfigured, each cell buzzing with flame. I stood on the grass with the lights in it, grass that was wholly fire, utterly focused and utterly dreamed. It was less like seeing than like being for the first time seen, knocked breathless by a powerful glance. The flood of fire abated, but I'm still spending the power. Gradually the lights went out in the cedar, the colors died, the cells unflamed and disappeared. I was still ringing. I had been my whole life a bell, and I never knew it until at that moment I was lifted and struck.

ANNIE DILLARD

... the prayer that struggles toward God in obscurity, in trial, beating down the phantoms.

THOMAS MERTON

"On weekday mornings," says my friend Richard, a Catholic banker in Manhattan, a husband, and a father of three who loves to sing loud in church, "I read the two Scripture passages for the day's liturgy. Sometimes I read the 'homilet' from [biblical scholar] Carroll Stuhlmueller's books from which I get the list of readings.[1] I tend to view the Scriptures as literary texts, more drama and polemic than theology. More recently, I have tended to spend some time writing instead, with a fountain pen on unlined paper." In a life full of meetings, reports, and office technologies, Richard relishes "the sensuous experience of intimate writing. The ability to draw arrows and circles, precomputer hypertext."

Elena's life in the Boston area and her relationship to writing and prayer may at first seem quite different from Richard's. A Jewish poet and artist, a former journalist whose doctoral dissertation in sociology dealt with the topic of women's voice, especially among artists and activists, my friend Elena too writes as a spiritual practice, both for herself and for her audiences. "Most of my journal writing does have divine intention of one sort or another," she answered when I asked whether there was an explicit connection between her writing and her faith. "Sometimes it's writing to God; I've had experiences of writing prayers. More often it has to do with dreams and with archetypes I connect with through my dreams. I also use my writing a lot to connect with nature and the greater cosmos, and that's the most spiritual act for me. I have a place where I sit when I do this, our big third-floor picture window. I check in with that view, look at the trees or a particular piece of sky, and describe what it evokes."

Even when she is not writing to God in her journal, Elena's writing is close to prayer. Speaking of her public writing, which includes poetry, fiction, and nonfiction, Elena continued, "I really believe that there's this realm, this world within me where characters live and stories exist and images merge and arise, and writing gets me in touch with that place. I'm not sure," she added, "whether I write *in order to* get in touch with that place or whether being in touch with that place makes me write; it's kind of a reciprocal thing.

"This realm of the imagination is divine. I feel that's what God has given me to work with, and that part of my task is bring it out from whatever hidden area it's in, into the everyday."

Elena and her husband, Tom, recently became the parents of a five-year-old Guatemalan girl, Isabel, but Elena's involvement with children and youth predates this new stage in her family life. She has worked and played with children from toddlers in daycare centers to youth in community organizations. More recently, for two years in a row, Elena developed and facilitated a weekly poetry workshop for adolescent girls, teenagers between the ages of thirteen and eighteen. These young women are involved in a community-based national organization whose local chapters, Elena said, "are dedicated to empowering girls and young women from a very young age." Lynn, Massachusetts, where the teenagers live, is "an old deserted mill town with a large immigrant population." The young poets are mostly children of Cambodian immigrants and also include a few from other Asian backgrounds, a few African Americans, and two teenagers whose family immigrated from the Dominican Republic. Elena does not know much detail about their religious background; some, she says, come from Buddhist families; a few are Christian.

Bringing the divine realm of the imagination into the everyday is, Elena said, "also what I'm trying to do when I work with these young women, to help them find that place within themselves— whatever that is for them—and for them to know there is something deeper than the day-to-day culture they are constantly grappling with and feeling the need to conform to. My experience of them is that they seem to live in two different spaces. One is a space at the community organization that is quite healthy but very very active— playing sports, doing service—and somewhat pressured. And then there is the trouble they get into, a lot of depression and, because these are often first-generation immigrants' children, a lot of conflict and division they carry within themselves. They feel very sad. They feel a need to break from their parents, yet they love their parents, they want to protect their parents and their culture. They don't get much chance to engage in introspection and meditation and contemplation in a healthy way that's not just plunging into depression. I think writing is a way for them to do that."

For the sixty- to ninety-minute period she spends with the teenagers, Elena just creates "that quiet space where the goal is to be in touch with themselves and to express whatever they find. It's quite a structured space, in fact, and we have certain sorts of rituals. We start off with a question: we go around the circle and everybody answers. It's always a question designed to tweak their imagination for a bit, to use words or ideas or images in a non-conventional way. 'If you were a kind of weather, what would that be and why?' Almost always those questions are connected to poems I bring: I always bring a poem by a well-known person to read with them.

"One time," Elena remembers, "only two girls showed up. I had brought Pablo Neruda's poem on the enemy within. I asked, 'Who is the enemy within you and who is the friend within you?' We had an amazing conversation. The room was quiet. One girl was talking about this light shining outside her window—like a streetlight— which is her talisman, the thing she connects with every night and talks to. 'My light,' she calls it. She has continued to write poems on that theme—such a spiritual image—getting in touch with both the deeper part of herself and also something outside herself she can connect with and feel protected by.

"On another occasion, a young woman started class saying she loved love poems. She wrote sappy poems to her boyfriend; I didn't see a lot of promise there. But at the end of the season she wrote an amazing poem about her family's escape from Cambodia. Writing had enabled her to connect with the world in a much larger way and to get beyond that limited view of herself, and also to integrate this pain her family had been through and use it and express it in a way that was very positive and empowering for her.

"So," Elena said, "I think that writing for them is not that much different than writing for me: it is both inward and outward. It's connecting with the inner place where their unique thoughts and feelings and images and stories exist, but it's also connecting with a world that's larger than themselves. It's also about sensuality and about action and about the body. It places them in a larger context, and it says you are not just *in* this larger context but you are *in relation to it*. Metaphor and imagery are about relationship; in writing about it you are discovering relationship and you're creating relationship. That's what I am trying to do with them and with myself. You are part of that whole 'dependent co-arising' Buddhists talk about, that 'interbeing' where different pieces of the world are constantly interacting with each other. We use writing as a way to illuminate that—without necessarily saying that that's what we're trying to do," she added.

Echoing Richard's sentiments, Elena said of her own writing, "I just love the act of writing. It's very sensual, comes directly from my heart onto the page with no mediation. Also, since I'm an artist as well, writing on the page is like drawing to me; it's adding another dimension of creativity; doing it on a computer would be taking that away."

Richard, Elena, the teenagers of Lynn: their writing opens up possibilities for prayer, some indirect, others more explicit. As I listened to their stories, it struck me that three dimensions of what they described were inherent in the act of writing and also in the act of prayer—even more so in writing that is or leads to prayer. This writing and this prayer are exquisitely intimate: just as ritual is fundamentally public, so writing is fundamentally private. We may conduct our private rituals, or our writing may become public, but the nature of writing and of ritual, and especially the process by which we arrive at them, reflects this basic difference.

The first dimension is the creation or setting apart of a space or time which is contemplative enough to permit writing. There is no bypassing this stage, in writing or in prayer. When Elena creates a hospitable space for her teenagers, when Richard swings his desk chair away from the computer, they are taking the step without which there is no writing, and in doing so, moving against the surrounding culture, against their schedules, toward their deepest self, the part where God lives and speaks.

The second dimension common to these activities is the use of the imagination in writing—and the writers' trust that imagination is a central, not an auxiliary or secondary, part of prayer. Richard and Elena both express appreciation for the sensuality of their writing. They are willing to step beyond the structures in their lives to let flow a new form of expression in which they are willing to discover the God of surprises. Imagination, that friend of writing, is also the friend of prayer, not its enemy.

Finally, the young women of Lynn, Elena, and Richard are in their writing engaged in the business of making connections, inside and out. Everywhere, in interviews for this book, in churches, bookstores, workshops, I see and hear the hunger for living a life that is not in pieces: mind to one side, body to the other, heart lost in space, nature and cosmos here, technology there, politics in one corner, spirituality on the opposite end. Writing, like ritual, knits or binds together, brings back the disparate pieces, re-members. The wholeness we seek in public rituals is the same wholeness we seek in the moving pen on smooth paper or the tap of fingers on the keyboard. "'You are a part of everything,'" Elena said. "I think that little children know that instinctively, and some of this gets taken away from them. Adolescence is the time when children are inculcated with the culture, and we live in a culture of separation and isolation and materialism, a culture that does not support the idea that you are interrelated and interdependent with all of reality. So to engage the girls in exercises and activities that let them discover or rediscover or reiterate that for themselves and get positive feedback for it is really important. It's not so much like an adult: 'This was taken away from me' and you need to restore it. With an adolescent it's more 'You don't have to let go of this.'"

There are many ways in which writing can be an aid to prayer. None of them requires that one be a professional writer, or that one "write well." They require only the space and time of which I just spoke, willingness to free the imagination even a little, and desire to live a life whose many dimensions flow into one another.

Richard's morning writing, accompanied or not by the reading of Scripture, is one way of moving into prayer. Two other recently popular forms of writing are not in themselves prayer, but can jump-start one's prayer or, to use a more organic image, loosen the soil in which prayer takes root. The first is the practice of "morning pages" devised by Julia Cameron in her course and book on creativity.[2] Timothy, a physician and writer in Boston who was raised a Catholic and is now without formal religious affiliation, writes "morning pages," which he calls "essentially a couple of pages of stream of consciousness. As someone who grew up in a family afflicted with 'smart people's disease,' that is, intellectualization cut off from deeper feelings, I have found that morning pages put me in touch with the deeper stuff in a way that's been hard to access otherwise. I often discover that something I hadn't suspected was lingering just below the surface (why else would I devote a page to it when I hadn't even known it was there?) and morning pages are often a place where breakthroughs and other epiphanies occur. By the way, morning pages are not a journal—I don't record where I went and what I did, though that's not prohibited. The point is that it's not a historical record. It's a process. I never go back and read what I wrote or let anyone else do so and I try not to censor anything. For me it's like daily therapy. I may find myself arguing both sides of some issue to figure out what I really feel."

Timothy writes his morning pages exactly as Cameron advises. Morning pages are not even a rough draft of further writing. They are more a way of clearing the clutter, making space for the writing, engineering, gardening, housework, nursing, or any other activity we may choose. Their function is, as Cameron writes in answer to the question "Why do we write morning pages?" "To get to the other side. . . . Above all," Cameron says, "they get us beyond our Censor," that inner voice or presence that keeps us from being free. Cameron's Censor sounds like a combination of Zen's "monkey mind" and Christianity's "temptation to despair," the tempting self-loathing that keeps us from discovering God's all-compassionate and forgiving presence. "Beyond the reach of the Censor's babble," Cameron writes, "we find our own quiet center, the place where we hear the still, small voice that is at once our creator's and our own."[3] It is easy to see the parallels between Cameron's exercise and the meditative practices that draw us to that same center where God dwells.

Cameron herself briefly alludes to this connection. "It may be useful," she writes, "to think of the morning pages as meditation. It may not be the practice of meditation you are accustomed to. In fact, you may not be accustomed to meditating at all. . . ."[4] Morning pages may be exactly the place to start a meditative practice, either as an end in itself or as a steppingstone to other forms of contemplative prayer. They can give us a taste for "the place where we hear the still, small voice."

Spiritual autobiography is another writing technique that is not itself prayer but can lead to prayer, an act of memory and storytelling that is freeing in some of the same ways as morning pages' stream of consciousness. Dan Wakefield, a novelist and non-fiction writer, has conducted workshops on and written about spiritual autobiography, a process he learned from the minister of his church in Boston, Carl Scovel. Both men have found a way to help the very private experience of writing find a communal or shared form. Wakefield writes of one of the simple exercises he has led, the writing of a short essay on a person important in one's life journey: a mentor, guide, or friend. After composing these essays in silence and privacy, workshop participants share them with one another aloud, with the proviso that "there should never be any coercion to read, and everyone should feel perfectly free to 'pass' on any or all opportunities to share in this way." Most participants, even newly assembled, do share what they have written. One young man "observed after doing the spiritual autobiography course that 'what I found is I could write something and read it to myself and it would probably have little impact, but if I'm with someone else and read it aloud, there's something about another person's presence that makes it "ring true." It's much more powerful.'"[5] It is also similar to what some call "faith sharing," in which usually no writing takes place, but participants in a group speak to one another about the movement of God in their lives and about their prayer. It is certainly possible to combine faith sharing with spiritual autobiography and experiment with ways to combine the two.

Some people keep a spiritual journal as an aid to prayer, or devote part of their journal to observing or chronicling their spiritual life, including their prayer. Keeping a spiritual journal is not the same as praying, but one can move from talking about one's spiritual life to talking to God—sometimes the line is a very fine one—as Elena does on occasion and as I have done in the past. I do not keep a journal much these days; letters to friends seem to have taken its place. When I did write a diary—which I did for years, from the age of ten or so— I found it easier after a while to speak to God, beginning, I think, in my very early twenties. (As far as I knew, I was an agnostic before that time.) For me, it took away some of the self-consciousness about "the reader over my shoulder" or about what posterity might think of my words, should someone discover and read them. I wrote more freely, I was more deeply myself, less self-conscious, when I wrote to God. For others, writing to God might have the opposite effect. During my conversion to Christianity and to Catholicism, which was a long process, my journal was a mix, addressed to no one in particular and sometimes to God, from one moment, paragraph, or page to the other. Was some of it prayer? Certainly. Was all of it prayer? No.

One can also record what is happening in one's prayer. I did this once during an eight-day silent retreat based on the Spiritual Exercises of Ignatius of Loyola, and I am glad to have this record. One can forget very fast what an encounter with God has been like, or what problems one may have resolved, and going back to one's own writings can help in the ongoing journey of prayer. "I keep a journal," Cheryl said to me, "but it isn't a super-spiritual component. It's more data entry, new breakthroughs or revelations on which I can look back ten years later."

From a record of one's spiritual discoveries to praying on paper is only a short distance. Try writing prayers or letters to God spontaneously, without censoring or second-guessing: letting the heart and hand lead. While I had been speaking to God in my journal for a few years, I began to "pray on paper" more intentionally during my first eight-day retreats. Some parts of the Spiritual Exercises lend themselves well to praying on paper, two especially: the colloquy, a dialogue with Jesus, and the time immediately after prayer (the Exercises generally have five periods a day of Scripture-based prayer) when one reflects on what has just happened in prayer. For me in those days of my mid-twenties, writing my prayer and my reflection on what happened in prayer was a way of focusing and calming the mind, either because I was dealing with so much in my "outside life" and my mind was wandering with the usual distractions, or perhaps—I am not sure—because I was already dealing with some symptoms of anxiety disorder, and the writing, physical and focused, steadied me and kept me from agitation and distraction.

Writing to God is one of many ways to pray. It can also be a way of jump-starting one's prayer in times when one cannot pray. One can express anger or questioning, frustration or loneliness, joy or puzzlement. It is not necessary to be spontaneous: one can use aids like the questions on pages 162–164. Cheryl devised a prayer notebook, which she has taught other people to design for themselves and use as well. Of the seven years "of growth and refinement" during which she developed the notebook's structure and prayed with it, she said: "The way I look at that period of time is that God took a huge mess of unruly impulses and began to organize them. I would sit down at the beginning of the month and say 'Show me how you want me to pray and show me who you want me to pray for.' I would just start listing people the Holy Spirit brought into my mind and put down their name and their need, general or specific."

Every morning, "or on average five times a week," Cheryl "would read the Bible, and after I read the Bible I would start praying." I did not just start going through my list; I would use ACTS [ACTS stands for a prayer sequence including Adoration (or in some cases Acclamation), Confession (or in some cases Contrition), Thanksgiving, and Supplication].[6] So I would start out with A, adoration: all the things I could praise Him for. Sometimes I would be creative about it and praise Him for anything starting with a P, like protection. Then I would go into C, confession, and ask Him to bring to mind the sins or things that had been displeasing to Him. And then T, thanksgiving, I would think of the things that I was thankful for. And finally S, supplication, and then I would get out my prayer notebook; one by one I would pray for the people I listed and things I listed for myself." Like many people who spoke to me about their prayer and many who write about Christian prayer, Cheryl quoted Paul's First Letter to the Corinthians: "We have the mind of Christ."[7] "I would say, 'Lord, show me how to pray for this person.' Sometimes I would come up with more things than I had written down. It released a creativity in me that couldn't have been discovered or harnessed any other way, and not just creativity in prayer: it would carry over into my daily life."

Cheryl offered further suggestions on structure for the notebook, focusing particularly on the prayer of intercession: "You can divide the prayer notebook by sections. You can have a family page and pray for specific things for your family, or devote Thursday to praying with the family. Or you can divide it by month" and address particular matters as Cheryl has: "others, self, vision, direction, work-related issues, and obedience, ability to trust Him more, wisdom, insight, praying for sharpening my intuition and increasing my sensitivity to others' personal needs, trustworthiness, being a truly humble person, knowing what true humility is, actualizing my own potential."

At the time of our conversation, Cheryl was at a low ebb, dealing with both clinical depression and a layoff at work. She did not have the energy to continue with her writing notebook, but had found a helpful substitute: "I picked up this book at a Christian bookstore that looked really interesting: it has prayers in it, and you put a person's name in the blank space, so I do that to help me get through this time. She listed some of the topics in the personal prayer section of the book she had found: "To walk in the Word; to walk in love; to receive Jesus as Lord; boldness; husbands; wives; single female trusting God for a mate; victory over fear; court cases"; and in the section on prayer for others: "Body of Christ, ministers, missionaries, success of a meeting, salvation for the nations and continents, peace of Jerusalem, American government, school systems and children, healing of the handicapped, deliverance from cults." In addition to topics, the books listed Scripture references. "I find this very powerful and helpful right now," Cheryl said.

There is also in prayer another helpful support through writing, what I call "the list on the side." I have not seen any mention of this in books—there are more disciplined ways of praying—but I have found it a great help. During retreats especially, and sometimes in other times of prayer, I keep a sheet of paper beside me. When distractions arise, I simply write them down, and return to my focus. For the most part, teachers of meditation and prayer recommend learning to do this with the mind—let the thought pass, observe it, let it go. When I meditate, I keep to that discipline: there is no paper next to the cushion where I sit cross-legged; what crosses my mind, my hands cannot help. But in prayer, in times when I have had either many worries and preoccupations or a demanding schedule before me, I have needed more of a crutch. I can more easily let go of my preoccupations by writing them. After I have written them down, they do not tend to take up so much inner space; and they are sitting on the page, to which I can return later, organize it, make of it a list. I may also return to it with a different mind, having prayed. I have come to trust the "if it is helpful to prayer, do it" rule. I find little need for this "list on the side" now. Five years ago it was indispensable to me. I do not know what next year will bring, or even next week, when I may take up the page and pencil again.

There are ways in which writing helps prayer. There are also ways in which writing is like prayer beyond the structural components of time, imagination, and connection. This is perhaps more true for those who, like me, write for a living or as part of their vocation. Two activities which are part of prayer for me are also, always, part of writing—and thus of writing-as-prayer. The first is wrestling with demons, or "meeting the depths." In both the times of writing and the times of prayer, especially long and concentrated times, but sometimes short ones or the times when I am approaching writing or approaching prayer, demons come to visit. Sometimes I recognize them, other times not; more and more often, I do. It is not that God and angels do not visit: they do. They are present, I am sure, even when in my limited perception I do not know it. Since the age of seventeen I have had near or above my desk a poster of Marc Chagall's painting of Jacob wrestling with the angel, from the first art exhibit I genuinely loved and visited at the age of fifteen. Perhaps it is the wrestling that is most significant here. But it is a fact that not all my wrestling partners are benevolent.

The second activity or event present in writing as in prayer is a combination of play, letting go, and gaining access to the riches of the unconscious. In prayer as in writing, discipline is only a framework: there is a letting go, a way in which one becomes recipient, channel, sometimes dance partner, abandoned flow. My friend Nancy spoke to me of this state, comparing it to the act of love; at the same time as she is utterly involved in it, she says, "I get out of the way." It is not only the monkey mind that interferes with the communion of prayer but the rational mind, perhaps akin to that "Censor" of which Julia Cameron speaks.

Sometimes I think I have experienced in writing the full range of what one learns in a life of prayer. Significantly, questions of production and worthiness come up in both places. Identified as I am with my writing, it is important for me to disconnect my sense of worthiness from what I am writing. What is it that makes me worthy and lovable before God? What I make and create? Or just that I am, not my "production"? I am my writing, I am not my writing. I am my prayer, I am not my prayer.

The act of writing can itself be a prayer. Sometimes it is pure gift—I am in a state of "flow," as if I were taking dictation from the

Holy Spirit, or in the writer's equivalent of that marvelous statement in the movie *Chariots of Fire*: "When I run, I feel God's pleasure." When I write, I feel God's pleasure. Other times are far less
ecstatic and involve a great struggle, sweat, and enormous acts of
the will: stay on the chair, stay focused, keep the mind alert, bracket
all other concerns. Writing as work, writing as grace.

CHAPTER TWENTY-THREE

When in Doubt, Sing:
Music as Prayer

When we sing, we pray twice.

ATTRIBUTED TO AUGUSTINE OF HIPPO

God picks up the reed-flute world and blows.
Each note is a need coming through one of us,
a passion, a longing-pain.
   Remember the lips
Where the wind-breath originated,
and let your note be clear.
Don't try to end it
Be your note.
I'll show you how it's enough.

Go up on the roof at night
in this city of the soul.

Let *everyone* climb on their roofs
and sing their notes!
Sing loud!

JALALUDDIN RUMI

One Sunday morning in September 1993 I attended a lively Latino Pentecostal church housed in a former synagogue in what had once been the German-Jewish section of Chicago. While the mostly Puerto Rican worshippers were singing "Dios Está Aquí" ("God Is Here"), I spotted a small sticker. It was attached to the gleaming red and white mother-of-pearl trap drums a young devotee was beating with an astonishing series of slams, rolls, and paradiddles. From my location about a third of the way back I could see the first word on the placard was "Music" and the last word was "Jesus." But the intervening words were in smaller print, and no matter how hard I squinted I could not quite make them out. My curiosity had been piqued, so after the service I slipped up to the band area to take a closer look. Now I could see the whole message. It said "Music Brought Me to Jesus."

HARVEY COX

P eggy, a seminary student in New York, was serving her field education placement in hospice ministry, visiting people who were near death, and their families and loved ones. Most of the patients lived at home and received hospice care in that setting, but the hospice also operated a small unit on a floor of a local hospital. "I would make rounds in the inpatient unit with people who were really close to death and whose families couldn't keep them at home or needed a respite. I had had a really hard day already," she remembered, "and I went in that time praying 'Please, God, let it be an easy day,' went up to the nurses, and asked whether anyone needed a visit. I was told Mr. N—— was dying and could I go in there till his wife came. So after a quick glance at the nurses' notes, I went in to a patient I had never seen before. He was in advanced stages of cirrhosis and past being able to talk to me.

"In instances like that where I felt totally unequipped, I would turn to the Spirit and plead for help and try to follow the directions. Which I did. So I started to sing 'Amazing Grace,' and then when I got tired of singing that, I sang 'Precious Lord, Take My Hand.' It goes 'Precious Lord / take my hand / Lead me on / let me stand. / I am weak / I am tired / I am worn.'—Boy, did I feel that myself—'Through the storm /through the night /lead me on to the light. / Take my hand / Precious Lord. / Lead me home.' It felt like a risk at the time. 'God, am I praying for this guy to die?' I wasn't. I just wanted to help him at whatever stage he was at. This could be projection on my part, but he did seem as I sang to be more peaceful. As I was singing 'Precious Lord,' a cleaning woman or orderly from the hospital came in, and I figured out she was his wife. She started to cry as I was singing 'Precious Lord' and saying, 'Thank you, thank you, thank you for being there and singing.' She said, 'I needed this too.' I was amazed the song was for all three of us. We all needed this song."

When in doubt, sing: Peggy's experience as a student chaplain in Manhattan singing to the dying and bereaved; my turn to song during my recovery from depression, as I groped for new ways to pray; my friend Diana's putting down her chopsticks in a Japanese restaurant in Berkeley and declaring, "My prayer had become stale, so I started singing it."

Virtually every Christian church sings: Byzantine polyphony, Gregorian chant, hymns and chorales of the Reformation, spirituals, shape-note singing, gospel—music is the compelling Christian art, matched only by the visual glory of icons and architecture. It is an authorial art—witness Isaac Watts, Charles Wesley, Johann Sebastian Bach, Olivier Messiaen, Andrae Crouch—but is also, like all of liturgy (the word means literally "the work of the people"), a popular, communal venture. Chant, David Steindl-Rast reminds us, "is a folk art: Its imperfection is part of its perfection. It accommodates all kinds of voices and vocal skill; in the monastery, chant is sung by whoever happens to be there and enters into its shared spirit. Imperfections are therefore inevitable, as they are in life. And this is the point: A remarkable transcendent beauty is generated when ordinary people, with their shortcomings, give themselves to the chant."[1]

"I have been singing since grade school," said Sylvia, a psychologist and member of both church and community choirs. "When I think back over all those years, a story comes to mind about the monks who used to sing loudly in prayer every day. They were joined by a young monk who had a gorgeous voice, and so gradually they all stopped praying to listen. And God was very sad. I don't remember the source of the story, but it says what praying in song means to me: doesn't matter what we sound like, God wants us all."

We learn our religion through music earlier than we learn it through reading texts. "As any person who had an early religious training will tell you," my friend Peter said, "the music came into their ears and their bodies before the meaning did." In his Jewish upbringing, Peter recalled, "I learned the Kaddish, both the mourner's Kaddish and the other forms,[2] long before I knew their purpose specifically and what the words meant. Anyone who hears the notes of the traditional form of that prayer has an immediate emotional response to it: four notes of the Kaddish and anyone with any familiarity will be put in that state of awareness, apprehension, fear of God. Although the prayer has no mention of death, in my mind it is associated with sadness, resignation, and acceptance. Only later in life did the more literal parts praising God and His magnificence and the wonder of creation come to the fore, with the appreciation of the life that was created."

I may well owe part of my conversion to Catholicism to Mozart. The Kent State killings occurred on May 4, 1970, my first year at Oberlin College. It was the day of my elder nephew's birth and three days before my eighteenth birthday. The Vietnam War had already come home; this time it was in the neighborhood: Kent, Ohio, is less than fifty miles from Oberlin. Our college closed down the following week and went to Washington. A U.S. citizen, I had just moved from Europe the year before and was still a bit of a stranger in my own country. I was passionately opposed to U.S. military involvement in Southeast Asia, but was uncomfortable with direct political action, both because I did not know the political system well and because I did not feel very secure in a political role. I had been demonstrating regularly against the war since my arrival at Oberlin the previous fall—in France, we did learn to demonstrate, and the May 1968 student and worker uprisings had taken place when I was in the eleventh grade—but I had no experience lobbying legislators, which many Oberlinians were planning to do during their Washington visit.

Then the Oberlin choir, under the direction of Robert Fountain, Dean of the Oberlin Conservatory, decided to put together a performance of the Mozart *Requiem* in three days and to take it to

Washington along with the rest of the protest. The conductor suspended the usual rules and did not require an audition. Music was something into which I could enter more easily than lobbying, as a still frightened and disoriented teenager seeking a way to make a difference in the social turmoil around me. And so I became a member of the soprano section of the Oberlin College Community Orchestra and Chorus that sang the *Requiem* at the Washington ("National") Cathedral after the massive antiwar rally on Sunday, May 10, 1970. For several days, and most of all during the performance, we lived inside the music and it inside us. Mozart's setting of the Catholic Mass for the dead settled in our bodies. I still know the music and the words by heart. At the end of the last bar of music, the cathedral bells began to toll. Spontaneously, we all bowed our heads, silent.

I had been singing for years, mostly informally: hiking songs in French girl scouts and songs of the civil rights movement in U.S. summer camp, international folk songs with my guitar as a soloist, a school choir or two. In that week in May I moved one step deeper into awareness of singing as an all-absorbing, unifying activity—in some ways the religious activity par excellence because of its ability to bind together all parts of one's being as well as disparate members of a human community. Singing the *Requiem*, we transcended ourselves, and at the same time were more than ever at our own center, bound by breath, passion, and discipline, mind and heart and soul.

Years later, in the late 1970s and early 1980s, I finally studied voice privately. I learned lessons in attention and focus I had not absorbed in any other setting. You cannot sing, really sing, and not put your whole self into the act. It is simply impossible to sing well and not concentrate. The mind cannot wander. The whole self is involved: physical posture, will, intellect, emotion, and the breath weaving them all together.

"I *love* music," my friend and colleague Tom answered when I asked about the place of music in his spiritual life. "The music I listen to most is the music that can move me somewhere; it lifts me up, takes me to another place. I can't listen to Mahler's *Resurrection Symphony* without crying." Peter said, "On my way to work, when I need to gird myself for the day, I often find myself singing the opening of Handel's

Messiah: 'Comfort Ye, My People' and 'Every Valley.' If there are people around, I keep it to myself [and don't sing aloud]. Regardless of what I may or may not have prayed earlier, it gets my energy up; it's heroic music, to say the least. It prepares me for the vicissitudes of daily life, particularly the ones I face in the restaurant trade and in my emotional life, and it always gets me on the mark. It works!"

Lisa, raised and still active in the Episcopal Church, is a lawyer in Boston and the mother of a young daughter. She is "trying to teach my daughter, who is two and a half, about Christianity by teaching her spirituals. I want to communicate the strength that early Afro-Americans drew from singing spirituals, as well as the basic Bible lessons communicated in their songs. I sing to her almost every night, and she is picking up the spirituals very quickly. The other night she started singing 'We Are Climbing Jacob's Ladder' on her own initiative. I'd only sung it to her twice before."[3]

Maggie, raised a Catholic and now a practitioner of Ch'an Buddhism, is a trained vocalist who favors jazz and works as a software interface designer in New Jersey. "From the beginning, I approached voice as a spiritual practice," she wrote. "Music puts us in touch with 'spirit,' and voice is the purest form of that spiritual expression. I am greatly moved by Roman Catholic hymns and Buddhist chanting; group singing joins us in a unity of spirit. Alone, I sometimes vocalize pure sound (no words) to express whatever I am feeling. I am usually motivated to this when I have a 'blues' feeling. Letting it wail never fails to cleanse me and restore my balance. A year ago," she added, "I was battling an addiction to marijuana (today I am thirteen months straight!). During this time I learned a gospel standard which I have sung many, many times; this song was an important aid in my recovery. Some of the lyrics are: 'I'm gonna live the life I sing about in my songs / I'm gonna stand right, always shun the wrong . . . I can't go to church, and shout all day Sunday,/ Then run around drunken and stoned on Monday,/ Got to live the life I sing about in my songs.'"

From Milwaukee, Ginny wrote: "I tend to seek out music in times of greatest joy, but also greatest sadness. When my husband died, I headed for our cheap little chord organ as soon as I got home from the hospital. My husband died while I was cooking his dinner. He was thirty, I was twenty-four. It was four years, eleven days, and two hours after our wedding. Our baby was born too soon and died six months before. My husband was building a transformer for his ham radio; something shorted out while his hand was on a metal instrument so the current completed before cutting off, and he died twenty minutes later. There was a sound like an explosion and I shouted to him; I could hear a weak 'Help' and ran to the basement. He'd been thrown against some uprights behind the workbench, and there was a compound fracture on his forehead; I didn't know about the electrical shock till I got back from the hospital. I grabbed old drapes and bedspreads from a storage area, to cover him and raise his feet against shock, then went outside and screamed for help till a neighbor heard me, and went to call the police. Then I knelt beside him, yelling at him to keep breathing—God, more than twenty years later I can hear this: 'Breathe, Bernie, keep breathing, you'll be all right. Don't give up. Breathe, Bernie,' over and over, eventually watching his face begin to turn blue. When the ambulance finally arrived (a small town, and a volunteer ambulance crew) just moments after I believe he died, I called them murderers, God help me. Then told them they had to help him. He never spoke a word after that 'Help,' but did squeeze my hand twice.

"When I got back from the hospital, I headed for our little organ. I'm afraid the neighbor assigned to keep me company thought I'd flipped from the shock. I just sat myself down and played 'Rugged Cross' and 'Rock of Ages.' A couple of times each. Then I headed to the phone for the necessary calls. I'm not going to suggest this kept me from falling to pieces. But it was an essential prelude to the calls. Believe me, I put the 'angry at God' to work plenty in the months following! But my initial reaction was a desperate *need* for God, hence the music. I do believe there's a deeper, more complete investment of self in singing; I needed that immersion; the silence of Centering Prayer was impossible."

Church musicians, professional and volunteer, have their own passionate involvements in music as prayer. Rachel Ann, a Catholic Filipina-American in her late twenties, sings and plays gospel music as well as classical and is as much at ease with Johann Sebastian Bach and Wolfgang Amadeus Mozart as she is with Tramaine Hawkins and Andrae Crouch. Rachel grew up in the South, where "gospel music must have seeped into my blood when my parents weren't looking. There is nothing quite so cathartic and redemptive as digging deep and asking for the assurance and release that only gospel can convey, rooted in its moans and groans born of pain." During her college years Rachel Ann directed a gospel choir: "What this meant was that, in general, I played the slow songs and directed the fast ones. Even now when I cannot express the depth of my pain and alienation, I turn to the slow songs I used to play: 'Precious Lord,' 'Uncloudy Day,' and 'Refuge,' among many others. I know a lot of the old songs, the gospel classics from the late seventies and early eighties; they are truly soulful, good for playing on the piano, alone, in a room. Sometimes I just need to be alone with God, weeping in that way."

"I am a lifelong choir member," Sylvia wrote, "so music is my highest form of prayer. I particularly enjoy watching people during communion. While we are all singing, I like to try to imagine what it is that God is seeing in each person, what brings each one to the worshiping community. When I am singing, whether in a choir or as a member of a congregation, I think it is the *comm-unio* of many voices joined that inspires me to feel one with God/other/self."

Tom is a tax lawyer in Boston who is active as a volunteer music minister, singing, conducting, and playing the piano. ("It's my outlet," he said. "Too many tax returns.") He spoke of a recent decision at his large urban church: "We have split our music ministry into three teams, so every team sings only every three Sundays. So there is a 'retro-choir' in the congregation two-thirds of the time; it gives us a radical sense of being part of the community, and it breaks down that invisible barrier between choir and congregation." He added: "For twenty years I've prayed through my fingers. Much of my prayer has been public. Much of it has involved galvanizing a community. Now much of my music prayer is being in the middle, singing harmonies from the congregation and just being a part of it."

Both Tom and Katie, who is a frequent music leader in several small worshiping communities, spoke of the communal dimensions of singing as Sylvia did, and of the shortcomings of church choirs and congregations. "The beauty of the song brings me close to God, but also to the community," Katie said. "The community needs work; there can be backstabbing; but coming together [in song] and *knowing* that God is present in that unifies us." Tom said, "I'm finding there's a power in the music that can get you even through the church politics, including the politics of the church choir."

He added: "I think that liturgical musicians are given to planning the music for their own funerals a lot: 'What music would sum up my entire life?'[4] It seems such a shame that you do all this planning and you aren't there to enjoy it," he quipped. "The piece of music that sums up my spirituality is 'How Can I Keep from Singing?' That song, written by a Quaker abolitionist community in North Carolina in the early 1800s, always speaks to me. It is certainly speaking to me now, in the midst of tremendous turmoil in our music ministry. 'What though the tempest round me roar/I hear the truth, it liveth . . . No storm can shake my inmost calm/While to that rock I'm clinging. . . .' In some ways it's the liturgical equivalent of 'I'm Singing a Happy Tune'—if I just sing it long enough perhaps it will come true." The other song they will probably sing at my funeral is 'Jerusalem.'"

I exclaimed, "That's the song from the first scene of—"

"—*Chariots of Fire.*" He quoted the lyrics: "'I will not cease from Mental Fight/Nor shall my Sword sleep in my hand/Till we have built Jerusalem In England's green and pleasant land.' [The hymn is] a poem by William Blake. 'Bring me my Bow of burning gold!/Bring me my Arrows of desire!/Bring me my Spear!/O clouds, unfold!/Bring me my Chariot of Fire!' He writes about a legend that Christ came to England after his resurrection, and asks, could it have been that God walked upon these green mountains where we now see the creeping edge of the industrial revolution? Did God at some point shine forth the divine countenance 'upon these dark satanic mills'? And from this he draws his vision, 'I will not cease from mental fight until we have built Jerusalem again.'"

"That's reign-of-God talk," I observed.

"Big-time reign of God," Tom answered. "You speak to anybody who is British and they will have grown up with this song in grade school. This piece of music has the effect on them that 'America the Beautiful' and 'Amazing Grace' put together would have on us. When I am in one of my more heroic modes it moves me like no other. It's the reason why the movie was built around it. For me it doesn't have any of the nationalistic overtones, but the vision of the new and the heavenly Jerusalem. God knows if we'll ever get there," he sighed. "We can't even finish the highway under the city of Boston. But," he added, "one step at a time . . ."

"The new and the heavenly Jerusalem." The reign of God— what traditional language calls the kingdom and some now name the kin-dom or the realm of God—is both the vision of the ultimate harmony we hold before our eyes and our efforts and longing to build the holy city now. England's "Jerusalem" hymn expresses a longing for a human and humane city and countryside after the Industrial Revolution; our own spirituals and their later revisions express longing for the freedom and dignity of African Americans.[5] Like the early labor movement, the civil rights movement is inconceivable without song—Fannie Lou Hamer singing "This Little Light of Mine," crowds at rallies singing "We Shall Overcome," marchers singing "Ain't Gonna Let Nobody Turn Me 'Round . . . Marchin' up to Freedom Land." Earlier in our history, the efforts of slaves toward their own liberation were coded into spirituals such as "Steal Away," "Oh, Freedom," "Follow the Drinking Gourd" (one of the first American songs I learned)—most of them songs with explicitly religious, biblical themes. "The basic idea of the spirituals," writes theologian James Cone, "is that slavery contradicts God; it is a denial of God's will. To be enslaved is to be declared *nobody*, and that form of existence contradicts God's creation of people to be God's children. Because black people believed that they were God's children, they affirmed their *somebodiness*, refusing to reconcile their servitude with divine revelation."[6]

During the summer of 1962, theologian Cheryl Kirk-Duggan recalls, the SNCC Freedom Singers sang "Ain't Gonna Let Nobody Turn Me 'Round" as a response when a Georgia judge issued an injunction in federal court banning all demonstrations. Participants in a mass meeting at Mount Zion Baptist Church in Albany, Georgia, learned and sang the song. Kirk-Duggan writes that CBS television "filmed the Freedom Singers being arrested and carted off to police paddy wagons, singing this song. [The song,] a song of defiance, says 'No!' to extensive caution that says one must wait until everything is safe before rallying for change. The protesters had to sing this spiritual, because they were in the middle of life-changing and life-ending crisis."[7]

PRECIOUS LORD, TAKE MY HAND

Precious Lord, take my hand,
Lead me on, let me stand.
I am tired, I am weak, I am worn;
Through the storm, through the night,
lead me on to the light.
Take my hand, Precious Lord,
Lead me home.

When my way grows drear,
Precious Lord, linger near,
When my life is almost gone,
Hear my cry, hear my call,
Hold my hand, lest I fall;
Take my hand, Precious Lord,
Lead me home.

When the darkness appears and the night draws near,
And the day is past and gone,
At the river I stand,
Guide my feet, hold my hand;
Take my hand, Precious Lord,
Lead me home.

THOMAS ANDREW DORSEY

Thomas A. Dorsey (1899–1993) began his musical career in blues and jazz
and went on to dedicate his life to writing gospel songs.

MUSIC IN LIFE AND PRAYER

Take some time, if you can, to answer these questions in writing, alone, or
communally, in a circle, with a group of friends or members of your congregation.

What is the place of music in your life?
What music? *(Do not censor your answer! This is not about dividing music between
"religious" and "nonreligious.")*
Why this music? What does it do for you or to you?

Is music a solitary experience for you? A communal experience? Both?

What are some of your earliest musical memories?

What are some of your earliest memories of singing as prayer or as a spiritual activity?

Any other significant musical moments or activities in your religious history and in your life history in general?

What is it like for you to sing as a prayer?

What does music or song do for you that other kinds of prayer don't?

Do you sing—or make music—in groups? What's it like?

Do you also sing or make music alone? When you pray?

How does music bring together body and spirit for you?

What kind of music do you love most?

What music helps you to pray? (*Again, do not censor your answer.*)

Now put this book down and sing—or play the drums, harmonica, piano, guitar, washboard, saxophone. Or put on a CD, turn on the radio, or call up a friend and go to that free concert in the park or community sing-along.

Next time you go to worship, see if this exercise has changed your experience.

HOW CAN I KEEP FROM SINGING?

The editor of the Quaker hymnal *Songs of the Spirit* says of "How Can I Keep from Singing?": "There are many ideas about the origins of this song. Pete Seeger reports it to have been an old Quaker hymn from North Carolina and it has been traced by a Young Friend to Indiana, perhaps arriving there with the migrations during the early 1800s. That it reflects the early struggles of Friends is plain to see, but its joyous optimism makes the celebration of life a real happening."

The United Church of Christ's *New Century Hymnal*, giving as a reference *Bright Jewels for the Sunday School* (ed. Robert Lowry, 1869), notes: "In various nineteenth-century hymnals this hymn was attributed to different poets, including Anna Warner. The earliest published source credits Robert Lowry as the composer, although Silas Vail later claimed the music. The third stanza was written by Doris Plenn in the 1950s when her friends were imprisoned during the McCarthy era."

1. My life flows on in endless song
    Above earth's lamentation;
    I hear the real though far-off song
    That hails a new creation.
    Through all the tumult and the strife
    I hear that music ringing;
    It sounds an echo in my soul,
    How can I keep from singing?

2. What though the tempest loudly roars,
    I hear the truth, it liveth;
    What though the darkness round me close,
    Songs in the night it giveth.
    No storm can shake my inmost calm
    While to that rock I'm clinging,
    Since love is Lord of heaven and earth,
    How can I keep from singing?

3. When tyrants tremble, sick with fear
    and hear their death knells ringing *
    When friends rejoice both far and near
    How can I keep from singing?
    In prison cell and dungeon vile
    Our thoughts to them are winging,
    When friends by shame are undefiled,
    How can I keep from singing?

4. I lift my eyes; the clouds grows thick
    I see the blue above it;
    And day by day this pathway smooths,
    since first I learned to love it.
    The peace of Christ makes fresh my feet,
    a fountain ever springing;
    All things are mine since I am Christ's—
    How can I keep from singing?

Some hymnals list as alternate words:
When tyrants tremble when they hear
The bells of freedom ringing

Mother and God

Mother and God, to You we sing:
wide is your womb, warm is your wing.
In You we live, move, and are fed,
sweet, flowing milk, life-giving bread.
Mother and God, to You we bring
all broken hearts, all broken wings.

Miriam Therese Winter

I will sing to the Lord
as long as I live;
I will sing praise to my God
while I have being.

Psalm 104:33

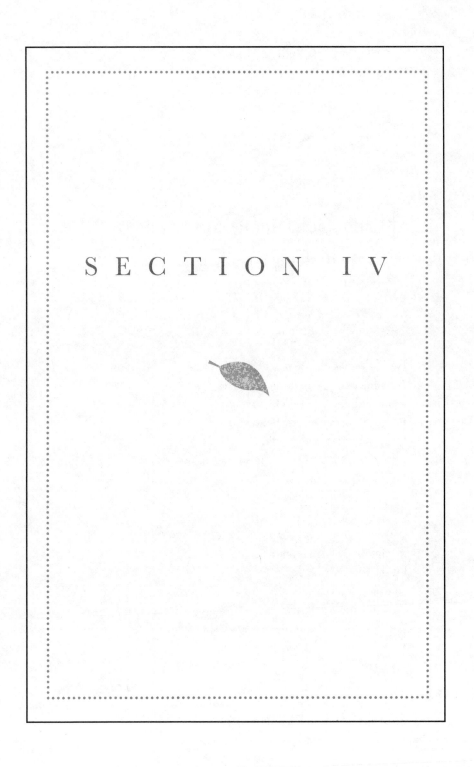

SECTION IV

CHAPTER TWENTY-FOUR

Faithfulness, Not Performance: Building a Daily Practice

Good-bye, Sir, excuse me, I haven't time.
I'll come back, I can't wait, I haven't time.
I must end this letter—I haven't time.
I'd love to help you, but I haven't time.
I can't accept, having no time.
I can't think, I can't read, I'm swamped, I haven't time.
I'd like to pray, but I haven't time.

MICHEL QUOIST

We give you thanks
for this food which is our life,
for the fruits of the earth,
conceived in darkness
rooted in the secret soil.
We offer you our part in the mess of creativity.
We wash, prepare, cook, present;
we eat and taste and enjoy with our bodies;
we clear away the mess.
We embrace with you the chaos that fulfils,
the secret labour that maintains life.

JANET MORLEY

I asked my father, a Unitarian Universalist, about his views and experience of prayer. He replied that he and my mother reject-ed the idea of "addressing prayer to some being up there who might say yes or no to entreaties. . . . Our prayer is more like self-examination and meditation, not petition or begging." Most of all, he said, prayer is present in events and activities not labeled "prayer." "Our prayer expresses itself in love, in work, in reverence for life and nature, in making human connections, in working for social justice, in helping others, in being a good friend. All these are forms of prayer for us. So is thrilling to good music, from Mozart to Errol Garner. Cooking is more than an art—it is also prayer. Baking bread is prayer. Our feeling of awe at a beautiful sunset is prayer." My friend Charles, a poet and arts administrator in Boston, raised a Catholic and no longer churchgoing, expressed kindred sentiments. "Some people," he wrote, "pray by praying. Some people pray by holding a door open for the person walking behind them. Or by tak-ing a deep breath and whistling 'Love Me Tender' when they're late and the subway car glides off just as they run to the platform. Or by cooking lasagna for a depressed friend. Or by humming the *Mission Impossible* theme song when they're stuck in traffic. Or by listening to Rostropovich play Bach's cello suites. Or by lending a frazzled coworker a hand. Or by apologizing for something they said, or did-n't say. Or by trying to remember what it was like to be three years old and happy to play in a mud pile."

When am I praying? When am I not? Is everything prayer? If everything is prayer, or potentially prayer, or infused with prayer, do I really need to set time aside for something called "prayer" that is dis-tinct from other activities? Benedictine monk David Steindl-Rast adds a layer of complexity to these questions with a story: "Suppose you are reciting Psalms. If all goes well, this may be a truly prayerful expe-rience. But all doesn't always go well. While reciting Psalms, you might experience nothing but a struggle against distractions. Half an hour later you are watering your African violets. Now, suddenly the prayerfulness that never came during the prayers overwhelms you. You come alive from within. Your heart expands and embraces those velvet leaves, those blossoms looking up to you. The watering and drinking become a give-and-take so intimate that you cannot separate your pouring of the water from the roots' receiving, the flowers' giving of joy from your drinking it in. And in a rush of gratefulness your heart celebrates this belonging together. As long as this lasts, everything has meaning, everything makes sense. You are communicating with your full self, with all there is, with God. Which was the real prayer, the Psalms or the watering of your African violets?"[1]

Steindl-Rast goes on to distinguish between prayers and prayer. "Sooner or later, we discover that prayers are not always prayer," he writes. "That is a pity. But the other half of that insight is that prayer often happens without any prayers. . . . If we want to do what Scripture tells us to do and 'pray continually' (Lk 18:1) we must distinguish praying from saying prayers. Otherwise, to pray continually would mean saying prayers uninterruptedly day and night. We need hardly attempt this to realize that it would not get us very far. If, on the other hand, prayer is simply communication with God, it can go on continually. In peak moments of awareness this communication will be more intense, of course. At other times it will be low key. But there is no reason why we should not be able to communicate with God in and through everything we do or suffer and so 'pray without ceasing' (1 Thess 5:17)."[2]

What matters, says Brother David, "is prayer, not prayers."[3] But here he and my father part company. Steindl-Rast continues: "If prayerfulness is all that counts, who needs prayers? The answer is simple: everyone. Prayers fill a need we all experience, the need to express our prayerfulness. We cannot be mindful without being grateful."[4]

Time set apart for "prayers"—or, more broadly, prayer practice—does matter, and it nourishes the times of spontaneous prayer, silent communion, or mindfulness-in-the-moment. "As the expression of our prayerfulness," says Brother David, "prayers make us more prayerful. And that greater prayerfulness needs to express itself again in prayers. We might not have much to begin with, but the spiral expands according to its own inner dynamics, as long as we stay with it."[5]

"Staying with it" is the key. In other words, pray daily, intentionally, in some form. Get a routine, any routine—one that suits you, not someone else. Then be faithful to it. Faithfulness is crucial here, not performance. This is not the spiritual Olympics, but regular exercise does make a difference. Steindl-Rast writes: "Some people stay healthy on a vegetarian diet, others on meat; some eat only once a day, others eat several times. One discipline may be as healthy as another, but without discipline in food and drink no one can stay healthy for long. The same is true for discipline in prayer."[6]

Shortly after Cardinal Joseph Bernardin of Chicago died, Terry Morgan, director of the priests' sabbatical program at the North American College in Rome, told the following story: Years before he came to Chicago, Bernardin had "a kind of a conversion experience, in his early Cincinnati years," about which he told Morgan years later and which has, Morgan said, "changed the way I 'do' my own day, every day. Archbishop Bernardin had been giving an intimate Day of Reflection to a handful of Cincinnati priests whom he had ordained a few months earlier: a kind of 'touch-up' retreat for the new guys. In the midst of one conference, on 'Practicalities of Prayer for the Diocesan Priest,' he had told the young priests that he had found that, as a busy bishop, his pastoral responsibilities did not really allow him to sit down for a block of time, even fifteen minutes, and simply pray. 'What I've learned to do is make my work my prayer,' he told the new priests." Bernardin told Morgan, "'Instead of taking in the wisdom of their bishop, three of them came up and told me they were flabbergasted. One told me he was scandalized.' The three new priests didn't just offer a protest. 'They told me that they would support me in any way possible to start a habit of setting aside a significant block of time each day for personal prayer,' he said. And they followed through. They came over and prayed with him. They sent notes of encouragement. They 'stayed on his case.'

"It changed my life," Bernardin told Morgan's sabbatical residents at the North American College. "It changed my priesthood, it changed my personal relation with Christ."

Morgan recounted that Bernardin told the priests "how he had begun to set aside the very first hour of his day for personal prayer. 'Usually, that hour begins at five-thirty. But if I have to get an early start, I just have to get up a little earlier for what has become the most important hour of my day.' 'Joseph our brother' didn't tell his story to us as Saint Joseph the Perfect, but rather as Joe, a brother priest who confessed that he had got so caught up in doing the Lord's work that even as a bishop he was oftentimes losing contact with the Lord. When he visited the house a month ago—to say

goodbye to the College and to Rome and to the Holy Father
[because he knew he was terminally ill] . . . he winked and asked me,
'Are you still getting up early, Terry?'"[7]

Richard wrote from New York, "My prayer is nonmystical.
Centering prayer makes me itch. Yet there are effects. When I neg-
lect the foregoing, I get cross, less engaged with family and friends.
Prayer does me good."

How does one build a daily prayer practice or routine? Making
time, or taking time, is naturally the first step. This, along with some
solitude, is nonnegotiable. Beyond that, experiment. Find what
works for you. This can take time and is a delicate task. Discipline is
also a matter of finding a comfort zone where you can exercise discipline. Steindl-Rast distinguishes between discipline and regimentation. Discipline is strong and flexible. Regimentation is rigid and
brittle. It is lifeless; discipline is life giving.[8]

"You need to be realistic about the possibilities," writes Nancy
Roth. "In looking at your daily schedule, for example, you may wish
you could set aside an hour in the early morning, but, since you are
home caring for your children, you may have only fifteen minutes
during their afternoon naps. You may wish to spend a half hour in a
quiet church each day, but you need to settle for the half-hour trip
on the commuter train. Be clever and imaginative. It is very likely
that your inhalation time," Roth writes, using her favorite metaphor
of breath, "is already there, waiting for you to discover it."[9] "What
may be challenging but doable for one person at one time in her or
his life may be nigh impossible at another time even for that same
person," Jon Kabat-Zinn writes of the practice of meditation.
"Perceptions of 'long' and 'short' are at best relative. The single
mother of small children is unlikely to have forty-five minutes at a
stretch for anything. Does that mean she can't meditate?[10]

"For those seeking balance in their lives," Kabat-Zinn continues,
"a certain flexibility of approach is not only helpful, it is essential. It
is important to know that meditation has little to do with clock time.
Five minutes of formal practice can be as profound or more so than
forty-five minutes. The sincerity of your effort matters far more
than elapsed time, since we are really talking about stepping out of
minutes and hours and into moments, which are truly dimensionless
and therefore infinite. . . . If you can only manage five minutes, or

even one minute of mindfulness at first, that is truly wonderful. It means you have already remembered the value of stopping, of shifting even momentarily from doing to being."[11]

Within the faithfulness to a practice of prayer are certain basic elements or anchors: time, space, a particular type of prayer. The division of time is a mark of prayer in every tradition: weekly, annual, seasonal celebrations—liturgical, related to nature, or both. In the course of the day, too, we mark the time with prayer. The Liturgy of the Hours is present in various forms in the Christian tradition—the Catholic Divine Office, Anglican Morning and Evening Prayer, ecumenical prayer books from Taizé, Iona, and other communities. In its original monastic setting it marked in prayer the times of day: the rising of the sun and its setting, high noon, deepest night.

Pick a time (or times) of day to pray—your time. Many people rise early to make sure they have uninterrupted time to pray. I suggested to a directee a simple exercise that I have now reminded myself to do: before you rise, take ten minutes to lie in bed and come to an awareness of your body—scan it from head to toe or toe to head, slowly, waking it up, stretching, wiggling, and giving thanks. Be aware of being alive, of being created—and of the Creator and Author of Life. Give thanks.

Nighttime is a traditional prayer time, not only for children who say their bedtime prayers, but for adults. The traditional prayer of the church alludes to the rest night provides, but also to the fears of the night, the resemblance of sleep to death, the need for assurance of protection. If morning is a time of waking up to creation, night is a time of resting in God, of giving over our rest as we have given over our activity.

Despite the long tradition of evening and night prayer in the Christian church, this may not be a good time for all: you may be too exhausted for prayer, or have commitments to a spouse or to children that preclude a time of recollection. C. S. Lewis wrote in *Letters to Malcolm: Chiefly on Prayer*, "No one in his senses, if he has any power of ordering his own day, would reserve his chief prayers for bed-time—obviously the worst possible hour for any action which needs concentration. The trouble is that thousands of unfortunate people can hardly find any other. Even for us, who are the lucky ones, it is not always easy. My own plan, when hard pressed, is to seize any time, and place, however unsuitable, in preference of the last waking moment. On a day of travelling—with, perhaps, some ghastly meeting at the end of it—I'd rather pray sitting in a crowded train than put it off till midnight when one reaches a hotel bedroom with aching head and dry throat and one's mind partly in a stupor and partly in a whirl. On other, and slightly less crowded, days a bench in a park, or a back street where one can pace up and down, will do."[12]

Between bedtime and morning there can be time for prayer, during times of wakefulness in the middle of the night. Having had occasional experiences of insomnia, I would not wish it on any person; but it is a reality for many. Why not use it for prayer? Since many physicians today recommend using meditation techniques to alleviate sleeplessness, one can also combine a time of prayer with a time of breathing, relaxing, and meditation, so that the time in the middle of the night is not only one of searching the Scriptures or wrestling with the demons, but also a time of learning and knowing stillness and peace.

Other moments of attention, thanksgiving, or petition punctuate the day: grace before meals, time out of doors, and the commuting time I have mentioned before. Katie sings her prayer in the car, often accompanied by taped music. Rachel Ann, a music lover like Katie, takes away the sound. "I often pray when I drive by myself," she wrote. "I could be stuck in traffic or on the open road, but [in either case] I turn off the music, clear my mind, and let things float up to God."

Even prayer times at work are possible, though the workday is not the ideal time for the major prayer of the day. The workplace can, however, be one of several places of prayer. My academic adviser, George Cummings, who is a theologian and a Baptist minister, urges his parishioners to "take a Jesus break" at the office. "You take a coffee break, right?" he says. "You have time for the cup of coffee and the talk by the photocopy machine and the water cooler: you can make time for Jesus."

Cummings expanded his congregation's understanding of the many places and opportunities for prayer in a sermon series on "The Practice of Prayer." In the first sermon of the series, he said,

"Some of us think that prayer is like those pretty little red boxes you see in buildings, marked 'for emergency use only.' The conditions under which we pray are in extreme emergencies. 'There's trouble in my life, and there's trouble at my door—Lord help me!' But this is not biblical," he warned, reminding his parishioners of "the three 'evers' of prayer . . . whenever, wherever, and whatever. . . . You don't have to wait until quiet time. Quiet times are necessary, yes! They are important, yes! But you can pray with noise all around you. You can pray right through the day, even on your job. One person asked me: Can I do that with people all around me? May I say this: Do you *think* with people all around you? Then why not pray with people all around you? You see, prayer without ceasing is this: it's staying right where you are—and retreating into the living center of your own soul's sanctuary."[13]

With "when" comes "where." Sometimes the space in which we pray is determined by the time we have chosen: in the early morning, a corner of our home—bedroom, bathroom, living room, kitchen, porch. We pray in both occasional space and intentional space. By occasional space I mean places where we happen to find ourselves—the car or subway of our commute to work, or the walk in the park during which we are surprised by new buds on the trees on a muddy spring day. These are the places of "praying as we are" or "praying where we are." Intentional space is the space we build to enhance our regular time of prayer, usually at home. It is a visual, architectural, and spatial anchor for daily prayer, one over which we have more control.

Cathy is particularly sensitive to her prayer environment: "I admit," she wrote, "I don't do well praying in a shabby surrounding. But that doesn't mean that the surroundings have to be opulent. Just whatever you do, do it well, with some creativity and quality; God deserves it and so do we." Cathy prays as well as works in her office, where the altar she has set up atop a bookcase holds a ceramic owl (for wisdom), a carved wooden Madonna from Switzerland, a candle, potpourri, memorial cards of people who have died in the last year, a photo of "stained glass with light streaming over the wall at the National Cathedral," a commemorative medal, and a marble chalice and paten.

Setting aside a prayer space provides an external sanctuary to nourish the internal one. The very act of entering that space can move one toward prayer. The space can be very simple: a flat surface with a visual anchor—cross, icon, candle, or more than one of these. Those whose tradition within Christianity does not encourage or celebrate the visual but privileges the word may simply light a candle, or keep a corner where the Bible rests in an honored place. It may be as simple as the bedside table, or a low bench on the floor by a cushion, or a coffee table by the rocking chair: a place set apart, with a symbol of one's faith, a solitary place that also ties one to the broader tradition and to the community of believers.

Nature continues to be a favorite environment for solitary prayer. Despite her love of church architecture and her gift for arranging beautiful indoor environments, Cathy observed: "Best of prayer takes place in the woods (except if mosquitoes are biting: one of God's goofs), on mountaintops, by the ocean, wherever there is a feast for the eyes to freely travel and caress the wonders of creation, to see the immensity and grandeur of God." "Prayer always seems to be connected to nature in some way for me," wrote Karen Nell, a mediator, consultant, and seminarian. For a few years she lived in a town outside Boston that was partly suburban and partly rural. "When I was living in the barn there and heating with wood, the patterns and disciplines of the seasons seemed to provide a framework or discipline for my prayer. Splitting and carrying wood, working in the garden, raking leaves, shoveling snow or just walking on the property—there was a rhythm that was meditative for me and always full of thanks for the beauty of that place and my life in it. I always felt that God led me to that barn as my place to heal, having just lost a sister, a business, and a marriage. I found reason to be thankful in every corner and at every turn. It was there I heard my call to ministry. Those patterns of thankful prayer and careful listening remain with me still."

Joe wrote from Philadelphia: "One of my favorite prayer sites is nature. I was raised in a home dominated by my maternal grandmother, who was part Lenni-Lenape, and much of our time for picnics and swimming was in the woods near a place called Indian Basin. That early influence led me to loving to pray alone in the woods when I was in the seminary. I found my own sanctuary sitting on a fallen tree stretching across a small ravine. The sacredness to me was akin to sitting alone before the Blessed Sacrament in a tabernacle." I heard a lot about prayer and water, almost exclusively from women. It all began when my friend Fran, a woman in her early sixties, confided that she practiced Centering Prayer in the bathtub. I began to include questions about prayer habits in my informal questionnaire, mentioning this as an example. Barbara C. wrote back from British Columbia: "The bath is a perfect place to pray! Asking Godde for cleansing, conversion, renewal, immersion in Godself, etc. Water is a very powerful image for me."

"My favorite places to pray," wrote Barbara from Atlanta, "are in nature and in churches. I really feel plugged in easily. My backyard is very woodsy and I like to pray and meditate there in the morning." She loves public spaces for private prayer: "Churches have been prayed in a lot and I like the feeling that it leaves behind in the energy. The older the church, the stronger the feeling. I could feel it in the churches of Paris when I was drinking and spiritually dead, that's how strong it was there. I like praying with others, and meditating with others. The more spiritually advanced they are the scarier/stronger it is."

Time and space: in them silence and sound live, other anchors for prayer. Find the balance of sound and silence that works for you. Try, if you can, to have at least some silence. Life, as Kit pointed out, is a noisy place. Try some silence, even or especially if it is hard for you. If this makes it too difficult for you to pray, wait a few weeks and come back to it. If silence frightens you there may be something important waiting for you there. Try it for a very short amount of time, and remember to breathe. Breathe deeply. Be attentive. What frightens you? Can you talk to God about it? Is it more comfortable talking with Jesus? Whom do you meet in the silence? Can you write about it? Can you notice it and sit with it? Try. See what happens.

As for sound: music is a wonderful way to move from the noise of the day into the time of prayer—and to make the transition back out. It can also dance at the heart of your prayer. I often find that in times of great joy, only music will do. A portable cassette player with earphones can help you pray at home in the middle of the night if you do not want to wake anyone, or on a walk to your errands. Some of us do not have the luxury of silence—we have a house full of children, or live in a busy urban neighborhood or a small town where privacy is rare. Are there ways to incorporate into prayer the noise in our life as well as draw some boundaries that will help us remove ourselves from it, if only for a few moments? Sometimes locking oneself in the bathroom is the only option for quiet in a house or apartment filled with family demands.

Having found a time, a space, a balance of silence and sound, you will choose from a variety of available anchors for your prayer. This book speaks of some of them: Scripture, other texts, song, writing, visual art, ancient prayers and newly composed ones, meditation and contemplative prayer. Notice also the relation between your time of solitary prayer and communal prayer. Are you more involved in one, less in the other? How? Why? How does one nourish—or fail to nourish—the other?

Barbara C., from British Columbia, wrote of her time with God, "I live alone, and start the day sitting quietly with a cup of coffee, like I would with a friend. We talk about all sorts of things—the coming day, what needs to be done, what might be bothering me, where I need healing, others that have requested prayer or who I want to pray for, thanks for a good and refreshing sleep, for another day, for the sunshine or soothing rain. Sometimes I try to read the Scriptures of the day's liturgy, but I often find them very dry and it is a struggle. Sometimes I put on a tape and pray with tai ch'i. Sometimes I worry that I'm too lazy. I used to set time aside and pray the Office, but that doesn't 'feel right' any more. I feel, in a certain sense, in the dark, and decided to trust the One I live with and 'go with the flow.'"

Distractions in prayer are part of the daily routine. I always begin the morning with ten yoga sun salutations, which wake up my body and focus me for prayer and for encountering the day. Sometimes I play music, but most of the time I do them in silence. It is amazing how the mind wanders in such a simple, short exercise. I try to keep attentive to what I am doing in the moment, and already a thousand things jump into my mind; from one moment to the next I am attentive to my wrists or to my lower back, and suddenly have lost my focus on the body and am thinking of the next telephone call. For some months now I have tried simply counting the sun salutations and otherwise staying focused on the body—the stretch of the hamstring, the opening of the lungs, the reach toward the ceiling or toward the floor. One sun salutation, two . . . The power of distraction is remarkable. I am often derailed somewhere around number four. I have decided to stick with the counting until I can in fact count to ten. It may take a year.

Distractions are not only the jumping "monkey mind." There is also one's own inner chaos; I run into mine periodically in the midst of the daily routine. This is a normal occurrence. It has come to bother me less and less because I know it is part of a normal relationship with God. One is always going to encounter some turmoil. I say hello to it when it comes up, and live with it. Of course, there are times when inside it feels like a desert, or like being lost or drowning, but for the most part there is that other reality, a kind of peace in the chaos underneath it all. Part of learning how to pray with one's own demons is learning how to avoid being derailed by them, and also how to recognize that peace which dwells below the surface. We can also trust that God prays within us even when we cannot pray in a way that seems adequate. Prayer is not just *our* doing. It is God's work within us and God's gift to us.

Some of these distractions really are temptations to keep us from praying. Use your own vocabulary: the Evil One, the powers and principalities, Satan, the devil, negativity. The fact is that powerful forces exist which pull us away from God, and often they are quite active. It may be that what we need is a change in routine; it could be that the distractions are a challenge to greater faithfulness. Discerning this is delicate; only practice and attention to practice can help us sort out the threads of our daily prayer, day after day, week after week, year after year.

Yves Congar suggests dealing with distractions by praying for them. In one of his last works, written when he was in his eighties after a life full of study and prayer, much of it lived with a chronic illness, he observed: "Sometimes one zigzags" during the course of prayer. One can overcome distractions "by orienting them toward prayer itself. If I think of So-and-So or of what has happened to me or of what I am about to do, why not make a prayer of it? Pray for So-and-So, for what I am about to do, for what has happened . . . why not?"[14]

✧

DISTINCTIONS

··

Let us distinguish parts within the whole
and bless their differences.

Like the Sabbath and the six days of creation,
may our lives be made whole through relation.

As rest makes the Sabbath precious,
may our work give meaning to the week.

Let us separate the Sabbath
from other days of the week,

seeking holiness in each.

MARCIA FALK

FROM KENYA:

··

A Morning Prayer

O God, you have let me pass the night in peace,
let me pass the day in peace.
Wherever I may go upon my way
which you have made peaceable for me,
O God, lead my steps.
When I have spoken, keep lies away from me.
When I am hungry, keep me from murmuring.
When I am satisfied, keep me from pride.
Calling upon you, I pass the day,
O Lord, who has no Lord.

An Evening Prayer

O God, you have let me pass this day in peace,
let me pass the night in peace.
O Lord who has no Lord,
there is no strength but in thee.
Thou alone hast no obligation.
Under thy hand I pass the night.
Thou art my mother and my father.

NIGHT

Lord Jesus Christ,
you are the gentle moon and joyful stars,
that watch over the darkest night.
You are the source of all peace,
reconciling the whole universe to the Father.
You are the source of all rest,
calming troubled hearts,
and bringing sleep to weary bodies.
You are the sweetness that fills our mind with quiet joy,
and can turn the worst nightmares into dreams of heaven.
May I dream of your sweetness,
rest in your arms,
be at one with your Father,
and be comforted in the knowledge
that you always watch over me.

DESIDERIUS ERASMUS (1469–1536)

As my head rests on my pillow,
Let my soul rest in your mercy.
As my limbs relax on my mattress,
Let my soul relax in your peace.
As my body finds warmth beneath the blankets,
Let my soul find warmth in your love.
As my mind is filled with dreams,
Let my soul be filed with visions of heaven.

JOHANN FREYLINGHAUSEN (1670–1739)

May God support us all the day long,
till the shadows lengthen
and the evening comes
and the busy world is hushed
and the fever of life is over
and our work is done—
then in mercy—

may God give us a safe lodging
and a holy rest
and peace at last.

ATTRIBUTED TO JOHN HENRY NEWMAN (1801–1890)

Now that the sun has set,
I sit and rest, and think of you.
Give my weary body peace.
Let my legs and arms stop aching.
Let my nose stop sneezing,
Let my head stop thinking.
Let me sleep in your arms.

TRADITIONAL DINKA (SUDAN)

TRY

True, meditation does require energy and a commitment to stick
with it. But then, wouldn't it be more accurate to say, "I won't stick
with it," rather than, "I can't do it"? Anybody can sit down and
watch their breath or watch their mind. And you don't have to be
sitting . . . [W]hen people say they can't meditate, what they really
mean is that they won't make time for it, or that when they try, they
don't like what happens.

JON KABAT-ZINN

FOR THOSE WHO CLEAN

Dear God, may those who sweep and clean
and take away our rubbish
Be assured of our love and our respect,
for you are the servant of all.

KATHY KEAY

My Lord God, I have no idea where I am going.
I do not see the road ahead of me.
I cannot know for certain where it will end.

Nor do I really know myself,

and the fact that I think I am following your will

does not mean that I am actually doing so.

But I believe that the desire to please you does in fact please you.

And I hope I have that desire in all that I am doing.

I hope that I will never do anything apart from that desire.

And I know that if I do this you will lead me by the right road,

though I may know nothing about it.

Therefore I will trust you always

though I may seem to be lost and in the shadow of death.

I will not fear, for you are ever with me,

and you will not leave me to face my perils alone.

THOMAS MERTON

I am not asking you tonight, Lord, for time to do this and then
that,

But your grace to do conscientiously, in the time that you give me,
what you want me to do.

MICHEL QUOIST

$\mathcal{S}$eeking Help:
Spiritual Direction, Retreats,
and Other Holy Resources

· ·

The very words "spiritual direction" can be offputting or seduc-
tive, as they conjure up the image of a clerical Svengali compelling a trembling soul to kneel on broken glass while reciting the
Miserere. Domination and submission are not what spiritual direction is about, but "holy listening," presence and attentiveness.

MARGARET GUENTHER

Monks are experts at doing nothing and tending the culture of
that emptiness.

THOMAS MOORE

$\mathcal{S}$ooner or later, we need to seek guidance in our prayer life—to
ask for help. Sometimes, this help is a question about how to
feed our hunger for intimacy with God. It may involve the
desire to make life decisions consonant with our faith and values. It
may be necessary because we find we can no longer pray as we used
to. Asking for this kind of guidance is difficult for many people,
either because they have trouble asking for help in other areas of
their lives as well, or because prayer, being even more intimate than

sex, is not easy to discuss with others, or even one other. We feel vulnerable talking about our inner life. Or perhaps we do not even have a language with which to talk about it.

Some people do not have access to spiritual resources providing support and guidance in prayer, or do not know that there are resources available to them: they are too busy, or they are economically struggling, geographically isolated, or at home with a new baby or an ailing parent or partner. In fact, resources abound, and in many forms: books, tapes, workshops, retreat centers and retreat facilitators, spiritual direction, and the more immediate resources of friends in faith.

Friends with their conversation and their companionship in the community of prayer are perhaps the most important and readily accessible source of support and guidance. The proliferation of small faith communities across the religious spectrum testifies to this. When I think of friendship and prayer, one face after another crowds my mind. I often think of my friends Bart and Susan. Fifteen years ago, Bart and I founded a church social action group together, with four nonnegotiable components: action, study, prayer, and parties. For several years we prayed spontaneously in small groups and in more solemn ways at Sunday Eucharist. We prayed for grace, forgiveness, justice, and strength to live out our convictions; we sang in praise; sometimes we just prayed. After Bart met Susan, the three of us attended worship services among our many other activities as friends; we said countless table graces together and I preached at their wedding. The morning after their first child was born, Bart called to tell me the good news and assure me that both mother and child were well. On that third day of the Gulf War, he talked of holding his little girl for the first time in the night and praying for all the children who were suffering from the armed conflict, on the other side of the world. A year or two later, Madeleine lisped through portions of the Lord's Prayer from her highchair. After her sister Lydia joined us, we often sat in church together with another friend and his two sons; we prayed with an eye on the children, alternately attentive and crawling over us and the wooden pews. We also talk about prayer together, though this is far from our only subject of conversation, and our friendship includes far more than going to church.

Sometimes spiritual friendships of this kind—one of life's great blessings—suffice. At other times or for certain people, a more formal and structured kind of spiritual companionship is helpful or necessary. This is spiritual direction, accompaniment by an elder, one not necessarily older in years but in some way experienced in the ways of prayer, skilled in listening and in asking questions that can help deepen our relationship with God.

As I mentioned in a note in the Introduction, "spiritual direction" is a misnomer. It is an old term that few still like but most still use, because of its long tradition and for lack of a better or more widely known word. It is primarily, as Episcopal priest and spiritual director Margaret Guenther calls it, "holy listening," attentive witness to the inner life with God. Leith, a married Episcopal laywoman who offers spiritual direction at the monastery of an Episcopal religious order of men, said, "Mostly what I offer people is a patient ear." Leith is also very clear about what spiritual direction is not. "Many people come, and what they ask for is discernment, as if a spiritual director had a direct line to God and God had a really particular opinion about how they should live their lives. I try to disabuse them of both of those ideas." Psychiatrist Gerald May writes that both the Eastern and Western Christian traditions generally assume "that the 'real' director is the Holy Spirit, manifested through the relationship in a graced way."[1]

May works with the Shalem Institute, one of the major U.S. training centers for spiritual directors which also offers spiritual guidance. He notes: "Amidst changing forms and emphases, Roman Catholic, Anglican, and Orthodox traditions have maintained some ongoing structures for spiritual direction. For Protestants, however, there have often been special theological problems with the idea of one person advising another on intimate matters of the spirit. Much of the concern here has to do with sacerdotalism, the possibility that the methods or personality of the spiritual director would supplant the role of Jesus as the prime mediator between God and the individual human being. Thus Protestants have characteristically tended to rely more on group spiritual guidance in faith-sharing meetings and on the private experience of prayer and personal scriptural reflection."[2] Nevertheless, a growing number of Protestants are seeking spiritual direction, often at Episcopal or Roman Catholic institutions. Leith notes the range of denominational backgrounds among her directees. In addition to Episcopalians, she and her colleagues at the monastery "see Baptists, Methodists, Roman Catholics, Unitarians, and UCC [members of the United Church of Christ]."

Spiritual direction provides a consistent witness to the inner life. For some, it is very much a "reality check." I can no longer count the number of times I have heard someone (including myself) say, "Oh, that happens to you too? You mean I'm not crazy?" Leith told me: "I have seen recently more and more people who have considerable unitive experiences with God and need somebody to talk about it, and want to have a context for it. Huge numbers of people have had extraordinarily powerful experiences of God in their lives and have had no one they could share this with, including their clergy." She added: "In the past, clergy were acutely uncomfortable with this kind of thing. As recently as the early or mid-1980s people would say, 'I can't talk to clergy about this; they refer me to a therapist.' They have these powerful experiences of God, they want to know more about it, they want to know they're not crazy, they want to be believed, and they don't want to be pigeonholed into some kind of clinical framework."

"More than any other religious experience including liturgy, spiritual direction has helped me grow close to God and come to understand who God is," said Rachel, the twenty-nine-year-old teacher in Connecticut. "Spiritual direction has enabled me to embrace the centrality of our relationship," she added, "both in the context of retreats and on an ongoing basis." "Spiritual direction," writes Kathleen Fischer, "is a conversation in which a person seeks to answer the question, 'What is spiritual growth and how do I foster it in my life?' The exchanges that comprise a spiritual direction relationship focus on awareness of and response to God in one's life. But since God is the deepest dimension of *all* experience, the conversation will range over every area of existence. Spiritual direction concerns the movement of our entire lives in and toward God."[3]

"One-on-one conversations," said Rachel, "are the most helpful part of spiritual direction for me. They provide the opportunity to explore God's activity in my life and my varied responses to it. This format establishes a safe environment that allows me to be open and honest in my self-reflection." She noted: "I find the 'nondirective' style difficult. I much prefer interaction and input from the director; otherwise it's like talking to a stone wall. I like it best when the person responds to me by pointing back to God's activity. I always find a lasting benefit if they can bring in Scripture, because I can return to that piece of Scripture with new eyes and continue to build insight.

"I also like spiritual direction because you can discuss images of God in a way that liturgy doesn't allow because the focus is not so personalized. It's not supposed to be about me—only in liturgy, it has all kinds of history, and that's the nature of it. There are certainly images of God in there, but in a one-on-one conversation the opportunity is there to really focus on who God is [for you] at that time." Rachel brought up two sets of images from her prayer and her experience of spiritual direction. The most recent, she said, was the tension she experienced between an image of God "filled with 'shoulds' and fear" and "the God who is alive and allowing creativity and allowing me to breathe," an image she finds "enlivening and opening." While these images are not necessarily male or female, Rachel stressed, they have in fact come to her in gendered form. "For me a very feminine image is Sophia[4] calling out in the streets, loving; the distant judging God is for me a very male God." She added, "When I'm feeling crushed and under pressure, my director does a very good job of saying, 'Which image of God is that?' When I get frightened and fearful it's that judging testing God [I think of] with whom 'you come up to these standards or you're not really justified, it's not honest for you to be happy or take pride in what you're doing,' as opposed to the 'give it a try, take a chance' God. I'm always so much happier when that's the image of God."

People define spiritual direction using a variety of concepts. Conversation is one. Spiritual friendship is another. There is a spectrum of opinions today about the relationship of friendship and mutuality to spiritual direction. Feminists especially have been partial to a model more closely based on friendship, though among feminists too there is diversity of opinion, and the tradition of spiritual friendship is as ancient as Celtic Christianity, perhaps even pre-Christian Celtic tradition.[5] Gerald May, on the other hand, is most emphatic about the basic asymmetry of the spiritual direction

relationship; his concern is that with a model more based on friendship might come loss of accountability, precision, and the occasionally necessary gentle confrontation.

One of my directees, whom I will call Donna and who, like
many women, is accustomed to "doing for others" and putting others before self, often asks me how I am. Of course I respond, but I
have to check myself so as not to get into too much detail, which I
know she is eager to hear. There are two reasons for my holding
back, or chiding myself silently when I do not. The first is a matter
of boundaries: I know that in other parts of Donna's life she has had
problems maintaining healthy boundaries. It is all the more important for me, while continuing to express clearly my support and
affection for her, to be vigilant about keeping the boundaries up
between us, for her sake, both for her psychological health and in
order for the spiritual direction to be able to function in a way that
will not compromise it. Which brings me to the second and fundamental reason: this spiritual direction relationship is *for her*. I have
often had to remind Donna of this, since her natural tendency is to
hold back from receiving.

Of course I come to our relationship as a whole human being; I
do not hide who I am, nor the fact that I may be, for instance, writing a book, recovering from the flu, or about to go on vacation. At
the same time, it is vital that I not be the focus of the conversation.
Ultimately, how I feel on a particular day does not and should not
matter. It matters privately, in that I need to be aware of it as we
move through the spiritual direction hour, to check for dynamics of
transference and countertransference—which are just as likely to
occur in spiritual direction as they are in psychotherapy—to bring
up my feelings in supervision if needed, to pray about them; but
they ought not to be a part of the conversation. The conversation is
about Donna and her relationship with God. This hour is for her, to
focus on this concern, and my task is to help her articulate what is
happening in her prayer and her relationship with God and to be
attentive to movements of the Spirit or of her own praying heart
which she may or may not have noticed, while at the same time
"getting out of the way." This is the midwife role, a metaphor I
often employ when explaining spiritual direction to people who
have never heard of it. "Well, 'direction' is a misnomer, midwife is

more like it" is my frequent shorthand. Many others use it, including Margaret Guenther, who notes that both men and women "can be sensitive midwives of the soul."[6]

Spiritual direction is also distinct from a conversation between peers, even though friendship and conversation inform it. On the growing edge of spiritual direction, however, is the small but increasing practice of group spiritual direction; this practice strongly trusts the maturity of the individuals involved and (especially) the movement of the Holy Spirit among them. It is in many ways an ancient practice, since Christians have for centuries met in small groups to reflect on their faith and to discern together the movement of God in their lives.

There is a marked difference between spiritual direction and psychotherapy, though mental and spiritual health are certainly related. Christian spirituality author Debra Farrington notes, "Therapists work with clients to help them understand the source of their anxieties or problems, and then seek to either resolve the problem or help the client respond to the problem in a healthier fashion. A spiritual director, on the other hand, may work with the same raw material, but his or her focus is on helping the client find God's hand or wishes in the client's life, rather than on resolving the problem per se."[7]

"There are many similarities between spiritual direction and psychotherapy," writes May, "but they are fundamentally different undertakings. In the modern state of flux among spiritual and psychological interests, it is very important to keep these distinctions as clear as possible. It is very tempting to blur these differences in the name of integration, but to do so is to risk psychologizing the process of spiritual direction. While the notion of combining psychological and spiritual care into a holistic approach to growth or healing is a noble ideal, in practice it takes great maturity and vigilance to avoid turning spiritual direction into a form of pastoral-psychological counseling that misses the spiritual mark."[8]

At the same time May, who is involved in the training of spiritual directors, would probably agree that it is important for spiritual directors to have enough clinical training to be able to identify depression and other mood disorders, personality disorders, and signs of substance abuse, to be comfortable with the subject of sexuality, and to be sensitive to the widespread realities of sexual abuse and other trauma. But always, writes Jesuit scholar and spiritual director Frank Houdek, "there is really one objective in spiritual direction: the development or growth of the individual seeking spiritual direction. The spiritual growth of the directee in faith, hope, and love is the explicit object, not a byproduct of spiritual direction."9 This spiritual growth is a delicate, private, intimate matter. Persons involved in spiritual direction frequently speak of it as a safe place to talk about our relationship with God. No subject is inappropriate, and the confidentiality of the relationship is as virtually inviolable as the seal of the confessional.

Spiritual direction began in some structured way in the early centuries of the Christian church, perhaps around the third century CE, with the desert fathers and mothers. Spiritual directors were not necessarily clergy. This changed over time, and until recently, when laywomen and -men began to offer spiritual direction, spiritual directors were frequently either clergy or members of religious orders of women or men. More and more spiritual directors receive training at such centers as the ecumenical Shalem Institute in Washington, D.C., the Jesuit-sponsored Center for Religious Development in Cambridge, Massachusetts, or the Sisters of Mercy–sponsored Mercy Center in Burlingame, California, all of which have trainees and clients, or directees, from a range of religious backgrounds. "There are now literally over a hundred training centers for this work," Leith noted. In spite of this, spiritual direction is still a fairly unregulated occupation.

Training, while increasingly necessary, cannot guarantee "good spiritual direction." "Spiritual direction," writes Houdek, "is an *art*. As such, I do not believe that spiritual direction, in its fullest and most authentic sense, can be taught, although it does utilize skills that can be learned. Even so, the gifts of grace, nature, temperament, and experience, which form the heart of spiritual direction, cannot be taught."10

How to find the right spiritual director? After the initial search—calling churches, monasteries, convents, retreat centers, the local divinity school or seminary, and spiritual direction training centers, or looking through one of the few directories that exist11—one may have to meet more than one person and "shop around" as one does for a psychotherapist. I always tell people, including people who

come to see me for the first time to explore the possibility of direction: "Go with your gut. If it says 'not this person,' it's probably
right." Two years ago, I attended a meeting at the Jesuit School of
Theology at Berkeley for students interested in being in spiritual
direction and for available directors. Those offering spiritual direction included men and women of different ages, lay and ordained,
vowed members of religious communities, single, celibate, and coupled, trained in a variety of settings. I was struck by the fact that all
of us, without exception, seemed to stress two points in the course of
our self-introduction: first, what a deep privilege it was for us to
serve in this ministry, and second, that we had no ego investment in
whom the person might choose as a director. If a person met with us
to "check us out" and we did not seem to be the right spiritual director for them, we hoped they would move on to find the right person,
with our blessing; our main concern was that they find the individual who would help them most in their spiritual life. A good spiritual director will be generous, both in sensing if someone else would
be better suited to help a particular person and in the openness to
sensing the movement of God in unexpected ways. "When you do
this work long enough," said Leith, "you begin to appreciate God's
versatility. You lose your own vested interest that God show Godself
in a particular way."

One may end up surprised in one's own choice of spiritual directors. After nearly two decades with only women spiritual directors
and one male retreat director, I ended up in spiritual direction, a
year or two before leaving Boston, with an older Jesuit priest. He
was gentle, wise, discerning, open to my experience as a woman,
and a real gift in my life. Rachel's first experience of spiritual direction took place in college, during a five-day silent retreat based on
the Spiritual Exercises of Ignatius of Loyola. "For a director I had
this wonderful old coot who was the legend of Georgetown," she
remembered. "He was wicked right-wing but I didn't know that.
[Rachel is politically on the left side of the spectrum.] He looked
like he was ninety years old, and I'm this socially active sophomore
living a college life just a little too much, lots of drinking, out all
night, and he was fabulous, the way that he listened and reflected
back and was not judgmental, gentle, working very much on how
God would view all this. I was heavily beating up on myself and he

directed the conversation so that the love was able to enter instead of just the self-hatred."

Who can benefit from spiritual direction and who tends to seek it? "Anybody is a candidate for spiritual direction if they want it," said Leith. Tom offers spiritual direction to approximately ten people on a regular basis. "Right now I think I have one of everything," he answered when I asked who came to him for spiritual guidance. "Religious [members of religious orders] and lay, gay and straight, female and male, very rich and very poor, Catholics, Protestants, and one Jew, and this all has happened over a period of five years completely by chance. I do have more women than men who come to see me. I am not sure whether this is true of other people who do spiritual direction."

Class privilege still plays a role in who has access to spiritual direction, not because it is expensive—some individuals charge for spiritual direction, but many centers offer it free of charge, especially those subsidized by religious orders—but because of who knows about it and of how religious communities and spiritual directors envision their ministry. My friend Skipp, a U.S. Jesuit who has spent much of his adult life in Brazil, said, "There's a basic bias against poor people because 'they don't have the time and don't have the intellect'—basic prejudices we have in all cultures—so 'don't waste your time' with them. Well, they do [have the time and the gifts]," he said, "even more so than other people." The location of spiritual direction practice is in fact beginning to change. "The work is happening not just in the highly educated segment of population I see, but in places like the South Bronx," said Leith. "The sad part," she added, "is that there *is* a certain segment of the population that says 'my spiritual director' the way they would say 'my personal trainer.'"

Skipp led the effort to found a center for the training of lay leaders in the city of Salvador, in Brazil's northeastern province of Bahia. "People only had to pay for the lights and the gas they used. They brought their own food and linens and did their own cooking. It was a beautiful place, formerly owned by a family of agronomists, with fruit trees, a very healthy place in many senses. In the slums there is literally no space—no community space, no green, very few trees, because they build on the sides of hills. We didn't restrict it to people from the Catholic community because there are so many movements and groups that need a space at a discount rate. The Jesuit province subsidized the house. We offered the space as well as our own programs, but not a lot of those. We let the community come to us. We acted as facilitators or resource people; if they wanted our help, we'd help."

One of the groups that came to the house was a group of very poor women from the slum next door. Skipp remembered, "We also had in the back of our minds that we would like to use the space to disseminate information and experience with Ignatian spirituality." Over the centuries the spirituality and Spiritual Exercises of Ignatius had gotten "interpreted in very static terms and become very elitist. In the last ten years in Latin America, retreat givers have been concentrating on debunking that. Poor people in slums have an incredible relationship with God, they are aware of their religious experience, and we can work with them with the Exercises." A group of Catholic sisters, the Religious of the Cenacle, were spending time in the community across the street from the center—"a very dangerous community," Skipp said, "lots of drugs, a couple of serious criminals." They came to know some of the women of the community, who began to visit the center. "A lot of them were washerwomen; it's the way lots of families support themselves." Besides taking in laundry, the women were also community leaders, "some because they were herbalists and had some knowledge of working with alternative medicine, some who took care of the little chapel in the slum where there was Mass once every two months: they would keep the people praying, keep the place clean, make sure there would be flowers in front of the image. Others knew how to deal with young people, especially the older kids, and help keep them out of trouble. One had a little store. Some were community organizers. Most of the women had husbands and children, and many were taking care of other people's kids as well. They were practical people; they weren't whiners; they were strong, very strong, and they suffered a lot.

"As we got to know them," Skipp continued, "we would invite them for little parties. The sisters would invite them to have a day without kids: they would put the kids in the mango trees and the mothers would sleep in the dormitories or be quiet in the chapel.

Then the women asked about the possibility of having some kind of retreat; they knew there were groups that did retreats and they didn't know what a retreat was. So we started giving them some spiritual exercises during an intensive weekend—not full time though, because they're mothers—to test the waters, to see if they could sustain a prayer time and then articulate afterward what happened. We were absolutely floored by the reaction. They had tremendous experiences of prayer. We gave them simple little exercises of creating a contemplative eye on the world, to go to a garden and let something capture their attention and then stay with it as long as they felt comfortable. When we came back for a sharing time—Did it work? Did you have trouble? What happened?—they were incredible in their descriptions of union with nature, the sense of God the Creator who was surrounding them, the color green reminding them of their younger years when they were left burdened by children and poverty. We found them extremely articulate.

"So we offered this group a formal way of praying the Exercises with some material recently developed just for this purpose by a priest in Colombia. They told us they would be able to come once a week to the center, to meet on Sunday afternoon. They promised they would try to do the prayer exercises every day, but this was a big thing since they had to find time and the slums are not very quiet." As the long-term retreat continued, the spiritual exercises included "two or three possible Scripture themes each week," Skipp recalled. "We ran into a problem because three of the eight women could not read, but we didn't solve the problem for them: we gave them the material and got Bibles for those who didn't have any. Two of the women got their children to read to them the little sheet we'd given them with the text of the next day, almost memorizing it, just like Ignatius tells you to prepare the night before for the following day. Another lady sought out another member of the group, and they prayed the whole retreat together."

The Spiritual Exercises also include contemplations of the life of Christ. "I've never seen people respond so easily to the application of the senses as a form of prayer," Skipp recalled. "They felt images or words or music and let them just bathe them at night before they went to bed. They became very articulate in the colloquies," sections of the Exercises in which the retreatant converses with, for instance, Jesus on the cross or in a particular Gospel scene. "The only direction we gave to them was talking about Moses: they do a lot of work on the Old Testament in Brazil with the poor. We'd say, 'Remember when Moses went into the tent and chatted with God friend to friend? That's how you should do the colloquies. Don't hide anything, God wants to see you just as you are.' And there were beautiful prayers; some of the women wrote them down and the ones who did not write remembered *everything*, since they live in an oral tradition. They would talk about how God was healing the holes in their lives, or that there were scars that hadn't healed yet and He was putting salve on them, or that they had rocks, or blocks, they were like a locked door to certain people, and He was putting a key in the door, wanting them to turn it."

Like the women of the Brazilian slum, most of us, privileged or economically poor, need time away. Jesus himself, the Gospels say, "went off to a lonely place and prayed" in the course of his earthly ministry. Why make a retreat? For the same reason we seek spiritual direction: to deepen our relationship with God. But also, in this more intense time away, to gain or regain the sense that our value lies in who we are and not in what we do. The retreat can be spread out over time in focused spiritual exercises or concentrated in a three-, five-, or seven-day time away. This is why retreats have traditionally taken place in monastic communities, those guardians of the culture of being.

Retreats also have what Guenther calls "an intentional austerity. The radically simplified environment discourages inner clutter. In most religious houses there is 'nothing to do'—no games, no distractions, no loud noises, no TV, no busyness. Instead, there is silence, simple food, adequate space, and the security of being surrounded by a praying community. For those of us who get trapped in crowded schedules, and fall into the dangerous and sinful delusion that we, the administrative assistants of a well-meaning but inefficient CEO God, are really the ones who hold up the world, even a brief retreat is a powerful corrective. When we have slowed down, we are able to look at ourselves and smile at our pitiful little constructs. Our humility is restored; at least for a little while, we are reminded of our true place in the order of things."[12]

After a time in that place apart, the senses come alive—both our bodily senses and our perceptions of the movement of the Spirit. There is little to do but pay attention, and so we do, to our hearts' desires, to the taste of the food, to the shape of clouds. At St. John's Abbey in Minnesota, on a brief trip two summers ago to lead a retreat for a group meeting there, I bathed briefly in the Benedictine spirit and joked that the local birds must be Benedictine: they sounded clear and pure, and one species ran across the grass, peeping and moving alongside the paths, unafraid of visitors. I am not from the prairie, nor do I naturally love it, but I learned to find it beautiful in its flat expanse and muted colors. The spirit of the place was spacious, generous; and so I made room for new ways of seeing.

For Rachel, the place of her first retreat was not as important as its structure, especially the quiet: "The silence of those days really invited me to experience God's love and forgiveness and embrace myself as a child of God." A common experience on retreats, especially first retreats, is to know the extent of God's love for us and of our own lovableness. "During that five-day retreat," Rachel said, "the relationship with God I began as a child raised in a strong loving Roman Catholic home became my own. Much of what was wrong at the time I made the retreat was a product of my own sinful choices. I *experienced* for the first time the overwhelming forgiveness and love of God. In the silence of those days, I heard the call to follow and believe that I am a child of God, forgiven and loved for who I am. This foundational experience has informed my spiritual life ever since. Nothing has been more real to me."

Retreats now come in all shapes, sizes, and flavors. Some retreats, like the charismatic "Believers' Retreats" Fred attended in western Kentucky during college, are noisier than others. Often retreats bring together particular groups whose shared identity or affiliation strengthens the experience of prayer, or who have similar needs: mothers of young children, engaged couples, lesbian and gay people, youth groups, divorced persons, parish leaders. One of the churches at which I worked offered what are often called "evenings of recollection" and we called "twilight retreats," an evening time of about two and a half hours during which even busy people could take some time to pray with Scripture, learn Centering Prayer, or reflect on the beginning of a liturgical season, and, always, remember who they were and Whose they were.

"I do at least two retreats a year," said Barbara. "They are AA retreats at a Jesuit retreat center. Oddly enough, my favorite thing is not the meetings or the fellowship, which are both great, but the chapel. I hate to admit that I find a certain spiritual experience in the traditional church setting as a place for serious prayer and meditation." On each retreat, Barbara said, "I take a serious problem, goal, challenge to retreat with me and pray, write, meditate, and listen. I always get an answer, and I never tell a single human being anything."

Although people who go on retreat are often the same people who either seek spiritual direction or have a focused discipline of prayer, for others, according to Leith, going on a regular retreat or day of recollection "works" better than establishing a prayer routine. "I've seen this with social activists. They're afraid they should be meditating an hour a day. It's not going to happen. They're people of profound faith, but they need a little more help with the inwardness. They're not going to stop being activists working for justice. I try and have these people not do a daily thing, but take a 'quiet day' every few weeks somewhere they can't be phoned. Trying to have them set up a daily routine was like spitting in the wind; if they got up ten minutes earlier they'd be on their computer!" This pattern may be as true, I thought, of executives or full-time parents. "If they take a quiet day without their laptop," Leith concluded, "they have a chance."

CHAPTER TWENTY-SIX

Discernment: First, Pay Attention

God be in my head, and in my understanding;
God be in my eyes, and in my looking;
God be in my mouth, and in my speaking;
God be in my heart, and in my thinking;
God be at my end, and at my departing.

PRAYER FROM A FRENCH BOOK OF HOURS, 1490;
ALSO FOUND IN *SARUM PRIMER*, SALISBURY, ENGLAND, 1527, 1558

Somebody's knocking at your door,
Somebody's knocking at your door,
O children, why don't you answer?
Somebody's knocking at your door.

AFRICAN AMERICAN SPIRITUAL

Colin is a widowed father of seven children, small business owner, and Charismatic Catholic with an easy capacity for friendship. "About ten days ago," he wrote me, "I was meeting with a divorced woman who was thinking about leaving the Catholic Church. She had some questions about the Faith and thought I would be a good resource. We had met twice before. She started the conversation off with a question about predestination.

371

Simple, eh?" he joked. "Well, I started to launch into my standard 'wonderful' insights into the question, when I felt certain God said, 'Shut up, Colin! Why don't you find out why she's asking that question?' To which my response was, 'She's asking because she wants to know the answer. Duh.' To which He said, 'Why don't you ask her?' So I stopped and asked her why she was asking this particular question and the conversation went a whole new, much more fruitful direction. She was worried about her children's salvation, so we shared about that and how that was not the burden the Lord wanted her to carry. She said at the end of the conversation, 'I'm sure glad you asked me why I asked that question, rather than just answering it.'"

Another story followed. Colin, a white man, lives in St. Paul, Minnesota. "Last Thursday, I was driving home at 1:15 a.m. I noticed a black man getting off of a scaffold in front of a new church, which struck me as odd. I drove on past. Then I felt God say, 'Go back and offer to help.' Yea, right! One-fifteen in the morning, in the inner city, me a white dude walking up to a black stranger saying, 'Can I help?' and I don't even know if he is working or ripping the place off. But after wrestling it over with Him for a few more blocks, I turned around and drove back there. As I pulled up to the side door, the man came out and looked suspiciously at me. I got out and walked over and introduced myself. He wasn't quite sure what to make of it, but one thing led to another and I helped him put up some Sheetrock. He didn't belong to the church, but his sister did and they had hired him to remodel this former sauna parlor into a COGIC church.¹ At least he wasn't fazed when I told him I was a Catholic. When it came time for me to leave, he wanted to talk. So I sat there as he poured out his story, unmarried with seven daughters, trying to stay off the streets where he could make a lot of money doing drugs, had knife wounds which messed up one of his hands, but trying to get his life going in the right direction. I encouraged him—not so much to attend church, but that the struggle to do right is worth it. Shared with him briefly that my relationship with the Lord was important to me and that was why I was there that night. Then I left."

How do we hear the voice of God? In what form? How can we know, as Colin did, or as Peter did when he asked God whether his prayers of intercession helped keep his parents alive, that it is God's voice we hear? How do we really know, in our life and our prayer, whether it is God speaking to us or the forces of division, illusion, and evil—or simply our stomach growling? These are only a few of the questions involved in what is traditionally known as "discernment."

"The Lord often leads me by these nudges or pithy comments," Colin said, reflecting on his late-night encounter. "One way I have of recognizing His voice from the myriad of ideas that traipse through my head is that He almost always surprises me by what He says. He doesn't say what I expect Him to say. One time I was telling Him how tough it was to trust him and He said, 'No it's not, you're just feeling sorry for yourself.' It brought me up short, because that was exactly what was going on at that point. He wasn't making a universal statement that believing in Him was easy, just that at that moment that was not the issue." "Surprise," writes Brother David Steindl-Rast, "is a name for God."[2]

In order to be able to speak with such certainty—which I know to be neither arrogance nor triumphalism—Colin has developed an attentiveness to his own experience. He hears God because he notices God: not only who God is—the God of Surprises—but how God chooses to speak to him, Colin, in ways God does not speak to me or to Peter or to the woman or the man with whom Colin engaged in conversation.

I have always loved the biblical description of God's presence as the "still, small voice" that comes to Elijah the prophet after the enumeration of all the places where the Holy One is not: the great wind, the earthquake, the fire. Recent translations vary: one has instead "a low murmuring sound," another "a sound of sheer silence." Still another (see chapter 4, page 57) is "the soft, barely audible sound of almost breathing." I love this passage for its sheer poetry, but also for the reminder that in order to hear God, we have to quiet our agitation and tune our senses so finely that we can hear the sound of breathing, almost a silent sound. There are times, in our lives and in those of our biblical predecessors, when God is in fact in the mighty wind and the loud noise, but the daily discernment of God's presence and voice is often more subtle.

In my own prayer, I do not usually hear God say "Do this" or "Don't do that" in so many words. What does occur when "God has spoken" or "God is speaking" is a feeling of clarity and deep peace, a kind of synchronicity in which my inner and outer life feel connected and I feel an internal unity, a sense that parts of me are not at war with others. Sometimes, there is a voice; more "in my mind's ear," a voice within, than a voice from beyond. Yet it is from beyond: I barely have the language to name it. Inner as it may be, the voice's Otherness is unmistakable.

Hearing the voice of God is intimately related to living in the presence of God and being attentive to this presence. Skipp spoke to me of the way the Brazilian women of his neighborhood noticed the movement of God in their daily lives. "Many times before, when I've dealt with professional or middle-class lay people [in spiritual direction and retreats] they'd often complain, 'I didn't pray, nothing happened' or they'd feel guilty. I'd always say, 'Did you look at your day?' The women [of the slums of Salvador] didn't need me to say it; they did that naturally. One woman would say, 'I didn't pray.' And then another woman would say, 'Yes, you did, when you went to the market and you saw the blind lady the little boy robbed the mangoes from, and you gave her your mangoes and comforted her, that's prayer. And then do you remember the blind lady was sharing the mangoes with somebody else?' They were able to talk about the days when you don't pray: on those days God usually appears very forcefully in the context of life—in the community, the people, the family—and they began to pick up on this."

Often our efforts to discern the presence or movement of God are related to discerning God's will for us. How do we know this will? What is its relation to ours? How can we integrate our life decisions with our deepest faith and values? We often hit that spot: what profession or job to choose; whether to enter a marriage, or whether to leave one; coming out as a gay or lesbian person to family and friends; making decisions about Mom and Dad's eldercare; childbearing and child rearing; decisions about money and sex; determining how to vote. At critical junctures in life, and in smaller ways every day, we are faced—often stumped—with decisions. How do we make them? Where does God fit in? Does prayer have a role in this?

Ignatius of Loyola, the founder of the Society of Jesus, is a particularly rich resource in this area. Ignatian spirituality, which derives from Ignatius's practice, writing, and directing of the Spiritual Exercises, pays close (though not exclusive) attention to what is known in Christian, especially Catholic, religious jargon as discernment. The practice of "discerning the spirits" or "discerning the movement of the Spirit" of course predates Ignatius, who lived in the sixteenth century. The desert fathers and mothers of the early Christian centuries were well versed in this matter, and common folk often sought them out for spiritual guidance at critical life junctures and in the everyday.

"The classic example of discernment," said Ken, a Jesuit priest and spiritual director who also trains and supervises spiritual directors, "is Saint Ignatius's awareness while recuperating from his wounds [after a battle at Pamplona] of the pleasure that came from reading romances but didn't last, and the lasting consolation that came from reading the *Life of Christ* and the *Lives of the Saints*. He was noticing and paying attention to what he was feeling inside. If we notice each day where we feel consolation, we *become discerning people* rather than *going through a process of discernment*. If we are noticing where and how God is acting in our lives each day, we will become more aware of the choices need to keep making that fit with God's activity. My own feeling," he added, "is that we can make too much of the process of discernment as a series of steps and neglect to pay attention to what God is doing with us each day."

Ken understands one of his and his colleagues' aims in their work as helping people to "become discerning *persons*. Not focus on this decision or that." Discernment is a lifelong process. I view development of the discerning faculty as part of the prayerful practice of attention. Noticing what occurs in our prayer and in our daily life, being attuned—this leads, when necessary, to discerning decisions. "Too often," said Ken, "God's will can be some kind of master plan outside that we are supposed to discover and follow, rather than noticing the seeds planted within us (by God) which indicate paths to follow."

He added: "There will be times when we have to make a big decision. Then we may need to take time to (1) gather the data, (2) consider prayerfully the cons and the pros (cons first) of each choice, (3) pay attention to the feelings until the choice made seems to 'fit,' (4) and then see if the peace that follows perdures. At the time when

I was discerning whether to return to Jamaica or remain in Cambridge [Ken worked in Jamaica for many years], I prayed for clarity during an eight-day retreat. The clarity did not come but I did hear God say, 'I will show you step by step.' Shortly after the retreat, a series of small events (being invited to join the staff at the center in Cambridge, becoming more aware of how skin cancer was affecting me, learning that the person who took my place in Jamaica was succeeding, the regional superior just happening to be visiting Boston and my being able to talk with him about staying in Cambridge at least for a couple of years, etc.) [showed me a direction]. I trusted what God told me but I had to pay attention to the events that followed."

Our needing to discern, to sort out, to clarify what it is we see and hear, presupposes that some realities (actions, situations, institutions, either for a particular person or in all cases) are better than others. It also means that evil is present in the world and that discernment involves the development of a certain kind of vigilance. How does the reality of prayer in our lives sharpen our ability to "keep our antennae up" for what Christians have variously called sin, Satan, the powers and principalities, and the power of evil in the world?

While we all live with complex social and institutional manifestations of sin and evil, prayer and retreats are the setting where we can often first become aware of the movements of what Ignatius called the evil spirit. Skipp reported that during the initial weekend retreat, when his neighbors were beginning structured spiritual exercises, one of them said: "In the middle I got this bad idea—I wonder what my kids are up to?—but I shelved it and went back to prayer." Skipp observed: "That's what discernment is about: Which spirit do you follow? How do you follow your focus in prayer? What nourishes your prayer?" Later in the process, Skipp said, "It was amazing when we [actually] started talking about discernment. Someone would say, 'I was thinking about this and another thought came into my head and I got tired and felt, 'Can't do it anymore.' Another person said, 'That's the devil, he's trying to confuse you, and to make you depressed. He tried that on me but I just told him to "get away, Satan!"' So I'd ask: 'Say a little more. Has that happened before? What did you do then? Any times when you told him to go and he didn't?'

"In this discussion of the spirits," Skipp said, the women had none of the classical terminology at their disposal, "and actually they had nuances many more educated people didn't have. They could see how the Evil One works in the family, works in the community. When you're fighting for survival, you're always on your toes not to get taken advantage of. Sometimes you can get obsessed with this. They'd say, 'That's when the devil gets us.'"

Evil: we encounter it every day, sometimes well disguised. How does prayer either help us realize the evil in a situation, institution, structure, or human relationship, or help us contend with it? Bill, the practitioner and teacher of Centering Prayer, said, "Evil is always closing in, restricting, shutting off possibilities, alienating us from one another in some way, destroying, dividing, and limiting. My experience of God is involved with opening up possibilities, bringing people who may never have expected it closer together, building, creating, and being joyful. This doesn't mean God is not there in the horrible times; God is there, but always in an unexpected way that leads to something more and not a dead end. The problem comes when I try to determine whether the evil is within myself or someone else. Is this a limitation of my own that I'm trying to impose on others? Is it fear and dread that arise because of pain in my own past? Is it anger turned the wrong direction that is destructive? In prayer I try to see where the limitations, the divisions, and restrictions come from, and whether I can let go of them."

"The characteristic of God's action," writes English Jesuit Gerard W. Hughes, "is happiness and spiritual joy, and therefore it should be the characteristic quality of the Christian whose life is directed to the praise, reverence and service of God. [This] does not mean living on a perpetual 'high,' but may be compared to the ballast in a ship. With ballast the ship will roll in a storm, just as a person capable of true happiness and joy will feel pain in a crisis, but the storm will not capsize the boat which will quickly right itself, even when struck by a wave."[3] There is a kinship between this joy nourished by attentive prayer and the flexible equanimity of Buddhist mindfulness practice. Drawing on an example from outside the Buddhist tradition to illustrate this, Jon Kabat-Zinn writes: "The spirit of mindfulness practice was nicely captured in a poster of a seventyish yogi, Swami Satchitananda, in full white beard and flowing robes atop a surfboard riding the waves off a Hawaiian beach. The caption read: 'You can't stop the waves, but you can learn to surf.'"[4]

Faithfulness to one's prayer practice helps in the development of the discerning self as well as in the making of life decisions. So, too, do what Ignatius called "holy conversations." Holy conversations, Skipp pointed out, are exactly what his neighbors were having with each other. As time went on, they began to speak more and more in this way with members of their community, helping others develop the capacity to notice the movement of God in their lives and their prayer.

The communion of saints can enter into the practice of discernment as it does into intercessory prayer and prayers of grief and celebration. Rosemary, a Sister of Mercy and health-care administrator, wrote to me: "Since I travel a great deal, my daily routine is to call on the Sisters of Mercy who have died and whom I knew to protect and guide me in all I do. I have some conversation with them about a meeting I am headed for and say things like 'I am not thrilled about this meeting' or 'It is a difficult one and I need your insights and guidance for a successful outcome.' At the end of the journey I thank them for being with me."

The dead are very much alive for Rosemary, as they were for David in his encounters with his deceased loved ones. I found this at first to be a Catholic phenomenon; it was certainly in evidence among the women I interviewed a decade ago. I began to hear of it from others, though less often from those whose piety does not include devotion to the saints. Then, when I wrote asking questions about prayer of my mother, who is not a Catholic and has not been particularly influenced by Catholicism, I found she engaged in a process similar to Rosemary's—and for that matter, to Hillary Rodham Clinton's much-maligned "conversations" with Eleanor Roosevelt.[5] In a letter written the day of her seventy-eighth birthday, in the late summer of 1996, my mother confided, after answering my questions about her prayer and spiritual life: "I must add one kind of reflection-communion-search when in times of quandary. It is going back to my mother, and less often, but still, my father, and even my grandmother, for a kind of reinforcement, or searching.

There are other souls also, living or dead, whose words or actions or presence are of guidance for me." The nature of God and God's presence was of less concern to her: "That there is some life force I am aware, naturally. That gives me assurance of course. But I cannot waste my time to define it."

Discernment, then, is not necessarily a dramatic process. It is often conversational. Nancy and I were on the phone together, close to midnight on a Saturday, talking about retreats. She spoke of her use of Scripture and nature on her annual silent retreat and of concentrating specifically on one dimension of nature or location—water, a specific body of water such as a lake or a piece of the Pacific coast, the desert, the Grand Canyon, a volcano. What a wonderful idea, I said, and then wondered, what is that place for me? I like to hike and revel in the beauty of the wilderness, but I do not have the same attachment as Nancy to the vast and tall expanses of land in much of this country, especially the West. Where is my "natural home," I wondered out loud. Into my head popped the image of a vineyard. I thought of the Napa and Sonoma valleys north of San Francisco Bay, which I love, and of the familiar vineyards in Europe where I grew up, of reading about the vine and the branches from the Gospel of John, the other New Testament stories set in vineyards, and all the references to vineyards in the Hebrew Bible—to their care, pruning and watering, their economic role, their association with labor and with the wine of joy. As Nancy spoke of her home, I thought of nature in France, my first home, which is rarely as wild as in the United States, or as massive—though there are forests and mountains of great beauty. But much of nature is cultivated; though France is now a highly technological society, it has deep agricultural roots. It was easy, growing up there, to understand Jesus' use of examples such as wheat fields and vineyards: how much more they speak to us when we know them, when our bodies and senses and memories are rooted in a particular land, an occupation, a craft, a specific topography. "Consider the lilies" was an image neither precious nor quaint to Jesus' friends, nor was the mustard seed nor the vines and fishnets. My conversation with Nancy opened the door to my next retreat, which I will spend in vineyard country with biblical readings related to the land. Even before the retreat has begun, I know that it will be rich, and that it speaks to me of home, in the multilayered sense of that word. This particular encounter with God would never have happened without an ongoing friendship in which conversing about God and prayer is like daily bread.

❦

Good Jesus,
the water of your teaching
flows in silence.
Your gospel
is not poured into our ears
by an eloquent tongue,
but is breathed into our hearts
by your sweet spirit.
Your voice never strains nor shouts.
You do not force us to hear you.
You ask only
that we open our hearts to you,
and in tranquility your love enters our soul.

AELRED OF RIEVAULX (CA. 1110–1167)

EXCERPT FROM
"RULES FOR THE DISCERNMENT OF SPIRITS"

The Spiritual Exercises

Ignatius of Loyola's Spiritual Exercises, a classic of Western Christian spirituality, are the result of intense spiritual experience and of careful observation of this experience. It is best not to read them in isolation, without an opportunity to "make the Exercises" in some form, that is, to pray through them with guidance from one who is well versed in them. The same is true of the well-known "Rules for the Discernment of Spirits" which are part of "Week One" and "Week Two" of the Exercises (designed as a four-week process, but adaptable to many longer and shorter periods). With these cautions, I share with you some excerpts of the "Rules for the Discernment of Spirits" in a new, accessible translation, having found helpful in many circumstances Ignatius's definitions of consolation and desolation, the simple rule of "no major life decisions in times of desolation," and observations about the way the powers of evil can interfere in our lives. Read carefully, ponder, discuss with a spiritual friend or guide, see whether and how this applies to your prayer and life experience. The numbers in brackets indicate the paragraphs or sections in the original text of the Exercises.

From "Rules for the Discernment of Spirits in the First Week"

Rules for perceiving and understanding to some degree the different movements produced in the soul. . . .

[316.] Rule 3. Spiritual Consolation. I call it consolation when the soul is aroused by an interior movement which causes it to be inflamed with love for its Creator and Lord, and as a consequence can love no created thing on the face of the earth for its own sake, but only in the Creator of all things. It is likewise consolation when one sheds tears, moved by the love of God, whether it be because of sorrow for sins, or because of the sufferings of Christ our Lord, or for any other reason immediately directed to the service and praise of God. Finally I call consolation every increase of faith, hope, and love, and all interior joy which calls and attracts the soul to that which is of God and to salvation by filling it with tranquility and peace in its Creator and Lord.

[317.] Rule 4. Spiritual Desolation. I call desolation that which is entirely the opposite of what was described in the third rule, such as darkness of soul, confusion of spirit, attraction to what is base and worldly, restlessness caused by many disturbances and temptations which lead to lack of faith, hope or love. The soul finds itself completely apathetic, lukewarm, sad and as if separated from its Creator and Lord. For just as consolation is the opposite of desolation, so the thoughts coming from consolation are the opposite of those which come from desolation.

[318.] Rule 5. In time of desolation we should never make any change, but remain firm and constant in the resolution and decision which guided us before the desolation, or in the decision which we made in the preceding consolation. For just as in consolation it is the good spirit which guides and counsels us, so in desolation is the evil one which guides and counsels. Following such counsels we can never find the way to a right decision.

[319.] Rule 6. Though in desolation we should never change former resolutions, it may be very profitable to change ourselves by insisting on more

prayer, more meditation, and more examination, and by increasing our penance in some suitable way.

[322.] Rule 9. There are three principal reasons why we suffer from desolation. The first is because we have been lukewarm, lazy or negligent in our spiritual exercises, and so through our own fault consolation has been withdrawn from us. The second reason is because God sometimes wishes to test us, to see how much we are worth, and how much we will progress in the service and praise of the Lord when left without the generous reward of consolation and special graces. The third reason is because God wishes to give us a true knowledge and understanding of ourselves, so that we may truly perceive that it is not within our power to acquire or retain great devotion, ardent love, tears, or any other spiritual consolation, but that all this is the gratuitous gift and grace of God our Lord. God does not wish us to claim as our own what is the property of another, becoming inflated with a spirit of pride or boasting, attributing to ourselves devotion or other kinds of spiritual consolation.

[323.] Rule 10. When one enjoys consolation it is good to reflect how one will act during a time of desolation, and store up strength for that time.

From "Rules for the Discernment of Spirits in the Second Week"

[329.] Rule 1. It is characteristic of God and the good spirits, when they act upon the soul, to give true happiness and spiritual joy, and to banish all the sadness and disturbances caused by the enemy. It is characteristic of the evil one to fight against such happiness and spiritual consolation by suggesting false reasonings, subtleties and continual deceptions.

[334.] Rule 6. When the enemy of human nature has been detected and recognized by the trail of evil which marks its course and by the evil end to which it leads us, it will be profitable for one who has been tempted immediately to review the whole course of the temptation. One should consider the series of good thoughts, how they arose, how the evil one gradually tried to make the person leave the state of spiritual joy and consolation, drawing the person toward its own evil plans. The purpose of this review is that once such an experience has been understood and carefully noted, in the future one may be better able to guard against the customary deceptions of the enemy.

[335.] Rule 7. In souls which are progressing toward greater perfection, the action of the good spirit is delicate, gentle and delightful, like a drop of water

penetrating a sponge. The action of the evil one on such souls is violent, noisy and disturbing, like a drop of water falling on a stone. In souls which are going from bad to worse, the action of the spirits mentioned above is just the reverse. The reason for this is to be sought in the disposition of the soul, whether opposite or similar to the different kinds of spirits. When the disposition is contrary to a spirit, it enters with noise and commotion which are easily perceived. When the disposition is similar to a spirit, it enters silently, as when one enters one's own house when the door is open.

IGNATIUS OF LOYOLA (1491–1556)

DISCERNMENT: GUIDELINES FOR WOMEN

It is often hard for women to listen to their own needs; this can complicate the process of discernment, as can institutional, social, and family situations where women and men's relationships are distorted by inequality and other manifestations of sexism. With this in mind, spiritual director and author Kathleen Fischer has formulated eight guidelines for discernment especially for women. The quoted material is from Fischer's *Women at the Well.*

1. Listen to your deepest self.

   "Women do not typically need to hear the constant references to the dangers of self-love, selfishness, and self-centeredness which punctuate most discussions of discernment," Fischer writes. "Their choices go wrong because of an inability to love self well. Certainly women, like men, fail to love perfectly in concrete situations. But the roots of their failure lie less in overextension of the self than in a weak sense of any self at all."

2. Affirm your own as well as others' needs.

   "Another challenge women face is to affirm *both* the fullest development of themselves and the nurturing of relationships, in other words, to learn what it means in practice to be a self-in-relation. . . . Knowing is itself a process of human relationship; it is 'connected knowing.' This is as true of discernment as of other modes of knowing."

3. Do not confuse passivity with conformity to God's will.

   Confusion about God's will can lead to passivity in women in two major ways: first, women "can mistakenly think they are living out God's will when they are merely living out of a cultural pattern of conformity or helplessness." Second, confusion about God's will leads to passivity in women when we suppose—and this concept affects men as well—"that God's will is a detailed plan for every aspect of our lives, so that discernment is not a matter of adult reflection and decision, but a fear of finding the hidden preplan and then simply conforming to it."

4. Trust the insights that come from your body, intuition, and feelings.

    Listening to the Spirit "calls for attentiveness to *all* dimensions of the self, the emotional as well as the rational, the conscious as well as the unconscious. The resources stressed in this approach to discernment are ones which women's socialization has strengthened in them: intuition, bodily awareness, imagination, empathy."

5. Be aware of the social and cultural forces influencing a situation.

    The focus of interest in discernment, often emphasizing "inner states and the process of sifting through our affective experiences . . . needs to be broadened. It must include outer circumstances, social arrangements, and structures. It must situate our personal histories within cultural and religious history. . . . Approaches to discernment need to be based on the realization that healing society's inequities is the only lasting way to bring about spiritual wholeness for all persons."

6. Interpret your affective experiences in light of women's social conditioning.

    "If emotions are to offer clues to the influence of the good or evil spirit in our life, we must be aware of the way in which the experience of oppression has conditioned these emotional responses. . . . The goal of discernment is growth in the Spirit, not the maintenance of the present social or religious system. Movement to the new brings conflict all along the way. . . . Short-term discomfort may be necessary for moving out of destructive situations."

7. Try to generate alternatives when you feel trapped.

    "Imagining a different way of living is the first step toward change. When women's choices are circumscribed by existing patterns, it is helpful to brainstorm other possibilities. This is best done in collaboration with others, since imagining with a community leads to possibilities we might not have seen alone. . . . This aspect of discernment is also based on the realization that not all approaches work well in every situation."

8. Take account of the price of change.

    "Insight is not usually sufficient to bring about change. . . . This is a time for relying deeply on God's grace, asking her to be with us as we step over into life. We may have to cross the border between life and death many times . . . before we finally choose to stay in the zone of life. It is not easy to change established social structures or the personal patterns of a life-time. . . . Liberation is a process, and it is God's work as well as our own."

God in heaven,
you have helped my life.
to grow like a tree.
Now something has happened.
Satan, like a bird,
has carried in one twig of his own choosing after another.
Before I knew it he had built a dwelling place
and was living in it.
Tonight, my Father, I am throwing out
both the bird and the nest.

A Prayer from Nigeria

Seedlings

If any of the short sentences that follow appeals to you,
place it in your heart and ponder on its inner meaning.
This will cause its inner truth to germinate and grow.
Do not force it open with your mind.
That would only kill the seed.
Sow it where the soil is rich. Sow it in your heart.
And give it time.

You do not
have
to change
for God
to love
you.

Be grateful
for your sins.
They are carriers
of grace.

> Say goodbye
> to golden yesterdays
> —or your heart
> will never learn
> to love
> the present.

ANTHONY DE MELLO

SUSCIPE

....

Take, Lord, and receive all my liberty,
my memory, my understanding
and my entire will,
All I have and call my own.
You have given all to me.
To you, Lord, I return it.
Everything is yours; do with it what you will.
Give me only your love and your grace,
That is enough for me.

IGNATIUS OF LOYOLA (1491–1556)

Lord, I want to go where You want me to go
Do what You want me to do
Be what You want me to be
Save me!

I say this prayer every morning when I rise. It connects me to the singing in
my childhood church and helps me to try to submit my will to God daily.

MARIAN WRIGHT EDELMAN

CHAPTER TWENTY-SEVEN

Prayer and
the Needs of the World:
Spirituality and Social Justice

You are the salt of the earth; but if salt has lost its taste, how can its
saltiness be restored?

MATTHEW 5:13A

O God, to those who have hunger give bread,
To those who have bread give the hunger for justice

A PRAYER FROM LATIN AMERICA

Doing the just thing keeps praying from pessimism, which is not
faith, and praying keeps doing of the just thing from resignation,
which is not Christian either.

EBERHARD BETHGE

Thy kingdom come.

THE LORD'S PRAYER

Praying always raises the question: So what? Ought I not be spending time *doing*? How can I sit and pray when there is so much suffering in the world? What good does prayer do? Judaism, Christianity, and Islam, all traditions of action and justice, agree that prayer by itself is empty, not true prayer. "Is this not the fast that I choose," the book of Isaiah, sacred to both Christians and Jews, asks: "to loose the bonds of injustice, to undo the throngs of the yoke, to let the oppressed go free, and to break every yoke? Is it not to share your bread with the hungry, and bring the homeless poor into your house; when you see the naked, to cover them, and not to hide yourself from your own kin?"[1] "Shall I not tell you what is better than prayers and fasting and giving alms to the poor?" said the Prophet Muhammad. "It is making peace between one another."[2] Justice and peace are not adjuncts to holiness; they are holiness itself. "Justice," says Jesuit biblical scholar John Donahue, "is the holiness of God embodied in human relationships."[3]

All the same, our traditions urge prayer upon us as part of the path to holiness. What then is the relationship between the hunger of our hearts for God and the hungers of the world? What does it mean for us to pray for the well-being of our society and of our planet? How can we live the relationship between prayer and the realities of social and economic injustice that surround us? Swiss theologian Karl Barth urged his contemporaries to pray with the Bible in one hand and the daily newspaper in the other. His contemporary, German theologian Dietrich Bonhoeffer, like Barth a resister against the Nazi evil, spoke of "praying and doing the just thing among people" as a path for life.

Prayer and action for justice—"doing the just thing"—interweave; one will lead to the other. "Prayer for others takes you out of yourself," said my friend Tom, who has been working several months a year in one of the poorest neighborhoods of Lima, Peru. Speaking of his neighbors there, he asked: "Seeing the horrible conditions they live in day in and day out, how can you pray and live without doing what you can to eliminate what causes the suffering in the first place?" The reverse is also true: "How can you work against injustice and not pray?" Many of the community workers Tom knows in Lima—"miraculous," he calls them, "they keep going"—find strength in the circular movement of prayer leading to action leading to prayer.

Barbara, writing from British Columbia, put it another way. "I think that when we split our lives into 'contemplative' and 'active' we rob ourselves of wholeness. I believe that every person has a contemplative dimension, and that our contemplative prayer leads to service to our brothers and sisters."

In *Proclaim Jubilee! A Spirituality for the Twenty-First Century*, Maria Harris recounts an anecdote from a World Council of Churches meeting in Sydney, Australia. "Krister Stendahl, then dean of Harvard Divinity School, noted that whenever an issue was brought to the table, it got four characteristic responses: Latin Americans responded with customary passion; Africans asked what the implications were for the community; Asians reflected quietly in contemplative mindfulness; and North Americans inquired, 'What are we going to do?' The point of this recollection is not to set these responses in conflict. Instead, it is to note that we need all four perspectives. We need passion and community and contemplative being and active intervention when responding to suffering."[4]

My brother recently sent me an article about United Nations Secretary-General Kofi Annan's return from apparently successful negotiations with Iraqi leader Saddam Hussein. The article noted that Annan's staff cheered him wildly. "I did not do it alone," Annan responded. "There were millions of people around the world rooting for a peaceful solution and praying for us." He added—and my brother underlined—"You should never underestimate the power of prayer." A day later, I received from an activist network an e-mail message noting the way in which grassroots peace groups had recently challenged in public the U.S. government's positions and policies on Iraq, both representing and changing public opinion. I write these words in days of fragile peace, but the questions will remain: What "did it"? Prayer? Local activism? Global leadership and diplomatic skill? All of the above? In what proportion? Does it matter? To whom does it matter?

"Pray as if everything depended on God; act as if everything depended on you" the saying goes, sounding like a religious version of "Cover your bases." It is that, and more. To bring about justice and peace, we may have to move heaven and earth, imploring God as well as putting to good use every art and craft we have learned. I would also modify the saying, or rather add a postscript: "Then again, act as if everything depended on God." I do mean both: act as if everything depended on you, and act as if everything depended on God. The latter is the fruit of prayer. Our activisms will be far better off if we know our ultimate dependence on God, if we place our security with God and not with weapons, money, service, and social-change groups, or even our own talents and gifts. "I say you can't work for justice until you've turned poor," my friend Sonia said, quoting one of her favorite books, William E. Reiser's *Into the Needle's Eye*: "There is a poverty which the human soul experiences as it awakens to the fact that everything in the world belongs to God," writes Reiser. "This is the ultimate truth about us. No one learns this truth without first turning poor."[5] Prayer—especially nonutilitarian, "useless" prayer for God's sake as much as ours, prayer in our utter dependence—fosters a broader and deeper perspective: on the situation or crisis with which we are dealing, on our own egos, on the material goods we own and skills that help us to survive.

Praying for the needs of our world raises acutely the questions of evil and suffering, especially the suffering of the innocent. Peruvian liberation theologian Gustavo Gutiérrez notes that the real subject in the book of Job is not suffering itself, "that impenetrable human mystery," but how to speak about God in the midst of suffering.[6] It is also of course about conversing *with* God in the midst of this unjust suffering. In other words, it pertains not only to our view of evil and of God, but to our prayer in the midst of evil.

Unjust suffering, yes: Job has done nothing to bring about financial ruin, death of children, physical illness—just as the neighbors with whom Tom works and about whom Gustavo Gutiérrez writes have not brought upon themselves the deaths of children at an early age, poor sanitation, lack of access to formal education, exclusion from the political process. We do not have to travel to Peru to find this kind of suffering: it is present in the neighborhoods of our country, where too often we blame the poor for being poor.

How to pray in the face of this? We pray to a God who loves and welcomes all, yet we often understand this God to be biased. We read this bias in different ways, but if we belong to biblically based traditions, the bias is most often in favor of the poor, the dispossessed, the disenfranchised, and the marginal. The biblical traditions show partiality, inviting us to pray with images before our eyes and summons ringing in our ears: protect the orphan and the widow, proclaim liberty to the captives, feed the hungry, clothe the naked, comfort the brokenhearted, rebuild the ruined cities.

The profession of faith of the base communities of El Salvador, written and prayed from the perspective of socially disenfranchised women and men deeply committed to their Christian faith, shows both partiality and inclusion. It proclaims: "We believe that Christ calls us to communion and to live as sisters and brothers. We believe that we need to love one another, to correct one another compassionately, to forgive one another's errors and weaknesses. We believe that we need to help one another recognize our limitations, to support each other in the faith. We believe that the poor, the illiterate, and the sick, the persecuted and tortured, are closest to the Gospel of Jesus. Through them, Christ challenges us to work for justice and peace. Their cause is our cause. We believe that Christ is also present in those who are slaves to their passions, to vices, lies, and injustice, to power and money. We commit ourselves never to give up hope in the possibility of their conversion, to love them even though they slander, persecute, and kill us; to pray for them and to help them so that one day they may live simply and humbly in the way that the Gospel calls all of us to live."[7]

Conversion: this, of course, is what the making of justice requires, that justice the Jewish tradition calls *tikkun olam*, "the repair of the world," and whose pursuit the assembled Catholic bishops of the world called "a constitutive dimension of the preaching of the Gospel,"[8] that is, part and parcel of the message of faith and its living in the world. "This is what's hard," said Sonia. "You pray for leaders to get their act together and take care of the poor and for people's hearts to be open to helping others and to being helped themselves, but all of that ultimately can be very abstract as a prayer. What makes it concrete is thinking about your own life, and if you were going to take a step toward justice what would that mean. That means looking at some very serious issues like, do you realize you are poor and you are powerless and God is in charge, and if you don't realize this, what objects or lifestyle are helping you to be deluded? You know, the Armani suit that can lull you into the notion that you're fabulous."

When I raised the question of prayer and social justice with Tom, his first question was "If you are the recipient of injustice? Or if you are the one who sees the injustice?" He could have added "Or if you are a perpetrator of injustice? A bystander? A participant in an unjust structure or situation?" In other words, Tom was asking me, and us: from what location do you pray for the social order? It matters. Be aware of it. All things are not equal: as a privileged, white North American, my prayer is not the same, nor can nor should it be, as that of Tom's neighbors in Lima. My prayer is not separate from theirs, since as humans we are sisters and brothers before God our Creator. I may well meet some of them one day and break bread with them. Yet the Gospel calls us in different ways; they and I do not have the same relationship to the suffering they innocently endure: crushing, deadly poverty into which they were born and in whose grip they die too young, because of social structures that concentrate the wealth of their country into the hands of a very few. When we pray "Give us this day our daily bread" and "Forgive us our debts," our needs and understandings are radically different.

Sonia continued her reflection: "You need to pray about what's enough. I'm talking about income, the size of your apartment, how frequently you need to have Ben and Jerry's ice cream. If you believe in justice and you believe in peace, where are you putting your cash? Where is it going, for yourself and others?" Sonia is an educator who helps schools and school districts to consider how to strengthen student achievement and school communities. Her husband, David, is a writer and consultant in information technology planning with a strong interest in the ethics of computer use in contemporary business. They and their young son, Christopher, live in a two-bedroom walk-up apartment in Boston. "We need more space now that we have Christopher," Sonia said. "But most of America doesn't have the space we have. So we're thinking and praying not just about how big a mortgage we can afford, but about 'how do we live in a place where the mortgage wouldn't keep us from making our daily work a work related to social justice?'"

Katie and José Luis regularly worship with a community of refugees from Latin America who meet at a Catholic Worker house in Oakland. They come largely from El Salvador, but also from Guatemala, Mexico, Honduras, Belize, Nicaragua, and Peru. Their prayer, Katie observed, is born of their own situation, "being a community in exile in a very poor neighborhood and themselves poor and hardly educated." They pray with a lot of petitions "for people who are sick both here and at home, for people who have been mugged or beaten on the street, for orphans, for homeless people. It's not so much a lamentation, a crying 'Why?' but a holding up in prayer, bringing the people to mind. They pray for people who are without hope and do not know God—'For people who do not know You, Father'—and for help in 'bringing our children up right.' They pray 'Forgive us when we don't hear your voice and fail to do your will,' and there are a lot of prayers for people with *vicios*, vices: drink, drugs, violence. They are often very well-articulated prayers that sound like somebody wrote them."

The refugee community also prays in thanksgiving for those who have sheltered and otherwise helped them, for the blessings of daily life, and especially for the presence of community. Again and again there are prayers for mothers and children. There is also, Katie said, "a lot of remembrance: remembering people who have died in the war, people who are still living and struggling at home. There's a real sense of missing family, and of the time lost, a real achy spot, especially around mothers or children people had to leave behind. There's this devotion to people who are gone. They remember martyrs: they still commemorate [Archbishop Oscar] Romero and Rutilio Grande.[9] We always have the *¡Presente!*—we make present the people who have died."

Prayer on behalf of justice is often a summoning of "dangerous memory," a remembering described by German theologian Johannes Baptist Metz as revealing "new and dangerous insights for the present. . . . They are memories that we have to take into account, memories, as it were, with a future content."[10] The *¡Presente!* of the refugee community is this kind of memory, a bringing alive as much as a going back, with the dead bringing back the values and people and communities for which they died.

In the African American community, as in so many others, it is the memory of the ancestors that helps people "keep on keeping on" in the present, memories like that of Uncle Silas, a slave whose story is told by Dwight Hopkins of the University of Chicago Divinity School in his book *Shoes That Fit Our Feet*.

"One ex-slave," Hopkins writes, "tells a story about a white minister sent to preach, no doubt, the standard 'slaves obey your master' sermon to the blacks on the plantation. Uncle Silas, a 100-year-old slave, hobbled up to the front row and challenged the white preacher with a pointed inquiry: 'Is us slaves gonna be free in Heaven?' The preacher abruptly halted his religious instructions and eyed Uncle Silas with vile contempt and a desire to kill him for questioning the normalcy of white theological doctrine. However Uncle Silas did not budge and this time resumed the debate with a yell: 'Is God gonna free us slaves when we git to Heaven?' The white preacher withdrew a handkerchief, mopped the sweat from his pale white brow and replied, 'Jesus says come unto Me ye who are free fum sin an' I will give you salvation.' Undaunted Uncle Silas rebutted: '*Gonna give us freedom 'long wid salvation?*' The preacher resumed his homily and Uncle Silas remained standing during the rest of the service" (emphasis added).[11]

Stories like Uncle Silas's are told in times of worship, but the story itself is about prayer as witness. Prayer for the world around us is not just petition but often witness, both to concrete injustices and to the reality of hope beyond them. The retelling of Uncle Silas's challenge, the *¡Presente!* of the refugees, the silent Good Friday Quaker witnesses for peace of my Boston years, vigils against the death penalty, urban Stations of the Cross in an immigrant neighborhood, a Mothers' March Against Drugs filled with the sustaining prayers of several religious traditions—these are only a few of the witnessing prayers for justice that both sufferers and sympathizers bring forth from their hearts into their churches or streets.

Petition, prayer of discernment and clarification of values, remembering and witnessing—all these prayers for the world and its suffering are undergirded by visions. Prayer for justice is a visionary prayer. In the face of individual and collective suffering and of the corruption and evil of so many systems and institutions, alternative visions lead to a prayer of hope. They are also wonderfully concrete. We who claim the biblical traditions as our heritage have several visions at our disposal, especially the visions of *shalom*, of the kingdom or realm of God, and of the Jubilee. *Shalom*: this Hebrew word, still used today and rooted in the biblical text, means "peace"—not a negotiated and fragile peace held together by treaty, not the absence of war, but fullness: lion lying with lamb, calves fat, fields thick with wheat, enemies embracing, ruined cities rebuilt, former wastelands flowing with streams. Not one image of *shalom* but rather a multitude of images runs through the Hebrew Scriptures.

"Thy kingdom come," Christians pray in the prayer of Jesus. We pray urgently, and with awareness that this is God's kingdom of which we speak, not our own, that earthly rulers do not rule us. Jesus also speaks frequently of the coming of the kingdom in the Gospel accounts in both his call for conversion—a change of life—and his parables. Some today have begun to use less patriarchal, more inclusive language, first saying "reign" rather than "kingdom," and now, dispensing with royalty altogether, "realm," and more recently "kindom," a play on the old "kingdom" word expressing our relatedness: we are kin to each other—slum dwellers in Lima, students in Berkeley, sex workers in Manila, bankers in Tokyo, farmers in Ghana, artists in Australia, and clerks in Belarus. Despite the change in vocabulary, the vision is much the same. It looks a great deal like the one my friend Alex had in San Francisco's Tenderloin neighborhood. At the time a volunteer coordinator at St. Anthony Foundation—St. Anthony's has a food program serving about two thousand people a day—Alex "was just sitting there one day, watching people come in. St. Anthony's has the people with disabilities and the elderly enter first. They go in and sit down [right away]; everyone else who is able stands in line and goes through cafeteria style. I was watching these people, visibly bruised and beaten by life—they're struggling just to get into the dining room, limping their way in. At that moment I had a sense of the fullness of love, and of these folks being first in God's kingdom. That has always stayed with me. That's what we have to do in order to build a just society: these folks do have to go first and we have to seat them at the table first and listen to them and be with them. That's really where the kingdom is breaking through."

Katie said, "If I were to summarize what is the majority of the [Central American refugee] community's vision for a just future, I would describe a typical Salvadoran drawing, where they have a village with houses and the sun is out and you can see the five volcanoes [of this land], in the background there is a dove flying, there are people growing crops. It seems very basic, but clear, a vision of justice and harmony; I don't think they would call it the kingdom. It is a place where there is a home, a family, a school, a clinic, and community activity. I don't know why they don't lose that vision, that hope," she added, "but it's all over the place. We have a mural that all the men, women, and children helped to paint, in fact we have made several, and they always have bright colors, they always show animals, crops, children, clergy, farmers, everyone is working and working the land, with this vision of harmony and health and respecting your parents and being good guardians and caretakers of your children, and they just don't lose it, which boggles my mind, because they live in an ugly, dirty, violent, crowded, noisy neighborhood."

After barely noticing the Jubilee Year, the Bible's "Sabbath of Sabbaths," during college study of the Bible, I discovered it more than twenty years ago through one of my professors, Sister of Notre Dame Marie Augusta Neal. More recently, another former professor, Maria Harris, again placed the vision before my eyes and before a broader public. The Jubilee Year described in the twenty-fifth chapter of the book of Leviticus is a "Sabbath of Sabbaths." Just as every seventh day of the week is a day of rest, every seventh year the land lies fallow. After seven times seven years comes the fiftieth year, the Year of Jubilee, marked by more rest for the land, but also by forgiveness—of debts first, but also of grievance and sin—freedom for prisoners and liberty throughout the land, a just redistribution of resources and power, and, last but not least, celebration and jubilation. Harris warns against overspiritualizing this text, which contains a vital spirituality, "attentive to dailiness, flesh and blood."[12] This is the spirituality in which the prayer for justice bathes and which it sustains, where prayer is both sheer poverty and dependence and, in Sonia's words, "the never-ending work of trying to bring more alignment between what you hope for and how you live."

THE MAGNIFICAT OF MARY

My Soul proclaims your greatness, O my God,
and my spirit has rejoiced in you, my Savior,

For your regard has blessed me,
poor, and a serving woman.

From this day all generations
will call me blessed,

For you who are mighty, have made me great.
Most Holy be your Name.

Your mercy is on those who fear you
throughout all generations.

You have shown strength with your arm,
you have scattered the proud in their hearts' fantasy.

You have put down the mighty from their seat,
and have lifted up the powerless.

You have filled the hungry with good things,
and have sent the rich away empty.

You, remembering your mercy,
have helped your people Israel,

As you promised Abraham and Sarah.
Mercy to their children, forever.

LUKE 1:46–55

WHEN HE CAME (1.)

He needs you
That's all there is to it
without you he's left hanging
goes up in dachau's smoke
is sugar and spice in the baker's hands
gets revalued in the next stock market crash
he's consumed and blown away

used up
without you

Help him
That's what faith is about
he can't bring it about
his kingdom
couldn't then couldn't later can't now
not at any rate without you
and that is his irresistible appeal

DOROTHEE SOELLE

Grandfather Great Spirit,
all over the world the faces of living ones are alike.
With tenderness they have come out of the ground.
Look upon your children that they may
face the winds and walk the good road to the
Day of Quiet.
Grandfather Great Spirit
Fill us with the Light.
Give us the strength to understand,
and the eyes to see.
Teach us to walk the soft Earth as relatives to all that live.

LAKOTA SIOUX PRAYER

For the hungry and the overfed
May we have enough.

For the mourners and the mockers
May we laugh together.

For the victims and the oppressors
May we share power wisely.

For the peacemakers and the warmongers
May clear truth and stern love lead us to harmony.

For the silenced and the propagandists
May we speak our own words in truth.

For the unemployed and the overworked
May our impress on the earth be kindly and creative.

For the troubled and the sleek
May we live together as wounded healers.

For the homeless and the cosseted
May our homes be simple, warm and welcoming.

For the vibrant and the dying
May we all die to live.

A NEW ZEALAND PRAYER BOOK

Come Lord
Do not smile and say
you are already with us.
Millions do not know you
and to us who do,
what is the difference?
What is the point of your presence
if our lives do not alter?
Change our lives, shatter
our complacency.
Make your word,
flesh of our flesh,
blood of our blood
and our life's purpose.
Take away the quietness
of a clear conscience.
Press us uncomfortably.
For only thus
that other peace is made,
your peace.

DOM HELDER CÂMARA

God of peace,
let us your people know,
that at the heart of turbulence
there is an inner calm that comes
from faith in you.
Keep us from being content with things as they are,
that from this central peace
there may come a creative compassion,
a thirst for justice,
and a willingness to give of ourselves
in the spirit of Christ.
Amen.

A NEW ZEALAND PRAYER BOOK

A STORY FROM THE TALMUD AND QUESTIONS FOR US

When god had created heaven and earth
he loved both equally
the heavens rejoiced
and praised god's glory
but the earth wept

    did you hear the earth weep
    did you forget the dying fish
    was the old tree in your way
    did you miss the birds
    did you hear the earth weep

the earth gave three reasons for weeping
you keep me she said at a distance
but the heavens are close to you
and rejoice in your glory

    did you come to comfort the earth when she was ravaged
    did you join with the pack and reckon the booty
    did you see the beauty of her old face with all its crevices
    did you show everyone how god's closeness makes her shine
    did you come to comfort the earth

my nourishment said the earth
you've given over to the heavens

and the heavens are fed from your own table
    did you hear the earth's complaints
    to get rid of the lords above who wouldn't like that
    or to sit at a table with plenty for all
    did you forget that she can feed everyone
    did you hear the earth's complaints against the lords
whatever lives on me the earth said
is doomed to death
death that does not enter the realms of heaven
why then said the earth should I not weep
    did you hear the earth speak
    did you understand the language of the earth
    did you listen to the lies of the heavenly immortals
    did you share the earth's sadness
    did you hear the earth speak
according to the books god comforted the earth
but he didn't promise her closeness
better food or life free of death
don't be downhearted earth
someday you too he said
will be among those who rejoice
    did you ever see god give comfort
    except through you or me
    did you rejoice with the earth
    did you learn from her to rejoice
    did you see god give comfort
were you a comfort for the earth

        DOROTHEE SOELLE

CHRIST'S BODY

•••

Christ has no body now on earth but yours;
yours are the only hands with which he can do his work,
yours are the only feet with which he can go about the world,
yours are the only eyes through which his compassion
can shine forth upon a troubled world.
Christ has no body on earth now but yours.

ATTRIBUTED TO TERESA OF ÁVILA (1515–1582)

Bread for the Journey: A Blessing

Gather us in and hold us forever,
Gather us in and make us your own,
Gather us in, all peoples together,
Fire of love in our flesh and our bone.
Marty Haugen

In the Gospel of Luke, two grieving disciples are on the road to a village called Emmaus. Jesus is dead. They do not yet know that he is risen. When he begins to walk on the road with them, they still do not recognize him. They speak of the latest and most important news and of its impact on their lives, engage with him in holy conversation, pondering the Scriptures. "Stay with us," they tell the stranger whose words touch them in ways they do not yet understand. They sit and share a simple meal. As Jesus and they break bread, they recognize him, and he disappears. "Did not our hearts burn within us?" they say as they look back on their walk with him on the dusty road. Now they know it was him. It has taken time, attention, conversation, and nourishment to come to that knowledge. They have walked with sorrow, discouragement, and weariness. In the friendship of a shared meal, they have discovered the friendship that will never die.

Our prayer has its banquet days and its Emmaus days, and days and weeks when all we see and feel is the dusty road. The food comes from God. The road goes to God. Together and in solitude, we walk, hunger, thirst, remember, notice, and hope.

More than ever I find myself in the hands of God.

This is what I have wanted all my life from my youth.

But now there is a difference;

the initiative is entirely with God.

It is indeed a profound spiritual experience

to know and feel myself so totally in God's hands.

PEDRO ARRUPE (1907–1991)

Pedro Arrupe, Superior General of the Society of Jesus (Jesuits) from 1965 to 1983, composed this prayer after suffering a debilitating stroke, the effects of which he patiently endured for the final ten years of his life.

WE DID NOT WANT IT EASY, GOD

We did not want it easy, God,

But we did not contemplate

That it would be quite this hard,

This long, this lonely.

So, if we are to be turned inside out,

And upside down,

With even our pockets shaken

Just to check what's rattling

And left behind,

We pray that you will keep faith with us,

And we with you,

Holding our hands as we weep,

Giving us strength to continue,

And showing us beacons

Along the way

To becoming new.

ANNA MCKENZIE

GOD'S GRANDEUR

The world is charged with the grandeur of God,
It will flame out, like shining from shook foil;
It gathers to a greatness, like the ooze of oil

Crushed. Why do men then now not reck his rod?
Generations have trod, have trod, have trod;
    And all is seared with trade, bleared, smeared with toil;
    And wears man's smudge and shares man's smell; the soil
Is bare now, nor can foot feel, being shod

And for all this, nature is never spent;
    There lives the dearest freshness deep down things;
And though the last lights off the black West went
    Oh, morning, and the brown brink eastward, springs—
Because the Holy Ghost over the bent
    World broods with warm breast and with ah! bright wings.

GERARD MANLEY HOPKINS (1844–1889)

O God whose greeting we miss
and whose departure we delay,
make our hearts burn with insight
on our ordinary road;
that, as we grasp you in the broken bread,
we may also let you go
and return to speak your word of life
in the name of Christ, Amen.

JANET MORLEY

May holy Wisdom,
kind to humanity,
steadfast, sure and free,
the breath of the power of God;
may she who makes all things new, in every age,
enter our souls,
and make us friends of God,
through Jesus Christ,
Amen.

JANET MORLEY

ABBREVIATIONS USED IN
EPIGRAPH SOURCES AND NOTES

....

Bible Translations

ICEL International Committee on English in the Liturgy (Psalms)

JB Jerusalem Bible

KJV King James (Authorized) Version

NRSV New Revised Standard Version

SB/EF *The Shocken Bible*, volume 1, *The Five Books of Moses* (Genesis, Exodus, Leviticus, Numbers, Deuteronomy), ed. Everett Fox (New York: Schocken Books, 1995.)

Other Abbreviations

NZPB *A New Zealand Prayer Book/ He Karakia Mihinare o Aotearoa*

Notes

●●

Introduction

1. My colleague Fred Sanders views the process somewhat differently; his ideas have given me pause, though they have not fully convinced me. In his understanding, the relationship between doxology and doctrine, between prayer and the formal articulation of belief, is more of a perpetual loop (my term). I thank Fred for our conversation on this matter, and continue to ponder his insight.

2. "Spiritual direction" is really a misnomer, as most of its practitioners know. A spiritual director is probably more midwife than director. Nevertheless, the terms "spiritual direction," "director," and "directee" remain in use to describe the process of one person accompanying another on his or her journey of prayer by attentive listening and gentle assistance in discerning the presence of God and the movement of the Spirit in his or her life.

3. See John 15:12–17.

4. Jane Redmont, *Generous Lives: American Catholic Women Today* (New York: W. Morrow and Co., 1992).

5. Wade Clark Roof, *A Generation of Seekers: The Spiritual Journeys of the Baby Boom Generation* (New York: HarperCollins, 1993).

6. Many Jews and an increasing number of Gentiles refer to the destruction perpetuated by the Nazis from Hitler's rise to power in 1933 till the end of World War II in 1945, against all Jews as well as Polish patriots, Communists, homosexuals, Gypsies, mentally ill persons, and others, as the *Shoah*, originally a Hebrew word meaning "catastrophe." Cardinal Johannes Willebrands, president of the Holy See's Commission for Religious Relations with the Jews, notes of the term "Holocaust": "In the Bible this word indicates 'a sacrifice to God of an offering wholly consumed by fire.' Under no circumstances can the extermination of Jews in Europe between 1939 and 1945 be considered as a 'sacrifice to God' offered by the persecutors." Johannes Cardinal Willebrands, *Church and Jewish People: New Considerations* (New York: Paulist Press, 1992), 159.

7. Krister Stendahl, "From God's Perspective We Are All Minorities," in *Journal of Religious Pluralism* 2 (1993):10.

Chapter 1

1. Miriam Ashkin Stanton, journal excerpt and personal correspondence, November 1996.

2. John 15:12–17.

3. Thomas Merton, *Thoughts in Solitude* (Garden City, NY: Image Books, 1956), 47.

4. Luke 17:20–21.

5. Jon Kabat-Zinn, *Wherever You Go, There You Are: Mindfulness Meditation in Everyday Life* (New York: Hyperion, 1994), 22.

6. "Charge" is close, but does not capture the full meaning of the Hebrew word *mitzvah*: duty, commandment, but also joyful responsibility and celebration.

7. Julian of Norwich, *Showings* (Long Text), Classics of Western Spirituality, trans. and intro. Edmund Colledge, O.S.A., and James Walsh, S.J. (Ramsey, NY: Paulist Press, 1978), 225, 13th Revelation, chapter 27.

8. Romans 8:18–28.

9. I am grateful to Elena Stone for our conversations about these matters, and especially for her notion of nature as community. I am also grateful to my classmates Kirk Wegter-McNelly, for reflections on nature, science, and moral community; and Kimberly Whitney, for reflections on nature and spirituality.

10. David Toolan, "Praying in a Post-Einsteinian Universe," in *Cross Currents* 46, no. 4 (Winter 1996–97): 445.

Chapter 2

1. Kosuke Koyama. *Three Mile an Hour God: Biblical Reflections* (Maryknoll, NY: Orbis Books, 1980), 6.

2. Diana is practicing a modified form of the "Jesus Prayer" or "Prayer of the Heart," an ancient meditative prayer practice of the Christian East that is increasingly popular in the West.

3. A devotional practice in which participants focus their prayer on representations of fourteen scenes of Jesus Christ's passion.

4. A "catechumen" is a participant in the Rite of Christian Initiation of Adults who has never been baptized; a "candidate" is an RCIA participant who is already a baptized Christian and seeks full communion and membership in the Catholic Church. Some parishes also involve "returning Catholics" (Catholics who have been away from the church for a long while and wish to become actively involved again) in the RCIA, or have adapted the rite for them.

5. Nancy Roth, *The Breath of God: An Approach to Prayer* (Cambridge, MA: Cowley Publications, 1990), 149. In addition to her discussion of the Myers-Briggs typology, Roth also presents Friedrich von Hügel's typology of the three "elements" of religion: historical/institutional, intellectual, and mystical, pp. 149–151. For more on the Myers-Briggs Type Indicator (MBTI), which classifies people into sixteen personality types according to four polarities (Extroversion/Introversion, Sensing/Intuition, Thinking/Feeling, Judging/Perceiving), see Isabel Briggs Myers, *Introduction to Type* (Palo Alto, CA: Consulting Psychologists Press, 1980). For more on the MBTI and its relationship to prayer, with practical suggestions for specific temperaments, see Chester P.

Michael and Marie C. Norrisey, *Prayer and Temperament: Different Forms of Prayer for Different Personality Types* (Charlottesville, VA: The Open Door, 1991).

6. Roth, *The Breath of God*, 149.

7. See Abraham Joshua Heschel, *The Sabbath: Its Meaning for Modern Man* (New York: Farrar, Straus and Giroux, 1951), 2–24.

Chapter 3

1. Believers as well as scholars are beginning to change the nomenclatures "Old Testament" and "New Testament" to "Hebrew Bible" and "Christian Testament," with the former term gaining wider usage. The change reflects a theological shift away from a belief that the Christian covenant supersedes, or is superior to, the Jewish covenant. I use "Hebrew Bible" consistently to reflect this rejection of the first testament, or covenant, as somehow "old" in the sense of "less valid" or "no longer valid." I have chosen to continue to refer to "New Testament" in most cases since the implications of the term are not as exclusive. I am also in the process of rethinking this practice.

2. David Toolan, S.J., "The Catholic Taboo Against Schism: Strained but Holding," in *Religion and Intellectual Life* 7 (Fall 1989): 36–37.

3. See Thich Nhat Hanh, *The Long Road Turns to Joy: A Guide to Walking Meditation* (Berkeley, CA: Parallax Press, 1996), and references to *kinhin* (Zen walking) in Roshi Philip Kapleau, *The Three Pillars of Zen: Teaching, Practice and Enlightenment* (New York: Anchor, 1989), 36–37, 40, 136, 202, 265.

4. In Catholic parlance, "congregation" often means "religious order" rather than "worshipping community." Annmarie uses it here in this sense.

Chapter 4

1. Teresina Havens, *Mind What Stirs in Your Heart* (Wallingford, PA: Pendle Hill Publications, 1992), 6.

2. Peter reminded me during our conversations that in Kabbalah, the Jewish mystical and esoteric tradition, *Ruach* is also the primordial ether out of which the universe was fashioned. As such, according to Kabbalah, it exists out of time and is without materiality. For an introduction to Kabbalah, see Daniel C. Matt, *The Essential Kabbalah: The Heart of Jewish Mysticism* (New York: HarperCollins, 1995).

3. *The Schocken Bible*, vol. 1, *The Five Books of Moses*, trans. and ed. Everett Fox (New York: Schocken Books, 1995), 13, n.2.

4. Thich Nhat Hanh, *The Miracle of Mindfulness: A Manual on Meditation*, trans. Mobi Ho, rev. ed. (Boston: Beacon Press, 1975), 15.

5. See Herbert Benson, *The Relaxation Response* (New York: William Morrow, 1975), and *Beyond the Relaxation Response* (New York: Times Books, 1984); Joan Borysenko, *Minding the Body, Mending the Mind* (Reading, MA: Addison-Wesley, 1987); Jon Kabat-Zinn, *Full Catastrophe Living: Using the Wisdom of Your Body and Mind to Face Stress, Pain, and Illness* (New York: Delta, 1990).

6. Sometime after he wrote me, I asked Peter to tell me the origin of this practice and how to do it. He was not sure of the origin, but described further the three steps: stop, look, and listen; decide to change your regular hyperactive breath pattern: take a long, first breath, which marks the transition to conscious breathing, thinking of it also as a cleansing breath. Move then to focusing all your attention on that second breath, a centering breath. Finally let the third breath be meditative, reminding your body and mind, heart and soul, of the quiet that is yours to uncover.

7. Romans 8:26.

8. See Stanley B. Marrow, *Speaking the Word Fearlessly: Boldness in the New Testament* (New York: Paulist Press, 1982).

9. Roth, *The Breath of God*, 20–21.

10. Unity Church, which has congregations around the United States, stresses personal belief and "practical Christianity" as well as the power of prayer, and has recently drawn people dissatisfied with traditional Christianity. The Unity School of Christianity and the Association of Unity Churches are both part of the larger Unity movement, founded by Charles S. (1854–1948) and Myrtle (1845–1931) Fillmore.

11. Kallistos Ware, "Ways of Prayer and Contemplation I: Eastern," in *Christian Spirituality: Origins to the Twelfth Century*, vol. 16, *World Spirituality: An Encyclopedic History of the Religious Quest*, eds. Bernard McGinn, John Meyendorff, and Jean Leclercq (New York: Crossroad, 1997). See esp. 402–410.

12. Ibid., 403.

13. Ibid., 402–403.

14. Roth, *The Breath of God*, 51.

15. Ibid., 55.

16. Ibid., 8–9.

17. Thomas Keating, "Cultivating the Centering Prayer," in *Finding Grace at the Center*, Thomas Keating, M. Basil Pennington, and Thomas E. Clarke, (Petersham, MA: St. Bede's Publications, 1978), 30.

18. Havens, in an aside, notes the appropriateness of this word, from the Latin *spiro*, "to breathe," and *ad*, "toward."

Chapter 5

1. Prayer of praise, in both silent and noisy mode, is also this kind of prayer. There is something wonderfully "useless" about sheer celebration. In this respect, the rapidly growing Pentecostal churches have much to teach us.

2. Thomas Moore, *Meditations: On the Monk Who Dwells in Daily Life* (New York: HarperCollins, 1994), 19.

3. Author and spiritual director Kathleen Fischer provides a helpful explanation of this term and of its partner and complementary opposite, *kataphatic.* "Our spiritual lives take two interrelated paths to God. One path, traditionally called the *kataphatic* and exemplified by spiritual writers such as Teresa of Avila and Ignatius of Loyola, emphasizes our capacity to reach God through creatures, images, and symbols. It underscores the similarity between God and creation which is the basis for an incarnational and sacramental vision. . . . This *kataphatic* way has been the dominant approach in western spirituality.

   "Today, there is a revival of interest in another dimension of the tradition, that approach which sees all particular expressions of God as radically inadequate. . . . This path, which is called the *apophatic,* . . . finds expression in the writings of *The Cloud of Unknowing,* John of the Cross, Simone Weil, and Thomas Merton. It emphasizes that God is 'not this, not that' [an expression originally found in the sacred scriptures of India, in the Brhadaranyaka Upanisad], Because of the radical difference between God and creatures, God is best known in obscure awareness, and, at times, in darkness." Kathleen Fischer, *Women at the Well: Feminist Perspectives on Spiritual Direction* (New York: Paulist Press, 1988), 62–63.

4. Desmond Tutu, ed., *An African Prayer Book* (New York: Doubleday, 1995), xvii.

5. See Thomas Keating, "Contemplative Prayer in the Christian Tradition: An Historical Perspective," in Thomas Keating et al., *Finding Grace at the Center*; and Kallistos Ware, "Ways of Prayer and Contemplation I: Eastern," and Jean Leclercq, "Ways of Prayer and Contemplation II: Western," in Bernard McGinn et al., *Christian Spirituality: Origins to the Twelfth Century,* 395–426.

6. Keating, "Contemplative Prayer," in Keating et al., *Finding Grace,* 37.

7. Ibid.

8. Ibid., 37–39.

9. The English word "commandment" does not adequately convey the broader and more joyful meaning of the Hebrew *mitzvah.* (See also chapter 1, note 6.)

10. Robert Aitken and David Steindl-Rast, *The Ground We Share: Everyday Practice, Buddhist and Christian* (Boston: Shambhala, 1996).

11. Thich Nhat Hanh, *The Miracle of Mindfulness,* 4.

12. Roth, *The Breath of God,* 49.

13. See chapter 4, note 5.

14. Thomas Keating, "Cultivating the Centering Prayer," in Keating et al., *Finding Grace,* 28.

15. Merton, *Thoughts in Solitude,* 83.

16. Dom John Main, O.S.B., *Christian Meditation: Our Oldest and Newest Form of Prayer* (Kansas City, MO: NCR Cassettes, 1980). Three cassette tapes of talks by Dom John Main, including "Introduction to Christian Meditation," "A Theology of Christian Meditation," and "Twelve Talks for Meditators."

Chapter 6

1. I am grateful to Mary Donovan Turner for her original scholarship on theology of voice (as both distinct from and related to theology of the Word) and for our conversations on voice in theology and preaching; and to Elena Stone for her PhD dissertation, "Rising from Deep Places: A Feminist Exploration of Voice and Silence in the Lives of Fifteen Women Artists and Activists" (PhD diss., Brandeis University, 1994), her book by the same title (New York: Peter Lang, 2002), and many conversations on this topic.

2. Gloria Anzaldua, *Borderlands / La Frontera: The New Mestiza* (San Francisco: Aunt Lute Book Company, 1987), 69.

3. For a classic Orthodox commentary on the icon, see Paul Evdokimov, *The Art of the Icon: A Theology of Beauty*, trans. Steven Bigham (Redondo Beach, CA: Oakwood Publications, 1990), especially chapter 16, "The Theology of Presence," 177–181.

4. For an appreciation of icons by a Roman Catholic, see Henri J.M. Nouwen, *Behold the Beauty of the Lord: Praying with Icons* (Notre Dame, IN: Ave Maria Press, 1987).

5. In his correspondence and scholarly work, Kevin uses the spelling "ikon," which is becoming widespread among scholars of Eastern Christian art and religion. I have kept the more traditional and still current spelling "icon," except when quoting Kevin's letters to me.

6. Virgilio Elizondo, *Guadalupe: Mother of the New Creation* (Maryknoll, NY: Orbis Books, 1997), xix.

7. Virgilio Elizondo, *The Future Is Mestizo: Life Where Cultures Meet* (New York: Meyer-Stone, 1992), 58; see especially the whole of chapter 5, "My People Resurrect at Tepeyac." See also Elizondo's earlier *La Morenita: Evangelizer of the Americas* (San Antonio, TX: Mexican-American Cultural Center, 1980).

8. Besides Elizondo's works (see previous note), see also Jeannette Rodriguez, *Our Lady of Guadalupe: Faith and Empowerment Among Mexican-American Women* (Austin, TX: University of Texas Press, 1994), which has an extensive bibliography of Guadalupe-related scholarship, including primary sources on the Guadalupan apparitions; Roberto S. Goizueta, "U.S. Hispanic Popular Catholicism as Theopoetics," in *Hispanic/Latino Theology: Challenge and Promise*, eds. Ada Maria Isasi-Diaz and Fernando F. Segovia (Minneapolis: Fortress Press, 1996); and Timothy M. Matovina, "Our Lady of Guadalupe Celebrations in San Antonio, Texas, 1840–41," in *Journal of Hispanic/Latino Theology* 1, no. 1 (Nov. 1993): 77–96.

9. Margaret R. Miles, *Image as Insight: Visual Understanding in Western Christianity and Secular Culture* (Boston: Beacon Press, 1985), 146–150.

10. John F. Kavanaugh and Mev Puleo (photographs), *Faces of Poverty, Faces of Christ* (Maryknoll, NY: Orbis Books, 1991), and Mev Puleo, *The Struggle Is One: Voices and Visions of Liberation* (Albany, NY: State University of New York Press, 1994).

11. *Vos*, the second-person plural in Portuguese, like the French *vous*, is equivalent to the Southern "all y'all."

12. Donald M. Steele, A Homily for the Memorial Service for Mev Puleo, St. Augustine's Parish, Oakland, CA, 1996.

Chapter 7

1. Jean-Marie Déchanet, O.S.B., *Yoga in Ten Lessons* (New York: Cornerstone Library, 1965), and *Christian Yoga* (New York: Harper & Row, 1959).

2. Barbara defined a sponsor as "someone who is in AA and has sober 'experience, strength, and hope' to share, usually someone with more time in the program who has something that I want."

3. Barbara is referring to the twelve steps of Alcoholics Anonymous. See *Twelve Steps and Twelve Traditions: A Co-founder of Alcoholics Anonymous Tells How Members Recover and How the Society Functions*, available from any local AA group or from A.A. World Services, Inc., P.O. Box 459, New York, NY 10163; (212) 870-3400. Information about AA is also available at www.aa.org.

4. The AA website notes of the book, *Alcoholics Anonymous* (575 pages), which AA members call the Big Book: "Originally published in 1939, this is the 'book of experience' from which the Fellowship derived its name. It contains an analysis of the principles which led to the sobriety of the earliest members, together with a representative cross section of members' personal stories." Barbara said, "The 'Big

Book' is our affectionate name for the
book from which our society got its name.
It is our basic text."

5. Dan Wakefield, *The Story of Your Life:
    Writing a Spiritual Autobiography—A Step-By-
    Step Approach to Exploring Your Past and
    Understanding Your Present* (Boston: Beacon
    Press, 1990), 46.

Chapter 8

1. Jane Redmont, "A letter to Christopher
    on the occasion of his baptism, for now
    and for later," May 16, 1997, personal
    correspondence.

2. Mark 14:3–9, Matthew 26:6–13, Luke
    7:36–50, and John 12:1–8 all tell the story.
    Only in the Gospel of John is the woman
    identified by name, as Mary the sister of
    Martha and Lazarus. For scholarly per-
    spectives on these passages, see Elisabeth
    Schüssler Fiorenza, *In Memory of Her: A
    Feminist Theological Reconstruction of Christian
    Origins* (New York: Crossroad, 1983), xiii
    ff.

3. Ibid., xiii.

4. "Usable past" is a term common in con-
    temporary feminist theological scholar-
    ship. Behind this technical term is the
    struggle of women and men to appropri-
    ate those elements of their tradition that
    can bring meaning to their lives.

5. William L. Holladay, *The Psalms Through
    Three Thousand Years: Prayerbook of a Cloud of
    Witnesses* (Minneapolis: Fortress Press,
    1993), 8.

6. The gifts of the Holy Spirit are "seven in
    number according to the Catholic tradi-
    tion that is based on the numbering in the
    Septuagint [the Greek version of the
    Hebrew Bible] version of Isaiah 11:1–3,
    which added piety to the list of six gifts in
    the Hebrew version: wisdom, understand-
    ing, counsel, fortitude, knowledge, and
    fear of the Lord." Patricia M. Vinje,
    "Gifts of the Holy Spirit," in *The
    HarperCollins Encyclopedia of Catholicism*, ed.
    Richard P. McBrien (New York:
    HarperCollins, 1995), 560.

7. For more on the prayer of Patrick and its
    context, see Thomas Cahill, *How the Irish
    Saved Civilization: The Untold Story of
    Ireland's Heroic Role from the Fall of Rome to
    the Rise of Medieval Europe* (New York:
    Anchor, 1995), 116.

Chapter 9

1. Roth, *The Breath of God*, 21–22.

Chapter 10

1. See Abraham Joshua Heschel's *The
    Prophets*, vol. 2 (New York: Harper
    Torchbooks, 1975), especially the chapter
    titled "The Meaning and Mystery of
    Wrath," 61–64. "Anger and mercy are not
    opposites but correlatives," Heschel writes
    (p. 63). It is especially dangerous to fall
    into the stereotype of identifying the God
    of the Hebrew Bible ("Old Testament")
    with anger and the God of the Gospels
    and other parts of the Christian
    Testament with love. This portrayal is
    simply inaccurate.

Chapter 11

1. This abbreviated description—though I
    hope it will be of help to readers—is not
    an adequate description of clinical depres-
    sion and other mood disorders. For further
    reading, see *Depression Is a Treatable Illness: A
    Patient's Guide*, no. AHCPR 93-0553
    (Rockville, MD: Department of Health
    and Human Services); Demitri Papolos,
    MD, and Janice Papolos, *Overcoming
    Depression*, 3rd ed. (New York:
    HarperCollins, 1997); Colette Dowling, *You
    Mean I Don't Have to Feel This Way? New Help
    for Depression, Anxiety, and Addiction* (New
    York: Bantam Books, 1993); Dana Crowley
    Jack, *Silencing the Self: Women and Depression*
    (New York: HarperCollins, 1991). These
    are only a few of the available books on
    depression. If you think you may be
    depressed, please seek help from a mental
    health professional.

2. Isaiah 55:11.

3. "Communication and *Communio*," *America*, July 30–August 6, 1995, 22–24.

Chapter 12

1. The shooting took place in Boston's Morningstar Baptist Church. It led to the creation of an interracial and interreligious coalition of urban clergy and other church workers that continues to meet and work for an end to violence in the city.

2. Charles Sheer, "The Remarkable Faith of a Downcast Soul: Introduction to Psalm 42," in *Healing of Soul, Healing of Body: Spiritual Leaders Unfold the Strength and Solace of Psalms*, ed. Simkha Y. Weintraub (Woodstock, VT: Jewish Lights Publishing, 1994), 54–55.

3. Ibid., 55–56.

4. Diana L. Hayes, *Trouble Don't Last Always: Soul Prayers* (Collegeville, MN: The Liturgical Press, 1995), 10. Hayes quotes from Countee Cullen's poem "Yet Do I Marvel," in *My Soul's High Song: The Collected Writings of Countee Cullen* (New York: Anchor Books, 1991), 79.

5. See pages 336–337 for the text of this hymn.

6. John 11:35. For the story of Lazarus's death and raising from the dead, which is the context of this quotation, see John 11:1–44.

Chapter 13

1. Krister Stendahl, *Meanings: The Bible as Document and as Guide* (Philadelphia: Fortress Press, 1984), 239–40.

2. Merton, *Thoughts in Solitude*, 83–84.

3. Harvey Cox, *Fire from Heaven: The Rise of Pentecostal Spirituality and the Reshaping of Religion in the Twenty-first Century* (Reading, MA: Addison-Wesley, 1995), 82.

4. Speaking in tongues, ecstatic speech, or song.

5. Fischer, *Women at the Well*, 54.

6. This is also true of the Jewish tradition, which is undergoing a parallel struggle with, and study of, God-talk in general and prayer-language in particular.

7. Fischer, *Women at the Well*, 53.

8. In fact, someone has. The (Roman Catholic) Carmelite sisters in Oldenburg, Indiana (formerly in Indianapolis), have edited an inclusive-language Divine Office or Liturgy of the Hours titles *The People's Companion to the Breviary* (1997) in two paperback volumes, including readings for morning, daytime, and evening prayer, with petitions relevant to the day (available from www.praythenewsbook.com). In the Episcopal Church, the Order of Saint Helena (Augusta, Georgia) has also produced an inclusive language breviary (Daily Office of Morning and Evening Prayer) and Psalter. Information is available for the breviary (www.osh.org/writing/breviary.html) and for the Psalter (www.osh.org/writing/psalter.html).

9. Fischer, 62–64.

10. James Weldon Johnson, "Lift Every Voice and Sing," in *Lift Every Voice and Sing II: An African American Hymnal* (New York: Church Hymnal Corporation, 1993).

11. The word *mestizo* is used most often to describe the blending of Spanish and Indian during and after the Conquest, in the sixteenth century. Today, most Mexicans and Mexican-Americans are mestizos, a word with increasingly positive connotations that some apply to any person of mixed cultures.

12. See, for instance: Ruth C. Duck, *Finding Words for Worship: A Guide for Leaders* (Louisville, KY: Westminster John Knox, 1995); Elizabeth Johnson, She *Who Is: The Mystery of God in Feminist Theological Discourse* (New York: Crossroad, 1993); Catherine Mowry LaCugna, *God For Us: The Trinity in Christian Life* (New York: HarperSanFrancisco, 1991); Gail

Ramshaw, *Liturgical Language: Keeping It Metaphoric, Making It Inclusive*, American Essays in Liturgy (Collegeville, MN: The Liturgical Press, 1996); Ronald T. Witherup, *A Liturgist's Guide to Inclusive Language* (Collegeville, MN: The Liturgical Press, 1996); Brian Wren, *What Language Shall I Borrow? God-Talk in Worship: A Male Response to Feminist Theology* (New York: Crossroad, 1993); and one of the earlier classics, Sharon Neufer Emswiler and Thomas Neufer Emswiler, *Women and Worship: A Guide to Nonsexist Hymns, Prayers, and Liturgies*, rev. and exp. ed. (San Francisco: Harper & Row, 1984).

Chapter 14

1. *"Veni, Creator Spiritus,"* Come, Creator Spirit," a Pentecost hymn dating back to the ninth century CE, is also sung at the dedication of a church, for confirmation, and at ordinations. Bill is referring to the earliest musical setting of this invocation, a Gregorian chant melody.

2. Labyrinths have existed as art forms and sacred spaces in such varied places as ancient Greece and the Chartres cathedral. The past decade has seen a revival of interest in the labyrinth on the part of a range of people from churchgoing Christians to seekers of New Age spiritualities, especially an interest in walking the labyrinth as a meditative practice.

3. Cyprian, *Treatise on the Lord's Prayer*, in *The Anti-Nicene Fathers*, vol. 5 (Peabody, MA: Hendrickson Publishers, 1994), p. 457.

4. Fred is referring to the story of the healing of the ten lepers, only one of whom returned to thank Jesus (Luke 17:20–21).

5. Acts 2:13.

6. John 20:11–18.

7. Luke 24:1–12.

Chapter 15

1. James Martin, ed., *How Can I Find God? The Famous and the Not-So-Famous Consider* the Quintessential Question (Liguori, MO: Triumph Books, 1997), xiii. Portions of *How Can I Find God?* were both initially and subsequently published in the national Catholic magazine *America*.

2. Yves Congar, *Appelés à la vie (Called to Life)* (Paris: Les Éditions du Cerf, 1985), 17. Author's translation.

Chapter 16

1. Irene Nowell, O.S.B., "Praying the Psalms," in *The Revised Psalms of the New American Bible* (New York: Catholic Book Publishing Co., 1992), 277 (appendix).

2. Weintraub, *Healing of Soul, Healing of Body*, 17.

3. A traditional element in Indian music, a *raga* sets forth a theme expressing a particular religious feeling and a tonal system on which the musicians improvise a set of variations. The word comes from a Sanskrit word *rāgah*, meaning "color" or "musical mode."

4. Dietrich Bonhoeffer, *Psalms: The Prayer Book of the Bible*, trans. James H. Burtness, with a sketch of the life of Dietrich Bonhoeffer by Eberhard Bethge (Minneapolis: Augsburg Publishing House, 1970), 14–15.

5. William L. Holladay, *The Psalms Through Three Thousand Years: Prayerbook of a Cloud of Witnesses* (Minneapolis: Fortress Press, 1996), 356.

6. Ibid., 17–18.

7. Holladay, *The Psalms Through Three Thousand Years*. Other helpful sources are Bernhard W. Anderson, *Out of the Depths: The Psalms Speak for Us Today*, 3rd ed. (Louisville, KY: Westminster John Knox Press, 2000); John Bright, *A History of Israel* (Philadelphia: Westminster, 1981); and James L. Kugel, "Topics in the History of the Spirituality of the Psalms" in *Jewish Spirituality: From the Bible Through the Middle Ages* ed. Arthur Green (New York: Crossroad, 1988). I am also grateful to John Endres, S.J., for his course syllabus

and lecture handouts and for our conversation on Psalms, and refer readers to his article "Cry Out to God in Our Need: Psalms of Lament 34–44" in the Autumn 1996 issue (Number 87) of *The Way Supplement* (London, England) devoted to the Psalms.

8. Nowell, "Praying the Psalms," 268.

9. Psalm 6: 3–4. ICEL translation.

10. Psalm 22:27–28a, 30–31. NRSV translation.

11. Bonhoeffer, *Psalms: The Prayer Book of the Bible*, 14.

12. Psalm 150:3–6.

13. Marty Haugen and David Haas, *Psalms for the Church Year: Twenty-Four Seasonal Psalms* (Chicago: IGA, 1994).

Chapter 17

1. Alternate transliteration and pronunciation from Yiddish-speaking Eastern European communities. The use of the modern Hebrew pronunciation "Shabbat" is more recent and increasingly widespread.

2. The Orthodox Church and other Eastern Christian churches such as the Catholic Church's Melkite rite serve communion under the form of bread dipped in wine, served with a long-handled spoon.

3. Christian baptism usually includes several rituals after the water baptism, one of which is the lighting of a candle from the large Paschal (Easter) candle in the church, and the giving of this candle to the child's parents, often with the words "Receive the light of Christ, and keep it burning bright in your heart by faith."

4. The Advent wreath, traditionally made of evergreens, has four candles. On the first Sunday of Advent, one is lit. On the second, two are lit, and so forth until all four are lit. Thus, the light increases as we move toward Christmas. Three candles are purple and one pink, the latter lit on the third of the four Sundays, *Gaudete* or "Rejoice" Sunday.

5. A brief formal prayer that varies with the day, said as part of communal worship in many of the Western Christian churches.

Chapter 18

1. Matthew the Poor (Matta El-Meskeen), *The Communion of Love* (New York: St. Vladimir's Seminary Press, 1984), 18–20.

2. The Gospel of Matthew's Beatitudes: Matthew 5:3–12. The Gospel of Luke's Beatitudes, which includes curses or "woes": Luke 6:20–23.

3. For a fuller history, description, and meditation upon the Rosary, see M. Basil Pennington, *Praying by Hand: Rediscovering the Rosary as a Way of Prayer* (New York: HarperCollins, 1991), from which I have taken much of the information on the Rosary in this chapter. See also the booklet by Benedictine sister Joan Chittister, *In Pursuit of Peace: Praying the Rosary through the Psalms* (Erie, PA: Pax Christi USA, 1992).

Chapter 19

1. C. S. Lewis, *Letters to Malcolm: Chiefly on Prayer* (New York: Harcourt Brace Jovanovich, 1964), 27.

2. Ingrid Shafer (published anonymously), "Sermon for May 12, 1991," in *Good News Homily Service* 18:6 (New Berlin, WI: Liturgical Publications, 1991).

3. "Praying for Kagis," "Praying for Perpetrators," and "Praying for Faceless Others," August 23–26, 1996. Online posting, Association for the Rights of Catholics in the Church: Vatican2 E-Mail Forum. See http://astro.temple.edu/~arcc/vatican2.htm for information about joining this forum.

Chapter 20

1. Thelma Hall, *Too Deep for Words: Rediscovering Lectio Divina with 500 Scripture Texts for Prayer*, 3, 28.

2. Isaiah 55:1–3a.

3. Religious lists, websites, and other Internet resources abound. For books on some of the Internet's religious resources, see, among others, Debra K. Farrington, *Romancing the Holy* (New York: Crossroad, 1997), particularly the chapter "Spirituality Online," 97–117; Mark A. Kelner, *God on the Internet: Your Complete Guide to Enhancing Your Spiritual Life via the Internet and Online Services* (Foster City, CA: IDG Books, 1996); Thomas C. Fox, *Catholicism on the Web* (New York: MIS Press, 1997); and Jeff Zaleski, *The Soul of Cyberspace* (New York: HarperCollins, 1997).

4. Ephesians 3:16b–19 reads: ". . . that you may be strengthened in your inner being with power through his Spirit, and that Christ may dwell in your hearts through faith, as you are being rooted and grounded in love. I pray that you may have the power to comprehend, with all the saints, what is the breadth and length and height and depth, and to know the love of Christ that surpasses knowledge, so that you may be filled with all the fullness of God." See also Ephesians 1:17–19.

5. Congar, *Appelés à la vie,* 31. Author's translation.

Chapter 21

1. Gertrud Mueller Nelson, *To Dance with God: Family Ritual and Community Celebration* (New York: Paulist Press, 1986), 41.

2. Ibid., 7.

3. The two major movements to which Norberg and Webber point are the erosion of confidence in the ability of human reason to order existence, and the "shift from mechanical to organic models, from compartmentalization toward holism" in "fields as diverse as physics and astronomy, medicine and biology, international politics, ecology and religion." Tilda Norberg and Robert D. Webber, *Stretch Out Your Hand: Exploring Healing Prayer,* Leader's Guide ed., A Kaleidoscope Series Resource (New York: United Church Press, 1990) 11.

4. Norberg and Webber, *Stretch Out Your Hand,* 12. For an accessible, practical book written by three Catholic Christians who "are writing for anyone who wants to give and receive the healing love of God as he or she understands God," see also Matthew Linn, Sheila Fabricant Linn, and Dennis Linn, *Simple Ways to Pray for Healing* (New York: Paulist Press, 1998).

5. Roth, *The Breath of God,* 29.

6. See Thich Nhat Hanh, *The Miracle of Mindfulness*; Herbert Benson, *Timeless Healing: The Power and Biology of Belief* (New York: Fireside, 1996); Larry Dossey, *Healing Words: The Power of Prayer and the Practice of Medicine* (New York: HarperCollins, 1993); Larry Dossey, *Prayer Is Good Medicine: How to Reap the Healing Benefits of Prayer* (New York: HarperCollins, 1996); Dean Ornish, *Love and Survival* (New York: HarperCollins, 1998).

7. Dossey, *Healing Words.*

8. "Healing Prayer," *In Good Faith,* WCVB-TV Channel 5, Boston (ABC affiliate), July 14, 1996.

9. Following the Second Vatican Council, what the Catholic Church used to call the sacrament of Extreme Unction, celebrated only at the time of death or perceived danger of death, has become the sacrament of the Anointing of the Sick. The sacrament is still celebrated when death is close, but is celebrated even more often in times of physical and mental illness, before surgery, in communal parish celebrations, and at any time when individuals and communities of believers wish to celebrate and call upon God's healing power. The renewed rite is in many ways a return to the premedieval perspective on the sacrament as more ordinary than extraordinary; its celebration in the context of ongoing care and prayer also incorporates contemporary insights from pastoral care and pastoral theology. It takes its meaning from Jesus Christ both as healer and as one who suffers; like all Christian sacraments, it is best understood

from the perspective of the Paschal (Easter) mystery of the life, death, and resurrection of Jesus Christ.

Chapter 22

1. See Carroll Stuhlmueller.

2. Julia Cameron, *The Artist's Way: A Spiritual Path to Higher Creativity* (New York: Perigee Books, 1992).

3. Cameron, *The Artist's Way*, 12.

4. Ibid., 13–14.

5. Wakefield, *The Story of Your Life*, 25.

6. Both in my reading and in the course of my interviews, I have run across this acronym for four related types of prayer. It seems especially widespread among Protestant Christians, but also figures in Anglican Archbishop Desmond Tutu's *African Prayer Book*. Men and women from Pentecostal, Methodist, Reformed, and Presbyterian backgrounds as well as evangelical born-again Christians had been raised with this simple method of prayer or had adopted it as adults. Though no Catholics mentioned this method of prayer, after hearing about it from Anglicans, Protestants, and Pentecostals, I read that ACTS was also found in the old Baltimore Catechism with which pre-Vatican II Catholics grew up. I also found mention of ACTS in a book on prayer and personality types whose authors appear to be either Roman Catholics or heavily influenced by Catholic spirituality and prayer practices. They understand ACTS to belong to the third step of *lectio divina* and be "part of our personal response to God's Word," and guard against our using this method, in which the person praying speaks, to the detriment of those methods or moments of prayer when we are primarily in listening mode. "True prayer," they write, "is, first and foremost, listening to God speaking to us and then, secondarily, responding to God's words to us." Michael and Norrisey, *Prayer and Temperament*, 34.

7. 1 Corinthians 2:16.

8. Cheryl may have been referring to Germaine Copeland's *Prayers that Avail Much* (Tulsa, OK: Harrison House, 1989) or to its companion, *The Prayers that Avail Much Journal*.

Chapter 23

1. David Steindl-Rast, O.S.B., with Sharon Lebell, *The Music of Silence: Entering the Sacred Space of Monastic Experience* (New York: HarperCollins, 1995), 20.

2. The mourner's Kaddish is the best known of several forms of this traditional Jewish prayer. Other versions are the *hatzi* Kaddish and the scholars' Kaddish. For more on the Kaddish, see Anita Diamant, *Saying Kaddish* (New York: Schocken Books, 1998).

3. Lisa had spoken to me of her daily singing with her daughter many times by the time I referred her to my colleague Jim Castelli for a book interview on the subject of prayer. This quotation is taken from Jim's formal interview: "Lisa Wood interview," in *How I Pray*, ed. Jim Castelli (New York: Ballantine Books, 1994), 170–171.

4. My informal sample bears this out: several church musicians and people for whom music was a central part of religious life spontaneously mentioned their own funerals.

5. For a comprehensive study of traditional as well as "redacted" spirituals, "redacted" meaning rewritten in later periods of history to meet new social circumstances, see Cheryl A. Kirk-Duggan, *Exorcizing Evil: A Womanist Perspective on the Spirituals* (Maryknoll, NY: Orbis, 1997).

6. James H. Cone, *The Spirituals and the Blues: An Interpretation* (Maryknoll, NY: Orbis Books, 1991), 34.

7. Kirk-Duggan, *Exorcizing Evil*, 281, 283.

Chapter 24

1. Brother David Steindl-Rast, *Gratefulness, the Heart of Prayer: An Approach to Life in*

Fullness (New York: Paulist Press, 1984), 40.

2. Ibid., 40–41.

3. Ibid., 48.

4. Ibid., 49.

5. Ibid.

6. Ibid., 54.

7. Story reprinted with permission of the author, Terry Morgan, from "Roman Echoes," online communication, November 17, 1996.

8. Steindl-Rast, *Gratefulness, the Heart of Prayer*, 54.

9. Roth, *The Breath of God*, 26.

10. Kabat-Zinn, *Wherever You Go, There You Are*, 122.

11. Ibid., 123.

12. Lewis, *Letters to Malcolm*, 16–17.

13. George C. L. Cummings, "The Practice of Prayer" (sermon), Church by the Side of the Road, Berkeley, CA, March 7, 1993, and October 31, 1994.

14. Congar, *Appelés à la vie*, 12–13. Author's translation.

Chapter 25

1. Gerald G. May, *Care of Mind/Care of Spirit: A Psychiatrist Explores Spiritual Direction* (New York: HarperCollins, 1992), 8. See also William A. Barry and William J. Connolly, *The Practice of Spiritual Direction* (New York: Seabury, 1983), 16.

2. Ibid., 2.

3. Fischer, *Women at the Well*, 3.

4. The personification of wisdom (in Greek *Sophia*, in Hebrew *Hokhma*) is an image of God found throughout the Bible. Rachel may be referring to the eighth chapter of the book of Proverbs, which includes such passages as these: "Does not wisdom call, and does not understanding raise her voice? On the heights, beside the way, at the crossroad she takes her stand; beside

the gates in front of the town, at the entrance of the portals she cries out: 'To you, O people, I call, and my cry is to all that live. O simple ones, learn prudence; acquire intelligence, you who lack it. Hear, for I will speak noble things, and from my lips will come what is right; for my mouth will utter truth; wickedness is an abomination to my lips. . . . I love those who love me, and those who seek me diligently find me'" (Proverbs 8:1–7, 17).

5. Kenneth Leech, *Soul Friend: An Invitation to Spiritual Direction* (New York: HarperCollins, 1980), 49–51.

6. Margaret Guenther, *Holy Listening: The Art of Spiritual Direction* (Cambridge, MA: Cowley Publications, 1992), 86.

7. Farrington, *Romancing the Holy*, 49, n. 2.

8. May, *Care of Mind/Care of Spirit*, 14.

9. Frank J. Houdek, *Guided by the Spirit: A Jesuit Perspective on Spiritual Direction* (Chicago: Loyola Press, 1996), 8.

10. Ibid., 9.

11. Owing to the fluid and unregulated nature of spiritual direction, there is no comprehensive directory of spiritual directors. One organization, Spiritual Directors International (P.O. Box 3584, Bellevue, WA 98009, www.sdiworld.org), does publish a directory, but not all directors belong to SDI. One might also call some of the principal training centers for spiritual direction in the country; they are located in large urban areas, but their staff may know of resources in more isolated or rural areas. Three important centers are the Center for Religious Development (2240 Massachusetts Ave., Cambridge, MA 02140, www.ordcambridge.com), the Shalem Institute (5430 Grosvenor Lane, Suite 140, Bethesda, MD 20814, www.shalem.org), and the Mercy Center (2300 Adeline Dr., Burlingame, CA 94010, www.mercy-center.org).

12. Guenther, *Holy Listening*, 13.

Chapter 26

1. COGIC: the Church of God in Christ, a Pentecostal denomination whose membership has historically been (and largely remains) African American.

2. Steindl-Rast, *Gratefulness, the Heart of Prayer*, 123.

3. Gerard W. Hughes, *God of Surprises* (London: Darton, Longman and Todd, 1985), 137.

4. Kabat-Zinn, *Wherever You Go, There You Are*, 32.

5. David Toolan writes: "Jean Houston's guided meditation with Mrs. Clinton was not more 'spooky' [the term used by political commentator and former Jesuit John McLaughlin of PBS's *The McLaughlin Group*] than St. Ignatius's Spiritual Exercises—wherein one is asked to enter imaginatively (and thus actively) into a Gospel scene and thereafter to converse with the Virgin Mary and the persons of the Blessed Trinity." Houston, Toolan notes, "has never stopped believing that the universe is gloriously sacramental and that, however small our lives may appear, we stand among a great host, a communion of saints, with whom we may commune." David S. Toolan, "Hillary's Guru," *America* 175:5, August 31–September 7, 1996, 11–12.

Chapter 27

1. Isaiah 58:6–7.

2. Quoted in *For You, O God: Prayer and Reflections*, Loyola University Chicago Prayer Book (Chicago: Loyola University Chicago, 1995), 29.

3. John Donahue, S.J., during a class lecture in New Testament at the Jesuit School of Theology at Berkeley, reported by Therese M. Becker. I thank both Terry and John for this gem of a definition, which also reminds me of the language and spirit of Rabbi Abraham Joshua Heschel.

4. Maria Harris, *Proclaim Jubilee! A Spirituality for the Twenty-First Century* (Louisville, KY: Westminster John Knox Press, 1996), 11.

5. William E. Reiser, *Into the Needle's Eye: Becoming Poor and Hopeful Under the Care of a Gracious God* (Notre Dame, IN: Ave Maria Press, 1984), 47.

6. Gustavo Gutiérrez, *On Job: God-Talk and the Suffering of the Innocent* (Maryknoll, NY: Orbis Books, 1987), 13.

7. "Profession of Faith of the Christian Base Communities, El Salvador," in *Gifts of Many Cultures: Worship Resources for the Global Community*, eds. Maren C. Tirabassi and Kathy Wonson Eddy (Cleveland, OH: United Church Press, 1995), 119.

8. "Action on behalf of Justice and participation in the transformation of the world fully appear to us as a constitutive dimension of the preaching of the Gospel, or, in other words, of the Church's mission for the redemption of the human race and its liberation from every oppressive situation." "Justice in the World: Statement of the World Synod of Bishops, 1971," in *Renewing the Catholic Documents on Peace, Justice, and Liberation*, eds. David J. O'Brien and Thomas A. Shannon (Garden City, NY: Image, 1977), 391.

9. Archbishop Oscar Arnulfo Romero of San Salvador was gunned down and murdered in church while celebrating Mass on March 24, 1980. He had spoken out with increasing frequency and fervor against the repression—censorship, economic exploitation, killing—of the Salvadoran government and allied groups. Rutilio Grande, a Jesuit priest who lived among poor peasants in El Salvador, was murdered a few years earlier.

10. Johannes Baptist Metz, *Faith in History and Society* (New York: Seabury, 1980), 109–10, quoted in Harris, *Proclaim Jubilee!*, 63.

11. Dwight N. Hopkins, *Shoes That Fit Our Feet: Sources for a Constructive Black Theology* (Maryknoll, NY: Orbis Books, 1993), 27. Hopkins notes the source of this story as *Weevils in the Wheat: Interviews with Virginia*

Ex-slaves, eds. Charles L Perdue et al. (Bloomington: Indiana University Press, 1980), 184.

12. Harris, *Proclaim Jubilee!*, 2. See also Hans Ucko, ed. *The Jubilee Challenge: Uptopia or Possibility? Jewish and Christian Insights* (Geneva: WCC Publications, 1997).

Sources for Epigraphs & End-of-Chapter Selections

Frontispiece Epigraphs

v   Psalm 42:2–3, ICEL.

v   John 21:9–12a, NRSV.

v   "Collect," in NZPB. The Church of the Province of New Zealand [Anglican] / *Te Haahi o te Porowini o Niu Tireni* (Auckland: Collins Liturgical Publications, 1989. Copyright © Church of the Province of New Zealand), 464.

Chapter 1

10   Mark 1:35, NRSV.

10   Dwight N. Hopkins, *Shoes That Fit Our Feet: Sources for a Constructive Black Theology* (Maryknoll, NY: Orbis Books, 1993), 18, 26, 29.

10–11   Joan Redmont, Letter to author, August 30, 1996 (Vershire, VT).

19   Marcia Falk, "The Gift of Gratitude" (*B'feh Maley Shirah*), in *The Book of Blessings: New Jewish Prayers for Daily Life, The Sabbath, and the New Moon Festival* (New York: HarperCollins, 1996), 246.

19   "A Prayer from New Guinea," in *Gifts of Many Cultures: Worship Resources for the Global Community*, eds. Maren C. Tirabassi and Kathy Wonson Eddy (Cleveland, OH: United Church Press, 1995), 22–23.

21   Source unknown, in *Student Prayer* (London: SCM Press, Ltd., 1950), np.

22   Jon Kabat-Zinn, *Wherever You Go, There You Are: Mindfulness Meditation in Everyday Life* (New York: Hyperion, 1994), 22–23.

Chapter 2

23   Psalm 24:1, NEB.

23   Thomas Merton, "Some Predisposition for Prayer," a conference on prayer (source: Thelma Hall) [Language slightly adapted for gender inclusiveness].

32   Dom Helder Câmara, "Go Down," in *The Desert Is Fertile* (Maryknoll, NY: Orbis, 1976), 43.

33   "A Collect for Wednesday in Holy Week," in NZPB, 584.

33   William Cleary, "An Inchworm's Alleluia," in *Lighten Your Heart: Healing Psalms of Bugs and Beasts* (Mystic, CT: Twenty-Third Publications, 1995), 20–21.

34   Merton, "Some Predispositions for Prayer."

Chapter 3

35   Eric Liddell, character in *Chariots of Fire*, by Colin Welland, 1981.

35   Song of Songs; 4:1–3, in *The Song of Songs: A New Translation with an Introduction and Commentary*, trans. Ariel Bloch and Chana Bloch (New York: Random House, 1995), 73.

36   Exodus, 3:4–5 SB/EF.

44   Janet Morley, "Collect for Christmas Eve and Christmas Day" in *All Desires Known: Inclusive Prayers for Worship and Meditation*, exp. ed. (Harrisburg, PA: Morehouse Publishing, 1992), 6. Collects written in association with the Eucharistic lectionary of the Church of England's Alternative Service Book, 1980.

44–45   Morley, "Collect for the First Sunday of Christmas," in *All Desires Known*, 6.

49   Morley, "Blessing," in *All Desires Known*, 87.

Chapter 4

50	Genesis 1:1–5, SB/EF.
50	Acts 2:1–6, NRSV.
51	Romans 8:26, NRSV.
56	"Night Prayer," in NZPB, 168.
57	"Desiderius Erasmus," in *HarperCollins Book of Prayers*, ed. Robert Van de Weyer (New York: HarperCollins, 1993), 136.
58–59	Lawrence Kushner, *The Book of Words* [Sefer shel devarim]: *Talking Spiritual Life, Living Spiritual Talk* (Woodstock, VT: Jewish Lights Publishing, 1993), 27–29.
59	Falk, "The Breath of All Life," in *The Book of Blessings*, (Boston: Beacon Press, 1999) 160.
60	Kabat-Zinn, *Wherever You Go, There You Are*, 13–14, 19, 20, 21.
60–62	Teresina Havens, *Mind What Stirs in Your Heart: Pendle Hill Pamphlet 304* (Wallingford, PA: Pendle Hill Publications, 1992), 7–10. Passages by Penington are from Douglas Steere, ed., *Quaker Spirituality* (New York: Paulist Press, 1984), 147–150, 152–154, 156.
62	"Preface of Pentecost," in *The Book of Common Prayer According to the Use of the Episcopal Church* (New York: The Church of Hymnal Corporation, 1979), 200.
63	Morley, "Collect for the Ninth Sunday Before Christmas," in *All Desires Known*, 3.

Chapter 5

64	T. S. Eliot, "Burnt Norton," in *Four Quartets* (New York: Harcourt, Brace & World, Inc., 1943, 1971), 15–16.
64–65	Charlote Joko Beck, *Everyday Zen: Love and Work*, ed. Steve Smith (New York: HarperCollins, 1989), 25.
65	Author unknown, *The Cloud of Unknowing and The Book of Privy Counseling*, ed. William Johnston

	(Garden City, NY: Image Books, 1973), 48–49.
79	Laurence Freeman, *Light Within: The Inner Path of Meditation* (New York: Crossroad, 1989), xii.
79	"John Main," in *Christian Meditation by Those Who Practice It*, ed. Paul T. Harris (Denville, NJ: Dimension Books, 1993), 8.
80	Thich Nhat Hanh, *The Miracle of Mindfulness: A Manual on Meditation*, rev. ed., trans. Mobi Ho (Boston: Beacon Press, 1975), 16–17.
80	Brother Lawrence, *The Practice of the Presence of God* (White Plains, NY: Peter Pauper Press, 1963), 25.
81	Thich Nhat Hanh, *The Miracle of Mindfulness: A Manual on Meditation*, rev. ed., trans. Mobi Ho (Boston: Beacon Press, 1975), 23–24.
81	Psalm 131, ICEL.

Chapter 6

82	Bill Wallace, "A Prayer from Aotearoa/New Zealand," in *Gifts of Many Cultures*, eds. Tirabassi and Eddy, 53.
82	"Seventh Ecumenical Council (Nicea II, 787)," quoted in Paul Evdokimov, trans. Steven Bigham, *The Art of the Icon: A Theology of Beauty* (Redondo Beach, CA: Oakwood Publications, 1990), 3.
97	Dorothee Soelle, "Alternative TV," in *Of War and Love*, trans. Rita and Robert Kimber (Maryknoll, NY: Orbis, 1983), 171.

Chapter 7

100	Robert Aitken and David Steindl-Rast, *The Ground We Share: Everyday Practice, Buddhist and Christian*, ed. Nelson Foster (Boston: Shambhala, 1996), 124.
100	Morley, "Collect for the Fourth Sunday After Epiphany," in *All Desires Known*, 8.

110 Marian Wright Edelman, *Guide My Feet: Prayers and Meditations on Loving and Working with Children* (Boston: Beacon Press, 1995), 50.

111 Reinhold Niebuhr, "Prayer for Serenity."

111 Teresa of Avila, *"Nada Te Turbe"* (Let Nothing Trouble You), in *The Collected Works of St. Teresa of Avila, Vol. III*, trans. Kieran Kavanaugh and Otilio Rodriguez (Washington, DC: ICS Publications, 1985).

112 Dorothee Soelle, "When He Came (3.)," in *Revolutionary Patience* (Maryknoll, NY: Orbis Books, 1977), 9.

CHAPTER 8

113 T. S. Eliot, "Little Gidding," in *Four Quartets* (New York: Harcourt Brace & World, Inc., 1971), 59.

113 Mark 14:3–9, JB.

120–121 Psalm 23, KJV.

122–123 *"Veni Sancte Spiritus,"* trans. Jill Raitt, in *Image Breaking/Image Building: A Handbook for Creative Worship with Women of Christian Tradition*, eds. Linda Clark, Marian Ronan, and Eleanor Walker (New York: Pilgrim Press, 1981), 71–72.

124–125 Susan Cady, Marian Ronan, and Hal Taussig, "Litany of Praise to the Wisdom of God," in *Wisdom's Feast: Sophia in Study and Celebration* (San Francisco: Harper & Row, 1989), 94.

125 NZPB, 405.

CHAPTER 9

129 Morley, "Collect for the Fifth Sunday before Christmas," in *All Desires Known*, 4.

136–137 Kathleen Norris, "The Companionable Dark," in *Little Girls in Church* (Pittsburgh, PA: University of Pittsburgh Press, 1995), 54.

137–138 Soelle, "When He Came (10.)," in *Revolutionary Patience*, 16.

138 James Baldwin, "Trying to See the Light," in *Conversations with God: Two Centuries of Prayers by African Americans*, ed. James Melvin Washington (New York: HarperCollins, 1994), 253. See also "Untitled original," in *Gypsy and Other Poems*, etched portraits by Leonard Baskin (South Hadley, MA: Gehenna Press, 1989).

139 Morley, "For the Darkness of Waiting, Litany," in *All Desires Known*, 58–59.

140 Câmara, "Hope Without Risk," in *The Desert Is Fertile*, 15.

CHAPTER 10

141 Psalm 3:8–9, ICEL.

141 Morley, "Collect for the Twenty-first Sunday After Pentecost," in *All Desires Known*, 24.

149–150 Psalm 7, ICEL.

150–151 Cleary, ". . . the grace to shout . . . ," in *Psalm Services for Group Prayer* (Mystic, CT: Twenty-Third Publications, 1995), 58

CHAPTER 11

152 Psalm 31:10–13, ICEL.

152 Psalm 121:1–2, NRSV.

164–165 Psalm 121, NRSC.

165 "Aelred of Rievaulx," in *HarperCollins Book of Prayers*, 21.

CHAPTER 12

166 Psalm 137:3–4, ICEL.

166–167 Romans 8:35–39, NRSV.

167 "Liturgies of the Eucharist," in NZPB, 458.

176–177 Psalm 57, ICEL.

177 Rainer Maria Rilke, "Pietà," from "The Life of Mary," in *Selected Works: Vol II Poetry*, trans. N. K. Cruikshank (Norfolk, CT: New Directions Books, 1960), 219.

177–178 M. Shawn Copeland, "My Name Is Waiting," in *Woman, Survivor in the Church*, ed. Joan Ohanneson (Minneapolis, MN: Winston Press, 1980), 140–141.

178–179 Psalm 51, NRSV.

179 "No Lamb in the Thicket," in *Laughter, Silence and Shouting: An Anthology of Women's Prayers*, ed. Kathy Keay (London: HarperCollins, 1994), 148.

180 Christina Rossetti, "In Weariness," in *Laughter, Silence and Shouting*, ed. Keay, 131.

180 Morley, "Prayer at Times of Ending: At a Funeral," in *All Desires Known*, 87.

CHAPTER 13

181 Morley, "Collect for the Second Sunday in Advent," in *All Desires Known*, 5.

191–192 Kathy Galloway, "Out of the Depths," in *Laughter, Silence and Shouting*, ed. Keay, 139–140.

193 Psalm 42:1–6, KJV.

193–194 Psalm 42:1–6, NRSV.

194 Psalm 42:1–6, ICEL.

194–195 "Alternative Lord's Prayer," in NZPB, 181.

195–196 Kerry A. Maloney, "Common Questions on Inclusive Language," workshop packet, n.d. (Principal sources: Elizabeth A. Johnson, *She Who Is: The Mystery of God in Feminist Theological Discourse* [New York: Crossroad, 1993]; Catherine Mowry LaCugna, *God for Us: The Trinity and Christian Life* [New York:

HarperCollins, 1991]; Sharon H. Ringe, "When Women Interpret the Bible," in *The Women's Bible Commentary*, eds. Carol A. Newsom and Sharon H. Ringe [Louisville, KY: Westminister/John Knox, 1992]; Rosemary Radford Ruether, "Sexism and God-Language," in *Weaving the Visions: New Patterns in Feminist Spirituality*, eds. Judith Plaskow and Carol P. Christ [San Francisco, CA: Harper & Row, 1989]).

196 Morley, Collect for the Sixth Sunday After Pentecost, *All Desires Known*, 19.

CHAPTER 14

199 Isaiah 55:12, NRSV.

206–207 Morley, "Collect for Easter Day," in *All Desires Known*, 14.

207 Psalm 150, ICEL.

207–208 *Siddur* (prayer book), Congregation Beth El of the Sudbury River Valley (Sudbury, MA: 1980), 128.

208–209 "Benedicite Aotearoa," in NZPB, 63–64.

209–210 "An African Canticle," in *An African Prayer Book*, ed. Desmond Tutu (New York: Doubleday, 1995), 7–8.

210 George Simpson, "Sermon, Bethany Church, Randolph, VT, 1989," in *Gifts of Many Cultures*, eds. Tirabassi and Eddy, 13.

210 Thich Nhat Hanh, "Peace Is Every Step," in *The Long Road Turns to Joy: A Guide to Walking Meditation* (Berkeley, CA: Parallax Press, 1996), 74.

211 Psalm 126, ICEL.

CHAPTER 15

214 Marty Haugen, "Gather Us In," IGA.

214–215 Samuel G. Freedman, *Upon this Rock: The Miracles of a Black Church* (New York: HarperCollins, 1993), 158.

215 Matthew 18:20, NRSV.

226–228 Elena Stone, "Vigil," in *Sing Me Out of Exile*, unpublished collection, 1997.

228–229 Dietrich Bonhoeffer, "Life Together," in *A Testament to Freedom: The Essential Writings of Dietrich Bonhoeffer*, eds. Geffrey B. Kelly and F. Burton Nelson, rev. ed. (HarperCollins, 1995), 327.

CHAPTER 16

230 Psalm 18:2–3, ICEL.

230–231 Gabe Huck, Foreword, *The Psalter*, ICEL translation of *The Liturgical Psalter* (Chicago: Archdiocese of Chicago, Liturgy Training Publications, 1995), viii.

237–238 Psalm 139, NRSV.

239 Psalm 70, ICEL.

239–240 Psalm 121, ICEL.

240 "Psalm 65: A Version for New Zealand," in NZPB, 171.

CHAPTER 17

243 Mark 10:13–16, NRSV.

244 David Heller, ed., *Dear God: Children's Letters to God* (New York: Berkley Publishing Group, 1994).

255 Evangeline Patterson, "For My Children," in *Laughter, Silence and Shouting*, ed. Keay, 67.

256–257 Edelman, "O God of All Children," in *Guide My Feet*, 102–103.

258 Thich Nhat Hanh, "Walking with a Child," in *The Long Road Turns to Joy*, 36.

CHAPTER 18

259 Contemporary *Exsultet* (Easter Vigil Liturgy). Text based on prayer by James Dillet Freeman, music by Marty Haugen (Chicago, IL: IGA Publications).

259 Deuteronomy 6:5–9.

273 "A Celtic Blessing," Iona Community, Isle of Iona.

CHAPTER 19

274 Matthew 5:43–44, NRSV.

274 Bishop Pedro Casaldaliga, "Heart Full of Names," in *In Pursuit of the Kingdom: Writings 1968–1998* (Maryknoll, NY: Orbis, 1990), 200.

287 Ellery Akers, "The World that Is A Prayer," in *Witness* XI: 2 (Farmington Hills, MI: Oakland Community College, 1997), 9.

287 "Deliver Me," in *An African Prayer Book*, ed. Tutu, 81.

288 Cleary, "Prayer for People I Dislike," in *Prayers and Fables: Meditating on Aesop's Wisdom* (Kansas City, MO: Sheed & Ward, 1998), 142.

288 Carlo Maria Martini, in *Hearts on Fire: Praying with Jesuits*, ed. Michael Harter, (St. Louis, MO: Institute of Jesuit Sources, 1993), 75.

288–289 *The New Century Hymnal* (Cleveland, OH: Pilgrim Press, 1995), #850.

289 John Shea, "The Last Prayer of Petition Ever," in *The Hour of the Unexpected* (Niles, IL: Argus, 1977), 18.

CHAPTER 20

290 Psalm 78:1–4, ICEL.

290 Isaiah 55:10–11, NRSV.

291 Thelma Hall, *Too Deep for Words: Rediscovering Lectio Divina with 500 Scripture Texts for Prayer* (New York:

Paulist Press, 1998), 7.

297   Armand Nigro (adapted), "Praying
       with the Scriptures," in *Hearts on
       Fire*, 42.

297–298 Hall, *Too Deep for Words*, 28, 32 and
       paraphrase and summary of the
       four stages of *lectio* and the experi-
       ence of interior silence.

CHAPTER 21

299   Luke 13:10–13, NRSV.

299–300 John 13:2b–9, 12–15, NRSV.

300   Morley, "Collect for the Third
       Sunday After Pentecost," in *All
       Desires Known*, 18.

309   Morley, "Collect for Maundy
       Thursday," in *All Desires Known*, 13.

309   "A Collect for Maundy Thursday,"
       in NZPB, 585.

310   Diann Neu, "In Praise of Hands,"
       in *WaterWheel* (Silver Springs, MD:
       WATER [Women's Alliance for
       Theology, Ethics and Ritual],
       1989), 2:1.

310–311 Tilda Norberg and Robert D.
       Webber, "Praying for Another's
       Healing: Before We Pray for
       Healing—The Discernment
       Process," in *Stretch Out Your Hand:
       Exploring Healing Prayer* (New York:
       United Church Press, 1990), 57–58.

CHAPTER 22

312   Annie Dillard, *Pilgrim at Tinker Creek*
       (New York: Bantam Books, 1974),
       35.

312   Thomas Merton, *Conjectures of a
       Guilty Bystander* (Garden City, NY:
       Image Books, 1965), 43.

CHAPTER 23
WHEN IN DOUBT, SING: MUSIC AS PRAYER

325   Jalaluddin Rumi (Maulana Jala a-
       Din Rumi), "Each Note," in *The

Essential Rumi, trans. Coleman
Barks, with John Moore, A. J.
Arberry, and Reynold Nicholson
(New York: Harper Collins, 1994),
103.

326   Harvey Cox, *Fire from Heaven: The
       Rise of Pentecostal Spirituality and the
       Reshaping of Religion in the Twenty-
       First Century* (Reading, MA:
       Addison-Wesley, 1995), 139.

335   Thomas Andrew Dorsey, "Precious
       Lord, Take My Hand," in *Lead Me,
       Guide Me: The African American
       Catholic Hymnal* (Chicago: GIA
       Publications, 1987), #163.

336–337 "How Can I Keep From Singing?"
       in *The New Century Hymnal*
       (Cleveland, OH: Pilgrim Press,
       1995), #476. For an alternate third
       verse *see also Songs of the Spirit, Friends
       General Conference* (Burnsville, NC:
       World Around Books, 1978), 2.

338   Miriam Therese Winter, "Mother
       and God," in *WomanPrayer,
       WomanSong* (Oak Park, IL: Stone
       Books, 1987), 206; music, 207.

338   Psalm 104:33, NRSV.

CHAPTER 24

340   Michel Quoist, "Lord I Have
       Time," in *Prayers*, trans. Agnes M.
       Forsyth and Anne Marie de
       Commaille (New York: Sheed &
       Ward, 1963), 97.

340   Janet Morley, "Blessing Over a
       Meal Prepared Together," in
       Laughter, Silence and Shouting, Keay,
       39.

352   Falk, "Distinctions," in *The Book of
       Blessings*, 318.

352   "Morning Prayer, Kenya," in *An
       African Prayer Book*, ed. Tutu, 121.

352   "Evening Prayer, Kenya," in *An
       African Prayer Book*, ed. Tutu, 121.

353   "Desiderius Erasmus," in *Prayers at 3 A.M.: Poems, Songs, Chants, and Prayers for the Middle of the Night*, ed. Phil Cousineau, (New York: HarperCollins, 1995), 62–63.

353   "Johann Freylinghausen," in *Prayers at 3 A.M.*, ed. Cousineau, 64.

353–354 Attributed to John Henry Newman, in *For You, O God: Prayers and Reflections* ed. Lawrence Reuter (Chicago: Loyola University, 1995), 118.

354   "A Sudanese Evening Prayer (traditional Dinka)," in *Prayers at 3 A.M.*, ed. Cousineau, 12.

354   Kabat-Zinn, *Wherever You Go, There You Are*, 34.

354   "For Those Who Clean," in *Laughter, Silence and Shouting*, ed. Keay 83.

355   Merton, *Thoughts in Solitude: Reflections on the Spiritual Life and the Love of Solitude* (Garden City, NY: Image, 1968), 81.

355   Quoist, "Lord I Have Time," in *Prayers*, 99.

CHAPTER 25

356   Margaret Guenther, *Holy Listening: The Art of Spiritual Direction* (Cambridge, MA: Cowley Publications, 1992), 1.

356   Thomas Moore, *Meditations: On the Monk Who Dwells in Daily Life* (New York: HarperCollins, 1994), 1.

CHAPTER 26

371   "God Be in My Head," from *A French Book of Hours*, 1490; found in a manuscript collection of prayers dating from 1514. Also appears in *Sarum Primer* of 1558, a prayer book used in Salisbury, England.

371   "African American Spiritual," quoted in Edelman, *Guide My Feet*,

(Boston: Beacon Press, 1995), 51.

380   "Aelred of Rievaulx," in *HarperCollins Book of Prayers*, 20.

380–383 "An Inclusive-Language Translation of the Ignatian Rules for Discernment," trans. Elisabeth Tetlow, in *Women's Spirituality: Resources for Christian Development*, ed. Joan Wolski Conn, 2nd ed., (New York: Paulist Press, 1996), 288–294.

383–385 Adapted (summary and paraphrase) from Kathleen Fischer, chapter 6, "Discernment," in *Women at the Well: Feminist Perspectives on Spiritual Direction* (New York: Paulist Press, 1988), 113–132.

385   In *An African Prayer Book*, ed. Tutu, 44.

385–386 Anthony de Mello, S.J., "Seedlings," in *Hearts on Fire*, ed. Harter 33.

386   Ignatius of Loyola, "*Suscipe*," in *Hearts on Fire*, ed. Harter 84.

386   Edelman, *Guide My Feet*.

CHAPTER 27

387   Matthew 5:13a, NRSV.

387   "A Prayer from Latin America," in *Gifts of Many Cultures*, eds. Tirabassi and Eddy, 53.

387   Eberhard Bethge, *Prayer and Righteous Action in the Life of Dietrich Bonhoeffer* (Belfast: Christian Journals, 1979), 27.

397   "Canticle of Mary (Magnificat)," in *People's Companion to the Breviary* (Indianapolis, IN: Carmelite Monastery, 1997), interior back cover.

397–398 Soelle, "When He Came (1.)," in *Revolutionary Patience*, 7.

398   "Sioux Prayer," in *For You, O God*, ed. Reuter, 42.

398–399 A Litany for Midday Prayer," in NZPB, 62.

399   Câmara, "Come Lord," in *The Desert Is Fertile*, 20.

400   "Collect: Liturgies of the Eucharist," in NZPB, 464.

400–401   Soelle, "A Story from the Talmud and Questions for Us," in *Of War and Love*, 169–70.

401–402   Teresa of Avila, "Christ's Body," in *Laughter, Silence and Shouting*, ed. Keay, 93.

BREAD FOR THE JOURNEY: A BLESSING

403   Marty Haugen, "Gather Us In" (Chicago: GIA Publications, 1982).

403   Pedro Arrupe, in *Hearts on Fire*, ed. Harter, 66.

404   Anna McKenzie, "We Did Not Want It Easy, God," in *Laughter, Silence and Shouting*, ed. Keay, 146.

404–405   Gerard Manley Hopkins, "God's Grandeur," *Poems and Prose of Gerard Manley Hopkins*, ed. W. H. Gardner (Harmondsworth, UK: Penguin Books, 1963), 27.

405   Morley, "Collect for the Second Sunday After Easter," in *All Desires Known*, 15.

405   Morley, "Blessing," in *All Desires Known*, 47.

PERMISSIONS

Portions of chapters 10, 11, 13, and 15 originally appeared in the following articles in *America* (106 West 56th St., New York, NY 10019): "Pronouns, Poets, and the Desire for God," March 16, 1991, 298–99. "Praying in a Time of Depression," August 26–September 2, 1995, 14–20. "How Can I Find God?" September 30, 1995, 20–21 *[One of several short essays, James Martin, S.J., ed.]*.

Portions of chapters 14 and 16 were originally published as "From lamentation to jubilation—and in the in-between: praying the Psalms in daily life" in *The Way Supplement* 87:

124–33 (Autumn 1996) and are reprinted with permission of the Editors, *The Way* (Campion Hall, Oxford, OX1 1QS, England).

"The Word That Is A Prayer'" by Ellery Akers. First appeared in *Witness*, VOL XI, No. 2, 1997.

The Desert Is Fertile, (New York: Orbis Books, 1981)—Originally published in French as *Le désert est fertile* by Editions du Seuil, Paris. Copyright © 1977 by Editions du Seuil. Reprinted by permission of Georges Borchardt, Inc.

"Magnificat" from *People's Companion to the Breviary* © 1997 by the Carmelites of Indianapolis.

Material by William Cleary © 1995 Twenty-Third Publications and © 1993 Twenty-Third Publications.

"My Name Is Waiting" by M. Shawn Copeland. Reprinted by permission of the author.

Selections from *Guide My Feet: Prayers and Meditations on Loving and Working for Children* by Marian Wright Edelman. Copyright © 1995. Reprinted by permission of Beacon Press, Boston.

Excerpts from "Burnt Norton" and "Little Gidding" in *Four Quartets* Copyright © 1943 by T. S. Eliot and renewed 1971 by Esme Valerie Eliot, reprinted by permission of Harcourt Brace & Company.

Excerpts, as specified, from *The Book of Blessings: New Jewish Prayers and Rituals* by Marcia Falk. Copyright © 1996 by Marcia Falk. Reprinted by permission of HarperCollins Publishers, Inc.

Excerpt from "Contemporary *Exsultet*" based on prayer by James Dillet Freeman. Reprinted by permission of IGA Publications, Chicago, IL.

Excerpt from *Gather Us In* by Marty Haugen. Reprinted by permission of IGA Publications, Chicago, IL.

Mind What Stirs in Your Heart by Teresina Havens. "Shareright" 1992 Teresina Havens.

Selections from *Dear God: Children's Letters to God*, David Heller, ed. Reprinted by permission of Penguin/Putnam, Inc.

"God's Grandeur" by Gerald Manley Hopkins. Reprinted by permission of Oxford University Press.

Selections from *Laughter, Silence and Shouting* by Kathy Keay reprinted by permission of HarperCollins Publishers.

Excerpt from *The Book of Words: Talking Spiritual Life, Living Spiritual Talk* by Lawrence Kushner (Woodstock, VT: Jewish Lights Publishing, 1993). Permission granted by Jewish Lights Publishing.

Prayers by Janet Morley: © Janet Morley 1988, 1992. Reproduced by permission of Morehouse Publishing, Harrisburg, PA.

Material from *A New Zealand Prayer Book*, Church of the Province of New Zealand. Reprinted by permission.

"The companionable dark" from *Little Girls in Church* by Kathleen Norris © 1995. Reprinted by permission of the University of Pittsburgh Press.

Prayers by Michel Quoist. Reprinted by permission of Sheed & Ward, an Apostolate of the Priests of the Sacred Heart. 7373 South Lovers Lane Road, Franklin, Wisconsin 53132, 1-800-558-0580.

"Pietà" by Rainer Maria Rilke, from *New Poems* Copyright © 1964 by The Hogarth Press. Reprinted by permission of New Directions Publishing Corp.

"Each Note" by Jalaluddin Rumi Copyright © Coleman Barks, *The Essential Rumi*, HarperCollins, 1995.

Selections from *Of War and Love* by Dorothee Soelle taken from *Dorothee Soelle Im Hause Des Menschenfressers* Copyright © 1981 by Rowohlt Taschenbuch Verlag GmbH, Reinbek bei Hamburg. English translation appears by permission of Orbis Books, Maryknoll, NY.

Selections from *Revolutionary Patience* by Dorothee Soelle © Wolfgang Fietkau Verlag, Kleinmachnow. English translation appears by permission of Orbis Books, Maryknoll, NY.

"Vigil" by Elena Stone © 1997 Elena Stone from the unpublished collection *Sing Me Out of Exile*.

Selections from *An African Prayer Book*, Desmond Tutu, ed. Reprinted by permission of Bantam Doubleday Dell Publishers.

From *Wherever You Go, There You Are: Mindfulness Meditation in Everyday Life* by Jon Kabat-Zinn Copyright © 1994 Jon Kabat-Zinn. Reprinted with permission by Hyperion.

Jane Redmont is a teacher, spiritual director, retreat facilitator, feminist theologian, social activist, and writer. She is currently preparing for ordination as an Episcopal priest. A graduate of Oberlin College, Redmont has an MDiv from Harvard Divinity School and a PhD in theology from the Graduate Theological Union in Berkeley, California. She is the author of *Generous Lives: American Catholic Women Today* and has written articles and essays for many publications including the *National Catholic Reporter*. Redmont teaches religion and theology at Guilford College in Greensboro, North Carolina. She maintains a personal blog at actsofhope.blogspot.com.